Abdurrahman, 1979
(Kompas)

Above: Abu Hasan, Idham Chalid and Abdurrahman (Antara)
Below: Abdurrahman and Kiai Achmad Siddiq (Antara)

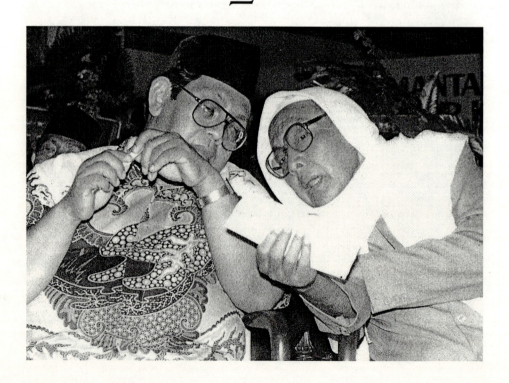

Below: Abdurrahman and Nuriyah on a visit to the Middle East in the early 1990s (family album)

Above: Abdurrahman and family in the Netherlands in the late 1980s (family album)
Below: Traditional family portrait, July 1999 (family album)

Abdurrahman and Soeharto shake hands in the early 1990s, observed by Solichah, Abdurrahman's mother (family album)

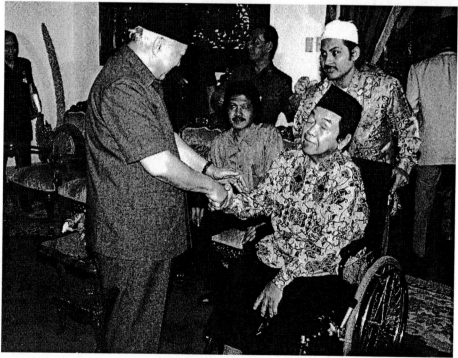

Abdurrahman shakes hands with Soeharto on 19 May 1998, when the group of nine *ulama* met with the president two days before his resignation. Al Zastron stands behind him.
(family album)

Above: Abdurrahman and Soeharto in November 1999, shortly after
Abdurrahman was elected president
(Presidential Archives)
Below: Abdurrahman and General Benny Murdani in the early 1990s
(Kompas)

Above: The 'four leaders of the reform movement' after their long-awaited meeting in Ciganjur, 10 November 1998. Left to right: Hamengkubowono X (the Sultan of Yogyakarta), Abdurrahman Wahid, Megawati Sukarnoputri, Amien Rais
(Kompas)
Below: Abdurrahman addresses a crowd of PKB supporters in May 1999
(author)

Abdurrahman, assisted by Yenny, casting his vote for president, 20 October 2000 (Kompas)

Abdurrahman being sworn in as president (Kompas)

Above: Abdurrahman — kitted out in navy jacket and beret — addresses officers of the Indonesian Navy in 2000 (Presidential Archive)

Right: Abdurrahman and East Timorese leader Xanana Gusmao meet in Jakarta in March 2000 (Presidential Archive)

Abdurrahman, flanked by Flalba, his police adjutant, and a smiling General Wiranto in early 2000 (Presidential Archive)

Abdurrahman with Sukirno, his airforce adjutant, and friends during his regular morning walk, July 2000 (author)

Above: Abdurrahman Wahid, accompanied by Yenny, talks with Akbar Tanjung during the annual session of the MPR in August 2000 (Presidential Archive)
Below: President Abdurrahman Wahid and B.J. Habibie in conversation; Yenny, Alwi Shihab and Bondan Gunawan walk behind them (Presidential Archive)

Abdurrahman checks the time on the talking watch given to him by Megawati, who is at his side (Presidential Archive)

Abdurrahman's four daughters: Anita, Inayah, Alissa and Yenny
(Presidential Archive)

Abdurrahman addresses a national Boy Scout jamboree in August 2000, flanked by
Navy adjutant Room on left of photograph and Police adjutant Halloa on right
(author)

Assembly members leave the chamber at the end of the annual session of the MPR, August 2000 (author)

Above: Abdurrahman relaxes with friends, including Djohan Effendi (left) and Wimar Witoelar (right) during the first week of the MPR session in August 2000 (author)
Below: Abdurrahman with friends, including (left to right) Djohan Effendi, Mohammad Sobary, the author, Marsillam Simanjuntak and Yenny, at his suite at the Hilton during the first week of the annual session of the MPR (author)

Abdurrahman standing between his mother and father, and behind his siblings and a friend of the family, circa 1952 (family album)

ABDURRAHMAN WAHID
MUSLIM DEMOCRAT, INDONESIAN PRESIDENT

GREG BARTON is a senior lecturer in the Faculty of Arts at Deakin University, Geelong, Victoria. Since the late 1980s he has researched the influence of Islamic liberalism in Indonesia and its contribution to the development of civil society and democracy. One of the central figures in his research has been Abdurrahman Wahid, whom Barton has come to know better than perhaps any other researcher.

This page intentionally left blank

ABDURRAHMAN WAHID
MUSLIM DEMOCRAT, INDONESIAN PRESIDENT

A view from the inside

Greg Barton

For
Siew Mee and Hannah
and
in memory of Herb Feith

A UNSW Press book

Published by
University of New South Wales Press Ltd
University of New South Wales
UNSW Sydney NSW 2052
AUSTRALIA
www.unswpress.com.au

© Greg Barton 2002
First published 2002

This book is copyright. Apart from any fair dealing for purposes of private study, research, criticism or review, as permitted under the Copyright Act, no part may be reproduced by any process without written permission. Inquiries should be addressed to the publisher.

National Library of Australia
Cataloguing-in-Publication entry:

  Barton, Greg, 1962– .
  Abdurrahman Wahid: Muslim democrat, Indonesian president.

  Bibliography.
  Includes index.
  ISBN 0 86840 405 5.

  Wahid, Abdurrahman, 1940– . 2. Presidents — Indonesia — Biography.
  3. Indonesia — Politics and government — 1998– . I. Title.

321.0092

Printer Kyodo Printing, Singapore

CONTENTS

Preface — 1
Acknowledgments — 5
Glossary and Abbreviations — 9
Prologue — 18

PART 1 *PESANTREN* AND FAMILY

1 Growing up in *pesantren* and politics, 1940–1963 — 37
2 Islam in Indonesia: modernists and traditionalists — 62

PART 2 THE MAKING OF AN INTELLECTUAL

3 Cairo, Baghdad and Europe, 1963–1971 — 83
4 The *pesantren* and reform, 1971–1982 — 102

PART 3 ISLAM AND MODERNITY

5 Abdurrahman and liberal Islam — 119
6 On the brink of change, 1982–1984 — 132

PART 4 CIVIL SOCIETY AND ISLAM

7 Reform and controversy, 1984–1990   147
8 Pushing the limits, 1990–1994   179

PART 5 POLITICS, REFORM AND THE PRESIDENCY

9   Contending with Soeharto, 1994–1998   209
10 Islam, politics and elections, 1998–1999   245
11 A brief honeymoon, 1999–2000   285
12 Regime change and the fight for survival, 1999–2001   330

Epilogue   359
Conclusion   366
Notes   386
References and Further Reading   400
Index   404

PREFACE

Few biographers like to imagine that their own subject is anything less than unusual and interesting. I certainly feel the same way about the focus of this biography for the most subjective of reasons, but I also believe that there are objective reasons for regarding Abdurrahman Wahid, or Gus Dur as he is known affectionately by tens of millions, as representing a most remarkable subject. I am also well aware that I have written a rather unusual biography.

By the conventions of the genre, a serious biography is generally hammered out in long sessions examining archives or interviewing dozens of people who knew the subject, all of which is documented in extensive footnotes. The approach that I have taken is somewhat different, for while this biography does benefit from extensive reading and research and from numerous interviews with a wide range of individuals, it deliberately focuses on the subject's own account. The reason is simple: I had a unique opportunity to observe and interact with Abdurrahman during a critical period of his life and was therefore in a position to give a firsthand account. I was privileged to be given remarkable access to Abdurrahman throughout his political campaign after the fall of Suharto and throughout his presidency; I spent hundreds of hours with him during this period, having already come to know him very well since first meeting him in the late 1980s. During his 21-month presidency I spent about seven months as his guest, rising most mornings at 4.30 am to spend the first three hours of the day with him. I was also able to travel with him around Indonesia, and occasionally abroad, and observe him at work as president.

It seemed to me that, because both Abdurrahman and his world of traditionalist Islam are frequently misunderstood, even within Indonesia, an account that attempted to understand the man and his world empathetically from his point of view would have significant value, especially if it drew on firsthand observation.

This does not mean that the approach I have taken is uncritical. On the contrary, I have wrestled with this material over many years and in the later chapters in particular this has led me to make a series of critical observations. This is made easier for me because the bulk of this book focuses on the period since I have come to know Abdurrahman and was able to observe many of the key developments described here. What this means, of course, is that this is a very personal and subjective account. This is both its strength and its weakness, but in this it is not so different from other biographies as might first appear. All biographies are essentially interpretations of an individual's life, and none is entirely objective in an absolute sense. Some benefit from decades — even centuries — of critical distance and vast bodies of earlier scholarship; others from direct access to more immediate sources. There are advantages and disadvantages with each. Consequently, although I believe that it is important that future biographers of Abdurrahman Wahid draw on material other than what I have used here, I don't believe that the approach taken here is any less valid.

Another defining characteristic of this account is that it is deliberately written to be accessible to as broad a readership as possible. As a professional academic I have found it the most challenging piece of writing that I have ever undertaken. I have spent years wrestling with trying to understand Abdurrahman and attempting to establish a coherent interpretation, so far as it is possible, of his convictions and behaviour. It seemed to me that there was little benefit in burdening the reader with an account of my struggles. Instead, I have tried to present the results of my research as straightforwardly as possible while also tying my reading of events into what I hope is a reasonably vivid narrative account.

I owe a great debt to many people with whom I have talked about Abdurrahman over the years; only a small number of them are mentioned by name in the acknowledgements that follow. Many of these conversations took the form of formal interviews, a number of which were recorded; others took the form of conversations of a kind that it did not seem appropriate to record. Indeed many of these conversations were so intimate that even to refer to them in footnotes was not appropriate. In recent years I have often had opportunity to meet with government ministers, religious leaders, intellectuals, activists, military generals, and other members of the Indonesian elite and have enjoyed many fruitful conversations. Few of these are referred to directly in this volume but all of them contributed, in some way or other, to my understanding of events. I have also been in the fortunate position of being able to accompany Abdurrahman and witness many of the events described here. Frequently I have found my observations of what I saw are at variance with contemporary accounts in the media. This does not mean, of course, that my recollection of events is always correct, or that it is always superior to media accounts. I have gained valuable insight both from reading accounts in the press and also from speaking directly with journalists. Nevertheless, I have oriented my account very much to what I have observed, in the hope that it communicates something to the reader that a secondhand account cannot do.

During the process of researching this volume I have experienced tremendous emotional pressure. I have seen Abdurrahman's strengths and weaknesses as few outside his immediate family have done. I have experienced extreme frustration and despair when he has made grave mistakes, as often happened during his presidency, and I have also seen something of the vision that drives him on. He has been a remarkably generous friend and has opened himself to me in a way in which few people would to a biographer. And while this account draws heavily, and therefore depends greatly, on firsthand observation and Abdurrahman's own recollections, there is no sense in which I have been directed to write anything at all. At no point has he, or anyone around him, attempted to influence what I was writing. Naturally, this degree of trust, combined with my own sense of what is fair and ethical, has left me with a sense of where it is reasonable for this biography to go. There are certain areas that, it seemed to me, because of their personal nature, that I had no good reason to investigate in this book at this time. There were other matters, such as the affairs of Abdurrahman's party, PKB, that I felt to be beyond the scope of this study, important though they no doubt are — this book is already too long as it is.

For all of my affection and respect for Abdurrahman, which has not been in the least diminished by his all too predictable failures in the political arena, I have tried to present what I understand to be the truth. Where there are doubts about historicity, such as the account of his early life, I have indicated this by acknowledging that what is being presented is his recollection or understanding of events. I am well aware that some of these recollections may later be shown to be at variance with what actually happened, but I regard them as being of value in attempting to understand Abdurrahman's life from his point of view. Although this work is shaped by its attempt to be an empathetic account, I have, as far as possible under the circumstances, tried to arrive at the truth as I wrestled with synthesising the masses of complex data before me. Those whose nature it is to think in an intuitive fashion will understand what I am saying. To those whose personal approach to analysis is less intuitive than the approach taken here, I can only say that I have done my best, in all sincerity, to arrive at what I am persuaded is the truth. It goes without saying that this has been done imperfectly; but if this book serves to provoke others into further research, I will feel that I have achieved something of value.

Greg Barton
Jakarta

ACKNOWLEDGMENTS

There are many people who have helped in the writing of this book but only some can be named here. Whether named or unnamed, I am deeply grateful to the multitude of people whose friendship, hospitality, advice and help I have experienced over the years.

The person to whom I owe the single greatest debt of gratitude is my wife, Siew Mee. She has patiently encouraged and endured not only during the years that went directly into the making of this book but also in the decade that came before, during which I undertook the research that forms the foundation of this book. I am deeply grateful, too, to our daughter, Hannah, for her stoic acceptance of the demands that my ongoing research has placed upon our family. Hannah's earliest memories include a seemingly endless series of rushed goodbyes in the middle of the night as I once again sped off to Jakarta, leaving her for weeks at a time. For years on end, all that she and Siew Mee knew of family holidays was joining me for whatever left over pieces of time they could grab during inter-semester fieldwork trips to Java. Even when I was physically at home with them, my mind was often elsewhere or I was locked in the study, making them as much as me prisoners of the demands of my chosen career. Consequently, it is no polite exaggeration to say that this book would not have been possible without their patient forbearance and generous sacrifice.

I am also deeply grateful to my parents, Jim and Edie Barton, whose support went well beyond kindly words of encouragement and finally became for me an affirmation that I really did have something worthwhile to contribute.

Alongside my own nuclear and extended family there is another family that has patiently bore my often unreasonable demands and repaid them with friendship and understanding and the gracious inclusion of me into their world and their lives. I am deeply thankful to Abdurrahman and Nuriyah and to their daughters Alissa, Yenny, Anita and Inayah. For years, Abdurrahman has responded to my clumsy probing into his personal affairs with patience and generous friendship. And Yenny, in particular, has gone out of her way more times than I can now remember to see that I had the access that I needed. That this continued unchanged even during the difficult months of his presidency is something that I still find remarkable. I also find it remarkable, and feel compelled to note it here, that at no time did Abdurrahman or Yenny or anyone else in the Wahid family ever try, directly or indirectly, to influence my account. Instead, they simply extended to me unfettered access and genuine friendship. To say that I could not ask for more helpful and trusting subjects falls well short of the mark — I could not ask for better friends.

There are many other friends in Indonesia, more than I can list here, to whom I owe a debt of gratitude to for their help, encouragement and friendship over the years. They include Munib Huda, Ratih Hardjono, Djohan Effendi, Mohamed Sobary, Henry and Martha Tong, Andy and Diena Trigg and Greg and Sarah Moriarty. I am also grateful for the professional help of Rohim Ghazali, Ahmad Suaedy and friends from Paramadina, NU and elsewhere who have helped me with my research over many years. In more recent times I have been extraordinarily helped and encouraged by friends such as Wimar Witoelar, Mark Hanusz and Dian Wirjawan and I am deeply grateful to them for their advice and understanding help.

Back in Australia, I am very grateful for the encouragement and support of many people who believed in me when my own confidence had long begun to waver. I particularly wish to thank Peter Browne, formerly from UNSW Press, for his wise counsel, his enormously helpful feedback and his unfailing encouragement. I am grateful too, to Janet Mackenzie for skillfully helping turn my prolix prose into something a little easier to read and to Felicity Raeburn and Edie Barton for their patient help with developing and refining my manuscript.

I also owe special debt of gratitude to Greg Fealy, Hamish MacDonald and Ed Aspinall for their careful work in pointing out the many flaws in my manuscript and their fearless advice to me. This book would be very much poorer without their contribution and I am grateful to them for saving me from going to print with a multitude of gaffs and mistakes. No doubt there will still be many things about this book with which they will take issue, some arising from difference in academic opinion and some from the limitations arising from this book's scope and focus; such is the nature of academic books, especially biographies. I am deeply appreciative of their patient scholarship and all that they have done to try and help me and this account. Needless to say, however, I take full responsibility for all errors, flaws and failings within this book.

This book was largely written in 2000, with several final chapters being added in 2001. The research, however, began in earnest in 1997 and over the past five years I have made numerous field trips to Indonesia which have directly and indirectly contributed to this book. This broader research would not have been possible without the support of the Australian Research Council (ARC) and my employer, Deakin University. I received two three-year research grants from the ARC to study 'The influence of Islamic liberalism' and 'Islam and civil society in Indonesia', and this book represents one of the direct outcomes of those research projects. I am also very grateful to Deakin University, and the Faculty of Arts and the School of Social Inquiry within it, for the understanding and flexibility that has been extended to me, allowing me to spend months each year away from campus on field work. I am particularly appreciative of the Dean's publication support scheme which made it possible for me to spend the first half of 2000 focusing almost exclusively on hammering out a manuscript.

I am also grateful for the permission from several parties for me to use material in this book. I thank the photographers at the Presidential Palace, Antara news agency, *Kompas* newspaper and the Wahid family for the use of some of their photographs. I also thank the *Age* and the *Sydney Morning Herald* for allowing me to use in the epilogue material that I earlier wrote for publication in their pages on 28 July 2001. Similarly, I am also thankful to Carfax Publishing for allowing me to use a revised version of an article I wrote for *Pacifica Review* (Vol. 13, No. 3, October 2001) in the conclusion of this book.

I also owe a debt of gratitude to the tireless, anonymous angel who runs the Joyo news service, without whose hourly deliveries to my 'Inbox' I would have been so much less well informed.

One of the somewhat unexpected pleasures of researching, writing about, and venturing to comment on contemporary developments in Indonesia has been the support and encouragement that I have received from colleagues. I am particularly grateful for the support that I have received from my colleagues in the Religious Studies/Comparative Studies program at Deakin — Ian Weeks, Barry Butcher and Peter Fenner. Not only have they covered for me when, often at short notice, I have had to make a trip to Indonesia during the semester, they have been unfailingly encouraging, as have Bryan Turner and Sue Kenny and many other colleagues at Deakin.

Outside my own university, I am thankful for the advice, assistance and friendship I have received from fellow Indonesianists and scholars of Islam, such as Robert Hefner, Arief Budiman, Abdullah Saeed, Andree Feillard, Martin van Bruinessen and Johan Meuleman. Each in their own way has significantly shaped my thinking about the issues covered in this book. A less direct, but still significant influence has come from other Indonesianists, especially those at Monash University, such as Barbara Hatley, Cyril Skinner, Paul Tickell, David Hill, John Legge, Merle Ricklefs and Herb Feith.

The sad news of Herb's untimely death on 15 November 2001 came just as I was preparing these comments. I cannot claim that Herb's scholarship shaped my own in any direct manner that I can easily delineate. I can say, however, that his very personality had an influence on me and many other scholars of Indonesia that was as profound as it was subtle. Herb was the model for us all of passionate, concerned, engaged scholarship. He was a *mensch*, an intellectual not afraid of actively engaging with his subject and with society. Only now am I aware of just how much he influenced me and this book. Thank you Herb. *Selamat jalan*.

GLOSSARY AND ABBREVIATIONS

abangan Muslims whose cultural and religious outlook is, to greatly varying extents, a syncretic amalgam of indigenous, animist, Hindu-Buddhist and Islamic elements. In the rural areas of Central and East Java a large proportion of the broader Islamic population is *abangan*.

ABRI Angkatan Bersenjata Republik Indonesia (Indonesian Armed Forces). This name was changed to **TNI** in May 1999 when **POLRI**, the police force, was split off from the military.

adat Customary law and practice which varies across the Indonesian archipelago and predates the coming of Islam.

Ansor A very large national organisation for young men affiliated with **NU**.

asas tunggal Literally 'sole foundation', in the early 1980s the phrase came to refer to the recognition of **Pancasila** as the underlying, fundamental ideological basis for all social, political and religious organisations in Indonesian society.

banser The uniformed activists of **Ansor** who guard congresses and other important occasions.

BI Bank Indonesia.

BRI Bank Rakyat Indonesia (People's Bank of Indonesia).

Bulog Badan Urusan Logistik (State Logistics Agency).

CIDES Centre for Information and Development Studies.
CPDS Centre for Policy and Development Studies.
CSIS Centre for Strategic and International Studies.
DDII Dewan Dakwah Islamiyah Indonesia (Indonesian Islamic Preaching Council). A radical Islamist organisation established in the late 1960s. Commonly referred to simply as Dewan Dakwah.
DPR Dewan Perwakilan Rakyat (People's Representative Council). Indonesia's 500-member parliament.
dwifungsi The important military doctrine of 'dual function', used to justify the military's role in politics during Soeharto's **New Order**.
fiqh Islamic jurisprudence.
Fordem Forum Demokrasi (Democracy Forum). Established in March 1991 under the chairmanship of Abdurrahman Wahid, a high-profile ginger-group of forty-five intellectuals and activists drawn from across the spectrum of Indonesian society.
FPI Front Pembela Islam (Defenders of Islam Front). A small but vocal radical Islamist group established in 1999.
Fraksi Reformasi (Reform Faction). The parliamentary faction representing **PAN**.
GESTAPU Gerakan September Tiga Puluh (The September Thirtieth Movement). The group alleged to have been behind a communist coup attempt in 1965.
Golkar Golongan Karya (Functional Groups). The state political party that was Soeharto's political vehicle during the **New Order**. After dominating Indonesian politics for three decades, Golkar's share of the vote dropped to about 22 per cent in the June 1999 elections.
GPM Geraja Protestan Maluku (Protestant Church of Maluku).
hadith (hadis) Sometimes referred to as the 'traditions' of the Prophet Muhammad, the *hadith* are important anecdotal sources for determining the Prophet's *sunnah* or personal history and pattern of living. The Sunnah augments the Qur'an as source of Islamic teaching.
haj The obligatory pilgrimage to Mecca that takes place at a set season each year.
haji Someone who has made the pilgrimage to Mecca.
halal A category of things or actions (generally concerning food) which are unreservedly deemed permissible for a Muslim to consume, use or do.
halaqah Islamic study circle or discussion group.

haram The opposite of *halal*, refers to things expressly forbidden in Islam.
HMI Himpunan Mahasiswa Islam (Association of Muslim Students). Indonesia's most important modernist student group; its alumni network **KAHMI** is also highly influential.
IAIN Institut Agama Islam Negara (State Islamic Institute).
ibadah Act or ritual of worship.
IBRA Indonesian Bank Restructuring Agency.
ICMI (Indonesian Association of Muslim Intellectuals).
ijtihad The individual exercise of powers of reasoning, interpretation and contextualised application of the Qur'an and the Sunnah, as opposed to simply accepting the consensus of earlier scholars.
IMF International Monetary Fund.
Interfet International Force East Timor. An Australia-led international peace-keeping force under UN auspices sent to East Timor on 20 September 1999 in the wake of violence following the self-determination referendum on 30 August.
IPS Institute for Policy Studies.
Islamism A radical political ideology arguing that Islam is inherently political and that there should be no separation between 'church and state'.
Jakarta Charter The short preamble to the 1945 constitution, containing the much contested phrase that 'the carrying out of Syari'ah is an obligation of all Muslims'.
jihad Striving, or struggling, for the purposes of God, either in the sense of a spiritual or moral struggle or in the sense of a just war.
jilbab Traditional Islamic woman's head scarf worn tightly so as to completely cover the wearer's neck and hair, much like the wimple of a Catholic nun.
KAHMI Korps Alumni HMI (HMI Alumni Corps). See **HMI**.
kiai A Javanese term applied to religious scholars (*ulama*), generally in the context of leadership within *pesantren* society.
Khittah 1926 Charter of 1926. A reform program spearheaded by Abdurrahman Wahid and Achmad Siddiq in the early 1980s, intended to restore **NU** in accordance with the vision of its founding fathers.
KISDI Komiti Indonesia Solidaritas Dunia Islam (Committee for World Islamic Solidarity). An alliance of the most radical elements from **DDII** with other hard-line Islamists.

KKN korupsi, kolusi, nepotism (corruption, collusion and nepotism).
Komnas HAM Komisi Nasional Hak-hak Asasi Manusia (National Human Rights Commission).
KOPASSUS Military special forces.
KOSTRAD Army Strategic Reserve Command.
LP3ES Lembaga Pengkajian Pengetahuan, Pendidikan, Ekonomi dan Social (Institute for Economic and Social Research, Education and Information).
madrasah Islamic schools. In Indonesia *madrasah* generally differ from *pesantren* in being day schools (not taking boarders) and offering a broad syllabus with a greater secular content. Previously, *madrasah* were identified with **Muhammadiyah** modernists and *pesantren* with **NU** traditionalists, but this distinction is blurring (though modernist *pesantren* remain rare) as many *pesantren* contain *madrasah*.
Masyumi Majlis Syuro Muslimin Indonesia (Consultative Council of Indonesia Muslims). The peak modernist Islamic political party in the 1950s.
Mazhab One of four orthodox **Sunni** schools of Islamic legal interpretation.
MIAI Majlisul Islamil a'laa Indonesia (Indonesian Supreme Islamic Council). A federation of Islamic organisations, including **Muhammadiyah** and **NU**, established in 1937.
Media Dakwah The official magazine of **DDII**.
modernism Islamic modernism refers to the movement in Islamic thought beginning in the second half of the nineteenth century, led by thinkers such as Muhammad 'Abduh of Al Azhar University in Cairo, which argued for 'opening the gates of *ijtihad*'. Besides insisting that the *umat* return to the Qur'an and direct *ijtihad* rather than 'blindly following' the classical commentaries, the modernist movement was also concerned with bringing about the reform of Islamic practice and thought, through educational reform. Having arisen partly as a response to the challenges of modernity, it also took the position that the Islamic world should not dismiss the achievements of Western civilisation but should rather 'take that which is good and reject that which is bad'. In this paradigm traditionalists are those in the Islamic world who opposed, or at least did not wish to be a part of, Islamic modernism. In practice the distinction usually shows in education, with the nature of an individual's education determining their intellectual outlook for life. Unlike traditionalists,

modernists, ostensibly at least, do not define their doctrinal position by reference to the four *Mazhab* and generally do not study the texts of classical Islamic scholarship. They also tend to be wary of mysticism and cultural beliefs and practices that suggest syncretism.

MPR Majelis Permusyawaratan Rakyat (People's Consultative Assembly). A super-parliament comprised of the **DPR** plus 200 appointees. Under Soeharto it was a rubber-stamp body that met once every five years. It now meets annually. The MPR elects the president and has constitutional authority over the president.

Muhammadiyah Founded in 1912, Indonesia's peak modernist Islamic organisation and one of the most successful modernist organisations anywhere in the world. It is said to have around 30 million members.

MUI Majelis Ulama Indonesia (Indonesian Council of *Ulama*). A small and highly political body sponsored by Soeharto in the 1990s.

muktamar congress. The five-yearly *muktamar*, or **NU** national congress, is the highest decision-making forum within NU.

munas musyawarah nasional (national consultation). The **NU** *munas* are held every five years, mid-way between *muktamar*, as a forum for *ulama* to deliberate on religious matters.

Muslimat The influential national women's organisation affiliated NU, founded in 1946.

neomodernism A progressive movement of Islamic thought arising after Islamic **modernism** but also deeply interested in traditional scholarship. Neomodernism argues for a holistic approach to *ijtihad*, informed by both classical scholarship and modern Western critical thought, in order to discern the overarching message of the Qur'an, and its application to modern society. It argues for a liberal, progressive understanding of Islam that accepts the pluralism of modern society, and seeks to make society more Islamic through education rather than through party-political initiatives, such as attempts to introduce legislative recognition of the **Syari'ah**, or even the establishment of an Islamic state.

New Order The name given to the Soeharto regime after it replaced the 'old order' of the Sukarno regime.

NGOs Non-governmental organisations.

NU Nahdlatul Ulama (The Awakening of the *Ulama*) Founded in 1926, Indonesia's peak traditionalist Islamic organisation; it is said to have 30–40 million members.

PAN Partai Amanat Nasional (National Mandate Party). Led by Amien Rais, PAN gained around 7 per cent of the vote in the June 1999 election, where it styled itself as a pluralist party with links to modernist Islam.

Pancasila A Sanskrit-derived neologism, literally 'the five principles'. Formulated during the Sukarno era but only championed with vigour after Soeharto came to power in the mid-1960s, Pancasila represents the core philosophy of the Indonesian state. The five principles are: (1) belief in one God Almighty; (2) humanity that is just and civilised; (3) Indonesian unity; (4) democracy guided by the wisdom of representative deliberation; (5) social justice for all Indonesians. In practice Pancasila functions as a political compromise that recognises the theistic convictions of the majority of Indonesians but delivers a modern secular (i.e. non-partisan with respect to the major faiths) model of the state. Often dismissed, particularly by Western commentators, as a collection of motherhood statements, Pancasila represents an important compromise in providing a critical ideological basis for Indonesia's plural society.

PBB Partai Bulan Bintang (Crescent Star Party). A small Islamist party, it gained around 2 per cent of the vote in the June 1999 elections.

PBNU Pengurus Besar Nahdlatul Ulama. The national leadership and headquarters of **NU**.

PDI Partai Demokrasi Indonesia (Democratic Party of Indonesia). Together with **PPP**, it was one of the two opposition parties permitted under Soeharto following the 'rationalisation' of parties in 1973.

PDI-P Partai Demokrasi Indonesia-Perjuangan Perjuangan (Democratic Party of Indonesia of the Struggle). The 'new PDI' formed in 1998 and led by Megawati Soekarnoputri, it is a secular, nationalist party. It gained almost 34 per cent of the vote in 1999, well ahead of **Golkar**, **PKB**, **PPP** and **PAN**.

pembaruan Reform, renewal. The *pembaruan* movement associated with Nurcholish Madjid in the early 1970s introduced **neomodernist** thought to Indonesia.

pesantren Boarding schools which emphasise Islamic education. Originally almost all *pesantren* had a rural base and provided a traditionalist Islamic education in traditional fashion. Over the past two decades, however, a number of urban and modernist *pesantren* have been established, and most *pesantren* today teach a mixed curriculum comprising secular as well as religious and Arabic-language subjects, delivered by methods similar to those of secular schools.

PK Partai Keadilan (Justice Party). A small Islamist party built on student support, it gained around 1 per cent of the vote in the June 1999 elections.

PKB Partai Kebangkitan Bangsa (National Awakening Party). The party of Abdurrahman Wahid. Although a pluralist party, PKB gets almost all of its support from **NU** members, and it gained around 12 per cent of the vote in the June 1999 elections.

PKI Partai Komunis Indonesia (Indonesian Communist Party).

PMII Pergerakan Mahasiswa Islam Indonesia (Indonesian Muslim Students Movement). Founded in 1960, PMII is the tertiary students' organisation of **NU**.

PNI Partai Nasionalis Indonesia (Nationalist Party of Indonesia). A Sukarno-era party, PNI was close to the president himself.

POLRI Polisi Republik Indonesia (The Indonesian Police Force).

Poros Tengah Central Axis. A coalition comprising **PPP** and the small Islamist parties plus **PAN**, and, for a while, **PKB**.

PPP Partai Pembangunan Persatuan (United Development Party). A largely moderate Islamist party, with **PDI** it was one of the two opposition parties permitted under Soeharto following the 'rationalisation' of parties in 1973. It gained around 10 per cent of the vote in the June 1999 elections.

PRD Partai Demokrasi Rakyat (People's Democratic Party). A leftist party appealing chiefly to students and younger people, PRD is the favourite scapegoat of conservatives.

priyayi Javanese Muslims with aristocratic connections whose personal faith and religious practice is a combination of *abangan* belief and courtly high culture.

PRRI Pemerintah Revolusi Republik Indonesia (Revolutionary Government of the Republic of Indonesia).

Rapat Akbar Great Rally. The term is sometimes used for **NU** rallies, such as the one on 1 March 1992 called to mark NU's sixty-sixth anniversary and to send a message to Soeharto.

RMS Republik Maluku Selatan (South Maluku Republic).

salat ritual prayer, to be performed at five set times each day.

santri Indonesian Muslims who are pious and orthodox in their devotional practice. Originally the term referred simply to students of the *pesantren*. The term's modern usage reflects the widespread usage of the paradigm of *santri* and *abangan* popularised by the American anthropologist Clifford Geertz in his influential book *The Religion of Java*.

Sekneg Sekretariat Negara (State Secretariat). Under Soeharto, a powerful super-ministry.

Semar The wise demigod of *wayang kulit* mythology who takes the form of a vulgar, flatulent, buffooning court-jester. Abdurrahman Wahid is often likened to Semar.

Shia The Shia understanding of Islam holds that Ali, the son-in-law of the Prophet, and his successors have a divinely inherited right to rule the Islamic *umat*. Followed by significant minority populations in modern Syria, Iraq, Afghanistan and Pakistan and the vast majority of those in Iran, but not, historically, in Indonesia. Shi'ites represent less than 10 per cent of the world's Muslims. See **Sunni**.

suksesi succession. Used in the late 1980s and 1990s to denote the transition that was to come at the end of Soeharto's **New Order**.

Sufism Traditional Islamic mysticism.

sunnah Literally 'path' or 'way'; used to refer to 'the way' or life of the Prophet Muhammad (as portrayed in the Qur'an and the *hadith* collections).

Sunni Literally 'the followers of the *sunnah*', used to mean all Muslims who are not Shi'ites. More than 90 per cent of Muslims around the world are Sunnites (or Sunni Muslims), as are almost all Indonesian Muslims. See **Shia**.

Syari'ah Islamic law.

Tanfidziah The name given to the executive boards of religious organisations such as **NU**.

tarekat Traditional Sufi brotherhood. See **Sufism**.

tassawuf The teachings of **Sufism**.

tauhid The doctrine that God is one and is unique.

TNI Tentara Nasional Indonesia (Indonesian National Army). It replaced **ABRI** in 1999 as a collective term for the three wings of the Indonesian military — army, navy and airforce — but excludes the police, who were part of ABRI

traditionalism See **modernism**.

ulama religious scholars; in Indonesian also used instead of the Arabic singular *alim*.

umat (ummah, ummat) Literally 'community' in Arabic, in Indonesia the term is used most often to refer to religious communities, especially the Muslim community.

wali A holy man, an Islamic scholar or saint with extraordinary spiritual powers.

wayang kulit The Indonesian shadow theatre. Centuries old and drawing on predominantly Hindu imagery and mythology from the *Ramayana* and *Mahabrata*, it continues to be popular in rural Java.

PROLOGUE

GOODNESS, IT'S GUS DUR

Late on the evening of Tuesday, 19 October 1999, a small group of officials, most smartly dressed in military uniforms, were going through an elaborate rehearsal for the swearing-in of Indonesia's fourth president. The ceremony the next day was to take place just a few hours after the members of the People's Consultative Assembly (Majelis Permusyawaratan Rakyat — MPR) had cast their vote to elect the president.

Earlier that evening the parliamentary building had been bustling with life as dozens of local and international television crews jostled for space in the balconies on each side of the Assembly hall. The hall itself had been filled with almost seven hundred Assembly members, numerous officials, and a large crowd of journalists and spectators who had packed the large rear balcony to overflowing. They had witnessed a surprising turn of events as the Assembly had effectively moved a vote of no-confidence in the embattled interim president B.J. Habibie by rejecting his end-of-term accountability speech.

While the city, and indeed the whole nation, wrestled with the news and wondered what it meant, the small group who had gathered in the auditorium late that evening went through the motions of the rehearsal seemingly unaffected by the remarkable events of several hours earlier. First came a practice run in case Megawati Soekarnoputri was elected. Those who would serve as her adjutants stood each side of her proxy, walked down the central aisle of the auditorium, and then positioned themselves on the podium as they would for the swearing-in ceremony. Next came the rehearsal for Habibie. Eager to get home, the small group was preparing to leave when one of the presidential adjutants, a recent appointee, asked an obvious question: 'Well, what about if it is Gus Dur?' After all, Abdurrahman Wahid was the third candidate. The only answer he got to his question, though, was a short round of laughter as the group left the hall.[1] No one could imagine that Abdurrahman Wahid, or Gus Dur as he is popularly known, could possibly get the numbers to become president. After all, in the June general elections, Megawati's Indonesian Democratic Party of Struggle (Partai Demokrasi Indonesia Perjuangan — PDI-P) party had won more than one-third of the votes. Abdurrahman's own party National Awakening Party (Partai Kebangkitan Bangsa — PKB) had gained less than 13 per cent, scarcely more than half that gained by Habibie's Golkar. Moreover, Abdurrahman was virtually blind, appeared decidedly ungainly on his feet, and had only recently recovered from the stroke that had almost killed him the previous year. There seemed little point in rehearsing for a Wahid victory.

Less than twelve hours later, the auditorium was once again buzzing with life. Tuesday's vote had produced an upset result, but what took place on Wednesday really caught everyone by surprise. In the early hours of Wednesday morning Habibie had announced that he was withdrawing from the race. Unexpectedly bereft of a candidate only hours before voting, Golkar was unable to produce a replacement. This left only Abdurrahman and Megawati to contest the presidency. Hours later, as vote counting commenced, most assumed that Megawati would cruise to victory. She did seize an early lead, but as the count settled down voting remained surprisingly close. Each had around 250 votes two-thirds of the way through the count. At this point, however, Abdurrahman opened up a small lead, which then accelerated. The tension of the previous evening returned in double measure. When counting closed, Abdurrahman had polled sixty more votes than Megawati. Megawati walked over to her old friend and placed her hand on his shoulder. Largely impassive, she appeared gracious in defeat; only a slight quiver at the corners of her lips and the moisture gathering in her eyes revealed something of her deep shock. In the midst of a gaggle of television crews Abdurrahman appeared calm and at ease. His wife Siti Nuriyah and daughter Yenny stood calmly beside Megawati, their faces barely betraying the shock that they felt. Amid a roar of applause and shouts of jubilation Abdurrahman was helped to his feet and escorted to the podium. Two days later his face was on the cover of the *Economist* beside bold yellow headlines declaring: 'Goodness it's Gus Dur: Indonesia's surprising new president.'

AN UNPRETENTIOUS LEADER

When I first met Abdurrahman in 1989 I was a rather gauche postgraduate student just starting on a PhD thesis examining liberal Islam. My Chinese Christian hosts in Jakarta thought this an odd topic, but when I mentioned Gus Dur's name they gave approving nods. Nevertheless, they were surprised when I declared that I was off the next day to meet with Gus Dur. It never occurred to me that an unknown foreign postgraduate student should have any doubts about walking in off the street and asking to meet with Abdurrahman Wahid. I was naive but, as it turned out, my confidence was not misplaced. From the first Abdurrahman was warm and generous with his time and showed little sign of impatience with my clumsy questions. He seemed as unpretentious as his surroundings, the dilapidated headquarters of Nahdlatul Ulama (NU). Located on a busy central Jakarta arterial road even more noisy and polluted than most, the building, both inside and outside, looked as if it belonged in some far-flung, impoverished rural backwater rather than in the nation's capital. It was the complete antithesis of the smart white tile-clad office block that was Muhammadiyah's national headquarters. A visit to the offices of the two organisations made it clear that the differences between them partook of the divide between city and village. The so-called 'modernist' Muslims of Muhammadiyah tend to be urban traders and white-collar professionals, and their straightforward, rational approach to their faith reflects an urbanity born of their environment. NU's 'traditionalist' Muslims, however, tend to be mystical by nature, and display a folk-religion approach to Islam that appears at one with their rustic milieu. And a more rusticated setting than NU's Jakarta office it was hard to imagine.

None of this appeared to deter visitors. There was a steady stream of visiting *kiai* (religious leaders) and *santri* (devout Muslims). It almost seemed as if the rundown and nondescript nature of PBNU (Pemimpin Besar Nahdlatul Ulama), as the organisation's national leadership and headquarters were known, was intended to make such visitors feel at home. Abdurrahman's office had been created by cheaply partitioning a large nondescript room. He sat behind a large desk that was invariably overflowing with books and papers; behind him stood a bookshelf filled with more books and papers. The titles of the books were often interesting: many of them were works of Western literature, including titles such as Salman Rushdie's *The Moor's Last Sigh*; others were recent studies on Islam or Indonesian politics.

From our first meeting he seemed to have no reserve about speaking with an unknown Australian postgraduate student and quickly opened up to talk about what he was doing and what he was trying to achieve. He appeared completely at ease and nonchalant, although it was clear from the number of phone calls and interruptions, together with the queue of guests waiting outside, that his schedule was, in fact, hectic.

He was chubby — indeed, more than chubby; his Buddha-like tummy was barely contained by the bursting buttons of his cheap batik shirt. In the late 1980s he wore clumsy, thick-rimmed, black spectacles. His left eye was almost closed over, and obviously the vision in his right eye was none too good either. He certainly could not be said to be photogenic. His teeth were crooked and somewhat yellowed and his hair a black wavy mess. Over the years I have taken many dozens, perhaps hundreds, of photographs of Abdurrahman, but few seem to do him justice. There is something about his magnetic presence that is rarely captured on film. The best photographs are those taken when he is laughing. For, despite his modest appearance, his presence commanded attention. It was not that he was imposing — the opposite was true – but his relaxed warmth and animated manner combined with his ready flow of wit and good humour made it impossible for me not to like him.

I was clearly not alone in these impressions. His office saw a steady stream of diplomats, often of ambassadorial or first-secretary level, as well as numerous teams of journalists from around the world. Almost always there were local journalist and activists from non-government organisations (NGOs) waiting for him in one of the front rooms, and the office seemed to be a hive of activity.

Despite Abdurrahman's relaxed and unassuming manner, the swirl of activities surrounding him, and the reaction of people whenever they met him, conveyed the impression that he was a very important man in

Indonesian society. Indeed, in 1990 the well-regarded weekly news magazine *Editor* named him their 'Man of the Year'. Their issue of 22 December that year ran fifteen pages about Abdurrahman. The subheading on the cover read 'The year of Islam's stirring in Indonesia'. The heading on the lead story read 'A mosaic whose name is Abdurrahman Wahid'; the subheading was 'Gus Dur, man of the year 1990, often controversial and not afraid to be independent'. This was a special issue of *Editor*, but it was hardly the first time that Abdurrahman's face had graced the cover.

By now Abdurrahman was already well known and his visage, usually laughing, frequently appeared on the covers of Indonesian news magazines such as *Editor* and *Tempo*. Even before becoming chairman of Nahdlatul Ulama he had been very much in the news, but the final years of the 1980s saw his prominence steadily increase. He was greatly admired for his outspokenness and frequently quoted because he would say things journalists themselves would never dare say. For example, in an interview with American journalist Adam Swartz in April 1991, Abdurrahman said, 'It is futile to argue with the government. There is no dialogue. They talk and talk. It is just a series of monologues. It's the rigidity of government policies which is what causes repression and this in turn causes sectarianism'.[2]

THE MAN BEHIND THE PERSONA

If there is a cardinal rule to understanding Abdurrahman, it is not to take him at face value. It is generally unwise to underestimate him for there is always more to him than meets the eye. It is equally unwise, however, to read him too literally. What he says is often not so much what he knows to be true as what he wants to be true. At best, this makes him an irrepressible optimist. At worst, he sometimes comes across as either disingenuous or deluded, or both. Having wrestled with understanding him for some years now, I have come to the conclusion that he is rarely as deluded as people imagine him to be, nor is he particularly disingenuous. Rather, his tendency to downplay the problems facing him in his statements, I am convinced, represents the extrovert workings of his habit of psyching himself up to meet completely intimidating challenges.

Whether this is good or bad I do not know. I do know that it is one trait that his friends would most dearly like to change, if only they could. As president it was frequently his undoing, giving rise as it does to the perception that either he does not understand or he does not care about the dire circumstances that he finds himself in. On the other hand, he is a survivor par excellence. Levels of intimidation and enormous challenges that would have broken other men have failed to break him. If, then, his projection of exaggerated self-confidence is essential for him to stay the course and not give in, its virtue outweighs the annoyance it causes. In any case, it seems to me that it is intrinsic to his 'rough diamond' nature. In Javanese terms he is more *kasar* (rough) than he is *halus* (refined). For better or worse, that is simply the way that he is.

Every now and then the vulnerable and very human Gus Dur behind the ever-confident public persona reveals itself. One such occasion came in November 1994, at a time when he was fighting for his life as leader of NU against the concerted strength of Soeharto's nefarious regime. At 3 am on Tuesday, 5 September, his future as leader of NU hung on the result of a ballot count that was nearing its conclusion.

Concerned about what might happen if Abdurrahman were not re-elected, I left the main Assembly hall used for the plenary sessions of the NU national congress, and sat under the canvas awning that filled the large square outside. There I ran into Yenny. I asked her about her father and remarked that when I had seen him earlier in the evening he had shrugged off concern about his situation and said that there was nothing to worry about, declaring that he was perfectly relaxed. Yenny's response indicated that this was not entirely the case. She explained that just minutes earlier she had been with her father, and as she had laid her head on his chest she had been surprised to hear how furiously his heart was pounding. Clearly, despite all his protestations, he too was feeling more than a little anxious about the outcome.

Another occasion when the vulnerable Gus Dur was on display occurred a little over three years after his victory at the NU congress. In January 1998 he was again fighting for his life, only this time the stakes were much higher and the challenges even greater. Days earlier he had suffered a stroke that very nearly killed him. When I went into his hospital room, I was not surprised to see him lying in bed, head shaven, and tubes in his arms. He was not yet out of the critical zone and was not really supposed to be having visitors.

His physical appearance was of course unsettling but what was really surprising was his presence of mind. Looking beyond the oddly helpless figure under the shaven head I found that he seemed to be the same man I had always known. I told him how a friend in Paris, Andrée

Feillard, had emailed me saying that she had heard the news of the stroke and, thinking that he had died, rushed into a cathedral that she was passing in the street and knelt at the altar to pray. I said, 'You know how unusual this is. Andrée after all is a French intellectual — they don't go to church, much less pray'. His reply came without hesitation and with a slight chuckle in his voice: 'In France all the best people are like that.'

From this and the exchanges that followed, it was clear that he had lost none of his droll wit. He did say, however, that he couldn't focus and that his eyesight was gone. It had not been good before the stroke, but now he now said that he couldn't recognise faces, and that he could see nothing but blurry patches of light and dark. Nevertheless, he was, as ever, characteristically upbeat. In circumstances such as these, it occurred to me, it would have been wrong to deny him his optimism. He needed every resource of strength and willpower that was available to him. A rational surrendering to circumstances is not necessarily a virtue when you are fighting for your life.

A third occasion when the 'vulnerable Gus Dur' was revealed occurred on the second day of the August 2000 session of MPR. Once again Abdurrahman was fighting for his life. He made an excellent address on the first day of the session, but on the second had to endure a full day of angry responses from the Assembly's eleven factions. The final speech before the dinner break was the most difficult one for Abdurrahman to sit through. It was the speech from the Reform Faction, which consisted of Amien Rais's National Mandate Party (Partai Amanat Nasional — PAN) and a series of small Islamist parties. In the language of the Qur'an, he was denounced as a hypocrite and an evil tyrant in an emotional speech that built to an hysterical conclusion.

Immediately the speech was over, we drove back to the Hilton Hotel. Abdurrahman had been ready for harsh criticism but the speech had gone beyond all expectations. Yenny asked me to go in and talk with him. 'You know my dad, he's a proud man after all and this sort of thing is really hurtful, he must be very upset', she said.

When I went in, Abdurrahman was sitting quietly in his suite. When asked, he simply remarked that the speech was 'nothing'. The tone of his voice and his posture, however, told a different story. It seemed as if a great weight was bearing down on his hunched shoulders and he was fighting to hold back a flood of emotion. As I reached out to grasp his hand across the table, something of what he had dammed up inside himself during those long hours seated on the podium began to trickle out. 'You know for three hours I was doing my best to stop from getting angry, but it was very hard during that last speech.' Having candidly confessed to the depth of his emotion, his mood began to change as we joked about the afternoon. Looking for a way to get him laughing, I joked that the speech from the Reform Faction suffered from three major deficits. Firstly, it was irrational; secondly, it was immature; and thirdly, it was immoral (a play on words that sounds much funnier in Indonesian than it does in English: *ada tiga yang kurang: kurang rasional, kurang dewasa, dan kurang ajar*). Hearing the joke Abdurrahman roared with laughter and, as the conversation broke into jokes and banter, his anger and frustration appeared to lift; by the time he was eating dinner and preparing to return to the Assembly, he was calm and in good spirits.

By chance I had lunch that day with Seth Mydans, the Southeast Asia correspondent with the *New York Times*. He reminded me of my comment the previous month, saying that Abdurrahman should not be underestimated and likening him to the 'drunken master' hero figure of *kung fu* lore, the apparently maladroit but surprisingly able character of film and fiction, that Abdurrahman had grown up with. I was deeply anxious about what might unfold over the next week and pointed out to Seth that my quote might well prove to be prescient but at this stage it could go quite the other way. I was not at all confident that the 'drunken master' could repeat his earlier success.

That evening Abdurrahman's old friend Marsillam Simanjuntak read out the second speech. From the outset it was clear that Abdurrahman was sticking to his policy of self-restraint and contrition. The speech began by accepting that the points of criticism from the previous day had been invaluable and that there was little to be gained in responding to them one by one, particularly some of the more angry points. Monday's speech had been surprising for its brilliance; Wednesday's was even better. It was exactly the right speech to make in response to the criticisms of the previous day. It repeated the tone of contrition from the first speech, acknowledged the need to learn from past mistakes, gently pointed out it was not fair to blame one person for every ill event in this culture, and then spoke positively and convincingly about the future.

As we drove back to Hilton I felt an immense sense of relief, which all those in the entourage around me seemed to share. The consensus was that the speech was even better than we thought possible and exactly the right response. I went into Abdurrahman's suite at the Hilton and he was in high spirits and obviously happy with the way things had turned out. On a morning walk several days earlier we had talked about my 'drunken master' comment, which Seth had written up in the *New York Times*, and this was clearly on his mind now. He turned to me and said, 'Well, it looks like the drunken master wins again', and chuckled.

RUNNING FOR PRESIDENT: A FOOLISH AMBITION?

When I approached him in the mid-1990s about writing his biography it naturally never occurred to me that Abdurrahman would ever become president. I felt sure that he would play an important role in civil society in the transition from the Soeharto era, but it seemed patently ridiculous to imagine him as president. The fall of Soeharto in May 1998, and the unexpectedly rapid transition to democracy — or at least to free and fair elections — only a little over twelve months later, did change things of course, but only by degrees.

When questioned about whether he had any chance of becoming president, Abdurrahman would typically reply in an ambiguous fashion. As early as July 1998 he told me, jokingly, or so it seemed at the time, that if there was no one else to do the job he might be prepared to do it. At the time I dismissed such talk as being somehow associated with his illness, his frustration at his loss of eyesight and struggle for recovery. While I could detect no major signs of personality change after his January stroke, it seemed to me that talk about becoming president might indeed represent precisely the sort of wishful thinking that many took to be a sign of deterioration in his mental health following his illness.

Even a month before the MPR was due to vote for Indonesia's first democratically elected president, however, the idea of 'President Wahid' seemed like a crazy long shot. By this stage Alwi Shihab, Abdurrahman's old friend and architect of his presidential bid, was feeling confident that they had the numbers to get Abdurrahman elected, but it did not seem likely to me. And if the truth were known, even Alwi was not completely certain.

On 29 September we were chatting in Abdurrahman's hotel suite when Alwi asked me to step outside in the corridor for a friendly chat. 'Frankly,' he said, 'what do you think our chances are? Do you think that the Central Axis will really back Abdurrahman and that he could really be president?' Alwi seemed deadly serious in his question and I didn't know how to reply. I said that I hoped that the Central Axis would remain true to their word but I was not very confident. 'The important thing,' I said, 'is to work on building a good relationship with Megawati just in case the Central Axis support fails to secure Abdurrahman's victory.'

It seemed to me that Abdurrahman was setting himself up for a devastating fall. He seemed to be convinced that he would be president in October and yet it seemed so unlikely. After all, the alliance of forces from the former regime and the Islamic right that he was relying upon to back him were by no means his natural allies or friends. He had a long history of mutual antipathy with most of the key players. What made him feel that he could rely upon them now? Talking with Yenny and with Ratih Hardjono, a close friend of the family, I realised I was not alone in my concerns. Even Munib Huda, Abdurrahman's personal assistant, the epitome of the untiring, faithful servant, was privately expressing concern. 'Do you think he is doing the right thing?' he asked on several occasions. 'Do you think he can really make it? Does it make sense?' Yenny likewise was worried that everything might fall in a heap. But it was Ratih, perhaps most of all, who was worried about where Abdurrahman was heading. We sat talking over dinner on Friday, 1 October. I wanted to check some things for the biography, and Ratih was keen to talk. We were both in a similar frame of mind, deeply concerned about what was about to happen to our friend. Ratih ran through the various challenges and problems facing him and the reasons why it seemed almost certain that he would not become president. The situation seemed hopeless.

My hope was that he would win the position of Speaker of the MPR and at least be left with a consolation prize. When I spoke with friends around town, including newspaper editors and prominent intellectuals, many shared the same concern. There was deep respect and affection for Abdurrahman and a genuine fear that, when the MPR disbanded, he would be left with nothing.

The next day I was to fly home again. The MPR was to elect the Speaker of the Assembly. The proceedings ran over time, as they often did, and I had to go to the airport before the decision came through. From the airport I phoned Munib, only to learn that Amien Rais had been successful in winning the position. I was crestfallen. 'Don't worry,' explained Munib. 'That is what he wanted. He endorsed Amien.' 'But why? What's he doing?' I asked. The answer should have been obvious enough.

When next I met with Abdurrahman it was 16 October, just four days before the presidential election. Despite my fears, Abdurrahman was in great spirits and completely confident that he would be president. On the night of Sunday, 7 October, the long-awaited meeting of senior *kiai* took place. As I sat with Munib outside the meeting, he again questioned me, 'Do you think he's really doing the right thing? Can he pull this one off?' The *kiai* warned Abdurrahman about the risks in proceeding but grudgingly gave him their support. For Abdurrahman that was enough.

The next day he invited me to join him on a visit to see Amien. As we walked into Amien's expansive 'presidential suite', given to him on account of his election as Speaker, he greeted us warmly. 'Greg, Gus Dur is the only one who can do it. He is the only one who can bring Muslims and non-Muslims and everyone together. Everything depends on him. He is our only hope.' Amien said the words with what seemed to be true conviction. Alwi had been working furiously behind the scenes and it seemed certain now that the whole of the Central Axis force would back Gus Dur's candidature.

As it happened, after we had spoken for a while, Amien received some official visitors. They were members of a Dutch parliamentary delegation, many of them born in the Maluku Islands, and were in Jakarta trying to raise support to combat the violence that continued unabated in Ambon. Abdurrahman turned to Amien and invited him to respond to the questions. 'You know all about it, you know what to say,' he said. And indeed Amien did. Amien spoke as if he were a protégé of Abdurrahman. He talked about the difference between religious sentiment and so-called religious violence and argued cogently and persuasively for tolerance, understanding and patience. It really did now seem as if Amien was on Abdurrahman's side, and as if Abdurrahman was going to be president. On the drive back to the Nahdlatul Ulama headquarters my mobile phone rang. It was my wife. I briefly told her what had been going on and passed the phone to Abdurrahman. He explained in detail and with great delight what had occurred, laughing out loud at the irony of the situation. 'Don't forget,' he said, 'you are to come back and visit us and stay at the palace.' 'Will you really be president?' she asked. 'Oh yes, yes,' he said. 'It's all fixed.'

EVERYTHING CHANGES, NOTHING CHANGES

When Abdurrahman was elected president on Wednesday, 20 October, he and his family were taken away under a tight security cordon and escorted to the palace complex. Given that he had to negotiate the formation of a new cabinet and do one or two other things, I thought it best to wait a couple of days before trying to make contact. By Sunday evening I felt it might be time to contact Abdurrahman who was, by then, ensconced in the State guesthouse in the palace complex. (The palace had not been used as a residence during the Soeharto and brief Habibie presidencies and therefore was not ready for occupation.) Just how one contacted a president, however, I was not at all sure. Neither Yenny nor Ratih was answering the phone, and I could not imagine presidential security being impressed by my line about being a friend of the president.

I called Mohamad Sobary, an old friend of Abdurrahman, and suggested that we just turn up at the palace complex early the following morning, saying that the president had asked to see us. When we approached the front gates we repeated our story and were ushered in. Downstairs, after passing through the outer line of security, we repeated the same falsehood, asking them to pass on to the president the information that we had arrived. With any other president this would have been an arrogantly bold approach but with Abdurrahman it seemed strangely appropriate. Indeed, before too long, we were ushered upstairs into the grand apartments previously occupied by Habibie and by visiting heads of state.

My apprehension about losing an old friend proved false. Despite the evident pressures of office that had already begun with the difficult task of selecting a new cabinet, Abdurrahman appeared as relaxed and jovial as ever. He seemed glad to see us and I was reminded of his words over lunch the previous Monday, though it felt as if a decade rather than a week had passed since that modest meal. He had made a point then of explaining seriously that when he became president — he was by this stage taking it for granted that he would be president — his schedule would be difficult, with protocol much heavier than anything in the past but that he wanted to continue to maintain contact with old friends. He proved true to his word. There's something about Abdurrahman's personality which means that contact is not just a blessing to his friends, but also necessary for his own stability and good health.

PRESIDENTIAL DREAMS

In the first weeks of his presidency the one thing that struck almost everyone who met with him was just how relaxed and comfortable Abdurrahman appeared. There was no question that the challenges he was facing were enormous, and he was not deluding himself about the scale of the task before him, nor was he worrying about things he could not change. Instead, he seemed positively excited about those things that he might be able to change. At one point I said to him, 'You are enjoying this aren't you?' He laughed and said, 'Of course!' I continued, 'It seems to me that the chance to put in place all those things you've long dreamed and talked about is really exciting'. 'Yes,' he said, 'now is the chance to really do something.' He was of course greatly constrained in what he could do, but he did know the direction that he wanted to take. The area of foreign policy was part of this vision. Much more than many of his peers, Abdurrahman was at home in a wide variety of cultural and social contexts. One of his immediate priorities was to promote Indonesia to the West. He wanted to gain the confidence of the West, together with important Middle Eastern and Asian powers, in the new and democratic Indonesia. One of the factors driving this was his concern about Aceh. Recognising the potential for the shipment of funds and even arms from sympathetic elements in the Middle East, and elsewhere in Asia, he made a point of seeking to persuade key parties to support him in his efforts to negotiate a solution to the conflict in Aceh, rather than fanning further militant activity.

One of the dreams that Abdurrahman brought with him to the presidency was of healing the rift that had torn apart Indonesian society in the mid-1960s when ordinary citizens, including NU youth, joined with the army in hunting down communists and killing them in cold blood. This was brought home to me on the second Saturday after his election. I returned to visit him, again with Mohamad Sobary and also with an old friend from Paris, Andrée Feillard, who has written extensively about Nahdlatul Ulama and Abdurrahman. A few days earlier, when asked where she was staying, Andrée had explained she was at the home of Hardoyo, a well-known dissident who had been jailed for eight years early in the Soeharto regime. Abdurrahman's response was, 'Well, please ask him to come along, please bring him with you next time.' When driving with us to the palace complex, Hardoyo drew our attention to a vacant block of land about two kilometres from the palace and quietly explained that this was the location of the military prison in which, under Soeharto, he had been kept for eight years.

On arriving at the palace complex, Hardoyo was clearly overcome with emotion. 'I haven't been here for years, not since 1964,' he said. 'I used to come here and listen to Sukarno speak. Since that time it has been impossible to ever imagine coming back.' His warm reception by the new president, complete with an invitation to stay for lunch, overwhelmed Hardoyo.

Understandably, he was also delighted to have snapshots taken as we sat and talked with Abdurrahman. Immediately afterwards, I had the roll of film processed and handed him the prints. He was delighted, and as he held up a photograph of himself and the new president he said, 'I'm going to enlarge this and put it on the wall of my front room. Just let any of those army people try and cause any trouble now. I'll point to this photograph and then they'll see'.

Over the following weeks Abdurrahman made a point of inviting a succession of former dissidents and political prisoners to meet with him at the palace complex. It was as if he wished to emphasise that this was a new era and that past wrongs had to be owned up to and addressed.

A PARADOXICAL PRESIDENT

It is easy to enumerate the many paradoxes that make up Abdurrahman Wahid. What follows are but a few. Firstly, he is a figure greatly underestimated, but also extremely well respected and enormously popular. In recent years he has also acquired the new label of 'frail and half-blind', but the stamina that he displays in cruising through an unrelenting schedule of travel and meetings, the same restless energy that he has displayed all of his life, suggests that he has the constitution of an ox. Although his eyesight has all but failed, his sparkling rhetorical performances testify to a sharp intellect and prodigious memory that go a long way in compensation. As a traditionalist Javanese *ulama*, or Islamic scholar, there is a side to Abdurrahman that is parochial. However, he is also fluent in four languages and can read in another three, and has a wide understanding of their related cultures. Linked to this is the paradoxical reality that Abdurrahman is both deeply ecumenical and passionate about Islam. He speaks of respect for all faiths but was for fifteen years head of the world's largest Islamic organisation, and was regarded by its tens of millions of rustic peasant members as a living saint. How deep then is his cosmopolitanism and to what extent does he live out the pluralism that he preaches?

The paradoxes continue. As an individual, Abdurrahman is by any measure physically plain. Yet those who spend time in his company remark on how seductively charismatic and magnetic he can be. Physical appearances aside, his is clearly a mind of rare agility and sharpness. Partly because of this. and also because of his supreme sense of destiny, many say that he is more than a little egocentric. Those who know him well, however, argue that he is remarkably humble and genuinely unpretentious. To what extent is his strong drive to be in the centre of political change simply an egocentric lust for power and to what extent is he a genuine idealist?

One trait which annoys people, perhaps more than anything else, about Abdurrahman, is his tendency to shoot from the hip. He is given to recklessness and often appears careless in his approach to making public statements. Yet, when it matters most, he is also capable of being extremely canny and careful in what he says. Similarly, he often gives the impression of flying by the seat of his pants, and of not working to a clear plan or method. Nevertheless, when one reviews his career in public life, including the first year of his presidency, it seems that he does have a long-term vision about what he wants to achieve. What sort of visionary is he?

Given the complexity of his personality, it is not surprising that observers frequently differ widely in their assessment of his behaviour and capability. Whereas in the late 1990s some saw him as a leader in decline, a man who was once great but was now living on past glories, others saw him as one of Indonesia's most powerful leaders. Even as he prepared to face the biggest test of his public career, the special session of the MPR on 1 August 2000 that would determine his political fate, he refused to give up hope of negotiating a deal that would save his presidency. His enemies, publicly at least, dismissed his determination as mere delusion. Others, more out of compassion than malice, simply wondered aloud why he did not simply give up. For Abdurrahman himself, however, giving up was never an option. He saw himself locked in mortal combat with the forces of the former regime, both civilian and military, who he felt were determined to do anything to stop the onward process of reform. If one was to believe his enemies he was, at best, a tragic, quixotic has-been who saw dragons where sane men saw windmills.

So what should we make of Abdurrahman Wahid? Was his victory simply the freak outcome of unusual circumstances, or was it a masterful political play? It is too early yet to form a definitive judgment of Abdurrahman's performance as president, although it is clear that for all concerned his presidency proved to be deeply disappointing. It is equally clear, however, that he is in many respects a remarkable leader and a deep and complex individual. There is much more here than meets the eye.

This page intentionally left blank

PART 1

PESANTREN AND FAMILY

This page intentionally left blank

ONE

GROWING UP IN *PESANTREN* AND POLITICS, 1940-1963

PESANTREN ORIGINS

It is unlikely that the crowd of friends and family who joined Abdurrahman to celebrate his sixtieth birthday at the Bogor Palace on Friday, 4 August 2000, realised that he was not, in fact, born on 4 August, even though he always celebrated his birthday on that date. As with so many aspects of his life and person, things are not quite what they seem. Abdurrahman was indeed born on the fourth day of the eighth month. But the month in which he was born was Syaban, the eighth month of the Islamic calendar.[1] In fact the fourth of Syaban 1940 was actually 7 September.[2] Abdurrahman was born in Denanyar, near the city of Jombang, East Java, in the *pesantren* home of his maternal grandfather Kiai Bisri Syansuri.

A *pesantren* is a religious boarding school run on a communal basis. Most are located in rural settings and service poor farming communities. The *pesantren* are led by *ulama*, or religious scholars, also known as *kiai* in Java. Because the approach to Islam in the *pesantren* is essentially that traditional in Java for centuries past and emphasises Sufism, or Islamic mysticism, the *kiai* are accorded considerable respect as spiritual teachers and guides. Since the formation of Nahdlatul Ulama (NU) in 1926, the vast majority of *pesantren* have been affiliated in a loose network under it. Nahdlatul Ulama (the name means the 'revival of the *ulama*') is a traditionalist Islamic organisation that is strongest among ethnic Javanese, both within Java and in areas where they have settled outside Java, such as South Sumatra and Central Kalimantan. NU's greatest strength is East Java, especially the East Java town of Jombang, the home of both sides of Abdurrahman's family.

KIAI BISRI SYANSURI AND KIAI HASYIM ASY'ARI

Abdurrahman's grandfathers, Kiai Bisri Syansuri and Kiai Hasyim Asy'ari, are held in great reverence in NU circles, both because of the role that they played in founding NU and because of their standing as *ulama*. Uncharacteristically for traditionalist *ulama*, Kiai Hasyim Asy'ari, and more so his son Kiai Wahid Hasyim, who was Minister for Religious Affairs under Sukarno, were respected within urban, middle-class society because of their close involvement with the nationalist movement that led the revolutionary struggle against the Dutch following the end of the Second World War. Because of this, both men are remembered officially as 'Pahlawan Nasional', or National Heroes. Their names, together with those of the other National Heroes, are commemorated in street names in central Jakarta.

Abdurrahman's paternal grandfather, Kiai Haji Hasyim Asy'ari, was born in Jombang in February 1871 and died in Jombang in July 1947. He was one of the founders of NU in 1926. He was much respected as an Islamic leader in traditional, rural society where he was known to be an inspirational teacher and learned scholar, but he was also a committed nationalist. He numbered among his friends many of the leading figures from the pre-war nationalist movement.[3]

Kiai Hasyim Asy'ari's family proudly claim descent from the sixteenth-century Javanese King Brawijaya VI, who in popular belief is regarded as one of the last kings of the great Hindu-Buddhist Javanese kingdom of Majapahit. More importantly, the legendary Jaka Tingkir, the son of Brawijaya VI, is believed to have introduced Islam to the northeast coastal region of Java while his son, Prince Banawa, is remembered as a recluse who turned his back on the court to teach Sufism. This lineage is regarded as immensely auspicious in traditional Javanese society, where modern academic quibbles about the veracity of this history, and of Kiai Hasyim Asy'ari's links to it, are less important than the perception of authority that it confers.

After studying in his family's *pesantren* until the age of fourteen, and then spending a further seven years moving from one *pesantren* to another across East Java and Madura, Hasyim went to Mecca in 1892. There he became an expert in studies of the *Hadith*, the anecdotal accounts of the Prophet Muhammad's life and teaching. He was eventually to conclude his studies in Mecca under the famous West Sumatran teacher, Syaikh Ahmad Chatib Minangkabau. Many of Syaikh Chatib's students, who included Kiai Bisri Syansuri, went on to become *ulama* of great standing in Indonesia. After seven years studying in Mecca, Hasyim returned to Jombang with the aim of establishing his own *pesantren*. For this he chose the village of Tebuireng, then some distance from the city of Jombang, which eventually swallowed it up.

Despite the advice of friends not to choose Tebuireng, then a hamlet where brothels and bars prospered on the wealth generated by the local sugar mill, Kiai Hasyim Asy'ari persisted, arguing that *pesantren* should play a role in transforming the surrounding society and encouraging piety in those to whom Islam had been alien. His *pesantren* was opened in 1899 and soon achieved a reputation as a centre of learning. Hasyim Asy'ari introduced a number of innovations to *pesantren* teaching which were subsequently widely copied, including structured classes, systematically tiered learning, and critical discussion within class. The curriculum at Pesantren Tebuireng was steadily developed and by the 1920s came to include instruction in modern languages, including Malay and Dutch, and classes in mathematics and science. At the same time Hasyim Asy'ari's reputation grew steadily greater as a reformer of Islamic thought and practice. After the formation of NU, he was made Rais Akbar, which literally means Great President, as head of the organisation's Religious Advisory Council. After his death the title was never used again; his successors were known instead by the title of Rais Aam, or General President. He was also accorded the rare honour of being titled Hadhratusysyaikh, or the Great Teacher. Many people outside the *pesantren* world remember him better, though, as a nationalist and a staunch critic of Dutch colonialism.

Abdurrahman's maternal grandfather, Kiai Haji Bisri Syansuri, although less well known in secular urban society than Kiai Hasyim Asy'ari, was also active in the nationalist movement.[4] Bisri Syansuri was born in September 1886 on the northern coast of Central Java, an area rich with *pesantren* as a result of its early conversion to Islam before the

Hindu-Buddhist interior of the island. Along with Hasyim Asy'ari, he was regarded as one of the key figures in the establishment of NU. In 1917 he introduced the *pesantren* world's first class for female students at his fledgling *pesantren* in the village of Denanyar, outside Jombang. After studying under Kiai Hasyim at Pesantren Tebuireng for six years and then in Mecca for two years, he served an apprenticeship in Pesantren Tambakberas for two years, and then established his own *pesantren* in Jombang. In time Pesantren Denanyar was to become as well known as Pesantren Tambakberas and Pesantren Tebuireng, although varying from them in style as it reflected the personality of its *kiai*. Like Hasyim Asy'ari before him, Bisri Syansuri took an expanse of land barren in every sense, and over time turned it into a thriving community of farming, learning and spiritual development. Bisri Syansuri had proved himself to be not only an expert scholar of *fiqh*, or Islamic jurisprudence, and a gifted educational administrator but also an able agriculturalist. His *pesantren* in Denanyar became known for its disciplined, ordered approach to scholarship and communal life.

KIAI WAHAB CHASBULLAH

Another key figure who was to have much influence in Abdurrahman's life was Kiai Wahab Chasbullah.[5] Born in Tambakberas in 1883, Wahab Chasbullah was a second cousin and former student of Hasyim Asy'ari. Like Hasyim Asy'ari and Bisri Syansuri he had studied in Mecca under the famous Syaikh Chatib Minangkabau, and before that with the equally well-known Kiai Cholil in Bangkalan on the island of Madura, across the strait from Surabaya. It was at Kiai Cholil's *pesantren* that Wahab Chasbullah first met Hasyim Asy'ari, who was a generation older. Wahab Chasbullah came from Jombang, where his father, Kiai Chasbullah, ran Pesantren Tambakberas. Despite their very different personalities, Wahab Chasbullah and Bisri Syansuri, who were only a few years apart in age, quickly struck up a lasting friendship. Instructed by Kiai Cholil to study in Jombang under his former student Hasyim Asy'ari, Wahab moved from Bangkalan to Tebuireng, where he joined Bisri Syansuri again for four years. In 1912, with their *pesantren* studies completed, Wahab Chasbullah and Bisri Syansuri were ready to make the *haj* pilgrimage. The two men, now in their late twenties, travelled to Mecca together. After completing the pilgrimage they stayed on, as was the custom of *pesantren* graduates, for a further two years of study, mostly under teachers from the East Indies including Syeikh

Chotib. During this time Wahab Chasbullah's younger sister, Chadijah, made the pilgrimage to Mecca with her mother. Sensing an attraction between his old friend Bisri Syansuri and his favourite sister, Wahab did his best to encourage what he considered to be an ideal union. Fortunately his mother shared his judgment of the pairing: Bisri Syansuri and Chadijah were married in Mecca before returning to Jombang together, leaving Wahab Chasbullah to carry on his studies alone for a final few months.

Returning to Java in 1914, Wahab Chasbullah chose to make a base for himself in the cosmopolitan port city of Surabaya. There he successfully conducted a range of businesses, became wealthy and mixed widely, befriending many within the nationalist movement. In many circles Wahab is remembered for his flamboyant and eccentric lifestyle. Short, wiry and dark-skinned, he was full of energy and radiated charismatic charm, amplified by a quick wit and a finely tuned sense of humour. He had more than a dozen wives, perhaps even more than twenty (though never more than four at once!) and rode around East Java on a Harley-Davidson motorcycle, the tail of his trademark white turban dancing behind him in the wind. Although a broad-minded thinker more inclined to the spirit of the law than the letter of the law in interpreting Islam, he was greatly respected as a religious scholar. He was accepted as a liberal and eccentric thinker given to emphasising the principles rather than the detail of Islamic legal thinking, just as Bisri Syansuri was respected for his strict approach to personal piety and his renowned jurisprudential and administrative skills.

KIAI WAHID HASYIM

Abdurrahman's father, Wahid Hasyim, was born in Tebuireng, Jombang, in June 1914.[6] The first son born to his parents, he was the fifth of ten children. According to Abdurrahman, while carrying him his mother became seriously ill and vowed that if her pregnancy was successful she would take the child to Kiai Cholil in Madura. Her health returned, her son Wahid Hasyim was born without any difficulties, and she duly took him to Madura to get the blessing of his father's old teacher. The incident was seen by many as portending greatness for the child. Born into the *pesantren* home of one of Java's most famous *kiai*, Wahid Hasyim had no need to travel far to study. His father was a highly regarded teacher who took learning seriously, but he was also democratic in disposition and gave his children considerable freedom in determining their course of study. As a small child Wahid Hasyim learnt to read the Qur'an aloud, and by the age of seven had read it from beginning to end (although, of course, not yet understanding the classical Arabic in which it was written).

Wahid Hasyim studied in his father's *madrasah* (in Indonesia a *madrasah* is a religious day school, often located within a *pesantren*). By the age of twelve he had completed his formal *madrasah* studies with sufficient mastery to assist his father in teaching other students. He was gifted with a prodigious memory and made a hobby of memorising classical Arabic poetry. At the age of thirteen he left Tebuireng to travel from *pesantren* to *pesantren*, as was customary. Somewhat unusually, however, he stayed just days rather than months or years at each of the *pesantren* he visited.[7] Staying just long enough in each *pesantren* to secure the blessing of the *kiai*, he quickly returned home to Tebuireng and, with his father's approval, spent the next four years in private study. His father Kiai Hasyim Asy'ari, atypically for a *kiai*, had married a daughter of the Javanese aristocracy. Thus Wahid Hasyim grew up in a home in which his mother was determined to ensure that her offspring were equipped to take their part in elite urban society rather than remain confined to the rural world of the *pesantren*. She arranged for her son to be given tuition in English and Dutch by the European manager of a local sugar mill. At the age of eighteen he sailed to Mecca and studied there for two years.

Returning home to Tebuireng in 1934, he began to teach in his father's *pesantren* and to develop his ideas regarding what had become for him a passion: how to marry modern education with classical Islamic learning. This took concrete form when he established his own modern *madrasah* within Tebuireng. By 1938, keen to become politically active and participate in the nationalist movement, he searched for an organisation to attach himself to. After much consideration, he decide to channel his energies into NU. Previously he had despaired of the traditionalist organisation, saying: 'NU represents an association of old men who are slow to act, they neither feel nor act in a revolutionary way.'[8] Nevertheless, after considering the alternatives, he eventually concluded: 'Those internal factors, that previously I regarded as being obstacles to progress, may in fact be the reverse, aiding progress.'[9] He had come to the conclusion that, for all its failings, its lack of modern intellectuals and revolutionary spirit, NU with its vast grassroots network had great potential. Choosing a political party or organisation to become involved with was, he wrote: 'Like choosing a life-partner, the one who could satisfy absolutely in all areas, in beauty, in intelligence, in housekeeping, in companionship, in deportment, and so on and so forth, is certainly not obtainable in this world.'[10]

WAHID HASYIM AND SOLICHAH

According to Abdurrahman, in the late 1930s Wahid Hasyim was regarded as one of Jombang's most eligible bachelors. Good-looking and bright, Wahid Hasyim had to deal with numerous offers of marriage made to him by fathers from leading families on behalf of their daughters. For several years he rejected all offers. Then one day in 1939, Wahid, now twenty-five, attended the wedding ceremony of a relative, and noticed a young girl dressed in ordinary work clothing carrying a bucket of water to wash dishes in the kitchen behind the festivities. This was Solichah, daughter of Kiai Bisri Syansuri. By all accounts she was not a classic beauty, and yet there was something about her that attracted his attention. The next day he went to Kiai Bisri and asked for his permission to marry his daughter Solichah. Although not yet sixteen, she was, by the standards of the day, just coming of age and ready for marriage, especially to such a desirable husband. Kiai Bisri gladly gave his permission and they were married that year.[11]

By all accounts Wahid Hasyim and Solichah fell deeply in love. Within a year they had their first child. When she married, Solichah was too young to have been extensively educated but she possessed a natural curiosity, an agile mind and a strong will. She had been educated in her father's school, but like many *madrasah* students first learnt to read and write in the Arab script, which was then used for Malay as well as Arabic. Wahid Hasyim taught her to read the Latin script, the medium for Dutch and Indonesian, the local Malay dialect chosen by the nationalist to become the language of the new nation.[12]

Like most Javanese *santri*, or orthodox practising Muslims (the majority of Indonesian Muslims, who are to varying degrees nominal in their practice of Islam are referred to as *abangan*), Abdurrahman took his father's name at the end of his own. Following Arab practice, he is Abdurrahman 'son of' Wahid, just as his father was Wahid 'son of' Hasyim. But as with most of his peers, his official birth name is different again. (Just as many Westerners are reluctant to use their middle names, the official birth names of many Javanese Muslims often remain little known outside their immediate families. This is, in part, because these names are often elaborate and essentially symbolic in intent and not intended for daily use. Indonesians habitually refer to people by one name only and often prefer a simple contraction or sobriquet.) Perhaps Wahid Hasyim, as an excited first-time father, was filled with the first flush of paternal optimism, or perhaps he was indeed preternaturally prescient. In any case the name he gave his first-born, Abdurrahman Ad Dhakil, was a heavy name for any child to bear. Taken from a heroic figure from the Umayyad dynasty, Ad Dhakil literally means 'the conqueror'. The original Ad Dhakil established Islam in Spain and set up a civilisation that would last for centuries.

Wahid and Solichah wasted no time in building a family. Within weeks of Abdurrahman Ad Dhakil's birth, Solichah was pregnant again. Abdurrahman's sister Aishah was born in June 1941, and she was soon followed by another boy, Salahuddin, born in September 1942.

By the time that Salahuddin was born, the Japanese had over-run the Dutch East Indies and interned the European population. In some areas the nationalists seized the opportunity to push forward with their own revolutionary ambitions, but the Japanese had no time for such diversions. They wanted a compliant, obedient and above all productive population to serve their war-time interests. In enforcing their rule they arrested a number of nationalist activists, including Kiai Hasyim Asy'ari. Abdurrahman recalls that, because his grandfather refused to bow in the direction of the rising sun or worship the emperor, he was beaten so severely by the Japanese that he eventually lost the use of his right arm.[13] Later, however, they realised that arresting the popular *kiai* had been a mistake. In attempting to develop lines of control over the civilian population, they had decided that Islam was one of the key elements of society untainted by Dutch colonialism. Traditionalist Islam in particular, with its network of *pesantren* across Java, represented, for the Japanese, an invaluable social network. Kiai Hasyim Asy'ari was recognised as a key figure in this network and the Japanese sought to make amends, releasing him from captivity.

JAKARTA

In March 1942 the Japanese had established Shumubu, the Office for Religious Affairs. By way of compensation to Kiai Hasyim Asy'ari for his imprisonment, they asked him to take charge of Shumubu. This presented him with a dilemma. To refuse the Japanese would be to risk inflaming suspicion; to accept would smack of accommodation, both for himself as a senior *kiai* and for NU. Hasyim Asy'ari came up with a clever solution. Arguing that he was needed in Jombang and that to commute between Jakarta and Jombang would be too arduous for his aged frame (he was, after all, in his seventies and he had never recovered full movement in his right hand), he proposed that his oldest son, Wahid Hasyim, be allowed to act as his proxy. Wahid Hasyim was already a prominent nationalist. In 1939 he had become involved in the Supreme Islamic Council of Indonesia (MIAI) and had pioneered the development of the Hizbullah, a military wing training young men for the coming revolutionary struggle. Suggesting that the Japanese draft him to head Shumubu was an elegant solution. It allowed Wahid Hasyim to operate in Jakarta together with the other 'above-ground' nationalists like Sukarno and Hatta without arousing Japanese suspicions.

So, in late 1944, when Abdurrahman was just four years old, he accompanied his father to Jakarta. Abdurrahman's brother Umar had been born in January of that year and Wahid Hasyim elected to leave his young family behind in Jombang while he went ahead with his oldest child and set up in Jakarta. During this time Wahid Hasyim and Abdurrahman lived in Menteng, the central Jakarta suburb favoured by leading businessmen, professionals and politicians.

Living there put them in the centre of things; when, for example, they prayed at the nearby Matraman mosque, they would regularly meet nationalist leaders such as Mohammad Hatta. It was also convenient for people to meet with Wahid Hasyim. Abdurrahman recalls that at this time he would often answer a knock on the door at around eight o'clock in the evening and find a strange man dressed in dark peasant garb who would ask whether he could come in and talk to his father. The visitor and Wahid Hasyim would often talk for hours. At his request, Abdurrahman called him Uncle Hussein. Only years later did he come to know the identity of his father's old friend. He was Tan Malaka, the famous Communist leader. Even though Wahid Hasyim was effectively leading the largest Islamic organisation in the country, he made a habit of maintaining good relations with all sections of society, including Tan Malaka and other Communists.

In October 1943 the Japanese abolished the Supreme Islamic Council of Indonesia and replaced it with an umbrella body that they named Masyumi. As with Shumubu they asked Hasyim Asy'ari to head this organisation, but once again he asked that his son, Wahid Hasyim, deputise for him. While in Jakarta Wahid Hasyim developed Masyumi into a credible component of the nationalist movement and in doing so met regularly with Sukarno and Hatta and other leading nationalists. He became involved in the formulation of the Nationalists' 1945 constitution and, Abdurrahman believes, with the development of the state philosophy of Pancasila.

THE REVOLUTION

Following the Japanese surrender, father and son moved back to Jombang where Abdurrahman stayed for the duration of the revolution. During the revolutionary struggle Wahid Hasyim visited Jombang periodically but spent much of his time in hiding. He was also kept busy by his work as an adviser to the revolutionary leader, General Sudirman. Abdurrahman recalls his father returning regularly to the family home late at night after having been in hiding for a week or two, and remembers dressing the recurring sores that plagued his father at the time. The young Abdurrahman would be instructed by his mother to boil up a lotion made from frog skins and apply it to his father's weeping sores. By morning his father would be gone again.

For many Indonesians the period of the nationalist revolution between 1945 and 1949 was time of considerable hardship and instability. For Abdurrahman, however, life in the *pesantren* in Jombang was far from unpleasant. His mother may have been privately fretting about Wahid Hasyim and his friends, but Abdurrahman was too young and too far from the conflict to see the revolution as anything but an adventure. Nevertheless he recalls that, with her husband largely absent, Solichah faced considerable difficulty in supporting the family through this time. To make a little money to buy necessities, she sold sweetmeats and snacks from a small cart in front of her house.

While Wahid Hasyim spent most of this period hiding from the Dutch, his aged father refused to be bothered by the threat of the Dutch targeting nationalist *kiai* such as himself. At one point early in the struggle, a delegation was sent from the nationalist leaders in the field to ask Kiai Hasyim Asy'ari to withdraw from Jombang for fear that he might be targeted by the Dutch. His response was to call his son Yusuf and ask for instruction in firing Yusuf's old pistol. 'Who knows?' he said, 'I should be able to knock off at least one or two Dutchmen with this pistol if they try to come into this compound.'[14] As it happened, Kiai Hasyim, now in his mid-seventies, was ailing and passed away in July 1947.

RETURN TO JAKARTA

In March 1948 when Abdurrahman's sister Chodiyah (Lily) was born, their father was away still busy in the struggle. Finally, when a lasting peace was signed with the Dutch, Wahid Hasyim was able to rejoin his family. His involvement with the new government now made it necessary for the entire family to relocate to Jakarta. In December 1949 Wahid Hasyim and Abdurrahman moved back to Jakarta to set up house in advance of the rest of the family. Wahid Hasyim had been appointed Minister for Religious Affairs and went on to serve in this capacity in four other cabinets before finally stepping aside in April 1952.

Wahid Hasyim and Abdurrahman spent the first few months staying at a hotel in Menteng. Abdurrahman recalls that in the mornings his father made a point of walking him to his nearby primary school rather than leaving this task to the household servants. Wahid Hasyim was an easygoing and unassuming man. His friends knew him as someone who loved to joke and make light of difficulties. As a father he was affectionate but often quiet and to the young Abdurrahman seemed serious. Nevertheless, Abdurrahman recalls his father playing football with him in the backyard, and it appears that he enjoyed having his company in Jakarta. Typical of Javanese fathers of his generation, Wahid Hasyim remained a benign but somewhat distant figure to his son.

It seems that Wahid Hasyim was also a patient father, especially when it came to dealing with his firstborn. Abdurrahman's older relatives recall him being an exuberant and irrepressible child — which is to say, he was frequently naughty. They recall him, on occasion, being bound by rope to a flagpole in the front yard as punishment for a practical joke gone too far or some other misdemeanour. Before he was twelve he had twice broken an arm, on both occasions as a result of his penchant for climbing whatever tree was in sight. On the first occasion the branch on which he had perched himself broke under his weight. The second incident saw him come close to losing his hand. He had taken some food from the kitchen and retreated with it to the comfortable seclusion of a fork between two large branches high up in the canopy of a large tree. After making himself comfortable, he fell asleep and rolled out of his perch. He recalls that the fracture that resulted was so severe; leaving bone protruding from the arm, that the first doctor his father took him to feared that he might lose his hand. Fortunately, some deft manipulation and a large splint enabled the break to mend. The experience appears to have done little to mend his ways, however, for he continued to be reckless and impulsive.

During this period in Jakarta, Wahid Hasyim exerted considerable influence over student leaders and other figures around him. This could be seen in the fact that a group of ten met regularly at his house, including an earnest young man by the name of Munawir Sjadzali. Some indication that Wahid Hasyim was less serious than he appeared and not lacking in a sense of humour comes from his instruction to the young Abdurrahman not only to serve tea and biscuits to this regular group of young cadres but also to lace together the shoes of those whom he observed to have fallen asleep.

Given his background and the circles in which he moved, Wahid Hasyim had a deep appreciation of traditional Islamic culture. Even so, he had a broad circle of friends; the household was full of an eclectic mix of regular guests, including a number of Europeans. Such intercourse was helped by the fact that, as a result of his mother's efforts, Wahid Hasyim was fluent in English and Dutch.

A good friend of Wahid Hasyim's in Jakarta was a German convert to Islam by the name of Williem Iskandar Bueller. Wahid Hasyim often arranged for Abdurrahman to spend afternoons after school at Bueller's house and it was through Bueller that Abdurrahman first gained his love of classical music, the works of Beethoven in particular. From the first day that Abdurrahman heard Beethoven's music played on Bueller's gramophone, he was enraptured. Although Abdurrahman's father was a cosmopolitan and a polyglot who filled his house with books and magazines, his taste in music was confined to traditional Islamic songs and Qur'anic recitation. Wahid Hasyim never came to share Bueller's taste in music, but he was more than happy for Bueller to teach his son to love the classical European composers. Although it was well known that Bueller was homosexual, Wahid Hasyim either did not know or did not care. In any case, Abdurrahman was not about to repeat to his father the dark mutterings of his driver about his father's German friend. Bueller, and his gramophone recordings, had opened a new world of music to him and he did not want to lose it.

Although his father was a government minister and well known in Jakarta circles, Abdurrahman never attended any of the elite schools usually attended by children of government officers. His father gave him the choice to do so but Abdurrahman preferred to attend ordinary schools, saying that the elite schools made him feel uncomfortable. He began his school life studying at the nearby KRIS Primary School in central Jakarta. He spent two years in third and fourth grade at this school before shifting to the Matraman Perwari Primary School, close to the new family home in Matraman, central Jakarta.

At this stage his education was entirely secular. He had, of course, learnt some Arabic as a child, sufficient at least to read the Qur'an aloud, but it was not until his teenage years that he started on a systematic study of Arabic. He and his siblings fondly recall the family home in Matraman, not only for its many interesting guests speaking assorted languages but also for its abundance of books, newspapers and magazines. Indonesian society, even middle-class society, did not have a library culture. Unlike, say, the middle class in India, most urban Indonesians did not read widely, and it was relatively rare to find large personal libraries even in the homes of well-known Jakartan families. Wahid Hasyim's Matraman home, however was an exception. Similarly, where many *santri* households would not think of subscribing to Catholic-owned or other non-Muslim newspapers, the house of Wahid Hasyim was different. The children were encouraged to read whatever they wished and to openly discuss their ideas. Wahid Hasyim was constantly frustrated by the small horizons of many *santri* and strove to ensure that his children would grow up to become different.

WAHID HASYIM

Wahid Hasyim clearly loved his community, but he often despaired of the small-mindedness that held it back. As Minister for Religious Affairs he was troubled by what he saw to be a growing attitude of dependency on the department, of being *manja*, behaving like spoilt children. Nevertheless, he was not, by nature, inclined to let himself be troubled by things that were out of his power to control. In 1952, having survived five cabinets, Wahid Hasyim lost his position in one of the frequent reshuffles that occurred during this period. As minister he had been ultimately responsible for organising the 1951 *haj* pilgrimage. Unfortunately arrangements for the Indonesian pilgrims that year went badly wrong and several thousand were unable to get to Mecca. The debacle gave rise to no-confidence motions against Wahid Hasyim in the parliament and generally did nothing to advance his reputation. As a result he was happy to step aside from the ministry for a time.[15] Many of his friends were upset that he was no longer in the cabinet. Wahid Hasyim, however, was characteristically sanguine. 'We are disappointed that Gus Wahid is no longer sitting in cabinet', one group of friends said. 'No point being disappointed,' Wahid Hasyim replied. 'I can still sit in my house. I have got quite a few chairs and a nice long couch. It's just a question of choosing.' 'Yes, but we are disappointed that the government is no longer making use of our leader ...' 'Well, if the government is not getting any benefit from me then let me get the benefit myself ...'[16]

In these years in Jakarta Abdurrahman spent a lot of time with his father, often accompanying him to meetings and witnessing the rich world in which he lived and the easygoing and unpretentious way that Wahid Hasyim moved through it. Wahid Hasyim made a point of having Abdurrahman with him when he could, both because he enjoyed his company and because he saw this as an important part of Abdurrahman's education. And so it was that on Saturday, 18 April 1953, Abdurrahman was with his father as they were being driven to an NU meeting in the town of Sumedang, several hours southeast of Jakarta on the Bandung road, which runs through the range of volcanic mountains that constitute the spine of Java. Wahid Hasyim was in the back of his big white Chevrolet with his friend the publisher, Argo Sutjipto, while Abdurrahman sat in front with the driver.

Between Cimahi and Bandung they met rain and the busy single-lane mountain road became slick. Their driver was hurrying trying to make up for lost time but, as they rounded a gentle bend at speed, the big white car skidded. Struggling to regain control, the driver, unaccustomed to the powerful American car, repeatedly overcorrected. A truck coming up the mountain road towards them saw what was happening and pulled up on the shoulder of the road to give them space. Unfortunately, as the Chevrolet drew close, it spun and slammed rear first into the stationary truck. It hit with such force that Wahid Hasyim and Argo Sutjipto were thrown from the car. Abdurrahman and the driver were unhurt but climbed out of the car to find both of their companions badly injured and unconscious. Wahid Hasyim had suffered serious head injuries and his forehead, one side of his face and his neck were lacerated and bruised. The accident had occurred at around 1 pm but it was not until around 4 pm that the ambulance from Bandung arrived. Abdurrahman sat for hours on the side of the road watching over his father's inert form. After they were eventually picked up and taken into the hospital in Bandung, Abdurrahman spent the night at his father's bedside. Late that night his mother joined him in the sad vigil. At 10.30 on Sunday morning, Wahid Hasyim succumbed to his injuries; his friend Argo Sutjipto followed him several hours later. Wahid Hasyim, the hope of so many in Indonesia, was gone. He was thirty-eight years old. Abdurrahman was just twelve.

Although in shock after the accident, Abdurrahman retained a certain presence of mind. As he sat beside his unconscious father by the car, he recalled that his father had earlier told him that he had hidden a large amount of cash in a small cushion on the back seat. Remembering this, he retrieved the cushion from the car and clung onto it tightly. Hours later in the hospital he refused all requests to let go of it; those around him assumed that he clung to it out of grief. Only when his mother arrived did he release his grip.

As he was growing up Abdurrahman knew that his father was a popular and influential man, but it is hard for a child to put such things in perspective. The extent of the respect and affection in which Wahid Hasyim was held only became clear to him as they began their sorry journey back to Jakarta with his father's body. As the procession drove through the streets of Bandung and out onto the highway, Abdurrahman was amazed to see large crowds of people lining the streets to pay tribute to Wahid Hasyim. In every town and hamlet, the streets were lined with mourners who had waited patiently in the hot sun to witness the man that they had loved make his last journey home. The story was repeated the next day when the funeral procession departed from the family home in Matraman and slowly made its way to Halim airport. Abdurrahman recalls seeing the streets of Jakarta packed with people come to witness Wahid Hasyim's final pilgrimage to East Java. In Surabaya he recalls the crowds along the roadside being even more packed than they had been in the national capital, as they were also in every little village and settlement all along the eighty-kilometre drive to Jombang. To the grieving twelve-year-old, their patient presence by the roadside spoke volumes about their love for his father. Almost half a century later Abdurrahman describes being overwhelmed by the realisation that they had loved his father so. He recalls wrestling with what it meant and thinking: 'What could one man do that the people would love him so? Was there any finer achievement in life than this?' The bitter-sweet memory was never to leave him.[17]

SOLICHAH TAKES CHARGE

Solichah was three months pregnant with Hasyim, their sixth child, when she bowed grieving over the body of her husband, the kind and gentle man who had seemed so full of promise. When the last of the official visitors had left, when the *kiai* had done with their mourning and the period of state grieving was over, Solichah, who was twenty-nine years old, was left to fend for the children and herself, as well as pay the upkeep on the substantial residence in Matraman purchased when her husband was a minister. To continue living in the family home meant working hard to look after her family. She had no profession or career to fall back upon and six children to support, one at her breast. Nevertheless, as the widow of Kiai Wahid Hasyim she was unlikely to be neglected and had a strong social network to fall back on. Moreover, she was a determined and resourceful woman. Making use of her extensive connections within East Java and Jakarta, she set herself up in the business of trading rice and was able to secure a number of government contracts.

Solichah may not have been the natural intellectual that Wahid Hasyim had been but nor was she an ordinary housewife. She may have married young with little schooling, and her days may have been centred on her young family, but she had also been Wahid Hasyim's closest friend and confidant. By all accounts their partnership of fourteen years had seen her grow and develop in ways beyond her peers back in East Java. She had developed a passion for reading and had become accustomed to keeping abreast of current affairs. She was an active partner in her husband's career and increasingly began to play a modest role herself, especially within NU circles. Following his death her influence steadily increased, and she became an important figure within her community. At home she continued to encourage in the children the sort of free and spirited debate about issues that Wahid Hasyim had stimulated. They were made to feel that that they could and should engage with the many visitors who continued to come to the house and were encouraged to read the papers and the books that were scattered throughout the home.

By this stage Abdurrahman was addicted to reading and seldom went anywhere without a volume in his hand. When he could not find what he was looking for in the household library, he was allowed to scour Jakarta's second hand bookshops to feed his habit. The many friends of the family were also a useful resource when it came to chasing reading material.

Solichah was the sort of woman who automatically inspired respect, not least from her eldest child. Outside the family her sense of bearing and quiet confidence, reinforced by the charisma of her late husband, elicited respectful treatment. Within the family, and especially from Abdurrahman, there was simply no question of going against her, at least not in her presence. For Abdurrahman, Solichah's authority had an added dimension. He was the eldest son of Kiai Wahid Hasyim, Kiai Hasyim Asy'ari's eldest son. Not only was he his father's heir; he was the hope of his family. According to the culture of traditionalist Islamic society, the eldest son was expected to follow in his father's footsteps. For the son of Kiai Haji Wahid Hasyim, and grandson of the Hadhratusysyaikh, the Great Syaikh, there was never any doubt that Abdurrahman Ad Dhakil would study in the *pesantren* and then study further in the Middle East, and there was every hope that he would live up to his name. Salahuddin, Umar and Hasyim could make their own choices, preferably becoming professionals, but Abdurrahman was to follow in the footsteps of his father as a religious scholar and leader of his people.

In the eyes of Solichah, Wahid Hasyim had been the perfect man. His death in April 1953 led her to transfer all of her ambition and her aspirations to Abdurrahman. For her it was natural that Abdurrahman should work out the labour earlier commenced by his father and fulfil what, for her, was a certain course of destiny. Wahid Hasyim was held up to the young Abdurrahman as the example of the man he must become and his life as an example of the path that Abdurrahman must follow. Abdurrahman for his part, although he had a reputation for being playful and disobedient, was always respectful and obedient to his mother, at least in her presence.

ABDURRAHMAN LEAVES HOME

In the short term Abdurrahman did not prove himself to be an outstanding student. In 1954, the year after he had graduated from primary school and moved to junior high school, or SMEP, he was forced to repeat his first year because he failed to prove himself in class tests. This early failure was apparently the result of spending too much time watching football and not enough time doing his homework. Bright enough to succeed but prone to laziness, Abdurrahman had never had to study hard for anything up until this point. He soon became bored in class when he found what was being taught insufficiently challenging to engage his attention. He was still grieving for his father, but he was not the sort of child to show this; instead he filled the void with his dual passions of watching football and losing himself in the world of books.

Today, when asked how the death of his father affected him, Abdurrahman denies any link between his poor performance in school the following year and his struggle to come to terms with his father's death. He simply says that he was lazy and distracted by football and movies and failed to apply himself to his studies. As an adult he seldom, if ever, acknowledges having suffered self-doubt or depression at any time in his life. Even so, there are clues that the death of his father, whom he was closer to than any of his younger siblings, was an enormous blow. Certainly, although never anything more than down-to-earth in his description of him, he always speaks of his father with the deepest admiration and affection.

In 1954, with his mother struggling to look after six children by herself and Abdurrahman doing poorly in school, he was sent off to Yogyakarta to continue his studies at junior high school. While there he stayed in the home of a friend of his father's, Kiai Haji Junaidi. Interestingly, Kiai Junaidi was one of the relatively few *ulama*, or religious scholars, involved in Muhammadiyah during this period and, significantly, was a member of the Majelis Tarjih, or Religious Advisory Board of Muhammadiyah. This might seem unremarkable, but at that time, and even more so in the decades that followed, there was relatively little mixing between Muhammadiyah modernists and NU traditionalists. Just as NU was, and is, the main organisation representing Islamic traditionalism in Indonesia, so almost all modernist Muslims are linked to Muhammadiyah. The modernists differ from the traditionalists in their approach to interpreting the Qur'an, in their attitude to mystical practices and beliefs, and in their cultural integration into modern urban life.

Muhammadiyah was founded in Yogyakarta in 1912, as a result of the rise of the modernist movement in the Middle East, with a vision of reforming and modernising Islamic thought and practice. It was successful as an organisation and as the guiding force in a cultural and educational movement. The traditionalist *ulama*, or *kiai*, who ran the *pesantren* eventually came to recognise that if they did not organise themselves in a similar fashion then their culture and approach to Islam, and particular their *pesantren*, would quickly lose public support. Consequently, in 1926 NU was formed. The traditionalists within NU were concerned that the success of Islamic modernism might see their approach to understanding Islam, with its heavy reliance on classical scholarship and deep appreciation for Sufism, gradually lose influence within Indonesian society, but they were not completely opposed to the ideas of Islamic modernism. And, in time, many of the key elements of modernism reform were picked up and incorporated into NU circles. This was particularly the case with the modernist approach to education, with its strong emphasis on a modern, secular curriculum, in their successful, and rapidly expanding, network of day schools. The traditionalists were keen to preserve the *pesantren* system of religious boarding schools, with their communal way of life and commitment to Sufism, but they established modernist-style *madrasah*, or secular day schools, within the *pesantren*, that were strongly influenced by the modernist approach to education.

Many Muhammadiyah and NU leaders had good personal relations, and a good deal of co-operation occurred between the two organisations. Many from both organisations were active in the nationalist movement. During the Japanese occupation, the two were forced to function together under the rubric of an organisation that eventually came to be called Masyumi; after the occupation ended, they continued to work together in politics. NU and Masyumi leaders co-operated under Masyumi, which now became the major political party representing Muslim interests.

NU abruptly broke away from Masyumi in 1952 because of growing antipathy between the two organisations, which came to a head over negotiations for cabinet positions in March that year. Members of the traditionalist NU generally felt that the modernists within Muhammadiyah and elsewhere looked down on them as 'country bumpkins' or unsophisticated villagers. It was remarkable that the son of the former leader of NU should stay in the home of one of the leading figures in Muhammadiyah. This early experience, itself the legacy of his father's catholic outlook, was to prove formative for Abdurrahman. Pak Junaidi's house was located in the Kauman, the *santri* Muslim quarter of Yogyakarta, close to the royal palace, the birthplace of Muhammadiyah.

A PESANTREN EDUCATION

To round out Abdurrahman's education it was arranged that he would travel three times a week to Pesantren Al-Munawwir in Krapyak, just outside Yogyakarta, to study Arabic with Kiai Haji Ali Ma'shum. Kiai Ali Ma'shum was born in March 1915, one year after Kiai Wahid Hasyim, and was famous for his egalitarian ethos.[18] On the one hand he gave no special treatment to the sons of prominent *kiai* who were entrusted into his care — indeed, just the reverse. On the other hand he mixed freely with his students and was in the habit of dropping by their quarters at mealtimes to check on their cooking, occasionally sampling it uninvited. He also kept a wide circle of friends, mixing freely with Muhammadiyah leaders, government officials and the Yogyakarta royal family. Until he came to Jakarta, Abdurrahman's Arabic had been largely passive. He already spoke good English, however, and could read Dutch. It was in Yogyakarta that his reading really took off and he read with a voracious appetite. By the mid-1950s Yogyakarta's character as a university city was already well defined, and for a bibliophile like Abdurrahman the city's second-hand bookshops were rewarding centres of pilgrimage.

When he completed Junior Economic High School in Yogyakarta in 1957 Abdurrahman commenced formal full-time *pesantren* studies at Pesantren Tegalrejo in Magelang, an hour's drive north of Yogyakarta, remaining there until mid-1959. The *kiai* in charge of his studies there was Kiai Khudori, another of NU's grand old men. At the same time Abdurrahman also undertook part-time studies at Pesantren Denanyar in Jombang under his maternal grandfather, Kiai Bisri Syansuri.

Abdurrahman confirmed his reputation as a gifted student by completing in his two years at Pesantren Tegalrejo a course of study under Kiai Khudori that most students would have required four years for, even though he had spent most of his time outside class reading Western books.[19]

In 1959 he moved to Jombang full-time where, until 1963, he studied at Pesantren Tambakberas under Kiai Wahab Chasbullah, as well as remaining in regular contact with Kiai Bisri Syansuri. During his first year at Tambakberas he was encouraged to begin teaching; he went on to teach at the modern *madrasah* established within *pesantren* complex and also became its headmaster. Throughout this period he continued to make regular trips back to Krapyak, where he would stay in the house of Kiai Ali Ma'shum. It was during this period from the late 1950s through to 1963 that Abdurrahman's formal studies in Islam and classical Arabic literature were consolidated. In *pesantren* circles he was regarded as a remarkable student. His studies, which drew heavily on powers of memory, presented relatively few challenges for Abdurrahman who, although inclined to be lazy and ill-disciplined in his studies, possessed a near photographic memory.

At this time he combined his intellectual pursuit of Islamic learning with a very different approach to knowledge and insight. By now he was deeply drawn to the Sufistic, mystical side of traditionalist Islamic culture and had formed the habit of making regular pilgrimages to graveyards and tomb sites to pray and meditate, usually in the middle of the night. Sometimes the two approaches to learning overlapped. In Jombang, for example, he was successful in committing to memory a standard classical book on Arabic grammar. Even though the string of verses that he memorised contained no outstanding religious insights, such was the importance of Arabic and the memorisation of Arabic texts that for a student to master such a book was considered to be of great religious merit. When setting himself the task of memorising this text Abdurrahman had vowed to make a pilgrimage, on foot, to various tomb sites south of Jombang, culminating in a site on the rugged, sparsely populated, south coast of Java. Success duly came and he set out on his personal pilgrimage, heading south via back roads lest he should be recognised and given a lift. The journey to the coast by foot was well over one hundred kilometres and took him many days. It was uncomfortably beyond the natural limits of his less than athletic physique, but his stubborn determination ensured that he made it. Nevertheless, when early in the return trip he was recognised by the occupants of a passing car, he gladly accepted the offer of a ride back to Jombang.

THE CINEMA, WAYANG KULIT AND CERITA SILAT

Because *pesantren* studies came so easily to him, and indeed because he rarely had to apply himself with great effort to anything he studied, Abdurrahman always had plenty of time to read. Not all his reading or cultural pursuits were religious. It was while in Yogyakarta that he first began to be a 'serious student' of the cinema. In fact for much of the year he was at the movies almost every day, not exactly the sort of behaviour expected from one who might follow in the footsteps of some of Indonesia's most revered religious leaders. Recognising this, Abdurrahman attempted a hopelessly transparent ploy. When his regular movie-buddy called for him outside his room in Kiai Junaidi's house, it was agreed that they should talk loudly of being late for a meeting of Ansor (the NU youth wing). While he was later to develop a serious appreciation of cinema culture, at this stage Abdurrahman simply watched almost every film that came through Yogyakarta with little discretion. Nevertheless, even as a teenager with a gluttonous appetite for new movies, Abdurrahman's appreciation of film was a more serious affair than that of most of his peers'.

It was also in Yogyakarta that he first began to take an interest in *wayang kulit*, the traditional Javanese shadow puppet theatre that was frequently performed in and around Yogyakarta but rarely performed in the national capital. While in Yogyakarta and Magelang he sought out *wayang kulit* performances and was generally able to see one every two or three weeks, often travelling a considerable distance to do so.

Like many other teenagers, Abdurrahman had a lively interest in what might be regarded as pulp literature, but for him even this reading often had a serious element. He developed an enduring passion for *cerita silat*, stories about martial arts warriors either written by Indonesian Chinese writers or translated into Indonesian from the writings of overseas Chinese. *Cerita silat* are generally published in short novella format and run in series through fifteen or more slim volumes. It's difficult to make an argument for regarding them as serious literature, but it is interesting that, in reflecting upon his early passion for *cerita silat*, Abdurrahman describes the extent to which the elements of Chinese philosophy that pervade the stories were influential in his thinking.

A key theme that runs through *cerita silat* is that of the loyalty of a student for his master. In the stories the students learn as much from their masters in terms of spiritual development and character formation as they do in terms of physical martial arts skills. In the world of *cerita silat*, fidelity to one's master and pursuit of the good is frequently tested but is ultimately rewarded. In many respects the world of *cerita silat*, while thoroughly Chinese in nature, parallels the world of the *pesantren* where fidelity and respect for one's *kiai*, or spiritual master, is of the utmost importance and where the formation of character is part of the core business of education.

As a teenager Abdurrahman also developed a keen interest in stories relating to the Second World War. Some of these stories he read in serialised form in local newspapers, syndicated from Western papers, others in magazines and books where he would study with interest the great battles of the recent war and the personalities who shaped those battles. He was also drawn to battles of a different kind and from this point on developed an interest in American politics. He liked biographies of American presidents and found their tales of personal struggle in development and maturation absorbing. His favourite American president was, and remains, Franklin D. Roosevelt, whom he admired for his drive and social vision, but he also has an abiding respect for the unpretentious Harry Truman.

READING

As Abdurrahman moved from Yogyakarta to Magelang, and then Jombang, and from childhood to youth he began to enter more seriously into two realms of reading that were henceforth to occupy his attention: European social thought; and the great English, French and Russian novels. When he was in Magelang he began to read the writings of Europe's leading social theorists, mostly in Indonesian and English but not infrequently in French and sometimes in Dutch and German. He read whatever he could get his hands on, sometimes bringing back books from his father's library in Jakarta, or being given them by friends of the family who knew well his appetite for reading. He was also able to find interesting titles in the Yogyakarta bookshops catering for students at Gadjah Mada University. As a teenager he began to grapple with the writings of Plato and Aristotle, important thinkers for medieval Islamic scholars. At the same time he wrestled with Marx's *Das Kapital* and Lenin's *What is to be done?*, readily available in Indonesia when the Indonesian Communist Party was making great advances. He was also much intrigued by the ideas of radical social engagement advanced in Lenin's *Infantile Communism* and Mao's *Little Red Book*.

For Abdurrahman, the most engaging topic of study, though, was not politics or philosophy studied in some abstract fashion but the nature of being human. Then, and throughout his life, he has had a deep passion for understanding the complexities of human nature. Just as he learnt in the *wayang kulit* stories to value ambivalence, so too in the great literature of the European novelists he learnt to value the complexities and shades of grey that make up human nature.

This love of humanity, which he nurtured through his reading of literary classics, was complemented by his passion for film. Such was his love of literature and learning generally, and his powers of memory, he continued to read throughout his *pesantren* years, finding it easy to read many books, reading some in a single night, without noticeably disturbing his formal studies.

Given this voracious appetite for new ideas and wide-ranging curiosity, it is hardly surprising that at a certain point in his development Abdurrahman was forced to grapple with his own religious identity and place in the world. What is surprising, given his deep interest in liberal Western social theory, is that in his early twenties he dabbled with, as he later put it, Islamic fundamentalism. His reading had persuaded him that the problems besetting humanity required a comprehensive response. He found much in Marxist thought that was persuasive but was troubled by Marxism's antagonism towards religion. Although he was wary of the simplistic and ill-informed social analysis that was popular among politically active Muslims in Indonesia during the 1960s, he nevertheless hoped to find in Islam an answer to the problems of injustice, poverty and oppression. He began to read the works of the postwar Islamists in the hope of finding a comprehensive and coherent political vision. He read Said Qutb, Said Ramadan, Hasan Bana and explored the ideas behind the Arab world's leading Islamist organisation, Al Ikwan Al Muslimun, or the Islamic Brotherhood.

In early 1962 his mother's younger brother Haziz Bisri, who was an admirer of Al Ikwan, encouraged Abdurrahman to establish a branch of Al Ikwan. Abdurrahman toyed with the idea, but this venture into fundamentalist thought was soon interrupted by his move to Cairo to undertake further studies in November 1963. By then he had begun to grow bored with most Islamist titles, finding them repetitive and superficial. He soon started rejecting all expressions of Islamism or fundamentalism, seeing them as contrary to the true spirit of Islam, but not before he had dallied with these ideas while in Jombang and in Cairo, and worked out his own position on them.

NURIYAH

In Jombang Abdurrahman had an encounter that was to prove more consequential than any of his literary encounters with the famous writers whose work he was so voraciously devouring. As a teenager Abdurrahman had never had the time, or the personal inclination, for romance. Though he liked to watch football and go to the cinema, he was ever the spectator and he remained a bookish youth. Moreover, he lived in a religious world that actively discouraged its brightest sons from entering into teenage romance. Consequently, even as a young man in his twenties he had never dated, much less had a girlfriend. In a way, any spirit of youthful rebellion on Abdurrahman's part was channelled into his brief flirtation with radical Islamism.

Until this point the only women that Abdurrahman had fallen for were those who had stared down at him with a smouldering gaze from the silver screen. When he began teaching at the *madrasah* in Tambakberas in the early 1960s, however, he was drawn to a young student called Nuriyah. One of the most attractive girls in her class, Nuriyah was also sharp and independently minded and drew the attention of more than a few young men in the *pesantren* community. So it was surprising that she should take any interest at all in this bookish and somewhat awkward teacher, already chubby and burdened with 'coke-bottle bottom' glasses.

Nevertheless, Nuriyah was a product of the *pesantren* community herself and a child of Jombang: it was not easy for her to reject out of hand the advances of the son of Kiai Wahid Hasyim and grandson of Kiai Bisri Syansuri and Kiai Hasyim Asy'ari. Nor did she find Abdurrahman wholly unattractive. His intellect and sense of purpose caught her attention early on. But he was certainly no film star and he had to work hard for some years yet to secure her affection. In November 1963, he left for Cairo, Egypt. He had a scholarship from the department of religious affairs to attend the famous thousand-year-old university of Al Azhar in Cairo.

TWO

ISLAM IN INDONESIA: MODERNISTS AND TRADITIONALISTS

'MUSLIM CLERIC BECOMES PRESIDENT'

When Abdurrahman was elected president in October 1999 the watching world did not know what to make of the news that Indonesia's first democratically elected president was a 'Muslim cleric'. The result had been no more expected than had Ayatollah Khomeini's revolutionary victory over the Shah of Iran in 1979. The parallel, or course, went no further than that. Those who knew of Abdurrahman knew him to be a committed liberal, just as they knew the religious scene in Indonesia was very different to that in Iran. Nevertheless, the unexpected ascendancy of this 'Muslim cleric' to the helm of the world's third-largest democracy was a reminder of how little attention had been paid by political analysts to Islam in Indonesia. This should alert us to the fact that to understand Abdurrahman we need to know something about the religious world that he inhabits. Before following Abdurrahman on his journey to the Middle East, then, we would do well to spend some time coming to an understanding of the world of Indonesian Islam. There is an unhelpful tendency in the West to see the Muslim world as a monolith, but as with Christianity, Islam exhibits great diversity, and regional culture plays a great role in shaping religious expression, behaviours and attitudes.

SANTRI AND ABANGAN

Indonesia is a majority Muslim nation, the world's largest. With approximately 85 per cent of its total population of 220 million confessing to be Muslims, Indonesia is home to around 190 million Muslims. But being Muslim in Indonesia means different things to different people. In Indonesia a broad distinction is generally made between *santri* and non-*santri* Muslims. This follows the usage made famous by Clifford Geertz, though originally the term *santri* simply referred to a student of a *pesantren*.[1] *Santri* Muslims are those who uphold 'the five pillars of Islam'. Not only do they, like all Muslims, confess that 'there is no god but God and Muhammad is His prophet', but they also pray regularly, fast during Ramadan (the Muslim fasting month), pay *zakat*, or tithes, and aspire to one day make the *haj* pilgrimage to the holy cities of Mecca and Medina. In short *santri* Muslims are orthodox in their practice of Islam. Non-*santri* Muslims — sometimes referred to as *abangan* Muslims — on the other hand, although they may aspire to one day become more pious and regular in their devotions, are regarded, at least by many *santri*, as being nominal Muslims. A third, much smaller grouping, the *priyayi* (descendants of the aristocracy of the old courts), are much like the *abangan* in their adherence to elements of Hindu-Buddhist belief, but they differ in two main ways from the *abangan*. Firstly, their mystical worldview is overlaid with both the burden and the refinement of their class. Secondly, their modern culture was shaped by their long association with the Dutch and their urbane preference for modern Western education and white-collar work. Not that many years ago the *abangan* and *priyayi* probably significantly outnumbered the *santri*, especially in cities. Since the late 1970s, however, there has been a broad revival of interest in Islam and the ratio appears to have altered significantly as many *abangan* and *priyayi* became *santri* in the 1980s and 1990s. Until recently, Arabic names distinguished the *santri* from the *abangan* and *priyayi*. Now *santri* are to be found even behind the long and imposing Sanskrit-derived names of those who previously identified as *priyayi*.

THE ISLAMISATION OF INDONESIA

Islam is a relative latecomer to the archipelago and the recentness of its arrival shapes its expression there. Indonesia is a place in which we paradoxically know little about the process of conversion but in which the memory of conversion, particularly in the interior of Java, belongs to the not too distant past. Indeed, it can be argued that Indonesian society is still in the process of Islamisation. This view is frequently expressed by traditionalists and modernists alike. Certainly it is an important part of the ethos of the world of traditionalist Islam.

Many of today's *pesantren*, such as the two founded by Abdurrahman's grandfathers outside Jombang, were deliberately established in areas reputed to be irreligious and dangerous. As the *pesantren* grew in numbers, previously nominal Muslim, or *abangan*, villagers were persuaded of the benefits of a more pious lifestyle. Jombang is located in the interior of East Java, equidistant between the Indian or Southern Ocean and the shallow Java Sea to the north that for over a thousand years has functioned as a maritime freeway; it links Java with Sulawesi, Borneo, the Malay peninsula, Sumatra, and the world beyond. It was in the busy seaports of that northern coast, one or two hundred kilometres northwest of Jombang, that Islam first took root in Java. In the farming towns and villages of the interior, however, the Islamisation of Java was, during the lifetimes of Abdurrahman's grandfathers at least, unfinished business. When Bisri Syansuri, as a boy from the solidly Islamic northern coast, married into the Jombang family of his friend Wahab Chasbullah, and eventually established his own *pesantren* on the outskirts of Jombang, he was conforming to a generations-old pattern. Such unions, whereby bright young *ulama* from the Islamic heartlands of the northern coast were encouraged to strike out as pioneering *kiai*, building new *pesantren* in the interior, was one of the mechanisms by which the interior of Java was Islamised.

Stories such as Kiai Bisri Syansuri's pick up a theme found in the tales of the Wali Songo, the fabled nine saints or apostles who are said to have spearheaded the conversion of Java several centuries ago. The theme, of course, is as old as religion itself. It is also one that is felt to apply to modern Indonesia. Modernists and traditionalists alike describe this phenomenon as the *santri*-fication of Indonesian society.

When did Islam first come to the archipelago?[2] The simple answer is that we really don't know. Tombstones with Arabic inscriptions dating back more than seven centuries have been found in several places across the western half of the archipelago, but it is not clear whether these were signs of the early emergence of Islamic settlement or simply mark the final resting place of foreign Muslims. It is even possible that they represent nothing more than the discarded ballast of passing trade vessels, which carried heavy items such as tombstones for ballast on their outward journeys. In any case, we do know that one of the first major Islamic kingdoms to emerge in the archipelago was the Sultanate of Melaka. According to one of the oldest existing Malay books, the *Sejarah Melayu* (Malay Chronicles), the first King of Melaka converted to Islam early in the fifteenth century, as the result of a dream. He was also said to have been mysteriously circumcised in his sleep, and thus delivered from one of the major stumbling-blocks to conversion! Whatever the historicity of this account, it is clear that early in the fifteenth century a sultanate centred on the port city of Melaka quickly grew to exert power, not just over much of the Malaysian peninsula, but also over parts of the East Sumatran coast, the island of Borneo, and possibly even parts of Java. From this stepping-stone Islam spread along natural trade routes to the coastal cities of northeast Java and Sumatra. Large parts of inland Java, however, were not completely or substantially Islamised until well into the seventeenth and eighteenth centuries, and in some cases much later. Consolidation continued into the nineteenth and twentieth centuries. In comparison with most of the Islamic world (with the exception of sub-Saharan Africa) Islam came but recently to Indonesia.

More important, perhaps, Islam appears to have come by largely peaceful means. We will never know the details of this history and the precise mechanisms by which the peoples and societies of archipelagic Southeast Asia converted to Islam because too little archaeological evidence remains. It is a monsoonal region straddling the equator, dominated by port cities in which the principal structures were wooden buildings, and these frequently built on stilts over muddy estuaries; precious little survives to satisfy the inquiring minds of archaeologists and historians. It is commonly thought that one of the major mechanisms for conversion that occurred was friendly contact with traders sailing to the archipelago via India. Some of these traders originated from the Arab world or from Persia, but many others came from India. As there is much evidence in India to suggest that Islam there was strongly influenced by Persian Sufi thought, it is likely that many of the merchants and travellers who introduced Islam to Southeast Asia were Sufis.[3] This probably played an important part in the appeal of Islam to the Malays, Javanese and others who converted to Islam in the fourteenth, fifteenth and sixteenth centuries. Conversion to Islam, for many people, may have been understood as 'upgrading' their faith, linking up with a higher civilisation and a spiritually more potent form of religion.

MODERNISTS AND TRADITIONALISTS

Within the *santri* community a distinction is made between modernists, most of whom belong to the organisation Muhammadiyah, and traditionalists, the vast majority of whom belong to NU. On Java the traditionalists outnumber the modernists, particularly outside the big cities, but on other islands the situation is very different. In most of Sumatra and in southern Sulawesi the modernists easily outnumber the traditionalists. Confusing matters further, on Java the students of the *pesantren* are called *santri*. This probably reflects the pre-twentieth-century origin of the term *santri* and the missionary role of the *pesantren* in Islamising Java.

In many respects the terms 'Islamic modernism' and 'Islamic traditionalism' are confusing and unhelpful. When Islamic modernism first came to Indonesia at the beginning of the twentieth century it was a progressive and reformist movement, but by mid-way through the century there were signs that parts of the modernist movement were becoming conservative. In other words, modernism started as a movement to change the behaviour and thinking of Muslims so that they would be better able to deal with the modern world as well as becoming better Muslims. In time, however, the movement became focused on preserving the distinctiveness of its people and their practices against the influences of an increasingly secular world. By the end of the century the modernists were divided into a moderate, but quiescent, majority and a conservative and outspoken minority. At the same time, although rural traditionalists continued to be culturally conservative, many of their sons and daughters, having graduated from *pesantren* and gone on to higher studies, were at the forefront of progressive thought and religious reform. There are many social and political reasons for this partial reversal of roles but the single most important reason is education. The *pesantren* and State Islamic Institutes (Institut Agama Islam Negara — IAIN) maintained education in classical Islamic scholarship, including Sufism, while introducing theologically literate students to critical Western thought in a way that encouraged a synthesis of the two intellectual traditions. The great majority of the modernists, however, grew up with limited theological literacy, not learning Arabic or studying the classical texts, and therefore not able to participate in the critical re-examination of Islam that was taking place in the IAIN, the tertiary-level colleges that sought to marry modern critical thinking and Islamic scholarship, and NU non-governmental organisations. At the same time Soeharto's attempts to win the political support of conservative modernists during the 1990s provided ideal conditions for the dissemination of sectarian political thought.

MYSTICISM AND TRADITIONALISM

The traditional expression of Islam as found in NU melds a mystical Javanese worldview, an *abangan* and *priyayi* worldview, with the core teachings, doctrines and practices of Islam.[4] We can conceive of a continuum in which *abangan* and *priyayi* mysticism, involving as it does elements of pre-Islamic Hindu-Buddhist belief and the local Javanese religion, merges, by stages, into the Sufistic mysticism of orthodox or *santri* Muslims. Nevertheless, an important distinction is made in the minds of Islamic thinkers such as Abdurrahman Wahid, between the pantheism inherent in the least Islamic forms of *abangan* and *priyayi* mysticism and the monotheism found in traditionalist Islamic Sufism. Even so, there is a recognition on the part of many traditionalist Muslims, and certainly on the part of intellectuals like Abdurrahman, that even in pre-Islamic belief, shot through as it is with pantheism, there are important elements of truth. This is perhaps the most fundamental difference between modernist and traditionalist approaches to Indonesian culture.

Liberal Islamic intellectuals such as Abdurrahman and most NU *ulama* are open to learning from other traditions, including those traditions which were at the heart of Javanese and Southeast Asian spirituality before the arrival of Islam. This is congruent with a conviction widely held in traditionalist circles: that unless something is expressly proscribed in the Qur'an and the Sunnah then it is permissible as long as it is consistent with the principles and values laid down in the Qur'an and the Sunnah. Whereas, for many conservative intellectuals from a modernist background, if something is not referred to in the Qur'an or the Sunnah, then it should be regarded with caution. If it contains elements which are at odds with Islamic monotheism then it is to be avoided at all costs. Consequently, modernists avoid anything suggestive of communication with the dead. Similarly, they are wary of speculation about any spiritual entities save for God alone.

It is for this reason that, when the modernist movement began to make inroads into Indonesia in the early part of the twentieth century, many aspects of traditional Islam were regarded as contrary to the true doctrine of Islam. The modernists took particular issue with the traditional practices of *ziarah* and of prayers to departed saints. *Ziarah* means to make a pilgrimage, normally to the tomb sites of dead saints, in order to pray and worship in the hope of gaining particular power, blessing, guidance or insight, or simply to repay a vow. Related to this are a host of meditative practices that involve reciting sections of the Qur'an or special prayers in graveyards or beside tombs, often at night. The modernists argued (and as a consequence so too did many Orientalist writers, or Western scholars of Islam and Muslim society, who relied upon them as informants), that such practices were heterodox. Such an approach to Islam represented, they asserted, a dangerous syncretic mixture of pre-Islamic Hindu-Buddhist and animist belief with Islamic ideas. This argument was often made in ignorance of the fact that practices such as *ziarah* are to be found throughout the Islamic world, even in places where Islam has been the dominant religion for more than thirteen centuries. The modernists, both in Indonesia and elsewhere, were, among other things, effectively championing a textually based understanding of Islam that set itself against 'folk Islam' — the more mystically inclined Islam of peasant farmers.

MODERNISM AND REFORM

Islamic modernism emerged in the second half of the nineteenth century. For Indonesian modernists the single most important reformist thinker was the Egyptian scholar Muhammad Abduh, who at the beginning of the twentieth century taught at the University of Al Azhar (the university in Cairo where Abdurrahman studied for two and a half years). Muhammad Abduh argued that one of the principal reasons that Muslim societies had been so easily conquered by Western colonial powers was the stagnation of thought that had, for centuries, held back the development of Muslim society. The traditionalist approach to theology and jurisprudence in the Arab world, he asserted, was fundamentally opposed to innovation and new ideas. Instead of encouraging creative thinking it stressed the importance of intellectual submission to collective authority, or *taqlid*. Among the traditionalists this took the form of adherence to one of the four orthodox *mazhab*, or schools of Islamic jurisprudence. This position, Abduh argued, was antithetical to the development of modern thought. It is time, he argued, for the 'gates of *ijtihad*', or personal interpretation, to be opened once again. *Ijtihad*, together with fresh and creative approaches to problem-solving, rather than *taqlid*, and the simple, unquestioning acceptance of established opinion, was to be the foundation for modern Islamic thought. Allied with this was a general emphasis upon rationality and, specifically, the importance of taking a rational approach to applying the core ideas of Islam to modern life. Abduh's discourse about *taqlid* and *ijtihad* was primarily concerned with theological or jurisprudential thought. Nevertheless, he saw intuitively that this was the root of the matter that affected every branch of intellectual endeavour. He argued that if Muslims were to study Western science and Western thought as a whole, with special attention to science, technology and medicine, then Muslim society would make rapid gains. To ignore such areas of modern thought was, he asserted, to risk stagnation and give up the chance of ever escaping the cycle of poverty and general backwardness that gripped most of the Islamic world.

In the early twentieth century Abduh also argued vigorously in favour of a more modern approach to education. At one level this meant modern educational methods, including such radical innovations, as they were then regarded, as using blackboards, chairs and desks. All these things were in sharp contrast to the traditional *madrasah* (as religious schools were known throughout the Islamic world). In Indonesia the term generally denotes Modernist day schools or schools within *pesantren*. In the Dutch East Indies, where the colonial powers of the day cared little about encouraging modern education, the traditional *pesantren* or *madrasah* were the chief means of education available to peasant farming communities, who were the majority of the population. Only a small elite were able to avail themselves of modern secular education, for the Dutch - unlike, say, the British in India — were not interested in building up a vast civil service of educated clerks, and established relatively few schools.

The message of Abduh was taken up with enthusiasm in Indonesia and quickly took organisational form. In fact, in some parts of the archipelago, such as West Sumatra, there had been some significant antecedents to twentieth-century modernism. When the ideas of Islamic modernism were brought to the main island of Java, they quickly found a home. But initially they were not accepted in the major urban centres like Jakarta and Surabaya, which were predominantly secular and Westernised in important respects, because they were the domain of the minor aristocracy, or the *priyayi*, who had come to dominate white-collar work, nor in the rural areas where traditional Islam still held sway, but in the domain of the *petite bourgeoisie*, the small traders.

In particular it was in Yogyakarta, a small city in Central Java, where modernism really took off. In 1912 Kiai Haji Ahmed Dachlan founded a new organisation which he called Muhammadiyah, meaning those who follow Mohammad. The ideas of Muhammadiyah and of modernism generally were quickly and popularly received. Many *ulama* regarded them with favour and saw that much was to be gained by learning from them. In part, however, the popularity and rapid spread of modernism through the growth of Muhammadiyah ultimately alarmed many of the traditional *ulama*. Their concern was that the day might soon come when the *pesantren* no longer had sufficient power of attraction to draw in new generations of students, and as a result, future education might be dominated by modern Muhammadiyah-style schools and modern, essentially secular, *madrasah*. Nevertheless, the early modernists enjoyed good relations with many of the traditionalist *ulama*, which is not so surprising when it is remembered that they came from similar backgrounds.[5]

TRADITIONALISM AND THE SOCIOLOGICAL DIVIDE

While the initial differences between modernism and traditionalism centred on matters of doctrine and religious practice, particularly concerning practices that the modernists regarded as syncretistic and heterodox, in the long run the main distinction became a sociological one. In the first half of the twentieth century *priyayi*, white-collar workers, and *abangan*, labourers, servants and factory workers, dominated the cities. In the cities *santri* Islam was something of a scarcity: the *santri* themselves were regarded as rural and backward looking, and certainly not middle-class. In due course Islamic modernism made serious inroads into the urban centres, presenting a more urbane and acceptable expression of *santri* Islam.

For these and other reasons, the *pesantren* had developed historically as essentially rural institutions. Over time the small towns and villages to which they had attached themselves became caught up in the creeping spread of urbanisation. East Java is still one of most densely populated rural areas in the world, and during the twentieth century population growth in villages, regional towns and cities saw many settlements merge. Towns such as Jombang, for example, steadily spread to the point where villages like Tebuireng, which had previously been well outside the town limits, became incorporated into the town proper. Consequently, many *pesantren* that had previously identified with a village community came to be physically located within a larger urban complex. Still, the cultural milieu of these *pesantren*, and even the surrounding small and middle-sized urban centres that they inhabited, remained steadfastly rural. When Abdurrahman was a student, Jombang was a country town rather than an aspirant city. One of the reasons why the *pesantren* were so closely identified with village life was that a majority of *santri* were children of peasant farmers. These students could not afford to attend one of the growing number of *madrasah* run by Muhammadiyah, or one of the few Dutch schools established during the colonial period for sons of the *priyayi*.

For poor subsistence farmers with little money to pay for the educational needs of their sons and daughters, there was almost always the option of the *pesantren*. In the *pesantren* those who could not find the cash for fees could generally negotiate some other form of exchange. Even those who had nothing to give might still find a *pesantren* that would take their children. In the *pesantren* world a culture of philanthropy prevailed and most *pesantren* carried their share of students whose parents could not afford to pay the fees and living expenses. When they could, even these very poor families would bring farm goods. Other members of the village also contributed to *pesantren* when they could, for the *pesantren* were important social institutions and contributing to them was a religious duty.

The *pesantren* themselves were not entirely without resources. Many of the *kiai* who ran the *pesantren*, as well as many others who were associated with them, were engaged in small-scale business. They were able to take advantage of a complex web of trading relationships that stretched across rural Java from Surabaya to Jakarta. Moreover, where sufficient land was available it was possible for a *pesantren* to be almost entirely self-sufficient, growing rice and other food crops like vegetables and spices, and raising ducks, chickens, goats and other livestock. Often a large *pesantren* was able to accumulate considerable wealth over the years. Ostensibly this wealth was concentrated around the family of the *kiai*, but in practice the *kiai* thought of himself as a steward, and in most cases the wealth was reinvested in the *pesantren* community. In practice some *kiai* were much better stewards than others, just as some were clearly more selfless than others. Those that were poor managers struggled to grow their *pesantren*. Those that were skilled in trade and business, on the other hand, came to command impressive financial empires, and for some these became ends in themselves. Even for the more noble and selfless among the *kiai* there was no doubt that material expansion was a sign of God's blessing, and few *kiai* were indifferent to opportunities for growth and accumulation of wealth. Underlying this is a cultural framework of patron–client relations that has been a dominant feature of Southeast Asian society for centuries, if not millennia. Political independence and the emergence of national political structures served to tie traditional, local-level patron–client relations into the fabric of national politics, and in this NU came to play an important role in determining the division of resources.

As money became available, endless building programs transformed *pesantren* from their initial *pondok* or 'hut' status to the point where the larger *pesantren* had three- and four-storey buildings, modern classrooms, large mosques and well-equipped study complexes. But, whether they were large complexes with thousands of students and extensive campuses, or the humblest of *pesantren* with just a few hundred students, almost all *pesantren* were linked to village life. Even those few dozen *pesantren* located in large cities such as Jakarta, Bandung or Surabaya continued to have a rural feel to them.

If the *pesantren*, and by extension the world of NU and traditional Islam, partook of village life and a rural cultural milieu, it was increasingly the opposite case for Muhammadiyah and Islamic modernism. Muhammadiyah, as we noted above, began in the Kauman, or *santri* quarter, of Yogyakarta, in 1912. By the middle of the century Yogyakarta was a university town, filled with tens of thousands of students drawn from all over the archipelago. It was also home to one of the few remaining sultanates from the pre-independence period, and consequently was a cultural centre for Javanese life. It therefore reflected more the culture of *abangan* and *priyayi* urbanites than it did the culture of rural Java.

Although many Muhammadiyah members were upwardly mobile and striving to enter the professions, to their credit when they did achieve high income they saw to it that Muhammadiyah was well supported in its charitable programs. As result, Muhammadiyah was able to develop a remarkable network of health clinics, hospitals, schools and orphanages spanning the archipelago.

WAHID HASYIM AND MASYUMI

Abdurrahman's father Wahid Hasyim was exceptional in that he had a wide range of non-NU friends, including many non-*santri* and non-Muslim friends. Unlike most of his peers in NU, he felt at home in the national capital and moved easily in Jakarta's elite circles. Consequently, Wahid Hasyim was well suited to his role as senior nationalist leader, and then government minister. Prior to the departure of NU from Masyumi in 1952, Wahid Hasyim had played a key role in maintaining good relations between modernists and traditionalists. Perhaps, had there been more *kiai* like Wahid Hasyim, a modern, integrated Islamic identity, neither wholly modernist nor wholly traditionalist, such as began to appear at the end of the twentieth century, might have developed more quickly. As it was, however, they were straddling a gap that only widened during the bitter political struggles of the 1950s and 1960s.

For several decades after NU was founded in 1926, relations between modernists and traditionalists were reasonably good, especially at the level of national leadership. As we have observed, NU was founded not so much to compete with the modernists as to protect the *pesantren* system and traditional Islamic culture, including particularly those Sufistic aspects of traditional Islam which the modernists dismissed. Because many of the early leaders in Muhammadiyah were *pesantren*-trained, a natural affinity existed between NU *ulama* and their counterparts within Muhammadiyah.

When the Japanese occupied the Dutch East Indies in 1942 they looked to *santri* nationalists as people they could work with in the administration of the territory. The Japanese reasoned that those who were trained in Dutch schools, whether church or secular, were likely to harbour sympathies to the Netherlands and Europe in general. To find reliable partners, they turned to the *santri*. In October 1943 they established an umbrella organisation for all Muslim groups that they called Masyumi. It replaced the Supreme Islamic Council of Indonesia, an organisation established in 1937, and headed by Wahid Hasyim, to provide a common forum of discussion for modernists and traditionalists. During the Japanese occupation the NU and Muhammadiyah nationalists worked side-by-side so well that they felt it good to maintain their relationship by turning Masyumi into a political party for all *santri*.

THE 1945 CONSTITUTION AND PANCASILA

The Japanese surrender presented the nationalists with a brief interregnum in which they were free to act before the Dutch returned to reclaim their colony. Needing to move quickly, the nationalists hastily cobbled together a draft constitution. The '1945 constitution' which resulted from this scramble to prepare for independence is a brief and vague document that ascribes strong powers to the presidency. It was announced on 18 August 1945, the day after the nationalists declared independence. Several months later a decree was issued transforming the system of government to a parliamentary one. Then in 1949, following ceasefire negotiations with the Dutch, a new constitution was drawn up describing a federal system of government. The foisting of this federal model of governance on them by the Dutch was resented by the nationalists. They seized the opportunity the following year to replace the 1949 constitution with a new temporary parliamentary constitution, based on a unitary republic and a largely ceremonial presidency. In announcing the 1950 constitution it was agreed that an elected 'constitutional assembly' would be formed to draft a permanent constitution. This body, the Konstituante, was only able to be formed after the new nation's first elections, which took place in 1955.

One of the central issues that was discussed in the Konstituante was the position of Islam in the constitution and the Indonesian state. Many within Masyumi, though probably still only a small minority, were strongly in favour of Indonesia being an Islamic state. Others were prepared to settle for a state in which Islam was recognised as the official religion. This option horrified most non-Muslims and *abangan*. Even some moderate *santri* were concerned about the prospect of the state being given the power to rule on religious matters. It raised the possibility, they felt, of authoritarian intervention into matters of conscience. Ever since the declaration of independence in 1945, moderate nationalists led by Sukarno and Hatta, and including Wahid Hasyim, argued that Indonesia's social and religious pluralism meant that it would be neither wise nor just to set Islam apart from the other religions observed in Indonesia. This attitude disappointed a small minority of Islamists, mostly from the modernist community.

As it became clear that the Japanese occupation would shortly end, and that the nationalists had to prepare for independence, debate about the guiding principles of the new state intensified. In June 1945, there were consultations with other nationalist leaders, including, apparently some religious leaders (Abdurrahman maintains that his father Wahid Hasyim was a key contributor, but no written records of the consultative process are available so it is difficult to know exactly what happened). Then Sukarno proffered a solution. He announced a doctrine for the new state which he called Pancasila (Sanskrit for 'five principles'); it offered a state philosophy which was neither secular nor sectarian. The five principles of Pancasila were: belief in one supreme deity; just and civilised humanity; the unity of Indonesia; democracy informed by the wisdom of representative deliberation and consensus; and social justice for all Indonesians.

For many *santri*, this compromise solution did not sufficiently acknowledge the special place of Islam. After some weeks of lobbying, the committee responsible for drafting the new nation's constitution agreed to include a seven-word amendment to the first *sila*, or principle, of Pancasila so that it read: 'belief in the one God with the obligation for all Muslims to carry out the requirements of the Syari'ah'. It was further agreed that this statement, which became known as the Jakarta Charter, should be included in the preamble to the new constitution. Sometime between late June and 18 August 1945 when the new constitution was announced, however, the 'seven words', 'with the obligation for all Muslims to carry out the requirements of the Syari'ah', were dropped. Conservative *santri* were furious with Sukarno for dropping the 'seven words' and fought for the next fourteen years to have them put back.

Although many within NU also argued strongly in favour of retaining the Jakarta Charter, Wahid Hasyim believed that to do so would open the door to sectarianism in national politics. When Abdurrahman began his own public career decades later and took a stand opposing any attempts to link 'church and state', he felt that he was carrying on the work of his father.

NU BREAKS AWAY

Under Sukarno Wahid Hasyim was appointed Minister for Religious Affairs. His tenure ended, as we have seen, following a cabinet reshuffle in 1952. At the same time relations between the traditionalists and modernists within Masyumi, which had long been tense, rapidly worsened. While NU figures like Wahid Hasyim were acknowledged as well able to work alongside their modernist counterparts and to make an equal contribution to Masyumi, there was a widespread perception among modernists that men like Wahid Hasyim were the exception rather than the rule in NU. And the managerial ability of even Wahid Hasyim had come under a cloud following the disastrous handling of the 1952 *haj* pilgrimage during his tenure as minister. They regarded most traditionalists as unsophisticated rural peasants. Few of the traditionalists had a Dutch education — or indeed any form of modern education — and only a few were comfortable in European languages or in Jakartan society. The modernists used this to argue that their people should be given prominent roles in the running of the party and in future cabinet posts. The traditionalists felt this to be offensive and erroneous. More particularly, both were concerned that, unless the ministry of religious affairs went to one of their own, they had little hope of exercising influence in the cabinet.

Things came to a head in April 1952 when NU declared that it was going to break away from Masyumi and establish itself as an independent political party. Consequently, when the first general elections were held three years later, the modernists and traditionalists contested the elections through separate parties. The result was that neither Masyumi nor NU gained sufficient votes to exercise much power in their own right, with each party getting around 20 per cent of the vote (20.9 and 18.4 per cent respectively). It's not hard to see that, if the two communities had been able to work together, a united Masyumi would have been easily the largest and most influential party to emerge from the 1955 elections. Despite the best efforts of Wahid Hasyim, who had worked hard to save the ailing relationship, this was not to be, and once the two had begun to go their own ways the gap continued to widen.[6]

SUKARNO, ISLAM, THE STATE AND PANCASILA

During the late 1950s leading Masyumi figures became increasingly strident in their protest against Sukarno's autocratic style of government. This steadily worsened when Sukarno, in 1959, announced that he was dissolving the Konstituante and reverting to the 1945 constitution in the name of 'Guided Democracy', having two years earlier been encouraged by the military to invoke martial law.

The reaction of the Masyumi politicians to Sukarno's return to the 1945 constitution was to challenge Sukarno's legitimacy and boldly criticise the failures and shortcomings of the Sukarno government. One of the issues that most upset the more radical elements within Masyumi was that, with the return to the 1945 constitution and the disbanding of the Konstituante they saw no hope of achieving their goal of a constitution which acknowledged the role and authority of Islam within the state. Ironically it was the traditionalists, instinctively falling back upon the traditional Sunni quiescent, or pragmatic, approach to politics, who were to prove much more successful in navigating the difficult conditions of the late Sukarno period.[7] Whereas the modernists were inclined to take a stand on principle, to draw a line in the sand and refuse to budge, the traditionalists were willing to bend to the demands of Sukarno's government just so long as the interests of their party and their people were protected, and they survived to fight another day with NU continuing as a political force.[8]

Sukarno eventually lost patience with the modernists, and in January 1960 he banned Masyumi. The final straw for Sukarno was that, while he was on an overseas visit in 1958, several senior Masyumi figures had travelled to West Sumatra, where many of them had family connections, and were seen to be offering support to the rebellion there in favour of the Revolutionary Government of the Republic of Indonesia (Pemerintah Revolusi Republik Indonesia — PRRI). Sometimes described as a separatist movement, this rebellion was not a genuine attempt to break away, but an attempt to change the government in Jakarta with the assistance of local military officers disgruntled with the commanders in the national capital. The affair was made greatly more serious, however, by the inept intervention of the CIA, who apparently sought to use it as an opportunity to topple Sukarno. Not surprisingly, Sukarno denounced the Masyumi leaders as opportunistic and disloyal, and from that point on they had little scope to influence his government. The NU politicians were at least able to preserve their position of influence within his government and, in particular, they retained the prized religious affairs portfolio.

THE *PESANTREN* NETWORK

One reason traditionalist Islam remained largely outside the domain of elite politics and elite life was the essentially rural nature of the *pesantren* network. It was not just that the *pesantren* were geographically located in rural areas; culturally their orientation was towards religious society and peasant communities. This cultural orientation was both reflected in, and a product of, the *pesantren* curriculum. The *pesantren* were remarkably successful in preserving classical Islamic learning throughout the turbulent changes of the twentieth century. For too many years, however, the downside of this was that *pesantren* graduates had too few choices for further education and employment. Traditionally the *pesantren* graduates either went on to work in the *pesantren* themselves or engaged in small-scale trading or farming while carrying out religious duties on a part-time basis.

Another aspect of traditional Islamic culture which served to limit the role of *pesantren* graduates in elite society was the way in which NU negotiated political engagement. Throughout the 1950s much of the full-time work of party politics was carried out by professional politicians, many of whom did not have a *pesantren* background but who nevertheless were accepted, for reasons of expediency, as representing the *ulama*. Originally this was necessary because it was difficult to find people with suitable linguistic and other skills to function as professional politicians in Jakarta. Later the role of professional politicians had become entrenched. To a certain extent it has been reflected in the bipartite division of general national leadership between the Syuriah, or Supreme Religious Advisory Council, and the Tanfidziyah, the Executive Board, although in practice the details have been rather more complex than suggested by that division. Very few *ulama*, even within the political wing of NU, have been able to engage successfully in elite society in Indonesia over a long period of time.

Reinforcing this is a cultural orientation influenced by centuries of Sunni Islamic political thought. In this respect at least, traditional Islam in NU is typical of Sunni Islam around the world. In Sunni thought, being too close to power was often regarded as dangerous, and yet it was necessary to negotiate a position with the power of the day in order to protect the community. Here the emphasis was on the minimisation of harm and the avoidance of danger. In other matters the emphasis sometimes shifted to the maximisation of benefits for the community. This pragmatic outlook reflects the experience of traditional *ulama* in all corners of the Muslim world. Democracy is a recent arrival in most nations of the world, particularly Muslim nations, and it has made little sense to stubbornly take a stand in the political arena on a point of principle. Better to negotiate access to power and exploit whatever leverage is available to look after the interests of the community. In Indonesia, this has meant that NU *ulama* have been content to leave politicking to the professional politicians paid to represent them.

Some sense of this thinking can be found in the famous response of

Kiai Wahab Chasbullah when challenged in the early 1950s by the modernists about the capacity of NU to engage in practical politics. Asked whether NU had the human resources to succeed in national politics, Wahab Chasbullah is said to have replied: 'If I buy a new car the car salesman doesn't ask "Sir, can you drive?" Such a question is unnecessary because if I can't drive a car I can post an advertisement: Driver Wanted. Without doubt there will soon be a queue of candidates in front of my door.'[9]

Ironically, even half a century later NU finds itself better at winning votes than it is at filling positions of leadership. One of the dilemmas confronting Abdurrahman Wahid as president was that he found few within NU's still predominantly rural constituency who are well equipped to contribute to national politics. And, although he had better grassroots support than most politicians, he had to struggle to prevent his emotional rural supporters from appearing to be a dangerous rabble.

This page intentionally left blank

PART 2

THE MAKING OF AN INTELLECTUAL

This page intentionally left blank

THREE

CAIRO, BAGHDAD AND EUROPE, 1963-1971

ARRIVAL IN CAIRO AND AL AZHAR

Mecca may be the city of pilgrimage, but Cairo, one of the great cities in the Arab world, was in the 1960s the city of learning for Indonesian Muslims. For centuries many have travelled to the Middle East both to make the *haj* pilgrimage and to undertake study. Although small centres of learning, led by Indonesian-born *ulama*, sprang up in Mecca, Medina and throughout the Middle East, Cairo increasingly became the city of choice for many Indonesian students.

For these students the magnet was the thousand-year-old University of Al Azhar, the oldest university in the world, centuries older than Oxford, Cambridge, the Sorbonne and the other ancient universities of Europe. It was also the centre of some of the Islamic world's most modern ideas and, under Muhammad Abduh, one of the pioneering centres of the modernist movement. It was through students studying at Al Azhar that Islamic modernism was introduced to Indonesia, and it is from the generations of Indonesian students studying at Al Azhar that many of Indonesia's best Islamic intellectuals have come.

Although Abdurrahman looked forward to his studies there with great eagerness, he was to be bitterly disappointed. The golden age of

Al Azhar had peaked decades earlier and by the mid-1960s first-year undergraduate classes at the old university did not have a lot to offer that was new or fresh for a bright graduate of some of Indonesia's better *pesantren*.

Abdurrahman relates the story that when he arrived at Al Azhar he was informed by university officials that he must join a remedial Arabic class.[1] From his studies in Jombang in 1960 he had certificates showing that he had passed studies in Islamic jurisprudence, theology and related subjects, all of which required an expert knowledge of Arabic, but he had no papers to show that he had passed basic Arabic language. As a result he was consigned to a class of raw beginners, many of whom were students newly arrived from Africa, scarcely knowing the Arabic alphabet let alone able to engage in conversation. Abdurrahman's response was simply to avoid the classes. As a consequence he recalls that he spent most of 1964 doing everything else but formal studies, succumbing to the attractions of Cairo's numerous football matches, large libraries, French cinemas and lively café discussions. If Al Azhar proved a disappointment for Abdurrahman, the same cannot be said for Cairo. It was a big, ancient city and he was enthralled.

AN EXCITING NEW WORLD

Cairo under Nasser in the mid-1960s was enjoying something of a golden age. For all its pollution and bustle, it was still a scenic city with a feel and mood quite unlike any Indonesian city. Even in the student quarter of old Cairo where Abdurrahman lived, many of the stone buildings that lined the narrow laneways were centuries old. Numerous small mosques and prayer houses, built during a golden age of Islam before the European renaissance, could be found throughout the heart of the old city. Java has no ancient stone cities in whose streets one could walk and feel somehow linked to generations past, but it does have numerous small ruins and even more numerous graves. As a *pesantren* student, much given to *ziarah*, or pilgrimages to gravesites, Abdurrahman had developed a strong sense of connection to historical sites and believed intuitively in the enduring presence of those who had once lived there. Even for a Western tourist a visit to Cairo can be an emotional experience. For a naturally curious young Muslim student from Java with a Sufi sensitivity for the past, Cairo was a wonderfully rich city in which to live.

In Cairo in his mid-twenties, Abdurrahman felt free. As a teenager in Yogyakarta his life had been relatively carefree, but as the oldest son of the late Kiai Wahid Hasyim his every move was watched, including his surreptitious visits to the cinema. As a *pesantren* student in Magelang and Jombang, he felt even tighter social constraints . Although Al Azhar had proved disappointing, it was in a strange way a liberating experience because it gave him the freedom to spend his time the way he wanted, unhindered by tight schedules or the watchful eyes of small-town Javanese society.

In Cairo Abdurrahman found that he could watch the best of French cinema, although he had to wait for the new releases from Europe. Besides enjoying European, English and American movies, Abdurrahman spent much of his time in Cairo at the American University library, a library greater than any he had ever seen. Even though he had grown up in a home full of books, and his unusual network of family and friends had allowed him much better access to varied reading material than most of his peers, obtaining the books that he wanted had often been a struggle. Cairo was a different world; its libraries were filled with more books than he had ever seen before. When not reading at the American University library, he was often at the Cairo University library or at the French library. He recalls reading compulsively, even when walking around the house or to the bus stop. In the absence of a book, a scrap of newspaper or an old magazine was enough to completely absorb his attention. He had always been a fast reader, and even as a *pesantren* student in Java he had found time to read. In Cairo his relative freedom and his uncluttered schedule, thanks to his delinquent approach to university classes, enabled him to read as much as he wished.

Presented with a vast array of books that he had never seen before, he recalls that his reading tastes expanded with each new discovery. In Cairo, for example, he read most of William Faulkner's oeuvre. Perhaps Faulkner's attraction for him was the appeal of exotica, for the America of Faulkner was a world away from the *pesantren* of Java. He also read and enjoyed the novels of Ernest Hemingway. During his *pesantren* years he had developed a love of Arabic poetry, but his preference in European literature was mostly for prose. Nevertheless he read both the prose and poetry of Edgar Allan Poe, and the poems of John Donne, committing to memory large parts of 'No Man Is an Island'. He also began to read the work of André Gide and Kafka, and previously unobtainable titles by Tolstoy, Pushkin, and the other European novelists whose work he had started to read when still in Java.

He explains that he had taken with him to Cairo some of his most prized books, including works by Marx and Lenin, which he reread and discussed with fellow students and intellectuals in the cafés of the great city. He found Cairo alive with literature, learning and new ideas. The government of Nasser provided an optimistic and relatively open intellectual environment. Abdurrahman may not have been studying in the universities of Europe, as he had longed to do, but his time in Cairo did bring him into contact with the world of European thought, and he was able to exchange ideas on a scale not possible in Indonesia.

When Abdurrahman was not reading and taking part in café discussions, he spent the hours that he should have spent in class organising Indonesian student affairs. Soon after arriving in Cairo he was elected chairman of the Association of Indonesian Students, which linked students across the Middle East. He recalls spending a great deal of time travelling and meeting with Indonesian students in the region and involving himself in student affairs. Like virtually all Indonesian students in Cairo he lived in a student residence in a section of the student quarter known as 'the Indonesian Village'. Not all Indonesian students were entirely comfortable speaking Arabic and mixing in Arab society without a break, and returning home at night to a 'little Indonesia', replete with familiar sounds and smells, was an essential part of the survival mechanism of most students. For students from Southeast Asia such communal living had for centuries been an important part of the experience of studying in the Arab world. Abdurrahman's grandfathers, for example, had lived in the Malay-Javanese quarter while in Mecca and had spent much of their time there studying under famous teachers from Java and Sumatra.

In 1964 Abdurrahman and a friend, Mustofa Bisri, established a magazine for the Association of Indonesian Students. Abdurrahman wrote regularly for the new magazine, just as he had been in the habit of writing for magazines such as *Horizon* and *Majalah Budaya Jaya* when living in Jombang during the previous three years. He also regularly addressed meetings of Indonesian students and quickly established a reputation as a witty and provocative speaker and essayist. His favourite essay topics were Indonesian politics, the future of Indonesia, and Islam and modernity. Like his father before him he spent his student years in the Middle East feeling extremely ambivalent about NU. There was no question that he had a strong affection for the *pesantren* world, but many aspects of traditional Islamic society in Indonesia troubled him deeply. In some ways his earlier misgivings about the limited thinking of many *ulama* found reinforcement in Cairo. He was also worried by signs that Indonesian society was becoming dangerously polarised. President Sukarno was increasingly leaning to the left and aligning himself with the Indonesian Communist Party (PKI), while conservative elements in Indonesian society, including NU, were moving to the right.

Along with all this intellectual activity, Abdurrahman was able to indulge another great love, soccer. Typically, though, he endlessly studied, analysed and dissected the movement of play, the strengths and weaknesses of teams and their strategies. He was the sort of soccer fan for whom strategy and game play was the real attraction. In soccer-mad Egypt he had plenty to feed his passion. He recalls that he had ready access to extensive newspaper and radio coverage of regional and European league matches as well as plenty of local games to watch.

Abdurrahman may not have attended many of his Arabic classes, but he did have the good sense to show up for the final examinations. Not that he bothered studying for these exams; he could not see any point. Not only was he fluent in spoken Arabic and had strong reading skills but he had also years before memorised the grammar primers that set down the complex rules for writing Classical Arabic. Ironically, his many hours spent in smoky cafés instead of class had provided the perfect finishing school for his language development. Any previous weaknesses in his active Arabic-language skills had now been largely cured. When university officials read his Arabic examination papers they acknowledged that a mistake had been made and that he should never have been relegated to the remedial class. At last he was able to enter the university's Higher Institute for Islamic and Arabic Studies.

MORE DISAPPOINTMENT AT AL AZHAR

Having waited so long to begin his studies, he was soon disappointed again. The Higher Institute for Islamic and Arabic Studies, he felt, failed to live up to its name. He was forced once more to study many of the classical texts, the *kitab kuning* or yellow books as they were known in Java, that he had already studied in Jombang and Magelang. Not only that, the approach to studying these texts was essentially rote learning. These classes were, once again, too boring to hold Abdurrahman's attention and he continued to roam. Had he come to

Al Azhar as a graduate student he might have had a different experience. Al Azhar was still home to some of the Muslim world's best religious scholars, and guided reading and research under the right supervisor might well have served to engage Abdurrahman. The undergraduate curriculum certainly did not. A more conscientious student would still, no doubt, have reaped some benefit from undergraduate studies at Al Azhar, as in fact many other Indonesian students had proved. But the approach taken there was certainly not to Abdurrahman's taste and could not hold his interest, especially when the world outside the ancient university held so many distractions. Al Azhar was quintessentially an Islamic university and was fiercely proud of its long history. It was not inclined to incorporate elements of modern Western learning into its teaching program. Instead it proudly taught classical subjects much as they had been taught for centuries, giving priority to memorisation over analysis. While Abdurrahman had excellent powers of memory, rote learning itself held no appeal for him.

A JOB AT THE EMBASSY

After a year or so in Cairo, Abdurrahman found regular employment in the Indonesian Embassy. As a bright young student leader with good language skills he was useful to the embassy. The fact that he came from a well-known family may also have had something to do with his appointment. He settled into a steady routine of working every morning at the embassy. The position was a great boon for Abdurrahman: it supplemented his scholarship and ensured that he had plenty of pocket money for the cinema and the bookshops. Work in the embassy also satisfied his desire to socialise, providing a natural opportunity to mix with a wide variety of people, to exchange ideas and to keep up with the latest news from Indonesia.

Towards the end of 1965, work in the embassy was to present him with unexpected challenges and some trauma. By the middle of that year, Abdurrahman recalls, he confided in Mustofa Bisri that he feared that tensions between the left and the right in Indonesia would lead to violent confrontation and large-scale loss of life. The Indonesian students in Cairo followed events from home as best they could, but their information was limited to what could be gleaned over the short-wave services or picked up from visitors. Abdurrahman, however, was in a unique position to monitor events. The Indonesian Embassy in Cairo, the main Indonesian diplomatic post in the Middle East, received a regular stream of telex messages and reports from Jakarta. Abdurrahman explains that from time to time he was called upon to translate these reports into Arabic or English and, as a result, he had ready access to the latest information from home.

After the alleged Communist coup attempt took place on the evening of 30 September 1965, a relatively little-known officer, Major-General Soeharto, appeared with exquisite timing, and more than a little help from the CIA, to 'save President Sukarno and the Indonesian nation from the threat of Communism'. What followed was a nightmare, one of the twentieth century's great human tragedies. General Soeharto's deft victory over the 'coup leaders' marked the beginning of a crackdown on the PKI, and alleged Communist sympathisers and fellow travellers throughout the country. In the pogrom that followed numerous personal vendettas were carried out, often neighbour against neighbour, in the name of crushing Communism. As many as half a million people died, perhaps many more, and many of these at the hands of people whom they knew well. The pattern of killings varied from region to region, with local issues clearly playing an important part. In East Java, the heartland of NU, one of the key issues was the Communist demand for accelerated land reform. This demand threatened the viability of many *pesantren* and the personal wealth of not a few *kiai* and NU families. In the hysteria following the alleged coup attempt, the anti-Communist pogrom was justified as a pre-emptive strike in self-defence. That the Communists were largely passive victims who seldom attempted to fight back did not seem to be acknowledged. With assistance from the military, whose appearance in a district was generally taken as providing authorisation to act, gangs of youths rounded up suspects and killed them en masse. In East Java and other NU areas these gangs were often part of the NU youth movement Ansor.

In the weeks following the alleged coup attempt, the Indonesian Embassy in Cairo ordered Abdurrahman to begin preparing reports on fellow students. The embassy had instructions from Jakarta to assess all Indonesian students studying in the Middle East in order to determine their political leanings. The purpose was clear; the Indonesian military under General Soeharto wanted to root out Communists and their fellow travellers and prevent them 're-infecting' Indonesia. Abdurrahman was assigned the onerous task of writing detailed reports on Indonesian students throughout the Middle East. He was selected for this, he explains now, because he was judged to be reliable and well-qualified, having an extensive knowledge of Indonesian students in the region through his work with the Association of Indonesian Students. He also had strong writing skills and was known to have read the works of Marx.

In Indonesia the majority of the alleged Communists involved with the PKI were unfamiliar with all but the most basic ideas of Communism. They had picked up whatever conceptions they had of the movement secondhand from popular speakers and pamphlets. Abdurrahman admired the utopian vision of Indonesian Communists and their concern for social justice, but rejected Communism as being romantically naive. He also admired Sukarno and was deeply impressed by his concern for the *rakyat*, the common people. In this he recalls that he was influenced by his uncle from Jombang, Wahab Chasbullah, who was a devoted supporter of Indonesia's first president.

Although by no means a Communist himself, Abdurrahman understood and respected Marxist thought and, he acknowledges, this put him in an unique position to assess his fellow students. It also presented him with a crisis of conscience. Even though the news reaching the students in Cairo was distorted by the disturbed political situation in Indonesia and the considerable limitations on foreign news services, Abdurrahman's position in the embassy gave him access to up-to-date and reasonably complete reports. This included much that was not made public at the time and often information which disturbed him. He was well aware that his own organisation, NU, and especially Ansor, in which he had previously been active, were involved in numerous brutal killings and in the massacre of innocents. He also knew that he was expected to deliver on the embassy's request and that failure to produce the reports would put him under suspicion.

During this violent period he was required to write dozens of reports on fellow students. He says now that he was able to clear the names of many students who had been under a cloud by pointing out that their interests in Marxist thought were academic rather than indicative of ideological commitment. By his own account he was fortunate that he was living in Cairo and writing about students studying in the Middle East, for it was not too difficult to argue that *santri* students of Islam in the Middle East were not likely to have an active political interest in Communism. After all, most of the Indonesian students in the Middle East at the time came from a NU *pesantren* background, and NU as an organisation, and Ansor in particular, was energetically engaged in crushing Communism, as was Muhammadiyah. Consequently, Abdurrahman recalls, it was relatively easy to argue that none of the students under investigation represented a threat to Indonesian society. In some few cases it was necessary to stress the *santri* credentials of the minority of students undertaking secular, rather than religious, studies but, Abdurrahman maintains, he was never placed in a position where he could not defend the student he was reporting on.[2] Nevertheless, as he talks about it three and half decades later, it is clear that the exercise was disturbing and stressful for him.

MORE DISAPPOINTMENT

Abdurrahman's easy success with his Arabic-language exams in late 1964 left him with a dangerous sense of confidence about his ability to dispense with the ordinary disciplines of university study. As a consequence, when he found undergraduate Islamic studies at Al Azhar to be almost as tedious as the basic Arabic course, he fully expected to be able to repeat his pattern of work without difficulty. His life was full enough anyway without having to sit through first-year classes, and he figured that some perfunctory revision at the end of the academic year would be enough to secure passes in the final exams. In this he badly miscalculated. For one thing, the university authorities who administered his scholarship were unimpressed with his attendance record. Secondly, he underestimated the amount of preparation required to pass the end-of-year exams. Moreover, if he had commenced his first-year studies in mid-1965 somewhat preoccupied, he concluded them in mid-1966 totally distracted by the pressing developments that followed the 30 September 'coup' in 1965. A more disciplined student might have been able to redeem the situation, but Abdurrahman's efforts were too little and too late. He failed one of his two core units and was told that he would have to repeat the year, and very likely without a scholarship.

At this stage he had been in the Middle East for two and a half years but had little to show for his time. He recalls that he was also feeling depressed about what had been taking place in Indonesia during his absence. The involvement of NU and Ansor saddened and disturbed him; he despaired that his community would ever be mature enough to leave behind its primordialism and unhealthy self-righteousness. At the same time he was feeling stressed by his work with the Indonesian Embassy and fearful that, no matter how carefully he had written his reports on his fellow students, they might still be used for purposes of persecution and oppression.

He recalls that at this time he was also beginning to wonder about the troubled relationship between religion and the state. His experience in Egypt gave him further grounds for despairing that Muslim society could successfully avoid polarisation and extremism. And if Egypt could not manage this, then what hope had the rest of the Arab world? He had followed the Egyptian state's treatment of Islamist thinker Sayyid Qutb with interest. By this time Abdurrahman had tried the Islamist writers and ultimately found Islamist thought to be extremist and naive. He had studied the works of Hasan al-Banna (who had founded Al Ikhwan Al Muslimun, the Islamic Brotherhood, in Egypt in 1928 under the banner of 'returning to the Qur'an and the Hadith' to solve society's ills), Ali Shari'ati (the radical Iranian writer whose ideas were a source of inspiration for the Iranian revolution) Sayyid Qutb and other Islamist writers. One of the things that he found hardest to accept was their lack of openness to truth from any source other than those they defined as allowable. As we have seen, Abdurrahman's father Wahid Hasyim had been a pluralist and his mother had continued to maintain an open intellectual and social atmosphere in the family home after her husband's death in 1953. Abdurrahman had grown up believing that, while the Qur'an and Hadith were the ultimate sources and reference points for 'religious truth', there was much truth, including religious truth, to be found across the spectrum of human cultural production, whether in the stories of the *wayang kulit* or in the novels of Dostoyevsky. To have embraced Islamism would have meant radically questioning his epistemology and his entire worldview. Moreover, having examined the writings of the Islamists he was unconvinced that their plan to transform society was a workable and as desirable as they maintained it to be. For Abdurrahman Islamism, like Communism, failed to offer a comprehensive and humane answer to society's problems, no matter how sincere its proponents.

Abdurrahman recalls that soon after arriving in Egypt he became convinced that Sayyid Qutb was fundamentally mistaken in his views. Nevertheless, he admired the man for his moral courage in the face of overwhelming opposition. He was also repelled by the brutality of the Nasser government in its suppression of Sayyid Qutb's colleagues in the Islamic Brotherhood. He says that for this reason he made a point of joining with the hundreds of other students who gathered to pray outside Sayyid Qutb's prison on the day that the Egyptian state hanged its 'troublesome cleric'.

To Abdurrahman, Al Azhar seemed mired in the past. Sayyid Qutb and the other Islamists were obsessed with religious extremism, and the government of Nasser seemed equally obsessed with nationalist extremism. Meanwhile, back in Java, NU had allowed itself to descend into the sort of hatred and hysteria that turned civilised men into cold-blooded murderers. He recalls that for a while he toyed with the idea of returning to Java and becoming a human rights activist. He recognised, however, that without a university degree he would always be limited in what he could do in Indonesia and he had seen enough of Cairo to know that there was much that he could learn in the Middle East.

NURIYAH

Throughout these years in Cairo, Abdurrahman recalls, he kept up a steady stream of correspondence with Nuriyah. He interpreted the regular arrival of her letters as meaning that at least she had not totally rejected his interest in her. She was an able and witty correspondent and over several years a relationship developed that was far deeper and more substantial than the uncertain friendship that they had known in Jombang, when Nuriyah had often rejected the gifts of books that he presented to her. Despite its hesitant start, the relationship deepened through their correspondence and by 1966 the pair were certain that they wanted to get married. Or, more accurately, Nuriyah had accepted that Abdurrahman really was to be her partner in life. She recalls that at one stage she had even consulted a fortune-teller to inquire whether the chubby, bespectacled, bookish Abdurrahman was really the man for her or whether she should look elsewhere.[3] The fortune-teller's response had been clear. 'Don't bother looking anywhere else; this one is your soulmate.' The response had unsettled Nuriyah as she was uncertain about her feelings for Abdurrahman. But his letters did much to turn that around, as did her own development and reflection on what it was that she was really looking for. She was under considerable social pressure to accept that Abdurrahman would be a good husband. Although rural families often facilitated marriages, this was not an arranged marriage: it was up to Nuriyah to accept Abdurrahman's advances or reject them and look elsewhere. She was an attractive and vivacious young woman and had no shortage of suitors. Abdurrahman was hardly the most handsome man she knew, but the gentle personality and sharp mind so evident in his letters began increasingly to endear themselves to Nuriyah.

Finally, in the middle of 1966 he wrote to her and asked: 'Well, what about it: will you marry me?' Nuriyah's initial response was ambiguous and ambivalent. She wrote: 'Finding a partner is like life and death. God alone knows what will be.' Abdurrahman was not deterred and persisted in his correspondence, pouring out to Nuriyah his feelings of despair at the way things had turned out for him in Egypt. For a man who seldom admits to feelings of doubt, much less depression, it was significant that he wrote so frankly about his anxiety. Upon receiving his end-of-year examination results in the middle of 1966, he recalls, he wrote of his feelings of failure to Nuriyah. This time there was some good news. Nuriyah wrote back immediately with encouraging words: 'Why should somebody have to fail in everything? If you fail in your studies you might at least succeed in romance.' Abdurrahman immediately dashed off a letter to his mother asking her to formally approach Nuriyah's father for her hand in marriage.

A FRESH START IN BAGHDAD

Abdurrahman had some other good news as well: he was offered a scholarship at the University of Baghdad. It was a welcome opportunity to make a fresh start. Abdurrahman says nothing about why he was offered a second scholarship in the Arab world, but there is no doubt that he was fortunate to obtain one after having performed so dismally at Al Azhar. No doubt his membership of one of Indonesia's most prominent *ulama* clans helped his case, as did the efforts of his mother in Jakarta as a well-connected and spirited advocate. Perhaps, too, his reputation at the embassy in Cairo, and his work with Association of Indonesian Students around the region, helped in his application for a second scholarship.

Although Abdurrahman had been disappointed with his formal studies in Cairo, he had benefited greatly from the social and intellectual environment. Nevertheless, he says that one of the reasons that he was not reluctant to leave Cairo for Baghdad was that he was becoming disenchanted with Nasser's autocratic style and was feeling less at home. Indonesian students studying in Baghdad spoke of it as a cosmopolitan city, charged with a vitality that was felt both in the sciences and in the arts. It was said that intellectuals there enjoyed considerable freedom to exchange ideas openly and debate matters of philosophy and religion. This time Abdurrahman was not disappointed: he found Baghdad to be a rich centre of intellectual endeavour and learning. . .

The University of Baghdad had been established as an Islamic university but, unlike Al Azhar, by the mid-1960s it had begun to be transformed into a European-style university. The university benefited from the presence of many of the Arab world's best academics. Ironically, many of Abdurrahman's favourite lecturers were Egyptians from Cairo who found that Baghdad offered greater academic freedom and better rates of remuneration. Many were graduates of European universities and they sought to impose European standards on their students at the University of Baghdad. In this they were by no means entirely successful, but the intellectual atmosphere and expectations of students differed vastly from what Abdurrahman had experienced in Al Azhar. Critical thinking and extensive reading was expected in students and in their class papers. The result for Abdurrahman was genuine intellectual stimulation in place of rote learning, with a more rigorous work routine than he had ever known.

The University of Baghdad was eventually to prove an environment in which Abdurrahman thrived, but not before being rudely wakened from his old habits. He recalls that at first he thought he might just sample classes rather than commit himself to regular attendance. He was soon dissuaded from this approach and told that class attendance was monitored and was regarded as compulsory. Even at Al Azhar Abdurrahman's freelance approach to learning had led to the threat of his scholarship being withdrawn. Now in Baghdad it was made clear to him that he would not be able to pass his subjects without a satisfactory attendance record. In his first year at the university he befriended Mahfudz Ridwan, a boy from Salatiga, Central Java, who had earlier completed high school studies in Mecca. Mahfudz became a trusted and valuable friend, just as Mahfudz's lecture notes became valuable guides whenever test time rolled around!

Once he had buckled down to his studies in Baghdad, Abdurrahman's daily routine became much fuller and more rigid than it had been in Cairo. No longer was he free to wander the city at will. Nevertheless, he recalls that he still found time for the cinema, re-watching many of the French films he had seen in Cairo, and he still read constantly, often into the small hours of the morning. Most mornings he awoke sleepy from having read half the night but had no choice but to follow Mahfudz and his other housemates off to class.

From 11 am until 2 pm each day he would report for work at the office of Ar-Rahmadani, cloth merchants. Ar-Rahmadani was a small firm specialising in importing textiles from Europe and America. Abdurrahman's skills as a writer and translator saw him remain comfortably employed with the cloth merchants for the next three and a half years. Each afternoon Abdurrahman would be busy in the university library. Most of the subjects he undertook at university required regular and often lengthy class papers, generally with specific requirements regarding the number of reference works to be consulted. As a result, he says, he found he had to spend several hours working in the library each afternoon if he was to keep up his studies. He also continued to write regular essays for newspapers and magazines in Indonesia and remained actively involved in the leadership of the Association of Indonesian Students. In the evenings, though, there was still time for drinking coffee down by the banks of the Tigris River. Drinking coffee at the riverside cafés in the evening was a popular social pastime in Baghdad, and it gave Abdurrahman an opportunity for the sort of intellectual discussion he had previously found in the coffee shops of Cairo.

For three years in Baghdad he also undertook private studies in French at the French cultural centre in Baghdad. He explains that by chance he had met the centre's French lecturer at a party and decided to take up her invitation to join her class the next day. He found her classes to be unusually engaging because of her modern approach to language instruction and her passion for French culture, and soon became a regular student. When he commenced his studies with her he had spoken French reasonably well and had good reading ability, but had no formal study of French, being entirely self-taught. In Cairo his roommate, Mustofa Bisri, had made an earnest but entirely unsuccessful attempt to learn French. Much to Mustofa's annoyance, his failure, despite endless repetitions of the recorded exercises, was accompanied by Abdurrahman's rapid advances in spoken French as he parroted the recordings.

While his schedule didn't allow as much time for café discussions as had been the case in Cairo, such discussions were still very much a part of Arab intellectual life, particularly during the 'golden age' of intellectual activity in Baghdad during the late 1960s. Besides evenings in the cafés by the river, there was also time to talk with classmates at the university. Attached to the university library was a coffee and teashop and he recalls taking regular breaks from his studies in the library to drink tea and talk with friends. His classmates came from across the Arab world and beyond, including Indonesia and Malaysia, and many were later to rise to positions of prominence in their own countries. Most were bright students studying in Baghdad on Iraqi government scholarships and were good company.

Much like Cairo, the ancient city of Baghdad had enjoyed great prominence throughout Islamic history and held other attractions for Abdurrahman. In Baghdad and Iraq he found a city and a nation home to some of the most important historic tombs in the Islamic world. When he had time, which was generally on the weekends, he made a point of visiting these tomb sites and he recalls that on a number of occasions he stayed behind to pray through the night. With its rich history of Shiite and Sufi saints, Baghdad, even more than Cairo, was for Abdurrahman a magical place, and he filled his free hours seeking out new sites to visit.

STUDENT LIFE

During his first three years Abdurrahman lived with fellow Indonesian students. He and nineteen others rented a large villa in Baghdad and set up house there. Scholarship conditions and the availability of part-time work meant that they were reasonably well off and their large villa was comfortable, especially by student standards. The student house was characterised by a pleasant communal atmosphere and lively, mostly good-natured, exchanges. The students contributed to a pool of money for running household affairs, paying for maintenance and other expenses along with rent.

Once every twenty days each student took his turn to cook for the household. Abdurrahman's specialty was fish-head curry, a welcome delicacy for Indonesians a long way from home. Abdurrahman confesses that the choice was not entirely accidental. Early in his stay in Baghdad he had discovered a fish shop a short walk from the student house. He soon noticed that the Iraqis never ate the heads of fish, but threw them away or gave them to their pets. So one day he approached the owner of the fish shop and asked if he could have twenty heads from the large fish that were being cut up and prepared behind the counter. 'Why do you need so many fish-heads?' asked the surprised proprietor. 'Well it's because I have a lot of dogs.' 'How many dogs do you have?' 'Twenty,' said Abdurrahman holding back a laugh. A deal was done, and once every twenty days Abdurrahman returned to the fish shop and collected twenty large fish-heads. In token exchange he would give the shop owner a few coins, return home, and cook a delicious curry. The meal cost him next to nothing and he says that his housemates enjoyed it greatly. This went on for more than a year and was as near as possible to an ideal arrangement. And then one day, he recalls, the students had official guests from Indonesia. The Indonesian Embassy had proposed a special festive meal to be held at the student house. The students, in inimitable Indonesian fashion, formed a committee and set about preparations. One of Abdurrahman's friends was put in charge of the cooking and decided to prepare a fish dish to accompany the lamb and beef ones that had already been planned. He went down to the fish shop frequented by Abdurrahman. The proprietor recognised him and chuckling remarked: 'Your friend is a very strange man.' 'Why do you say that?' 'Because he keeps so many large dogs. Twenty dogs, just imagine that!' The friend returned home and was furious with Abdurrahman. 'How can you call us dogs?' he demanded.

Although it gave Abdurrahman great pleasure to turn the virtually worthless waste of a Baghdad fish shop into a prized meal, he explains that he was not primarily motivated by a desire to save money. His Iraqi scholarship, together with his wages from Ar-Rahmadani and his regular earnings from his essays and other writings made him comparatively well off. And in any case money held no intrinsic appeal for him. Provided that he had enough for books and the cinema, he cared little about money. In fact he says that he relied upon Mahfudz to manage his money for him. That Mahfudz saw fit to occasionally use his money to help out some of the poorer students did not worry him. He was more concerned about finding time to read than about money. Arrangements in the student house suited him perfectly. His good friend Mahfudz took care of day-to-day matters, his turn to cook came but once every three weeks, and he was left with plenty of time to himself to continue reading.

Abdurrahman enjoyed good fellowship with his housemates and with the other Indonesian students in Baghdad, and he also had a wide circle of non-Indonesian friends, including many other foreign students and local Iraqis. Abdurrahman enjoyed the cosmopolitan atmosphere that prevailed at the university and, being endlessly curious, he enjoyed cross-examining those who seemed to have an interesting story to tell.

AN UNUSUAL FRIENDSHIP

One of his closest friends was a colleague by the name of Ramin. Ramin worked with Abdurrahman at Ar-Rahmadani, writing and translating correspondence for the firm. Ramin came from the small Iraqi Jewish community in Baghdad. He was a naturally liberal and open-minded thinker and a keen student of the Cabbala, the Jewish mystical tradition. Ramin and Abdurrahman regularly found time to sit in a quiet corner discussing religion, philosophy and politics. One of their favourite haunts was the market beside the Hanging Gardens, where they could be sure of finding a quiet place to talk, undisturbed and unmonitored. It was from Ramin that Abdurrahman first learned about Judaism and the experience of the Jewish people. Ramin talked extensively about the experience of the Jewish Diaspora and particularly about the tribulations then being experienced by Jews living in Russia. He also talked of his own family history and how it was that his family came to be trapped in Iraq. From Ramin, Abdurrahman says, he learned respect for Judaism and also came to understand Jewish religious outlooks and the political and social concerns of Jews living in the Diaspora as a frequently persecuted minority.

AN UNUSUAL WEDDING

Throughout his time in Baghdad Abdurrahman, as chairman of the Association of Indonesian Students, continued to correspond with and occasionally visit Indonesian students throughout the Middle East. They were worried about political developments at home. Like their fellow students back in Indonesia they initially welcomed the new stability that Soeharto brought to Indonesia. They were concerned, however, about the dominance of the Indonesian Armed Forces (Angkatan Bersenjata Republic Indonesia — ABRI), and what it would mean for the future of democracy in the country. Abdurrahman occasionally expressed such concerns in his essays for the Indonesian press.

In mid-1968 Nuriyah, who by now had been formally engaged to Abdurrahman for almost two years, graduated from Pesantren Tambakberas in Jombang and was about to enter tertiary studies at IAIN Sunan Kalijaga, the State Islamic Institute in Yogyakarta. Unusually, for the time, she was offered a place in the faculty of Syari'ah or Islamic law, regarded as the most academically rigorous of all the IAIN faculties. For this reason, in the IAIN female students had earlier not been permitted to study in the Faculty of Syari'ah. (Abdurrahman is quick to point out that it was Wahid Hasyim as Minister for Religious Affairs who, in the process of establishing the institutions that would become the IAIN, decreed that female students should have equal access to all faculties along with male students.) When Nuriyah was studying in Yogyakarta most of the students in her faculty were male; she was one of a significant early group of female students. She had begun her studies at Sunan Kalijaga in 1967 after she completed her high school studies at Pesantren Tambakberas in Jombang in 1967.

Nuriyah's parents had decided that, before she went to live and study in Yogyakarta by herself, it would be best if she and Abdurrahman were formally married. However, there was a minor problem. Abdurrahman was eight thousand miles away in Iraq, and being mid-way through his studies he had neither the time nor the money to return for the wedding. A solution was found and the wedding proceeded in September that year. The solution led to unfortunate speculation on the part of those unfamiliar with the arrangements. Since he could not be present in person, Abdurrahman was represented by his grandfather, Kiai Bisri Syansuri. The sight of the 81-year-old *kiai* standing beside the young bride reportedly caused quite a stir. Although technically Abdurrahman and Nuriyah were now married, they regarded the arrangement as being more like a betrothal; they accepted that it would only be after they had both finished their studies that they could be together.

In his final year in Baghdad, Abdurrahman moved out of the large student house into a smaller house together with Mahfudz and another friend. The arrival of new Indonesian students in Baghdad had precipitated the move, and Abdurrahman's comfortable financial circumstances made it possible. For Abdurrahman the real advantage, he recalls, was that he had more time to read. In order to save time they continued to meet with the other students in the student house for evening meals, leaving Abdurrahman with uninterrupted time in the evening.

During his final two years in Baghdad Abdurrahman focused on researching the history of Islam in Indonesia. His lecturers had given him permission to write extensively on the topic of Indonesian Islam. He read all of the Orientalist sources that he could find as well as the local Indonesian accounts. Drawing on the surprisingly extensive resources of the University of Baghdad library, he became something of an authority on the subject.

EUROPE

In the middle of 1970 Abdurrahman had finished his four-year course at the University of Baghdad and moved from there to Europe, settling first in the Netherlands in order to search for an opportunity for further studies. He was hopeful, he says, of an opportunity to undertake postgraduate studies in the field of comparative religion and inquired initially at Leiden University. He had hoped that he would be able to secure a place for further studies and then bring Nuriyah with him to Europe. He was disappointed when he found that not only at Leiden but throughout Europe there was little recognition of his studies at the University of Baghdad. The European universities all laid down prerequisites that would require him to repeat his undergraduate studies. He was to spend almost twelve months in Europe, returning home in the middle of 1971 effectively empty-handed.

Although Abdurrahman had gained no formal qualifications from his studies in Europe it was an experience that he had been working towards for many years. Since his time in Yogyakarta he had made a study of Western thought. In Cairo he continued his studies. Similarly, in Baghdad, he was able to delve more deeply into critical Western social science and Western thought more generally, and his sojourn in Europe completed the experience. He felt his stay had afforded him a chance to study at firsthand the nature of society in the Netherlands, Germany and France and to engage in numerous conversations and discussions about society and thought in Europe itself.

Abdurrahman was to spend a total of six months in the Netherlands. Much of this time was taken in investigating openings at Leiden and in universities in nearby cities in both the Netherlands and Germany. During this period he sustained himself by working at a Chinese laundromat, learning to iron and fold clothes with industrial efficiency, helped in part by the music of Janis Joplin! From the Netherlands he moved to Germany for a further four months. He then spent two months in France before returning home.

FOUR

THE *PESANTREN* AND REFORM, 1971-1982

RETURN TO JAVA

Abdurrahman returned home to Java on 4 May 1971. He confesses that he was disappointed that his attempts to pursue higher education in Europe had failed so completely. He comforted himself with the thought that he had a good chance of being accepted in the respected Islamic studies program at McGill University in Montreal, Canada. He was clearly a bright student and it was not difficult for him to find referees and mentors to vouch for his suitability for postgraduate study. At the same time his family connections provided easy access to the Minister for Religious Affairs, so he was confident about obtaining a scholarship. McGill had a long-standing arrangement in which it received young Indonesian intellectuals who had been chosen to join the faculty of the State Islamic Institute system and guided them through a program of postgraduate research that drew on their knowledge of classical Islamic texts. Where the European institutions had hesitated to recognise his studies in Baghdad, McGill, he felt sure, would have no such qualms.

Once settled back in his mother's house in Matraman, near the centre of Jakarta, Abdurrahman was anxious to find out what had happened during his absence. It would be at least a year before he could go to McGill so he had plenty of time to tour the *pesantren* of Central and East Java. With Nuriyah completing her bachelor's degree at the State Islamic Institute in Yogyakarta, it would be September before they could host their wedding reception and properly start their married life, so he had time on his hands. Nuriyah joined him in Jakarta when she could, and he also travelled with her to Yogyakarta. As her classes finished she was busy preparing for final exams, but at least her schedule was more flexible and she was able to join him in many of his activities, including regular trips to Jombang.

Abdurrahman had not lived in Jakarta since he was a boy, and he recalls that he was eager to use the opportunity of being back in Matraman to get to know the city's intellectual communities. After several months he was invited to participate in the work of the Institute for Economic and Social Research, Education and Information (Lembaga Pengkajian Pengetahuan, Pendidikan, Ekonomi dan Social — LP3ES), one of the more promising non-government organisations to emerge in the 1970s. LP3ES was initially funded by the German Neumann Institute, and later received help from the Ford Foundation; it was intended to build up a centre for social research and critical thought in Indonesia. It attracted some of the country's best young intellectuals, mainly from social-democrat and progressive Islam circles, such as Dawam Rahardjo, Adi Sasono, Aswab Mahasin and Abdurrahman Wahid. One of its main achievements was publishing *Prisma*, for many years Indonesia's premier social science journal, to which Abdurrahman was a regular contributor.[1] A further attraction for Abdurrahman was that it showed a strong interest in the *pesantren* world and sought to combine it with community development. He recalls that he felt very encouraged by the considerable respect and recognition from the leadership at LP3ES for what he could contribute to the organisation. It was arranged for him to visit LP3ES once a fortnight, spending two to four days working in the Jakarta office. Abdurrahman provided LP3ES with an understanding of the *pesantren* world and traditional Islam, while they educated him in the practical and critical aspects of community development. The combination, Abdurrahman explains, suited him perfectly. When not working in the Jakarta office, he was free to tour Java. Abdurrahman's love of people was conveniently combined with a general interest in visiting new sites and in making regular pilgrimages to favourite old sites.

After their wedding reception in September 1971, Abdurrahman and Nuriyah settled down in Jombang and Abdurrahman continued to tour Java. He commuted regularly to Jakarta, spending several days each fortnight in the office of LP3ES. He was beginning to revise his earlier plans about studying at McGill. As he toured the *pesantren* he was struck by the extent to which their traditional value system was under attack. Many within the *pesantren* felt it to be imperative that the *pesantren* implement *madrasah* school programs with a state syllabus. Abdurrahman welcomed moves to reform the *pesantren*, but he was troubled by the extent to which traditional elements of learning were being neglected. He did not oppose the adoption of the state curriculum, but he was concerned that unthinking modernisation and rapid change, driven by the desire to secure state funding, might irreversibly damage the traditional values of the *pesantren*. He was also struck by the level of poverty in many of the small communities surrounding NU *pesantren*.

SOEHARTO'S NEW ORDER AND THE 1971 ELECTIONS

The Indonesian economy had been near collapse when Abdurrahman had left Java for Egypt in 1963. Sukarno's 'Guided Democracy' approach to economic and social management had contributed to the rapid disintegration of the economy. Things had deteriorated considerably in the lead-up to the September 1965 'coup' and under the effectual regime that followed. By the late 1960s, the new Soeharto government had made considerable progress in re-establishing order and laying down the foundations for economic growth. Nevertheless, in the early 1970s, the rural world of East and Central Java saw significant poverty and few obvious opportunities for development. Abdurrahman, now increasingly thoughtful about developmental issues through his discussions at LP3ES, saw potential for using the *pesantren* network and communities for community development. There were already worrying signs that the Soeharto government might prove excessively authoritarian, but in the early 1970s there was considerable intellectual and press freedom; with economic recovery and with Soeharto so evidently concerned about rural development, many were feeling optimistic about what could be achieved.

At the same time there was a confident mood within NU about the organisation's political profile and its ability to negotiate with the Soeharto government based on the results of the 1971 elections. These elections were the first held since the nation's only other elections in 1955. Not surprisingly, Soeharto's new political vehicle (the army did not like the idea of being associated with a 'party'), Golkar, had dominated the 1971 election results, gaining 63 per cent of the vote. By any ordinary measure the result would have been surprising, but Golkar's clean sweep was the product of a carefully organised campaign spearheaded by Ali Murtopo's Opsus, or Special Operations unit. Ali Murtopo was one of Soeharto's small clique of powerful personal staffers (*staff pribadi*, or *spri*), who wielded more power than most government ministers. It was Ali Murtopo's brief to handle 'political affairs'. The other key member of Soeharto's personal staff was Sudjono Humardhani, assistant for economic affairs. In the early 1970s Ali Murtopo and Sudjono Humardhani worked together to establish the Centre for Strategic and International Studies (CSIS). It quickly became a key research centre and was widely seen as the originator of many of the key policy initiatives in the early part of Soeharto's New Order regime. At this time both men were seen as having Soeharto's ear and being able to do more or less whatever they wanted to do. Not surprisingly, they were viewed with suspicion by many army generals.

By 1967 Soeharto had already moved to consolidate his power by making a series of institutional changes. The election scheduled for 1968 was postponed until 1971. The government announced that it would henceforth have the right to appoint one-third of the representatives to the People's Consultative Assembly, or MPR, the body charged with electing a president, and more than one-fifth of the sitting members of the DPR, or parliament. In that same year irresistible pressure was placed on the PNI, the Nationalist Party of Indonesia to replace its leaders with people who met with the government's approval. Similarly, Parmusi, the successor to Masyumi, was told that all of the senior Masyumi leaders would be barred from holding office in Parmusi. At the same time the government introduced the concept of *golongan karya*, or functional groups representing every sector of society, including the military, and explained that it was setting up an umbrella organisation of the same name, Golongan Karya, or Golkar, to channel the aspirations of every group in society. In other words, it was making Golkar the dominant political body in the nation. In theory Golkar would have to contest elections in the same way as any ordinary political party, but in practice it had unparalleled resources with which to coerce voter support. Not the least of these was the military's hierarchical network of surveillance and control, inspired by territorial warfare, which mirrored the civil bureaucracy from village level all the way up and operated like a fantastical Neighbourhood Watch.

Ali Murtopo's Opsus group intervened heavily in the run-up to the 1971 elections, using inducements and intimidation to ensure that every village and district head achieved their 'quota' of Golkar votes and hence earned the promised reward of extra development funding. Public servants were obliged to support the government by voting for Golkar, and the ever-present military representatives did their best to see that the communities which they supervised did 'the right thing'. The PNI and the modernists in Parmusi, both heavily discredited as a result of government meddling in their leadership ranks, saw their vote plummet in the 1971 election, with Parmusi gaining less than 6 per cent compared to Masyumi's 21 per cent in 1955. In contrast, NU's vote continued to hold up. NU gained around 18 per cent of the national vote in 1971, an almost identical result to its result in 1955, and in its East Java heartland it won 35 per cent of all votes cast. The 1971 results suggested that NU represented the largest political power outside Golkar. Now that it was in a position to directly challenge Golkar, it felt confident that the government would have to take it seriously.[2]

It was widely believed that Ali Murtopo was behind the government's 1973 push to collapse the nine opposition parties that had contested the 1971 elections down to two new putative opposition parties: the Democratic Party of Indonesia (PDI), representing the former PNI and other non-*santri* parties, and the United Development Party (PPP), representing NU, Parmusi, and the two smaller *santri* parties.

PESANTREN AND COMMUNITY DEVELOPMENT

In the early 1970s Mukti Ali, the new Minister for Religious Affairs, called for the rejuvenation of the *pesantren* value system and for the *pesantren* to act as change agents in Indonesian society in order to facilitate community development. In explaining his vision Mukti Ali, who was known to be a reasonably progressive thinker and a gracious mentor of young intellectuals, was fond of invoking the Qur'anic injunction, 'be among you a group which will do good deeds and carry out the obligations of religion and observe that which is prohibited in religion'. Mukti Ali took this text to indicate that small committed groups of religious visionaries could play catalytic roles in society and that this was part of the mission of Islam. Encouraged by the opportunities opening up in Indonesia, Abdurrahman explains, he decided to put off further studies and for the next few years concentrate on building up the *pesantren*.³

In 1972 Abdurrahman began giving regular lectures and seminars around Java. He also wrote columns for national news magazines like *Tempo* and feature articles for *Kompas*, the leading daily newspaper owned by Catholic Chinese interests.⁴ His columns in *Tempo* and *Kompas* were well received, and he quickly came to be regarded as an up-and-coming social commentator. As we have seen, he also wrote for *Prisma*, which had been established in the early 1970s to promote critical social thinking in Indonesia. His articles for *Prisma* and the seminar papers he gave at academic conferences allowed him to explore his ideas further.

STARTING OUT

As the first-born son of Kiai Wahid Hasyim and the grandson of Kiai Hasyim Asy'ari and Kiai Bisri Syansuri, Abdurrahman was closely watched by the senior *kiai* of Nahdlatul Ulama. His promotion through the ranks of NU, however, was by no means automatic. His heritage gave him a position of prominence and meant that much would be expected of him, but he still needed to prove himself. Abdurrahman was also becoming noticed in secular intellectual circles in Jakarta, but this was not necessarily of benefit to his reputation and standing within NU. Indeed, his interest in the arts and his friendships with actors and writers in Jakarta raised eyebrows back in Jombang. In the 1970s *pesantren* graduates seldom ventured into the 'dangerous', 'secular' domain of film and literature.

Life for Abdurrahman and Nuriyah in 1973 was good: their modest new home in Kiai Bisri's *pesantren* complex had been completed, and their first child Alissa had just been born. Abdurrahman enjoyed his work with LP3ES and was happy shuttling between Jombang and Jakarta, moving comfortably in both worlds and never staying too long in either. He also enjoyed the regular circuit of seminars and lectures that had become part of his life. Nevertheless, he and Nuriyah had to work hard to make ends meet. The honoraria that Abdurrahman received for his articles and public lectures did not provide sufficient money to meet the young family's expenses.

Short of money, Nuriyah recalls, she decided that she would have to do something to bridge the gap. She thought of preparing snack food at home to be sold each day to the thousands of students studying in Jombang. She chose *kacang tayamum* (sand-roasted peanuts), prepared by stirring peanuts through sand in hot wok. Every evening she and Abdurrahman sat at the kitchen table preparing the *kacang tayamum* for the next day. He filled small plastic bags, about twenty-five peanuts to the bag, and she sealed them by running the tops of the bags through the flame of a candle. This done, they would then prepare *es lilin* or 'ice candles'. Abdurrahman's mother had given him a Vespa motor scooter, which he used daily to deliver fifteen thermos flasks packed with the ice confectioneries to strategic points around town. The *es lilin* proved popular and quickly became known as 'Es Lilin Gus Dur'. Nuriyah's snack business was modest but successful and the steady income proved sufficient for them to keep their heads above water. In 1974 their second child, Zannuba Arifah Chafsoh, soon nicknamed Yenny, was born. The little family was not at all well off, even by the standards of the day when few people had much money, but they were surrounded by their extended families in Jombang, Abdurrahman was respected in the community, and they were happy.[5]

Abdurrahman recalls that the family finances improved later that year after Kiai Sobary, one of the senior *kiai* from Jombang who had attended the meeting at Kiai Bisri's garage the previous year, invited Abdurrahman to his house to talk. Kiai Sobary began by saying words to the effect of:

> Gus, your grandfather entrusted to me the Madrasah Alia and because of that I now want to ask you to teach Kaidah Fiqh [the elements of Islamic jurisprudence] because I know that you know much about Kaidah Fiqh. I did not realise it before but books I've never seen you have read and understood. I also understand that you have memorised the famous 54 legal maxims of Kaidah Fiqh. Please come and teach.

Abdurrahman countered by arguing that he was not qualified to teach Kaidah Fiqh, or the rules of Islamic jurisprudence. In the day schools within the *pesantren*, the *madrasah alia*, a teacher was allowed to teach only those subjects for which he had been awarded an *ijazah*, or certificate of competency, by a senior *kiai*. Kiai Sobary quickly responded: 'I'll give you the *ijazah*, I know that you are capable.' With this Abdurrahman embarked upon a teaching career at Pesantren Tambakberas that was to last for as long as he was living in Jombang.

Abdurrahman soon made his mark as an able teacher of Islamic law, his quick, dry wit making him a favourite with students. He recalls that the following year Kiai Sobary again approached him and said: 'You have succeeded in teaching Kaidah Fiqh, now teach Kitab Al Hikam.' Al Hikam is one of the classical Islamic texts on Sufism (Tasawuf). Again, says Abdurrahman, he declined to accept the old *kiai*'s offer and again Kiai Sobary persisted. The old man added to his insistence that Abdurrahman teach the Sufi text one further command. He made him promise that every thirty-five days he would visit his father's grave to pray and recite certain passages from the Qur'an.[6] This he dutifully did for many years, though few knew that he did so as such rituals are normally done in the middle of the night, sometimes continuing until dawn. Although in latter years such graveyards in Jombang attracted increasing numbers of pilgrims, in the 1970s he says that he rarely encountered others praying at the graveyard where his father was buried.

By 1977, when their third child Anita was born, Abdurrahman and Nuriyah had a settled and comfortable routine. Nuriyah was close to her family and friends and busy raising her three young children. Even though Abdurrahman's teaching provided a more reliable income, they were still continually short of cash. He recalls that this did not seem to matter so much in the communal environment of their *pesantren* home in Jombang. Abdurrahman enjoyed increasing respect both in Jakarta and Jombang and was in demand as a speaker and writer, but, at this point, not so much so that he was short of time for his family. This was just as well; they could not afford much household help and Abdurrahman had to assist Nuriyah in household chores. Because of the climate in Jombang, which was well known for being oven-hot and dusty, and because the overweight Abdurrahman had a poor tolerance for heat, Nuriyah explains that he was assigned tasks such as doing the laundry by hand, washing the dishes and mopping the floor, anything which involved water and afforded some chance to cool down.[7] In later years they were to have more money, but never again would Abdurrahman have so much time to spend with Nuriyah or the children as during the first five years of their married life in Jombang.

In 1977 he was approached to become Dean of the Faculty of Usuluddin at the University of Hasyim Asy'ari in Jombang, a position he gladly accepted. The university was an Islamic college named after Abdurrahman's grandfather. It had been established by a consortium of *pesantren* to provide tertiary education for *pesantren* graduates. One of its faculties was located in Pesantren Denanyar, another in Pesantren Tebuireng, and a further one in the city centre. It was no competitor for the state universities but, drawing on the strength of Jombang's *pesantren*, it built a reputation as an institution providing sound higher-level instruction to graduates of *pesantren*. Abdurrahman began to lecture in Tarbiyah, or pedagogy, and Usuluddin, or Islamic belief and practice. He explains that some at the university wanted him to teach other subjects, but this did not happen because he fell foul of university politics. He was stopped from teaching Syari'ah, or Islamic law, and Dakwah, or missiology, by the University Secretary who Abdurrahman felt seemed concerned to check the rise of this popular young teacher. It was, he recalls, his first major experience of having to battle unhelpful bureaucrats. The experience did not trouble him greatly. Blasé as ever, he ignored the slight and simply concentrated on what was at hand. At the same time he was also invited to teach one day a week in the *madrasah* at Tambakberas. Now thirty-seven, he had a steadily rising profile and his comfortable, easygoing life was rapidly becoming very busy.

A popular speaker, Abdurrahman frequently gave religious addresses on significant Islamic dates. Each Ramadan (the Islamic fasting month), for example, from 1973 until 1978, he addressed large assemblies of students in the Jombang area. He recalls that by 1978 several thousand people were gathering to hear his address each evening of the fasting month. That year his text year was Tafsir Djalalin, one of the famous medieval commentaries on the Qur'an. The book was conveniently divided into thirty *juz* (sections), and each evening he expounded on one. By the eve of Idul Fitri, the day of feasting that marks the end of Ramadan, he had arrived at Juz no. 27. That evening the local train from Jombang was forced to wait at the station because several hundred of the regular passengers were still listening intently to Abdurrahman as he concluded his instruction. Because there were three juz remaining, he promised to return at a later date and complete the series. Years later people were still asking when he would come back and fulfil his promise.

A SMALL ACCIDENT, AN ONGOING PROBLEM

That same year, while casually turning into the grounds of Pesantren Denanyar on his Vespa motor scooter Abdurrahman was struck by a car. Although he did not suffer any broken bones, the impact was severe enough to detach the retina in his left eye. Specialists in Jakarta advised that with sufficient rest the retina might re-adhere. Unfortunately, Abdurrahman was not good at staying still and before long he was up reading books, writing, and giving seminar papers. As a result the retina failed to re-adhere properly and he was forced to commence a cycle of regular specialist intervention and check-ups. Partly for this reason he began to make more frequent trips to Jakarta and also began thinking about the wisdom of relocating to the national capital. He underwent an operation on his eye, intended to help it heal and encourage the loose flap of retina to re-adhere to the back of the eyeball, and he had to go to Jakarta regularly to consult the specialists who were treating him. He recalls that later that year something else occurred, which suggested to him that the time might have come to leave Jombang and settle in Jakarta.

JAKARTA BECKONS

Kiai Bisri Syansuri approached Abdurrahman and invited him once again to consider joining NU's national Syuriah or Religious Advisory Council. This was Kiai Bisri's third request to Abdurrahman to join the national leadership of Nahdlatul Ulama. Abdurrahman had declined the previous requests on the grounds that he was not yet ready to take on that sort of work. He recalls feeling apprehensive about becoming caught up in NU national politics and being saddled with organisational responsibilities. He told his close friends that his ambition was to continue to develop as a public intellectual and not become tied to NU's organisational structure. But he became increasingly aware that he was unlikely to be able to pursue this desire, as he was expected to play a formal role in NU. The realisation was not, of course, a new one: his mother had impressed upon him from the time of his father's death in 1953 that one day he would have to take up his father's mantle and carry on his work. Although she did not make it clear what work it was that she expected Abdurrahman to take up, it seemed likely that it would involve a formal role in NU's national leadership.

Following Kiai Bisri's third invitation, Abdurrahman went to discuss the matter with his mother. Abdurrahman was well known for being headstrong and impetuous. His steady loss of eyesight in his left eye following his failure to take sufficient rest after the accident in 1978 is a clear example of the high costs of this stubbornness. Nevertheless, there was one person whom he rarely disobeyed and certainly never in her presence, and that was his mother. She had continued to exert a strong influence in his life even as he was developing his own career in Jakarta and Jombang. It was common for him to consult with his mother in Jakarta and ask her advice whenever he was faced with difficult decisions. When he raised this matter with her, he recalls that her response was quick and to the point: 'Grandfather has asked you twice. He is not the sort of man to ask anyone to do something twice, now if he asks you a third time, don't refuse him. It is your duty to do whatever he asks you to do.'

Abdurrahman complied with his grandfather's request and joined NU's central Syuriah. This meant that he had to be regularly in Jakarta for meetings of the Syuriah and for consultation with his fellow board members. As we have seen, he was writing for *Tempo* magazine and involved with other intellectual endeavours in the national capital. At the same time his eye specialists were struggling to recover some of the lost vision in his left eye, and he had regular consultations as they attempted different forms of treatment. For over a year he shuttled back and forth between Jombang and Jakarta on a regular basis.

NU, PPP AND NATIONAL POLITICS

Abdurrahman served on NU's Syuriah for several years under his grandfather Kiai Bisri Syansuri, who was Rais Aam, or head of the Syuriah. This experience served to reinforce in his own mind the scope and nature of the issues confronting Nahdlatul Ulama, as well as cementing his reputation as a promising young leader.

In 1980 Kiai Bisri died, and a large part of the reason for Abdurrahman remaining in Jombang went with him. The family decided to move permanently to Ciganjur, a suburb far to the south of Jakarta that merged into the rural hinterland surrounding the national capital.

The house where Abdurrahman, Nuriyah and their three daughters settled in Ciganjur was modest even by village standards. There were no other houses for some distance around it, and it was located in the middle of a large field that regularly flooded. During the monsoon season the house was permanently surrounded by mud inches deep. Making matters worse, it was very small, but it was all that they could afford. The move to Jakarta ended Abdurrahman's salary from teaching in Jombang, and his involvement with the Syuriah cut into the time that he could spend speaking and writing and further reduced his income. Moreover the cost of living in Jakarta was much higher than in Jombang. On the other hand, he was able to strengthen his contacts with Jakarta intellectual circles. The death of Kiai Bisri in April 1980 represented a significant loss to the organisation. For some years the Tanfidziyah, or the National Executive Board, which in theory operated under the authority of the Syuriah, had been the subject of intense criticism from many of the NU *kiai* and *ulama*. They felt that the Tanfidziyah was dominated by NU politicians and had for many years neglected the organisation's social and religious activities. The national head of the Tanfidziyah, or executive chairman of Nahdlatul Ulama, was Idham Chalid, who had occupied this position since 1956. In many respects Idham, working closely with the politically astute Wahab Chasbullah, had been successful in navigating NU through some extremely trying circumstances, particularly during the change of regime from Sukarno to Soeharto in the mid-1960s. By the late 1970s many felt that Idham's leadership, which by then seemed set to continue indefinitely, represented a significant liability to the organisation. He had been president of PPP since its formation in 1973, and many felt that he paid more attention to party political matters than he did to NU social and religious aspirations. The national structure of the organisation had deteriorated, and many felt that a change of leadership was needed to inject new vision into the organisation and facilitate the sort of reforms that were required to adapt NU to the modern era.[8]

In the eyes of many *ulama*, Kiai Bisri Syansuri's leadership of the Syuriah had helped to balance what they felt to be the lack of appropriate leadership being displayed by Idham Chalid in the Tanfidziyah. Bisri Syansuri had become head of the Syuriah in 1971, following the death of his friend and brother-in-law Wahab Chasbullah. It was only after significant persuasion and urging that Bisri Syansuri was willing to take on the mantle of Rais Aam. Having done so, however, he worked solidly attending to the religious interests of the organisation. He lacked Wahab's finely tuned political instinct, but was the equal of any in dogged tenacity. Moreover, unlike Wahab Chasbullah and his protégé Idham Chalid, Kiai Bisri did not believe in a 'pragmatic' approach to politics. Like most NU *ulama* he was reluctant to be involved in confrontation with the government, but unlike many of the NU politicians he did not believe in backing down on matters of principle.

Apart from tackling the government over its proposed 'secularisation' of the marriage law in 1973, Kiai Bisri also did much to secure a strong result for PPP in the 1977 election. As head of the PPP Syuriah (the Islamic party's religious advisory council) he was determined to stop the 'Golkarisation' of NU *ulama*. Though some were still induced to back the government's party, most who did experienced a marked loss of support within NU. Kiai Bisri even went as far as issuing a *fatwah* declaring that it was the religious duty of all Muslims to vote for PPP. The party went on to poll strongly in the 1977 elections, even out-polling Golkar in the national capital (43.5 per cent to Golkar's 39.3). The following year NU and PPP had a further opportunity to demonstrate their political independence. Kiai Bisri was angered by two issues that had come before parliament that year. The first was a proposal that *Kebatinan* and other forms of indigenous spiritualism be officially recognised alongside the mainstream religions. The second was the government's plan to commence a comprehensive program of indoctrination built around Pancasila.

Pancasila, the state's central philosophy, is in essence an essentially benign doctrine that offers a non-secular but non-sectarian 'civil religion' alternative to an Islamic state. During Sukarno's Old Order, Pancasila was accepted by many moderate *santri* Muslims as representing a political compromise that was not only acceptable but also desirable in comparison with the alternatives. Under Soeharto, however, Pancasila was used by the regime to enforce hegemony, with dissenting ideas or 'aberrant' behaviour being quickly labelled contrary to Pancasila. In time the regime began describe its approach to governance and elections as Pancasila Democracy, the inference being that it represented an approach peculiarly appropriate to Indonesian, or even Asian, values.

The NU *ulama* were upset with both initiatives in 1978 because they saw them as designed to undermine the status of Islam, bringing God's revelation down to the level of political doctrine and traditional spiritualism. When it came to expressing their displeasure, however, they had few options. Golkar's overwhelming majority in the parliament, reinforced by the presence of military and other appointees, made it pointless to vote against the proposals, despite PPP's strong showing in the 1977 elections. Moreover, the political climate had changed considerably since their victory in addressing the proposed marriage law amendments five years earlier. By 1978 articulating dissent was both difficult and dangerous, with the regime keeping the press on a short leash and brooking no sign of public protest. Frustrated and angry, the NU PPP parliamentarians, followed by members of other PPP factions, led a walkout from parliament. It was a symbolic victory of sorts, but it came at a price. Soeharto responded by engineering a declaration by Djaelani (Johnny) Naro, an Ali Murtopo crony, that he was replacing Mintaredja as PPP's chairman. Not surprisingly, Naro's declaration went unchallenged, and despite the lack of any formal process PPP had a new chairman.[9]

In 1980 NU again staged a parliamentary walkout, although this time Naro ensured that the other factions did not walk out with them. This walkout was not a protest over any religious issues but rather a protest against the government's refusal to enact any legislative guarantees that in conducting elections it would act in an impartial and non-partisan manner. NU was not alone in concerns about Soeharto's declining commitment to democracy and reform. The PDI parliamentarians were also unhappy, but did not go as far as walking out, and outside the parliament members of the Indonesian elite were also protesting. In 1979 and 1980 a group of fifty senior civilians and retired military officers, known as the Petition of Fifty, made a series of outspoken statements about Golkar's behaviour and particularly its use of the military for political purposes. Soeharto moved quickly to ensure that the media did not print their demands for reform or even their photographs.

Following the 1978 walkout and the accession of Naro to the leadership of PPP, NU began to experience increased pressure from the government and suffer an erosion of its position within the party. Much more than Idham Chalid, who was widely seen to be a political opportunist, Kiai Bisri was defiant in defending what he saw to be matters of principle, but by 1980 his health had seriously declined and he died that year, as we have seen. Many within NU, particularly within the *ulama*-dominated Syuriah, were unhappy with Idham's performance as chair of the organisation's executive, so the choice of a new leader of the religious advisory council was a matter of considerable strategic importance

By now much of Abdurrahman's time was taken up with work for the Syuriah, but he also regularly accepted invitations to talk at a variety of gatherings. Early in 1981 he was invited to join a team working on the government's Five-Year Plan. His team was assigned the responsibility of developing details relating to co-operatives. The following year Abdurrahman, who by now was well known among liberal intellectuals, writers and artists in Jakarta and respected for his essays and his knowledge of film and literature, was asked to become chairman of the Jakarta Arts Council. This was an unusual position for anyone from a *pesantren* background, let alone somebody in the national leadership of Nahdlatul Ulama.

INAYAH

In the same year their fourth child, Inayah, was born. She was to be their last child. Abdurrahman says that he was keen to have more children, Nuriyah decided that four was plenty. It was well known within NU that Abdurrahman's own father, Wahid Hasyim, was the fifth child after four girls. Consequently friends often teased him, saying 'You must have more than four'. Abdurrahman's standard response was 'Please tell that to my wife'. Every time he broached the topic of having more children, he was met with a sharp reaction from Nuriyah. This was hardly surprising: by this time his work commitments were such that Nuriyah was left to do almost all the housework herself (they could not afford to employ domestic help for more than a few hours each week). In Jombang Abdurrahman had helped in caring for the girls, but by the time they made the shift to Jakarta his schedule was too busy to allow him to spend much time assisting his wife. Fortunately, not too long after Inayah was born they were able to shift several kilometres north to the suburb of Cilandak, where they rented a larger and more comfortable house that could accommodate a family with four young children.[10]

PART 3

ISLAM AND MODERNITY

This page intentionally left blank

FIVE

ABDURRAHMAN AND LIBERAL ISLAM

THE JOURNEY TO LIBERALISM

When Abdurrahman left Jombang to study abroad, he was a youth wrestling with the question of how Islam could make a difference in the world; on the threshold of adulthood, he flirted with radical Islamism. Seven years later he returned home from his studies a man deeply committed to a liberal understanding of Islam. The influences that shaped his liberalism are not difficult to identify, and it is not surprising that the allure of the certainty and surety that radical Islamism promised was short-lived. The first influence was his family, where both nature and nurture shaped in him an open-minded and questioning intelligence. Secondly, he grew up immersed in the tolerant Sufistic world of Indonesia's traditional Islam. Thirdly, he was influenced by the cultural orientation of modern Indonesian society towards pluralism and egalitarianism.[1] Finally, he was deeply influenced by his reading and his studies in which he sought to synthesise modern Western thought with Islam. He was not alone in doing this, and when he returned home to Indonesia he joined forces with a small group of pioneering young thinkers who were wrestling with how to renew Islamic thought. To properly understand this journey to liberalism, it is important to understand something of the world in which Abdurrahman lived.

AN ENCHANTED WORLD

Abdurrahman grew up in an enchanted universe in which the spiritual was as real as the material. It was not just that God and the hereafter were the beacons for life: that much is true for all Muslims. In Abdurrahman's *pesantren* world, the world of traditionalist Javanese Islam, the spiritual was not confined to the life to come; it was also part of the here and now. Coursing through both were those who had never lived and would never die, beings that, though they might find a place in the taxonomy of orthodox Islamic cosmology, were also known by other names, names from a pre-Islamic Java. Many would regard Abdurrahman's understanding of traditionalist Islam in Indonesia, as a young Javanese Muslim, as a uniquely Indonesian amalgam of Hindu-Buddhist thought and Javanese 'animism', with a late overlay of Islam. But not only is this a simplistic view of traditionalist Islam in Indonesia, it also obscures the distinctiveness of Abdurrahman's position. Not all traditionalists grew up so conscious of the spiritual realm around them as Abdurrahman. In part this is because of the influence of his *pesantren* schooling. His five younger siblings didn't undertake *pesantren* studies, and only Hasyim, the youngest, shares the same mystical orientation as Abdurrahman. Even so, many *pesantren* graduates are less mystically inclined than is Abdurrahman. From an early age he became intensely interested in the spiritual world as it is presented in the Sufistic traditions of Java. As a teenager and young man he studied not only the Qur'an and the Sunnah, but also Javanese mythology. And while still a teenager he regularly prayed and meditated in graveyards in the middle of the night and made long and often arduous pilgrimages to pray at the tombs of Sufi saints. At the same time he displayed an openness to all manner of sages, seers and mystics that indicated a particularly deep interest in the unseen world.

As a traditionalist Muslim, Abdurrahman was inclined to embrace indigenous cultural expressions of religiosity. This was apparent in his attitude to the *wayang kulit*, or shadow theatre, which came from the pre-Islamic world of Hindu Southeast Asia. Abdurrahman respected it not only for its art but also for its spiritual content. The characters portrayed in the Javanese shadow theatre are drawn from the *Mahabharata*, the Hindu classic describing conflict between two clans of brothers, and from the *Ramayana*. The two groups of brothers in the *Mahabharata*-based *wayang kulit* stories are in many respects very similar. The major point of difference between the Pandavas, the heroes, and their militaristic cousins the Kuravas, is that they have developed spiritual insight and understanding, fostering in them a benevolent maturity not yet obtained by their opponents. Growing up in Central Java Abdurrahman came to identify strongly with the corpulent clown figure of Semar, the crude but wise buffoon from the *wayang kulit*. Semar is a demi-god who takes the form of a ribald, obese, razor-sharp court jester. Interestingly, both Sukarno and Soeharto, as *abangan* Javanese, grew up with the *wayang kulit*, and both identified strongly with this unlikely hero, who became for them a totemic figure. The name *Ramayana* means the story of Rama; the text describes the epic mission of Rama, an incarnation of Vishnu and one part of the triune Hindu godhead, to rescue his wife Sita from Lanka, the island stronghold of the demon king Ravana; he is assisted by his brother Laksamana and his friend the monkey god Hanuman.

In the world of the *wayang kulit*, conflict is not between good and evil, cast in absolute shades of black and white, but between the more good and the less good or, better still, between the spiritually developed and the spiritually undeveloped. For Abdurrahman the world of the *wayang kulit* stimulated an appreciation of the need for ambivalence and tolerance, and corresponded with the graduated and ambivalent understanding of spiritual development which underlined the philosophy of *pesantren* education. Abdurrahman considered the classic form of the *wayang kulit* tableau, in which the spiritually immature came face-to-face with the enlightened, as being parallel to *pesantren* education where the students sit in neat lines facing the *kiai*, their teacher. The aim of *pesantren* education was the moulding of raw spiritual material into something of maturity and consequence.

Abdurrahman's intellectual development was shaped by both classical Islamic scholarship and modern Western learning. These factors set the preconditions for him to develop his liberal ideas. As he travelled, read and debated ideas, Abdurrahman synthesised these two worlds of learning. He may have done this more completely than the majority of Islamic intellectuals in Indonesia, but he was not alone. Although he did not realise it at the time, he was to become a part of a new movement of Islamic thought in Indonesia.

NURCHOLISH MADJID: A KINDRED SPIRIT

Abdurrahman Wahid was not the only prominent Islamic intellectual to be born in Jombang in the twilight of Dutch colonialism. Eighteen months prior to Abdurrahman's birth in his grandfather's house in Pesantren Denanyar, Abdul Madjid, a Jombang *madrasah* teacher and farmer welcomed the birth of his first son, Nurcholish. As young men in the 1970s, and then as Indonesia's leading Islamic intellectuals in the decades that followed, Abdurrahman and Nurcholish developed their thought along similar lines, and the pair became known as Indonesia's leading exponents of Islamic liberalism. Understanding something of Nurcholish's life and thought is of great help in understanding Abdurrahman.

Though Abdurrahman and Nurcholish did not meet as children, their fathers were close friends and came to be related through marriage. Not only was Nurcholish's father, Abdul Madjid, a close friend of Wahid Hasyim, but he had also been a student of Kiai Hasyim Asy'ari at Pesantren Tebuireng. As a *pesantren* graduate, Abdul Madjid was a traditionalist by background even though he was not formally a member of NU. As a successful farmer he used his prosperity to found a small *madrasah* run along traditionalist lines but influenced by modernist ideas. It is a mark of Abdul Madjid's respect for Wahid Hasyim that he remained in Masyumi even after NU had split to form its own party in 1952. He did this, he said, because he believed that it was what Wahid Hasyim would have wanted. He knew that Wahid Hasyim had been disappointed by the breakdown in relations between modernists and traditionalists. Abdul Madjid's decision to support Masyumi resulted in a great deal of pain and suffering for him. He often returned from his rice fields in Jombang with tears in his eyes, as a result of accusations levelled against him both by the modernists who dominated Masyumi, and by the traditionalists who questioned why he did not want to become a member of NU. This did not deter Abdul Madjid from staying true to what he understood to be Wahid Hasyim's vision of uniting traditionalism and modernism. For this reason he was keen that his son Nurcholish would have an education that brought together the best of both elements.[2]

After studying in his father's *madrasah*, Nurcholish was sent to complete his studies at Pesantren Modern Gontor in Ponorogo East Java. Pesantren Modern Gontor was established with the aim of modernising *pesantren* education and was affiliated with neither Muhammadiyah nor NU. Gontor became famous for its insistence on high academic standards and scholarship, reflected in a standing rule that conversations among students could take place in either English or Arabic but not in Indonesian or Javanese. Gontor prided itself on its ability to produce well-grounded students equally at home in the traditional world of Islam and in modern Western society.³

Many Gontor graduates have gone on to make their mark in Indonesian society but perhaps none so successfully as Nurcholish Madjid. Nurcholish and Abdurrahman only got to know each other when Nurcholish visited the Middle East in 1969 following a visit to America sponsored by the US State Department. Nurcholish had been chosen for the trip to America as part of a US government scheme to encourage young Muslims to adopt a more open-minded attitude to the West and to America in particular. In Nurcholish's case the scheme was a great success as his visit marked the beginning of a lifelong love affair with the United States.

On his way home to Indonesia, Nurcholish took the opportunity to stop over in the Middle East. Unlike many of his friends from Jombang he had not had an opportunity to visit the Arab world, even though he had learnt to speak fluent Arabic. He visited Egypt, Saudi Arabia and Syria and then decided to cross from Damascus to Baghdad. His father had often talked about Wahid Hasyim's son Abdurrahman and suggested to Nurcholish that he take the opportunity to visit him in Baghdad. Much to the consternation of Indonesian Embassy officials in Damascus, Nurcholish, whose travel funds were all but exhausted, boarded a desert caravan bound for Baghdad. In the 1960s travel from Damascus to Baghdad for those on a tight budget was a hazardous affair using a mechanised equivalent of the Bedouin camel caravans. The driver of the agricultural tractor that pulled the train of carriages across the desert sands was a Bedouin who relied on his local knowledge to navigate a partly unmarked path through inhospitable wastes. When Nurcholish's caravan pulled into Baghdad, he was greeted by a welcoming committee headed by Abdurrahman. This first meeting, which had been much anticipated by both men, was the beginning of a long friendship.

Even at that stage Nurcholish enjoyed a high profile among young Indonesian intellectuals. He was national chairman of the influential, and largely modernist, HMI, the first chairman to be an IAIN student and come from a *pesantren* background. Nurcholish began his first three-year term as chair while studying at the IAIN Syarif Hidyatullah in Ciputat, South Jakarta. When he returned from his Middle East visit, he was re-elected for a second three-year term. However, months later, he was to find himself in the middle of controversy. Throughout his student days Nurcholish had been widely acclaimed as a spiritual successor to Mohammad Natsir, the influential Masyumi leader from the 1950s. In fact he was frequently dubbed 'the young Natsir', and was even regarded as a protégé by Natsir himself. Overnight he went from being respectable to controversial as many of his erstwhile supporters declared that his ideas were dangerous and ill-informed.

THE MOVEMENT FOR THE RENEWAL OF ISLAMIC THOUGHT

The reason for Nurcholish's sudden descent into controversy was a speech he delivered at an end-of-Ramadan gathering of students in Jakarta in January 1970. In what he assumed to be a closed-door student gathering, Nurcholish read from a carefully prepared paper in which he argued strongly for greater boldness and risk-taking on the part of young intellectuals. He asserted that many young Indonesian intellectuals were heartily sick of the wistful, backward-looking obsession with party politics prevalent among many of the Masyumi generation of modernists. What young Muslims really wanted, he claimed, was Islam, not Islamic politics. He argued that Muslim society in Indonesia, the intellectual leadership in particular, was at a crossroads. To continue to give priority to the unity of the *umat* would be to perpetuate stagnation and intellectual decline. The alternative, he argued, was to risk criticism, and even division, in order to promote new ideas and stimulate fresh thought within Islamic society.

If Islamic organisations represent the vehicles for Islamic ideas, why is it, Nurcholish asked, that people are not attracted to Islamic organisations? The reasons, he argued, are obvious. Islamic organisations are no longer attracting the kind of mass support that they once did, firstly, because the very nature of the thought that these organisations represent and actively disseminate has become stale. And secondly, because Islamic parties and their leaders have lost credibility in the eyes of the public. Summing up what he felt to be the feelings of the Islamic public, Nurcholish wrote:

> The answer to the above questions might be found by putting down the next question: to what extent were they attracted to Islamic parties and organisations? Except for a few, it is clear that they were not attracted to Islamic parties or organisations. Their attitude might be formulated thus, more or less: 'Islam yes, Islamic party no!' So if Islamic parties constitute a receptacle of ideas which are going to be

fought for on the basis of Islam, then it is obvious that those ideas are now unattractive. In other words, those ideas and Islamic thinking are now becoming fossilised and obsolete, devoid of dynamism. Moreover these Islamic parties have failed to build a positive and sympathetic image; in fact they have an image that is just the opposite. (The reputation of a section of the umat with respect to corruption, for example, is mounting as time passes.)[4]

This speech marked the beginning of a movement that came to be known as Gerakan Pembaruan Pemikiran Islam, or the Movement for the Renewal of Islamic Thought. Over the next few years Nurcholish produced a series of papers elaborating on this theme, as he and a group of young intellectuals met regularly in Jakarta to discuss new Islamic thought. Although he knew that what he was doing was controversial, Nurcholish had not expected his ideas to be seen as provocative as they were interpreted to be by many of the older generation of modernists. His erstwhile mentor Mohammad Natsir angrily expressed extreme disappointment with his young protégé, as did many of the other senior figures in modernist circles. Nurcholish became something of a *cause célèbre* within HMI. Some championed him as an emerging new thinker who would lead Islamic thought in Indonesia into a new era. Others saw him as having sold out, both to Westernisation and to the Soeharto regime. Indeed, among his critics he was quickly categorised as an 'accommodationist', as his call to forget party politics was interpreted as representing support for the Soeharto regime and betrayal of the modernist cause.[5]

Nurcholish was not by nature a radical. He found the criticism from his former mentor deeply painful. Several years later he wrote that he regretted that he had not stuck to his original strategy of 'smuggling in' new ideas and seeking to promote reform in an evolutionary fashion rather than confronting things head-on.[6] Whether the avoidance of controversy would even then have been possible is not clear, but Nurcholish's January 1970 paper was a bombshell that served to launch a new movement.[7] Throughout the early 1970s Nurcholish and his peers fleshed out the essentials of this new thought.

THE YOGYAKARTA CIRCLE

At the time that Nurcholish was travelling across the Syrian desert to meet Abdurrahman, unknown to them both, a small group from HMI was meeting quietly in Yogyakarta to talk freely about the renewal of Islamic thought.[8] This group met in the home of Mukti Ali, a senior academic at the Sunan Kalijaga IAIN in Yogyakarta, who played a mentoring role among progressive student intellectuals in the city. The small group met regularly at his house for discussion, and Mukti Ali encouraged his young friends to speak freely on whatever topic they chose. Leading lights in the discussion group were Djohan Effendi and Ahmad Wahib. Djohan came from a traditionalist *madrasah* background in South Kalimantan (he had learnt Arabic and studied the classical texts), and was also a student at the IAIN were he was studying in preparation for a career in the Ministry of Religious Affairs. Ahmad Wahib was not a theological student; he studied at the University of Gadjah Mada. Nevertheless, he too had learnt Arabic as a teenager in his devoutly Islamic family in Madura, the island adjoining Surabaya known as a stronghold of traditionalist Islam.

Djohan and Wahib were also active within HMI and took local leadership positions in the Yogyakarta branch where they ran training courses. They were keen to see the transformation of Islamic thought and the opening of a way for that reform, unfettered by what they saw to be the obsession of the former Masyumi leaders with party politics. At first they, like Nurcholish, tried to work underground to promote critical reflection without overtly challenging the prevailing orthodoxy. In time, however, they found themselves at odds with the central Java leadership of HMI Students. Things came to a head late in 1969 when both men decided, independently, to formally resign from HMI. Having tendered their resignations, they were pleasantly surprised to receive an encouraging letter from HMI national chairman Nurcholish Madjid praising them for the stance that they had taken.

In 1971, after graduating from IAIN Sunan Kalijaga in Yogyakarta, Djohan Effendi and Ahmad Wahib moved to Jakarta. Djohan went to work for the Ministry of Religious Affairs in Jakarta; he and Ahmad Wahib became active in Jakarta intellectual circles, where they came to know Abdurrahman and Nurcholish. Tragically in 1973, Ahmad Wahib, who had just commenced his career as a journalist with the weekly news magazine *Tempo*, was knocked down by a motorcycle and killed as he left his office one afternoon. In the early 1970s Mukti Ali was made Minister for Religious Affairs. He immediately began to work with Harun Nasution, the head of Syarif Hidayatullah IAIN in Jakarta, to launch a campaign of reforms within the IAIN. By the 1980s these reforms had produced significant changes in the culture of learning within the IAIN. The process of reform was greatly aided by the drafting of Nurcholish Madjid and several other young progressive intellectuals on to the faculty. This resulted in IAIN Syarif Hidayatullah in Jakarta, and to a somewhat lesser extent Sunan Kalijaga IAIN, leading the way to the reform of Islamic thought in Indonesia.

It is significant that the leading figures in this movement came from traditionalist homes, and as a result had been educated in *pesantren* and *madrasah* to the point where they could read Arabic and study the classical texts of Islamic learning. This enabled them to marry classical Islamic thought with modern Western thought to produce a creative synthesis. It was this same synthesis of thought which drove forward the process of reform within the IAIN and within the growing circle of young reformists in Jakarta led by Nurcholish and Abdurrahman. At the same time as these ideas were being propagated through discussion groups, seminars and conferences, these young intellectuals were also putting their ideas in print through essays in newspapers and magazines.

FAZLUR RAHMAN AND NEO-MODERNISM

The movement of thought that Abdurrahman, Nurcholish and Djohan were involved in was of intellectual significance, though few recognised it at the time. Because almost everything written by Indonesian intellectuals was written in Indonesian, rather than English or Arabic, few outside Indonesia were aware of the momentous innovations in Islamic thought that were being pioneered there. As it happened, the rethinking in Indonesia paralleled developments taking place elsewhere in the Islamic world. A largely unique aspect of the Indonesian situation, however, was that its proponents were not subject to political oppression in the manner of similar movements in Pakistan and Egypt, or even Malaysia. Ironically, it was in part because the New Order regime was so authoritarian that Islamic liberalism had an opportunity to develop freely in Indonesia. The aversion of Soeharto and the Indonesian military to political Islam caused them to look favourably on young liberal Islamic intellectuals such as Abdurrahman and Nurcholish. Like-minded intellectuals in many other Muslim societies were often forced to flee their homelands and relocate in Western countries if they wanted to continue writing about rethinking Islamic thought. This reality was brought home to the young Indonesian thinkers when they encountered a pioneering Islamic writer from

Chicago. The contact was to provide not just encouragement and opportunities for further education but also a new paradigm with which to understand the historical context, and significance, of what they were doing.

In 1976 Nurcholish Madjid was given an opportunity to spend nine months in a research seminar program at the University of Chicago; as a result of that visit, he returned to Chicago in 1978 to undertake doctoral studies there. The opportunity arose because of the visit to Jakarta by University of Chicago academics Fazlur Rahman and Leonard Binder. Fazlur Rahman was a Pakistani intellectual forced to flee his homeland in 1969 because of political hostility to his progressive ideas. In Chicago Rahman was free to develop his thought, and he evolved a paradigm of Islamic reform in which he argued that neither traditionalism nor modernism offered a way forward for the development of Islamic thought in Muslim society. Instead, Rahman argued that a combination of modernism and traditionalism was needed to lead the way.

Rahman argued that the intellectual vitality of early Islam was lost as Islamic thought ossified through being institutionalised.[9] As Islam had spread throughout the eastern Mediterranean, across northern Africa and eastwards into Iran and West Asia, Islamic civilisation and thought were opened to new ideas and influences. The expansion and flourishing of Islamic thought ground to a halt towards the end of the thirteenth century, primarily because individual interpretation or *ijtihad* was regarded as being dangerous and best avoided. Instead, the *ulama* advocated that the correct way of finding the truth was to confine oneself to the limits of the four orthodox *mazhab* or jurisprudential schools which, by this stage, had been integrated into well-documented positions. The result, in Rahman's estimation, was disastrous. The gates of *ijtihad* were closed, and creative and vital learning largely ceased. Islamic thought entered a period of stagnation.

The first signs of challenge to this stagnation, Rahman suggested, occurred in the late eighteenth and early nineteenth centuries. The revivalist movements of the Wahabi in Arabia and Sanusi in North-West Africa marked the beginning of a serious rethinking of the way Islam was practised. These revivalist movements, however, were essentially concerned with reformation only in the sense of going back to an earlier, 'more pristine', period of thought and civilisation. In other words, they were not concerned with the reinterpretation of Islamic thought so much as its purification. The revivalists warned against moral decay on the one hand and against the syncretistic melding of Islamic thought with local superstitious practice and belief on the other hand. In this sense they were fundamentally conservative, and even reactionary, in that they wanted to return Islamic society to an earlier golden age.

Next came modernism. At the beginning of the twentieth century, modernism, Rahman argued, marked the beginning of a genuine intellectual revival within the Islamic world. With modernism came the reappraisal of *ijtihad* and a conscious effort to reopen the gates of *ijtihad* and personal interpretation. Modernism was also inspired, as the name suggests, by the growth of modern thought and technology and its application in society to avert disease, to harness the powers of nature for human good, and to generally improve society. Modernism began as an essentially progressive movement: it was forward-looking and desired to see society become steadily better. It was a movement that was concerned about returning to some of the original purity of the world of earlier times. It was primarily concerned with creating a future that was different to and better than all that had come before. In time, however, the creative dynamism of modernism came to a halt also. By the middle of the century, as the modernists failed to attend to theological education and to reproduce new generations of intellectuals capable of engaging in *ijtihad,* and as they became absorbed in party politics and political change, the movement began to regress.

Rahman, writing about the Islamic world as a whole, argued that the intellectual decline of modernism in the second half of the century fed directly into the re-emergence of revivalism. To distinguish this revivalism of the early to mid-twentieth century from the revivalism of one and a half centuries earlier, Rahman applied the label neo-revivalism. It differed significantly from these earlier movements in that it was linked organically to the modernist movement. Neo-revivalism grew out of a decaying modernism and it merged elements of modernist concern with technology and science for the betterment of society with the wistful, backward-looking nature of the earlier, more puritan revivalist movements. The chief flaw in neo-revivalism was that it soon stagnated intellectually.

Thinkers such as Maulana Maududi, a Pakistani layman turned popular preacher, did much to accommodate this new form of revivalist thought. Maududi's ideas differed greatly from those of his compatriot, the famous modernist intellectual Mohammed Iqbal. Rahman argues that, whereas Iqbal's thought was characterised by original insight and the reapplication of Islamic concepts, Maududi's thought tended towards reductionism and the simplistic application of narrowly conceived Islamic concepts to an ailing society.

Rahman only mentioned Indonesia in passing and did not discuss developments there in detail. Nevertheless, following Rahman's line of analysis, it could be argued that in Indonesia the former Masyumi leader Mohammad Natsir increasingly adopted a position similar to that taken by Maududi and other neo-revivalist figures. In the 1950s he was regarded as a reasonably progressive thinker, but by the 1970s was a much more conservative figure. Even more conservative were many of the younger intellectuals who joined Natsir in Dewan Dakwah Islamiyah Indonesia (the Indonesian Islamic Preaching Council), a non-government organisation that he founded in the late 1960s out of frustration with the Soeharto regime's suppression of political Islam.

It was with thinkers such as Maududi that the Islamist movement properly began. In most respects Islamism coincides neatly with what Rahman defines as neo-revivalism. Neo-revivalism is concerned about improving society by taking it back to an earlier and purer form of Islam. It sustains itself on the optimistic hope that making society more Islamic will cause all of the social problems of modern life to drop away. At the same time it recognises the need to exploit and benefit from modern technology. It is not surprising that the majority of neo-revivalist and Islamist thinkers of the twentieth century were not theologically trained, but instead had studied applied sciences such as engineering. They had learnt to apply reductionistic modelling to complex real-world problems and as a result tended to believe that the complex ills of twentieth-century society could be reduced to a handful of spiritual ailments that could be easily remedied by applying formulaic prescriptions.

Rahman did not believe that neo-revivalism or Islamism represented a satisfactory answer to the challenges facing Muslim society. While he was ready to acknowledge the moral courage and dedication of many of the neo-revivalists, he felt that intellectually neo-revivalism represented a cul-de-sac. The movement sustained itself on the optimistic hope that, as soon as the appropriate Islamic solution was formulated and implemented, society would begin to improve. After many decades of this experiment failing to produce lasting results, however, many

Islamic intellectuals began to believe that perhaps something more was required.

That something more, in Fazlur Rahman's view, involved returning to classical Islamic learning and combining this with the best of modernism so as to produce a synthesis between classical Islamic learning and modern Western thought. In that way, Rahman argued, the core truths of Islam could be appreciated afresh and applied flexibly and creatively to modern society, generating a more profound and sophisticated spirituality and a more compassionate and tolerant Islam. He coined the term neo-modernism for this movement.

By the late 1970s, some commentators were beginning to apply the label neo-modernism to the Renewal of Islamic Thought movement in Indonesia.[10] The new movement of thought that emerged with Nurcholish, Djohan and Abdurrahman was indeed essentially a synthesis of classical Islamic learning and modern Western thought. They sought to combine the best of modernism and traditionalism to produce something new, something that would exceed the boundaries inherent in both traditionalism and modernism.[11]

SIX

ON THE BRINK OF CHANGE, 1982-1984

AHMAD SIDDIQ, PPP AND THE 1982 ELECTIONS

By 1982 Abdurrahman was working closely with Achmad Siddiq, a reform-minded senior *kiai*. The two men worked well together and enjoyed considerable influence within the Syuriah. Kiai Achmad Siddiq was twenty-four years older than Abdurrahman and became something of a father figure to the younger man. Like Abdurrahman, Achmad Siddiq had thought much about the need for reform within NU. He was one of the first NU *kiai* to talk openly about the necessity of *ijtihad* or personal interpretation of the Qur'an and the Sunnah. He too was something of a cultural broker. He was able to translate modern ideas into the language of traditional Islam and express them in a fashion that could be received by more conservative *ulama*. Together he and Abdurrahman formed an impressive team, and there was a growing expectation that they would take charge of the organisation in future.

Abdurrahman was encouraged in his endeavours by a number of young friends who had studied in *pesantren* at the same time as him and were now emerging as young *kiai* active in both the regional and national leadership. Some of them were Middle East graduates he had known during his studies in Cairo and Baghdad. At the same time several influential older *kiai* began to ask Abdurrahman to speak at their *pesantren* on the topic of renewal within NU.

In the run-up to the May 1982 national elections, Abdurrahman became busy campaigning for PPP. He was not particularly enamoured with PPP, but reasoned that in a system that permitted only three parties (apart from Soeharto's Golkar there was PPP and PDI), it was important to strengthen the two small opposition parties if some modicum of democracy was to emerge. Nurcholish Madjid had used the same argument in the lead-up to the 1977 election when he employed the analogy of a *becak* or trishaw — 'If one tire was flat on one of these three-wheeled pedicabs', he argued, 'you could go nowhere until the flat tire was fixed'. 'We must pump up the flat tyre', Nurcholish exclaimed by way of explaining his support for PPP in 1977.

While Nurcholish's support for PPP the 1977 campaign was not particularly surprising, Abdurrahman's support for the party in the 1982 campaign is more curious. After Djaelani Naro assumed the leadership of PPP in 1978, things had begun to go badly for NU politicians within the party. This was just as Soeharto intended, for after the infamous walkout of PPP politicians from parliament in 1978 he decided that it was time to begin to rein in the party, and particularly its outspoken NU figures. In the run-up to the 1982 election Naro was instructed to ensure that the total proportion of PPP seats assigned to NU was substantially cut back and to see that the more vocal NU politicians were given unwinnable positions on the party's card.[1] The regime's heavy-handed intervention in the affairs of PPP meant that there was little reason for NU to continue to support the party. Nevertheless, Abdurrahman fell back on Nurcholish's argument about the need to ensure that Golkar was presented with substantial opposition at each election to explain his support for PPP during the 1982 campaign.

BENNY MURDANI

Abdurrahman says that while campaigning for PPP he was detained many times by the police, who were under orders to obstruct opposition party meetings. He explains that each time he was taken into overnight detention he asked friends to inform ABRI headquarters that he had been detained. Each time this sufficed to secure his immediate release. By this stage Abdurrahman had achieved such stature as a moderate Islamic intellectual that certain officers in the military looked upon him with favour and saw in him a hope for developing a moderate Islam. They also recognised that he was likely to play a future leadership role in NU and sought to cultivate his friendship. The most important of these officers was General Benny Murdani. Benny, as he was widely known, was a protégé of Ali Murtopo and head of military intelligence. He had assisted Ali Murtopo in orchestrating the Indonesian invasion of East Timor in 1975 and worked with him closely on other Opsus projects. He was regarded as a tough soldier who felt little compunction in spilling blood when he felt violent means were called for, but he was also seen to be personally austere and professional. As a military intelligence czar and a Catholic general in an officer corps that was profoundly suspicious of militant Islam, he was deeply distrusted by most Muslim leaders, especially among the urban modernists. Abdurrahman did not shy from contact with Benny, although he has consistently maintained that he did not fully trust him and that the relationship was one of mutual convenience rather than real friendship.[2] It was to be an important relationship, all the same, for the following year Benny was appointed head of the armed forces. For Benny the relationship provided an entry into the Byzantine world of NU politics via a popular young intellectual who seemed to share many of the concerns of the military about militant Islamism. For Abdurrahman, 'friendship' with Benny made it possible to shape elite perceptions of NU and of himself, and to negotiate the regime's response to political developments. In a society as tightly controlled as Soeharto's Indonesia had become in the 1980s, a modicum of support from one of the ruling elite's several factions was not merely useful but essential if one wanted to play a role of any significance.

The regular police detentions failed to deter Abdurrahman from campaigning for PPP in 1982, but following the election he became increasingly disillusioned with the party and vowed never to campaign for it again. Abdurrahman focused on preparations for the upcoming *munas*, or national congress of *ulama*, planned for the following year. Moves were under way to bring about change within NU's national leadership. Idham Chalid, NU's executive chairman, had been greeted with hostility when he addressed the national congress of NU in Semarang in 1979. On that occasion Idham's profuse and eloquent apology and request for forgiveness was enough to ensure that he was re-elected as executive chairman. Events since, most notably Djaelani Naro's government-backed moves to emasculate the organisation within PPP and the failure of Idham to defend NU's interests within the party, had intensified the resentment that had been steadily building to Idham's leadership throughout the 1970s.³

THE *KIAI* MOVE AGAINST IDHAM CHALID

On 2 May 1982, two days before the national election, a group of four senior *kiai* from the Syuriah gathered in Jakarta and proceeded to Idham Chalid's house in the suburb of Cipete. Three of them were founding members of NU and as such commanded enormous authority. They were Abdurrahman's old teacher Rais Aam Kiai Machrus Aly, Kiai As'ad Arifin Syamsul, Kiai Ali Ma'sum and Kiai Masykur. When they met with Idham they asked him to step down 'because of poor health'. They were convinced that NU was in danger of becoming moribund and that a change of leadership was necessary if the organisation was to move forward. For too long, they felt, the politicians and technocrats within the Tanfidziyah had dominated NU, marginalising the *ulama* in the Syuriah. Idham, naturally enough, did not share their view and did not appreciate being pressured into stepping down. The request from the *kiai* was most irregular. But while it found no place in NU's constitution, their action was not at odds with the spirit of the constitution, which enshrined the principle that the Tanfidziyah was subject to the Syuriah.

As a result of discussions between Abdurrahman and Achmad Siddiq and other *kiai* from the Syuriah, the Syuriah established a forum of reform-minded *kiai* and younger intellectuals to wrestle with the many issues facing the ailing organisation. This forum of two dozen, which included many of NU's brightest minds (along with a few others who had political axes to grind, or at least patronage interests to protect) came to be called the Council of 24. It met on several occasions before finally deciding to appoint a smaller group of its members to work closely together to spearhead the reform effort. Seven men, including Abdurrahman and Achmad Siddiq, were chosen and charged with mapping out a plan for the reform of NU.

The news of Idham Chalid's resignation finally broke on 6 May. Abdurrahman and Dr Fahmi Saifuddin, another member of the so-called Team of Seven, the group charged with formulating reform within NU, decided to pay a courtesy call on Idham to try to defuse his anger towards the Syuriah. Abdurrahman recalls that he began by saying, 'Pak Idham; the matter of you stepping down as proposed by the *kiai* two days ago is not strictly constitutional'. Idham replied, 'Yes but I couldn't refuse those *kiai*, they are the biggest *kiai* in NU and the Tanfidziyah has always to listen to the Syuriah. What could I say in my defence to these *kiai* from the Syuriah?' To which Abdurrahman responded, 'Okay but that does not make it constitutional, and I believe in doing things constitutionally'. 'Thank you, thank you,' Idham said. Abdurrahman continued: 'Pak Idham, please understand that I am in the Syuriah and as a student of the *kiai* senior to me in the Syuriah I must follow their lead and cannot oppose them.'[4]

Both Abdurrahman and Idham recognised that they faced an impasse. Idham was not willing to simply relinquish his authority within NU, and yet the Syuriah *kiai* who had met with him were committed to proceeding with an interim collective leadership team until a new chairman could be elected at the next national congress of NU, in two years' time. Abdurrahman suggested a compromise arrangement that would permit the two camps to co-operate in the leadership of NU during the interregnum. Idham indicated that he agreed, and Abdurrahman concluded by saying: 'Okay, I will represent the *kiai* and you appoint Chalid Marwadi as your representative, and I will maintain communication with him from now until the congress.'

Henceforth Abdurrahman and Fahmi met regularly with Marwadi in order to co-ordinate the functioning of the national leadership of NU. Their efforts were only partly successful, however, and for the next two and a half years NU's national leadership was curiously bifurcated. Idham continued to act as national chairman despite his earlier acceptance of the need to resign when confronted by the four *kiai*, and on 14 May he issued a statement cancelling his earlier statement about resigning. This left the masses of NU confused and divided and the leaders split into two camps. Both camps maintained that they represented the official leadership of NU and handled correspondence simultaneously from two separate offices. The camp backed by the majority of *ulama* in the Syuriah was nominally led by the much-feared Kiai As'ad Arifin Syamsul. The two camps came to be identified as the 'Cipete camp' after the Jakarta suburb in which Idham Chalid lived, and the 'Situbondo camp' after the East Java home of Kiai As'ad. The Team of Seven was instrumental in brokering peace between the two camps. They were assisted in this by Abdurrahman's mother, Solichah, who used her formidable authority to persuade the two camps to co-operate.

PANCASILA AND ASAS TUNGGAL

During this period Abdurrahman continued to tour the country. Always an inveterate traveller, he had become even more active in visiting *pesantren* across Java after joining the Syuriah. In 1983 he made visits to NU strongholds in Java, in Sumatra, and in Kalimantan. He explains that he felt there to be a degree of urgency about visiting regional NU branches because he was aware of considerable confusion and anxiety about the ructions within the national leadership. He moved from *pesantren* to *pesantren* and met with NU branch leaders around the country, explaining the need for reform and urging them to recognise it.

At the same time Abdurrahman began to work with Achmad Siddiq on formulating a response to the issue of Pancasila. By 1983 Soeharto had begun to make it clear that he was pushing for the widespread acceptance of Pancasila as the *asas tunggal*, or sole basis, of all organisations. In early 1983, following the five-yearly meeting of the MPR which re-elected him president, Soeharto gave a speech in Riau in which he urged acceptance of Pancasila as *asas tunggal* by all groups in society, including religious organisations. Abdurrahman had intelligence from Benny Murdani that those organisations that resisted acknowledging Pancasila as their 'sole basis' would ultimately face 'irresistible pressure' from the government to yield.

Abdurrahman had for a long time been persuaded that Pancasila represented the best compromise to resolving the thorny issue of the relationship between 'church and state'. Throughout the 1970s and early 1980s he articulated his ideas in a series of essays and long articles, arguing that a constitution that formally legislated a role for Islam in the state would be bound to result in unpleasantness not just for non-Muslims and *abangan* Muslims but also for those *santri* Muslims who disagreed with the official religious line taken by the state. To involve the state in arbitrating on religious matters, he reasoned, would inevitably result in the state trampling on the freedom of conscience of many of its citizens. It was far better, he argued, for the state to keep its distance from religious matters and allow religious organisations to manage their own affairs. At the same time he acknowledged that it was inconceivable that, in the world's largest Muslim society, people would readily accept a constitution that failed to acknowledge the contribution of religion to society, especially in the wake of the 1965–66 crackdown on communism, with all the consequent emotion and phobia about atheism. This meant, Abdurrahman maintained, that Pancasila provided for the state to be non-sectarian but also non-secular, and consequently represented the best compromise possible.

In response to Soeharto's Pancasila speech in Riau, Abdurrahman met with Kiai Ali Ma'sum, by now Rais Aam, and proposed that the Syuriah should form a committee to discuss the position of NU and Pancasila. A committee was formed with Kiai Achmad Siddiq as chairman and Abdurrahman as secretary. They began meeting in June 1983 and met regularly until October that year, by which time they had finished their proposal. A special meeting was held at the Menteng home of Kiai Masykur, one of the committee members, in order to present the proposal. Over the five or so months they had carefully examined material from the Qur'an and the Sunnah and the *Kitab Kuning* in order to find support for accepting Pancasila as NU's *asas tunggal*. Their final formulation read: 'Islam is pluralistic and because of this implementation of Islamic teachings should be pluralistic, and this is in accordance with the tradition of NU.' This they saw as providing more than enough space to allow the adoption of Pancasila without it in any way being seen as a sell-out to the government.[5]

PLURALISM, PANCASILA AND PARTY POLITICS

The reformists led by Abdurrahman and Achmad Siddiq, and backed by their friends in the Team of Seven and the Council of 24, also argued that NU should withdraw from party politics and return to its original vision as enshrined in its *khittah*, or charter, of 1926, of being a social-religious organisation. The phrase 'return to the *khittah* of 1926' sounded grand and venerable. In reality Achmad Siddiq had first coined the phrase as recently as 1979. The withdrawal from party politics was based in part on a concern that NU's political activities had distracted it from its core business of education and religious activity. Certainly, many argued that the politicians and technocrats loyal to Idham Chalid paid far too little attention to these matters. But it was also based on the realisation that, after the regime's intervention into the affairs of PPP via Djaelani Naro, NU had become so marginalised that it made little sense to remain in the party. Abdurrahman and some other reformists within the Council of 24, harking back to Nurcholish's famous statement from 1970 — 'Islam yes, party-political Islam no!' — also believed that, in principle, a direct linkage between a religious organisation and a political party was unhealthy.

In response to this proposal, Abdurrahman recollects, Kiai Masykur, one of the grand old *kiai* from the founding generation, recounted a story about Kiai Hasyim Asy'ari in the early days of NU.[6] Kiai Masykur explained how Kiai Hasyim Asy'ari had written an article in the magazine *Suara Nahdlatul Ulama* in 1926, several months after the formation of the organisation. In it he argued that because the *kentungan* (the split cylinder struck like a gong and used in some *pesantren* to announce prayer time) was not mentioned in the Hadis of the Prophet, it was therefore *haram* or prohibited and should not be used to signal the time of prayer. Like many *kiai*, Kiai Hasyim argued that in matters of worship traditions should be preserved and innovation confined to matters of the social application of teaching, not basic modes of worship. Not everyone agreed with Kiai Hasyim Asy'ari, however, as even in the early days of NU a tradition of pluralism was strong. One month later after Kiai Hasyim's article had been published, another senior *kiai*, Kiai Fakhi, wrote an article to rebut it. He argued that Kiai Hasyim was mistaken because the principle that was being employed in this matter was that of *qias*, or reasoning and inference based on established principles. On this basis the Southeast Asian *kentungan* was okay as it fulfilled the function of drum in announcing prayer. In response to this, Kiai Hasyim invited the *ulama* of Jombang to meet him at his house and then he asked for both articles to be read aloud. When this was done he announced to the assembly, 'You are free to follow either opinion, because both are right, but I insist that in my *pesantren* the *kentungan* is not to be used'. Several months later Kiai Hasyim was invited to attend the celebrations of Maulid Nabi, the Prophet's birthday, in the coastal city of Gresik. Three days before he arrived, Kiai Fakhi, who was senior *kiai* in the Gresik district, distributed a letter to all the mosques and prayer houses asking them to take down their *kentungan* out of respect for Kiai Hasyim and to refrain from using them during his visit.

Kiai Maksyur suggested to the assembly gathered in his house that this was a perfect illustration of NU's pluralism: 'So in NU it is usual to have different views, and this is reflected in Pancasila, so we have to accept Pancasila.' Another *kiai* responded by saying 'How then could we explain why, when NU became a political party in 1953, it did not take Pancasila as its *asas tunggal*?' 'We should then trace matters back to the beginning and show that NU has always been pluralistic. For example Kiai Hasyim and Kiai Wahab were constantly quarrelling.'

The reformists prevailed and decided that henceforth NU would adopt Pancasila as its *asas tunggal*. They also decided that NU would no longer be a party-political organisation and that it would withdraw from the PPP and instead return to its basic charter or *khittah*. They labelled this new policy 'return to the *khittah* of 1926'.

THE SITUBONDO MUNAS AND ACCEPTANCE OF PANCASILA

One month later the *munas* or national congress of *ulama* was held in the *pesantren* of Kiai As'ad Arifin Syamsul in Situbondo, and the proposal regarding Pancasila was introduced to the broader NU community. The *munas* congresses were generally held every five years, just like the *muktamar* or national congresses of the entire organisation, but were regarded as subordinate to the *muktamar* because they involved only the *ulama* from the various religious councils throughout the NU branches and not the organisation's executives. Nevertheless, the *munas* were generally seen as undertaking important preparatory work for the larger *muktamar*. This was especially the case in 1983 when the *ulama* were mobilising support, both for their move against Idham Chalid and the technocrats who supported him and for their vision of reform. Abdurrahman recalls that Kiai Tolkhah Mansur from Yogyakarta, who had not participated in the Jakarta meetings, took the floor to address the *munas* assembly saying: 'I have my own view, I differ on this point.'[7] Abdurrahman immediately walked up to him and said in Arabic, 'Kiai, please use Arabic rather than Indonesian'. 'But why in Arabic?' 'Please just do it.' Abdurrahman was aware that military intelligence agents from Bakin (a central intelligence agency run by the military) were attending the meeting and carefully following every point of the discussion. He was concerned that if Kiai Tolkhah Mansur launched into a long critique of Pancasila it might lead to negative reports being filed about him. Fortunately, they could be quite confident that if they employed Arabic none of the intelligence agents (who were generally, at that time, recruited from among *abangan* and non-Muslims and certainly had not received a *pesantren* education) could follow their discussion. Abdurrahman recalls that they launched into an earnest but polite debate that ran from 10 o'clock that evening until 4 o'clock the following morning, when finally Kiai Tolkhah said, 'Okay, I can accept that, you've proved it to me'. Abdurrahman had been arguing that because Pancasila reflected the basic principles of Islam there was no need to have an Islamic state. Kiai Tolkhah replied, 'As Islam is more complete than Pancasila, of course Islam covers both the hereafter as well as this world'. Abdurrahman responded: 'Exactly, Pancasila is only concerned with this world.' He says that he had in mind the idea of Pancasila acting as a kind of civil religion but did not dare use the term because he knew that it would certainly be misunderstood by the assembled *ulama*.

Once Kiai Tolkhah had accepted Abdurrahman's point of view, he recalls, the assembly quickly came to a point of consensus about accepting Pancasila. Abdurrahman took the initiative and explained that, according to Kiai Masykur, in 1945 Kiai Wahid Hasyim had invited seventy *ulama* to meet at Pesantren Tebuireng to discuss the formulation of the constitution. They listed seventy principles and presented them to Sukarno, who used these principles and others to formulate Pancasila.[8] 'So on this basis we have to accept that there will be no end to discussions about these things. This might be the way of religious discussions but it is no way to run a state.' It was nearly 4 am when the discussion concluded, and the assembled *ulama* proceeded directly with the *Subuh* prayer. Abdurrahman and Kiai Tolkhah embraced each other warmly in front of the assembly. There was a sense of relief and euphoria that this difficult question had finally been dealt with and that the organisation was now moving forward. There was also a sense of relief that a possible confrontation with the government had been avoided and that the *ulama* had been able to resolve matters without compromising their principles.

After the discussion, Abdurrahman recalls, one old and influential *kiai* approached Abdurrahman and said, 'Ah, we remember Kiai Wahid and Kiai Bisri. You remind us of these two'. Abdurrahman politely asked, 'Did you understand what we were debating?' 'Yes, well, about half of it. But in any case it is good to have these things debated because for a long time we have been stagnant and have not been able to talk about important things while under the leadership of Idham Chalid. This is not the way to conduct an organisation. You should be the next chairman.' Abdurrahman responded, 'No don't ask me to do that. I'm happy with my life the way it is'. 'Yes but this can be arranged.' In the following months the senior *kiai* lobbied for Abdurrahman to be made national chairman. Kiai Achmad Siddiq, who had been Kiai Wahid Hasyim's secretary until the time of his death in 1953, had followed the debate with some apprehension. After it was all over he embraced Abdurrahman and, overcome with emotion, said: 'You know, Durrahman, in my view you are like your father. I knew your father for a long time, I knew the way he thought, what he thought about NU, and I think you are right, you are like him in so many ways.'

Part of the reason for the relief of the *kiai* at formulating a response to Pancasila was that they were no longer on a collision course with a government that was steadily ratcheting up pressure against Islamic elements that it judged to be recalcitrant. In September 1984 the military savagely put down a protest in the Jakarta port district of Tanjung Priok. The Muslim protest was, in part, directed against Chinese business activity in the port district and appears to have been fuelled by a resentment based on socio-economic differences. It allegedly started after soldiers rudely entered a local mosque without stopping to remove their shoes. Information about the incident was suppressed, but critics of the government believed that as many as several hundred people had been killed. Those killed were said to be members of extremist Islamic cell groups and were labelled as being dangerous radicals. There is good reason for believing that in fact the military had provoked the confrontation and fomented the violence in order to make an example of the Tanjung Priok group and to warn other Islamic groups not to resist the government.

Abdurrahman recalls that, shortly after the Tanjung Priok violence, Benny Murdani approached him and spoke about his anxiety about Islamic extremism. Abdurrahman was struck by the fact that General Murdani had contacted him and not other, more senior, *kiai*, and interpreted this as a sign that the government was backing him to become a future leader of NU. Even though he was close to Kiai Achmad Siddiq, he did not tell him about this encounter and kept the matter to himself.[9] Over the next twelve months Abdurrahman's standing in NU went from strength to strength. By late 1984, in the run-up to the national congress of NU in Situbondo, he had become something of a celebrity and he was invited to speak throughout Java, Sumatra and Sulawesi.

As the much anticipated congress drew near, Mahmud Djunaidi, an influential reformist and member of the Team of Seven, approached Gus Dur and said: 'We will make you chairman of NU.' Abdurrahman recalls that he replied: 'Okay, but I would like the liberty to choose my own leadership team — just elect the Rais Aam and myself.' But when the congress came, Kiai As'ad Arifin Syamsul, in whose *pesantren* they were meeting, said that he would form a commission composed of himself and six others who would decide on the composition of the new leadership group. In suggesting this he was invoking the historical example of the election of Islam's third Caliph twelve centuries before, an image that sat well with NU *ulama* fed up with the reign of technocrats. Abdurrahman agreed, thinking, he explains, that it would be a mere formality, and gave him his list of preferred members for the central leadership of NU. The list was then signed by Idham on the left corner, by Munawir Sjadzali in the middle and by Abdurrahman on the right corner. After the list had been through such a process, Abdurrahman expected that it would go forward unchanged.

Very early on the last day of the *muktamar*, after the assembly had formally adopted the decision of the *munas* regarding Pancasila and NU's return to its *khittah* of 1926, Abdurrahman drove to the town of Pasir Putih, fifty kilometres away, to meet with Idham Chalid in his hotel. He arrived shortly before dawn in order to have one final meeting with Idham and asked him whether there were any alterations that he wanted to make to the list. 'Please write any alterations on this and sign it.' Idham wrote in a new name, for the treasurer's post, and signed the paper again. Abdurrahman returned to Situbondo at around 10 am, stopping to talk with Kiai As'ad in his room where he gave him the countersigned list that was to guide the electoral college in formulating the new leadership team. Abdurrahman returned to his room and slept. At 1 pm he was awakened in time to join the plenary meeting under the great canvas pavilion erected for the *muktamar*. Kiai As'ad had already met with the six other members of the commission. After half an hour of waiting they appeared before the assembly. Kiai As'ad asked someone to read the names of NU's new central leadership. It was a completely different set of names from the list that Abdurrahman had signed. Virtually all of Idham's men had been excluded and replaced with men of Kiai As'ad's choosing. Abdurrahman stood up to protest, but Mahmud Djunaidi said: 'Please sit down, please accept it, otherwise it will be a real fight, a bitter fight.' Abdurrahman replied, 'Okay, but you had better have a talk with Idham'. Idham was phoned; he was already in Surabaya. He said, 'Please tell Abdurrahman not to worry. We won't do anything to contradict him openly, and there will be no fight'.[10]

In leaving matters to Kiai As'ad, Abdurrahman had clearly made a major political blunder. As expected, the prickly *kiai*, who had for the past two years led the fight against Idham Chalid's leadership, did back Abdurrahman, but his last-minute changes to the leadership list were unnecessarily antagonistic to Idham, since virtually no one from Idham's group was included in the new team. In a culture where confrontation is studiously avoided wherever possible and compromise is the cornerstone of politics, Kiai As'ad's vindictive treatment of his old foe was clearly as unwise as it was unnecessary. As he was soon to discover, Kiai As'ad's wilfulness wiped out, in one move, all of Abdurrahman's careful efforts in fence-mending with Idham, making the difficult task of reforming NU that much more difficult.

PART 4

CIVIL SOCIETY AND ISLAM

This page intentionally left blank

SEVEN

REFORM AND CONTROVERSY, 1984-1990

A NEW ERA FOR NU

The ascension of the duo of Abdurrahman Wahid and Achmad Siddiq to the national leadership of NU was warmly welcomed by many within NU, some of whom would have agreed on little else. Many *pesantren* students and young graduates were concerned that NU and its *pesantren* system risked being left behind by modern society to eventually become quaintly antiquarian and anachronistic.

Critics of the former executive chairman, Idham Chalid, felt that under his leadership the core activities of the organisation had been neglected while at the same time little had been done to check the erosion of its political interests within PPP. They rejected the people around Idham as being urban politicians little interested in NU's social, educational and religious activities. After all, they argued, NU, whose name meant the awakening of the *ulama*, was supposed to be a *jamiah diniyah*, a religious organisation — run 'by the *ulama* and for the *ulama*'. At the same time, Idham's apparent unwillingness to stand up to the calculated marginalisation of NU by PPP chairman Djaelani Naro incensed many *ulama*, not least those, like Kiai As'ad Syamsul Arifin, whose patrimonial prestige and power depended on political connections.

For many of the *pesantren* students and young graduates, however, these concerns were outweighed by the concern that NU and its *pesantren* system risked being left behind by modern society – much like America's Amish and Shaker communities. Unlike most of their seniors before them, this generation had the choice of matriculating from the *pesantren* to modern tertiary studies and careers in the cities and turning their backs on meaningful involvement within NU. If NU was in a terminal state of decay, they reasoned, what incentive was there to follow in the footsteps of their fathers and grandfathers and invest in an organisation without an exciting future? For many young people within NU in the 1970s it was easy to believe that the process of decay was running swiftly within the organisation and that within a generation NU would be reduced to an ineffectual curiosity on the periphery of modern Indonesian society. For such youth it was only the growing influence in the early 1980s of reformist younger *ulama*, led by Abdurrahman and Siddiq, that held out any hope that the organisation might once again play a central role in Indonesian life. Consequently, for those who looked for reform, and a creative and meaningful response to the challenges of modernity within NU, the 1984 *muktamar* marked the beginning of a new era.

It was not just those interested in intellectual and cultural reform, however, who welcomed the new leaders. The political pragmatists and many of the more intellectually conservative *ulama* who had been fearful of confrontation with the government were relieved that the reformists had succeeding in formulating a response to Pancasila that saw NU accepting the non-sectarian state philosophy without feeling that it was compromising its religious principles. They were relieved when President Soeharto and his government welcomed NU's new leadership team and felt comforted that the organisation appeared set to enter into a period of peaceful coexistence with the military-backed and Islam-phobic regime.

For many within NU, the decision to back the reformers at the 1983 *munas* and the 1984 *muktamar* at the expense of Idham Chalid and NU's involvement with PPP was also motivated by another desire: to have revenge on the people within PPP, both modernist politicians and some of NU's own people, including Idham, who were seen to have undermined NU's interests within the party. Some NU *ulama* were angry with what they saw to be the domination of NU by the non-*ulama* technocrats and politicians on the Tanfidziyah. For others the motivation to support the reformists was more a desire to recapture the support of the regime so that they could once again enjoy the business benefits that flowed from good relations with the government. There was also a realisation that continued opposition from the regime was having a detrimental impact on the organisation's enrolments and that NU had already suffered from steady erosion of its mass base. For NU's younger and more reform-minded members, exiting from PPP and breaking with party politics was essential if NU was to regain its vitality and its vision for social, educational and religious activity.[1]

Abdurrahman was convinced that it was important for NU to break with PPP for two related reasons. Firstly he felt that, given the regime's treatment of NU within PPP and its determination to block all political dissent, it was pointless for NU to remain within the party. It was far better, he felt, for NU to focus its energies on its civil society activities. Secondly, Abdurrahman was convinced that it was unhealthy to have direct links between religious associations and political parties. It was not that Islam (or any of Indonesia's other religions) should not seek to influence political developments; rather, direct involvement of religious bodies in party politics threatened to limit the freedom of conscience of their members and to encourage sectarianism within politics. He was mindful of the deleterious effects of the debate over the 'seven words' of the Jakarta Charter in the 1950s and 1970s, and of the obsession of many conservatives, both modernists and traditionalists, with making the state 'more Islamic' (or demanding that the state 'make' its citizens better Muslims). He was also painfully aware that NU antagonism to PKI in the political sphere had spilled over into unspeakable violence during the anti-communist pogrom of 1965-66.[2]

Many influential individuals and groups within NU were, at best, ambivalent about new leaders; one such person was Kiai As'ad Arifin Syamsul. Although he had led a charge on behalf of the *ulama* in the Syuriah against former chairman Idham Chalid, he was not so motivated by reformist ideals as by self-interest. He was concerned that Idham had caused the stagnation of the organisation, but he was even more concerned that Idham had not directed towards Pesantren Situbondo and Kiai As'ad the amount of government largesse that As'ad felt that he, as one of NU's most senior *ulama*, rightly deserved.

Kiai As'ad's vision was not the same as that of the progressives whose campaign against Idham Chalid he had backed. At the eleventh hour As'ad had broken faith with both Abdurrahman and Idham by directing the electoral college to ignore the earlier negotiated leadership list. In replacing all of Idham's men with men of his own choosing it may have seemed that he had advantaged Abdurrahman. Nothing could be further from the truth: not only did the switch leave the former chairman doubly antagonistic towards Abdurrahman, but it also left Abdurrahman with a deeply flawed and fundamentally divided leadership team.

Abdurrahman's response was simply to work outside his leadership team. This suited his independent and, some would say, stubborn frame of mind. Nevertheless, he found the experience of working with a partially antagonistic central board, which was divided in both the Tanfidziyah and the Syuriah between supporters and critics, to be fatiguing and discouraging. To compound matters, within a few months of the *muktamar* concluding, Idham Chalid, aggrieved by his lack of representation on the new board, launched into a low-key but unrelenting campaign against Abdurrahman.

Relations within NU's new central leadership may have been fractious, but at least the organisation was now enjoying a period of openness and good relations with the Soeharto regime.

THE NEW ORDER REGIME SUPPORTS ABDURRAHMAN

In 1984 the government, and even more so the military that backed it, was deeply sceptical of political Islam. In the 1960s and early 1970s the regime had tended to overlook NU, which it regarded as moderate and pragmatic, and had focused its critical attention on the modernists who were seeking to revive Masyumi in a new guise. In fact during the early years of the New Order the military had tended to see NU as an ally. By the early 1980s, however, the regime was defensive and on edge and more anxious than ever about the potential for Islam to channel dissent, and it regarded even NU with suspicion. There were several reasons for this. One was that Indonesian society was experiencing the beginnings of a revival of interest in Islam, and students, frustrated with a decade of government repression of political dissent on the campuses, were increasingly turning to mosques and Islamic study cells as forums for political discussion and activism. Another was that the PPP, in which NU played a major role, had performed strongly in the 1977 and 1982 elections. Although Golkar's position was never in doubt, when the PPP gained 28 per cent of the overall vote in 1982 — only a slight decrease in the 29 per cent it had gained in 1977, despite increased intimidation and intervention — it was clear that political Islam represented its greatest threat. The New Order regime had watched the development of progressive, liberal Islamic thought by young intellectuals like Nurcholish Madjid and Abdurrahman Wahid with great interest. It welcomed the emergence of this new expression of Islam with its emphasis on pluralism and its deep ideological commitment to separating 'church and state', especially when it began to make inroads into NU. Consequently, after the victories of the reformists at the 1983 *munas* and the 1984 *muktamar*, that saw the adoption of Pancasila as NU's *asas tunggal* and the withdrawal of NU from party politics, the Soeharto regime welcomed the new Abdurrahman–Siddiq leadership.

By the 1980s the authoritarian character of the Soeharto regime was firmly established. The Malari riots of 1974 marked a turning-point from an ambiguous semi-liberalism to an authoritarian regime with totalitarian aspirations. Full-blown totalitarianism was never attempted, much less achieved, for a number of reasons: the fundamental orientation of the regime was pragmatic, focused on maximising rent-seeking 'business' opportunities; the civilian and military elite were fractured into numerous competing elements; and incompetence (including 'intentional incompetence') often got the better of the conspiratorial ambitions of the security apparatus. Nevertheless, without the co-operation of elements within the regime's ruling elite it was simply not possible to operate on a national level. With perhaps as many as 35 million 'members', NU (followed by Muhammadiyah) possessed the most extensive social network outside the Indonesian military. Soeharto knew that the organisation's sheer size could make it, if sufficiently antagonised, impossible to control, even with his considerable resources. Consequently, heavy-handed intervention into NU affairs by the regime, of the sort that had worked so well in PPP and PDI, was risky. At the same time the political potential of the organisation was a continuing source of worry to a regime which was becoming steadily more intolerant of any expressions of dissent and which saw militant Islamism as its greatest threat.

The success of Achmad Siddiq and Abdurrahman Wahid and their Team of Seven at the 1983 *munas* was a matter of great interest to the regime. Especially interesting were two decisions: the recommendation that NU officials no longer be permitted to hold office within political parties, which in effect withdrew NU from practical politics; and the adoption by NU of Pancasila as its *asas tunggal*, or sole foundation. To

Benny Murdani and his colleagues it seemed that, if the reformers could prove as successful at the following year's *muktamar* as they had been at the *munas*, the regime's greatest anxieties about NU would be resolved overnight.

It was not that Idham Chalid's loyalty was in question — he had proved a faithful friend of the New Order regime from before its inception, and even in the 1980s continued to demonstrate his support by allowing PPP leader Djaelani Naro to ride roughshod over NU's interests. By 1982, however, it was clear to people such as Benny Murdani that Idham's declining popularity meant that he was rapidly approaching the end of his usefulness to the regime. Consequently, Benny and his colleagues in the security apparatus did their best to facilitate the rise of Achmad Siddiq and Abdurrahman Wahid. It is impossible to quantify the degree to which the security apparatus was able to influence the leadership vote at the 1984 *muktamar*. There is little doubt, however, that the perception that the regime was supportive of Achmad Siddiq and Abdurrahman Wahid was significant in shaping attitudes within NU.

ISLAMIC REFORM AND THE DEPARTMENT OF RELIGIOUS AFFAIRS

A number of substantial advantages flowed from NU's improved relations with the regime. Not least was a return to close co-operation with the Department of Religious Affairs. NU had long regarded the department proprietarily, and not simply because it wanted to retain control of official culture. The department was an important source of employment for the largely NU graduates of the *pesantren* and State Islamic Institutes. Such mundane concerns continued to prevail within NU, but for the reformists control of the Department of Religious Affairs also meant the ability to influence the State Islamic Institutes and secure a space for progressive intellectuals to write and teach unimpeded. In this they had the regime's support. It had actively encouraged the development of liberal Islamic thought when Mukti Ali was minister in the 1970s and had seen plenty to persuade it that fostering this sort of tolerant non-party-political Islam was its interests. Now, with the liberals on the ascendancy within NU, it was more than happy to facilitate their influence.

In 1983, not long before Abdurrahman became executive chairman of NU, a new Minister for Religious Affairs was installed. The reform-minded *pesantren* graduate, Munawir Sjadzali, was a welcome appointment. In the late 1940s he had been one of the group of young men who had been mentored by Wahid Hasyim, often attending the meetings in Wahid Hasyim's Jakarta home where a young Abdurrahman had been called upon by his father to serve tea. (And occasionally to tie up the shoelaces of those who had nodded off to sleep — at their first formal meeting in their new roles, Munawir reminded Abdurrahman that he had once been one of his victims.) Munawir Sjadzali was ideally suited for the post of religious affairs minister. He was by nature moderate and liberal, and a strong advocate of tolerance and inclusiveness. Although a modernist, he was familiar with the *pesantren* world and with classical Islamic scholarship. He was also an admirer of the neo-modernist ideas of Nurcholish Madjid and Abdurrahman Wahid and supported the progressive stance taken by Rector Harun Nasution of IAIN Syarif Hidayatullah. After becoming minister he moved quickly to encourage the sending of promising young IAIN staff (many of whom were educated in NU *pesantren*) to undertake postgraduate research degrees in Western universities, preferably in the social sciences. He was a strong advocate for one of the central concerns of neo-modernism, namely contextualised *ijtihad*, an interpretive approach to the Qur'an that was mindful of the unique cultural circumstances that prevailed during the Prophet's time, and the consequent need to make appropriate adjustments when applying Qur'anic teaching to contemporary society.[3]

Munawir Sjadzali directed his energies towards the reform of the State Islamic Institute system. Such reform directly benefited NU because the institutes offered the main opportunity of tertiary education for *pesantren* graduates. Many of these graduates, in turn, went on to play decisive roles within NU. In fact, many of the young reformers who had been part of the Council of 24 and the Team of Seven who had backed Abdurrahman and Achmad Siddiq were graduates of State Islamic Institutes. And now eleven of them were serving in NU's new central leadership team.

PANCASILA

In January 1985, following Abdurrahman's December 1984 *muktamar* victory, Soeharto had indicated his support for Abdurrahman by making him an official indoctrinator of Pancasila, a *Mangala Nasional*. In practice this meant that Abdurrahman was drafted onto the national board responsible for formulating the state position on Pancasila and the education of Indonesian schoolchildren about Pancasila. Like many aspects of Abdurrahman's relationship with the state, this appointment was strategically important but problematic for both parties. The support of Abdurrahman Wahid, son of Wahid Hasyim and grandson of Hasyim Asy'ari, and now chair of NU, would boost the legitimacy of Soeharto's Pancasila initiatives in the eyes of the Islamic community. At the same time, however, this appointment further advanced Abdurrahman's push to influence the Pancasila discourse and emphasise the tolerance and acceptance of social pluralism inherent in Pancasila. Prior to the entry of NU liberals the state enjoyed virtually total control of the discourse. Now Abdurrahman and Achmad Siddiq were able to turn the debate to their own advantage, reinterpreting Pancasila for their own purposes. In Abdurrahman's hands Pancasila came to represent a kind of civil religion that simultaneously promoted enlightenment values, including democracy and accountable governance, and protected freedom of belief for the individual.

NU's improved relationship with the government was complemented by an increasingly good relationship with the Indonesian armed forces (Angkatan Bersenjata Republik Indonesia — ABRI). ABRI, more than any other element in the regime, was cautious of political Islam and worried about the potential for extremism to erupt into widespread disorder. By Abdurrahman's own account, even before becoming chairman he had enjoyed a good working relationship with the military intelligence chief Benny Murdani. For Abdurrahman the relationship was not just a means of influencing thinking within the military, and occasionally trouble-shooting when problems arose at the local level. It also provide useful feedback, enabling him to gauge how far he could go in his criticism of the regime before risking confrontation. This was to prove particularly useful as the decade advanced.

Abdurrahman sought to engage with Soeharto while simultaneously maintaining a critical stand on social issues. For example, Abdurrahman was outspoken in his criticism of the government's handling of the controversial Kedung Ombo dam project in Central Java, funded by the World Bank. He was also a vigorous defender of Indonesia's ethnic and religious minorities. Nevertheless, he was also at pains to maintain good relations with the president. Initially this approach of constructive engagement worked well, and Soeharto appeared to welcome many of Abdurrahman's initiatives.

In the lead-up to the 1987 general elections Abdurrahman became increasingly critical of PPP, which was now dominated by modernists. This earned him the ire of many conservatives within NU who regretted NU's withdrawal from the party, but probably did much to cement his good relations with Soeharto. Indeed, following the 1987 elections Abdurrahman was appointed to the MPR by Golkar. Given that the MPR, which met only once every five years, was little more than a rubber stamp, the appointment was essentially symbolic, but the symbolism was important.

FAMILY LIFE

In 1987 Abdurrahman and Nuriyah shifted house again. Their new home was still a modest rented property and it was still a long drive from central Jakarta and the NU headquarters, but it did offer more room to raise four girls. By then Inayah was getting ready for school and there was no longer a baby in the house. Alissa and Yenny had already commenced high school, while Anita was nearing the end of her primary school years. They were, in many respects, a close family, but neither the girls nor Nuriyah saw as much of Abdurrahman as they would have liked.

With Abdurrahman's promotion to the chair of NU, life had become steadily more comfortable. The position did not attract a formal stipend, and the responsibilities that went with the job left little time for earning money through speaking or writing, but the family had begun to benefit from the philanthropic assistance of patrons and were able to settle down to a less precarious existence. Even though some of his backers included wealthy Chinese businessmen, the family still lived relatively modestly. Support from Chinese and other businessmen was mostly channelled into NU and *pesantren* projects. Abdurrahman had little interest in money and no great desire to improve his standard of living; it was not uncommon for him to give money away as soon as it was given to him. Indeed, when donations were given to him for the work of NU he often passed them to his aides to disburse without stopping to count what had been given, much less record the transaction. Unfortunately, for someone who could be a sharp judge of character and discerning observer when he put his mind to it, Abdurrahman was often surprisingly quick to trust those who sought his attention. Whether this was a negligent approach to management on his part, or a generosity of spirit that would give anyone a chance (and even a second or third chance) to prove themselves, the result was often that his trust in those around him was betrayed.

Since moving to Jakarta he had become busy with speaking engagements and NU business. After becoming chairman of NU he was busier than ever, often coming home late at night after meetings and travelling outside Java as often as twice a week. Even when he was home, much of his time was taken up with an endless stream of visitors. At some stage most of the major figures in national life — cabinet ministers, politicians, army generals, religious leaders of all persuasions, intellectuals, journalists, diplomats — made the long trip south to talk with Abdurrahman in his front room. Many were frequent visitors. But it was not just the power-brokers and opinion-shapers who made their way to his house. Almost every week a late-night knock on the door would announce someone seeking something, an ordinary Indonesian whom he had never met before, perhaps a peasant farmer or poor widow who had travelled across Java by train and bus to see him. Sometimes, not infrequently, they needed money, perhaps for themselves or perhaps to complete a new village mosque. Sometimes they wanted advice. Sometimes they wanted an auspicious name for their new-born child. Seldom were they turned away.

It was hardly surprising that Nuriyah and the girls looked for more from Abdurrahman than they were getting. But it was not just his busy schedule that was the problem. Abdurrahman, the extroverted rhetorician and gregarious joker, found it difficult to express his love to those close to him. While he was no distant patriarch or stern disciplinarian, he was uncomfortable expressing his feelings to his wife or daughters. There was no doubt that he enjoyed their company, but he did not do as much to demonstrate it as he could have. It is possible that his own experience growing up had not equipped him to express his feelings.

While Abdurrahman had enjoyed a close relationship with his father, his father had been a man of his time and had trouble displaying affection and intimacy with his son. The two spent a lot of time with each other but Wahid Hasyim spoke little to his son of his feeling for him. At the age of twelve, Abdurrahman had suffered the loss of his father; the following year he had left home and moved to Yogyakarta and then Magelang and Jombang to study. Consequently, as a teenager he had grown up more or less independently. He remained forever beholden to his mother, but his relationships with his siblings were more distant.

Even his relationship with Nuriyah had developed mostly through correspondence, with little occasion for intimacy until after they had known each other for over a decade. And even after they were married Abdurrahman still found it easier to express himself to Nuriyah by writing her letters. Invariably, if they had an argument or misunderstanding the resolution would come through an exchange of notes. When he wanted to apologise or tell Nuriyah how he felt, he would pen a letter and tuck it under her pillow.[4] All of this had left him ill-prepared for fatherhood. It was not that he was a bad father; in fact as Alissa and Yenny were growing up in the early days in Jombang he had been very involved with home and family. He had helped Nuriyah with household work and changed and fed the children, things that many of his peers would never have thought of doing. Nevertheless, by the time Yenny was in high school she began to feel that there was something missing in her relationship with her father, although she knew it was not a lack of affection by either of them.

When still in early high school Yenny wrote a long essay about her admiration and love for her father. She placed this essay in an envelope and left it on the table near the telephone so that he would find it. One day she decided to take the initiative and try to draw him out. She sat beside him on a couch in the family room and awkwardly reached out her hand to place it in his. He responded with a great degree of initial reserve but seemed to understand what she was trying to do, and indeed from that point on he began to try to display his affection for his family more than he had done in the past. Yenny and Alissa and Anita persisted in trying to get him to become more demonstrative by giving him cuddles and hugs, and over time he did become more open in his display of affection for them. By the time Inayah was in school, he was much more comfortable showing his feelings. He was no less busy, though, and the girls still resented the fact that the entire world, or so it seemed, had more call on his time than they did.[5]

CONTROVERSY

Until she had gone to high school Yenny had not really stopped to think about what it was her father did, or who he was. Upon entering high school in Jakarta she began to understand, partly because of the strangely respectful way in which fellow students and teachers received her, that as Chairman-General of NU her father was an important public figure. Also, at about this time he began to confide in Yenny and her sisters that his public role entailed a degree of risk and that there existed a real possibility of his being incarcerated. He told them that they should be prepared for whatever might happen. He had been arrested many times during the campaign for the 1982 general elections, as we have seen, but was only ever kept overnight. Now he had reason to believe that he might face much more significant opposition.

When Abdurrahman became chair of NU he had enjoyed a significant honeymoon period with the Soeharto regime, but he knew that it would not last. Before his first five-year term was over his critical stance on many social and political issues would see Soeharto's patience wearing thin. Nevertheless, he calculated that Soeharto would be reluctant to turn against him for fear of provoking a harsh response from NU's millions of members. In theory at least, Soeharto controlled every aspect of Indonesian society. The military's territorial warfare system was intended to ensure that scarcely a single village or neighbourhood in Indonesia was free from monitoring and control through a comprehensive network of surveillance and intimidation. Even though the system seldom worked quite as comprehensively as theory suggested, there was little doubt about the regime's ability to crush dissent. The territorial warfare system was ramshackle in places and not nearly as well-resourced as the military would have liked, but it still represented an unparalleled social network enveloping virtually the entire archipelago. The only entities able to rival this system were the mass-based Islamic organisations, NU and Muhammadiyah. NU, with its organic network of *pesantren* and *ulama* based in the villages, and its tens of millions of members, was beyond even ABRI's capacity to control. Abdurrahman also believed that Soeharto would be reluctant to move against him for fear of having to deal with a less moderate replacement. Soeharto was unhappy with Abdurrahman's dissident views but seems to have recognised that in most respects he was a moderate and was opposed to revolutionary methods. In that sense they shared a common desire to avoid social unrest and a common aversion to Islamism.

From the outset of his tenure as executive chairman of NU, Abdurrahman was often involved in open criticism of the regime's policies. He used his public profile to help other activists (most of them less known and more vulnerable to government intimidation and repression) to bring the message to the government that it needed to rethink its callous approach to compensating villagers displaced by the construction of the Kedung Ombo dam. The project was widely criticised on a number of grounds. Some held that it was environmentally untenable. Others argued that the confiscation of the land of peasant farmers was unjust and improper, particularly as they had not been successfully rehoused. The use of part of the confiscated land to build a luxury golf course was seen as further evidence of the self-serving nature of the Soeharto regime. Abdurrahman suggested to some friends in NGOs that they write to the World Bank outlining their concerns and asking the World Bank to be more responsible in its management of such projects.[6] Although the letter was Abdurrahman's initiative, its final form was somewhat different from what he envisaged, being strongly worded and personally critical of Soeharto. Soeharto demanded, and received, an apology from Abdurrahman after he had confronted him over the letter. Nevertheless, the incident left many of Abdurrahman's critics within NU openly wondering about Abdurrahman's potential to be a loose cannon endangering the safety of all within the organisation.

At the 1987 *munas*, several groups initiated moves to unseat Abdurrahman at the upcoming *muktamar*. Many NU politicians were angry at his attempts to undermine PPP in the 1987 government elections. Soon after this another incident occurred which was to be used repeatedly to question his commitment, not just to NU, but to Islam itself. According to Abdurrahman, an *abangan* NGO activist friend asked his advice on how he should address public gatherings as he had trouble in pronouncing the standard Islamic greeting, *assalamu alaykum*. Abdurrahman told his friend not to feel under pressure but instead to use the Indonesian expression *selamat pagi*, 'good morning'. He explained that the root of *selamat* was the same as that of the Arab word *salaam* and *selamat pagi* conveyed the same sense as *assalamu alaykum*, 'peace be upon you'. This exchange was overheard by a journalist, who wrote it up in a national newspaper the following day. It was then blown up by his critics, who asserted that he had advocated the dropping of *assalamu alaykum*, an important identity marker for *santri* Muslims, replacing it with the secular Indonesian *selamat pagi*. At the same time, others began to openly question his piety on the grounds that they rarely saw him pray or perform other ritual aspects of worship. Abdurrahman's refusal to defend himself emboldened his critics. Leading the charge against him was Kiai As'ad Arifin Syamsul, who, although helping get Abdurrahman elected in 1984, soon realised that Abdurrahman was not nearly as malleable as he had hoped when he helped him replace Idham Chalid.

NU, NGOS AND CRITICAL SOCIAL ANALYSIS

Abdurrahman's tenure at the helm of NU coincided with dramatic changes within the organisation. It is difficult to quantify the extent to which Abdurrahman's leadership contributed to these changes, but there is no doubting that many within NU believed that his greatest contribution was in helping change the culture of traditionalist Islam in Indonesia.

Although Abdurrahman was, in most respects, a poor manager and did little to reform the administration of the organisation, he did make a great contribution to transforming its intellectual culture. Perhaps his greatest contribution was to give people within NU, particularly young people, the confidence to explore new ideas and initiate new ventures. Despite his popularity among the organisation's youth, Abdurrahman avoided building direct mentor–protégé links between himself and younger leaders. Instead, he appears to have deliberately created an environment for them to engage in critical discussion, without directly seeking to guide their thoughts and actions. The younger generation, for their part, looked up to him as a charismatic and inspirational figure who gave them a licence to try new things and explore new ideas.

Following the accession of Achmad Siddiq and Abdurrahman to the leadership of NU, a variety of new and largely autonomous NGOs sprang up within the NU community. These new organisations were mostly the work of students and recent graduates, and they emerged more or less spontaneously across Java. It would appear that, in this respect at least, Abdurrahman's failure to introduce a professional style of management across the NU network was not entirely a bad thing. In comparison with NU, Muhammadiyah, for example, was run along more modern lines and this, together with Muhammadiyah's membership largely of urban-based professionals, civil servants and business people with relatively good incomes, saw it make progress in the area of community development. Muhammadiyah members are rightly proud of the many schools, orphanages, health clinics and hospitals that it has established. But in the last two decades of the twentieth century, when so much NGO activity was occurring in NU circles, Muhammadiyah produced virtually no new NGOs. Muhammadiyah leaders acknowledge that the spontaneous emergence of NGOs would never happen within

Muhammadiyah, where everything is centrally planned and closely vetted by a central board. The absence of strongly centralised organisational structure within NU seems to have encouraged initiative and creativity.

Most of the NGOs started by young *pesantren* graduates, often with the assistance of progressive *ulama*, were not formally linked with NU, but they played a significant role in transforming the culture of the organisation. Leading the way were the NGOs: P3M, Lakpesdam and LKPSM in Jakarta, and LKiS in Yogyakarta.[7] With the exception of P3M, these were all initiated in the second half of the 1980s during the first term of Abdurrahman's leadership of NU. In the 1990s NU youth set up more NGOs in cities across Java, such as eLSAD in Surabaya. In some cases Abdurrahman was directly involved in the establishment of these NGOs, but many sprang up without any assistance from NU's central board.

One NGO that Abdurrahman helped to form was P3M. Abdurrahman, along with a number of colleagues, decided to establish an organisation outside NU to encourage key young members to reflect critically on the role of *pesantren* and community development. This approach, they felt, would more effectively encourage initiative and independent thinking than if NU tried to do it itself. To a significant extent their approach succeeded.

After P3M's foundation, Masdar Farid Mas'udi, a promising young scholar, was selected to manage its day-to-day affairs.[8] He wrote a book which argued that *zakat*, the giving of alms and tithes, did not necessarily have to take place in the manner assumed by Muslim society. Masdar's radical suggestion was that a modern taxation system in a welfare state might be able to replace *zakat*. In other words, if Muslims paid their taxes and those taxes were responsibly used for welfare, the paying of taxes could be considered a religious duty and fulfilment of *zakat*. In a society in which the paying of taxes was frequently avoided, this proposal was not without merit. Nevertheless, it was widely criticised.[9]

P3M was one of only a few NGOs with which Abdurrahman had direct links, and over time, his day-to-day links with even this NGO were reduced. He often remarked that his distance from NU youth was a deliberate ploy to encourage them to think independently. This was a convenient excuse for somebody who, at the best of times, was neither inclined towards teamwork nor given to maintaining relationships in an organised and carefully planned fashion. Whatever the cause, it appeared that NU youth, more than almost any other group of Indonesian youth, demonstrated a high degree of independent and critical thinking. And this critical thinking certainly did not exclude sharp and rigorous criticism of their much-loved and admired chairman.

Abdurrahman's writing and public addresses were studied closely by NU youth. Abdurrahman's work, together with that of progressive thinkers like Nurcholish Madjid and Djohan Effendi, seemed to allow them fresh licence to engage in critical approaches to re-examining Islamic thought in Indonesia.

Major reform of the *pesantren* system had begun in the 1970s and continued throughout the 1980s and 1990s. The reforms focused on transforming the culture of teaching and learning within the *pesantren*, through changes both to the curriculum and to teaching styles. These efforts were broadly successful in closing the gap between the quality of education on offer in the best *pesantren* and that available in good secular schools, to the point that students in the more progressive *pesantren* were often not only more disciplined than their secular school peers but also more capable of independent thought. To a significant extent these reforms were encouraged, or accelerated, by Abdurrahman's leadership within NU. One of the practical results of these reforms was that many young members were able to graduate from *pesantren* and proceed directly to university studies. Many others entered the IAIN, and considerable numbers proceeded from there to undertake higher degree studies in Western universities. Making this possible was the quality and nature of education in the IAIN; although variable from campus to campus, it was often better than that available at equivalent Islamic institutions elsewhere in the Islamic world. Certainly, under Harun Nasution the postgraduate program of IAIN Syarif Hidayatullah in Jakarta, which drew many of the best IAIN students from across the archipelago, was one of the best such programs in any Muslim country.

The 1980s and 1990s saw many promising young intellectuals emerge.[10] It is not accidental that the majority of new liberal Islamic thinkers come from the ranks of *pesantren* graduates. Although many modernist thinkers have emerged in Indonesia over the past two decades, few are fluent in Arabic and hence few have intimate knowledge of classical Islamic sources. Thus they are unable to make significant, innovative contributions to Islamic thought and instead concentrate on economics and the social sciences. Younger *pesantren* graduates, those born in the 1960s and later, tend to strongly identify with the progressive ideas of Abdurrahman Wahid and Nurcholish Madjid. Some have taken upon themselves the label of neo-modernist or at least see themselves as representing a new approach to Islamic thought that is neither modernist nor traditionalist.

This would be interesting in itself if it were confined to theological thought. What has made it significant, however, is that these young liberal thinkers have moved from the re-examination of Islamic thought to examining a broader range of social issues. In short, many of these young people have become key players in Indonesia's developing civil society.

LKiS and several of the other progressive Islamic NGOs became active in writing and publishing. By the beginning of the 1990s a surprisingly diverse and extensive array of critical texts could be found in Indonesian bookshops. Besides a broad range of translations of seminal Arabic and Western thinkers, there emerged an increasing number of texts categorised as belonging to 'the Islamic left', as the Islamic progressives were sometimes styled. Interestingly, these texts not only displayed a progressive approach to religious thought but they also married this with critical analysis of political and social affairs.

Central to the emergence of this new generation of intellectuals was reform of the IAIN. The graduate faculties at the IAIN Syarif Hidyatullah in Jakarta and IAIN Sunan Kalijaga in Yogyakarta, in particular, became incubators of innovative and progressive new thought. Interestingly, these young intellectuals did not simply become religious functionaries, as did previous generations of graduates, but many also became involved in the media, in teaching and in the civil service. By the late 1990s a significant number of Indonesia's leading journalists and academics were *pesantren* graduates.

HALAKAH DISCUSSION GROUPS AND THE RENEWAL OF ISLAMIC THOUGHT

It is difficult to gauge the extent to which these changes can be directly linked with Abdurrahman's leadership, but there is no question that, in the perception of many of the young people involved, his leadership was a key factor. They point to his leadership of NU as playing a critical role in generating an open atmosphere for progressive thought. Nevertheless, Abdurrahman's personal attitude to renewal of Islamic thought needs to be placed in its historical context. He was hardly the first traditionalist thinker to support the idea of *tajdid*, or renewal. For a long time it was assumed that only the modernists were interested in *tajdid*, and that NU was opposed to the Islamic modernist movement on principle. In fact, many key NU leaders championed *tajdid*. This was particularly evident in the first generation of leaders where Abdurrahman's uncle Kiai Wahab Chasbullah and his friend Kiai Mahfudz Siddiq (chairman of NU in the 1940s and elder brother of Achmad Siddiq) were early advocates of the need for renewal of Islamic thought.[11] NU's seminal thinkers were not so much opposed to *tajdid* as they were concerned with defending classical Islamic scholarship and culture.

The key source of learning and guidance for traditionalist Islam, apart from the Qur'an and the Sunnah, were the *Kitab Kuning*. The *Kitab Kuning* is a diverse collection of texts thought essential to a basic Islamic education. It contains books on such mundane matters as Arabic grammar; it also includes the standard medieval commentaries on the Qur'an and classic texts on *Tasawuf*, or mysticism, as well as guides to *ibadah*, or ritual, and a whole range of other matters. A section of the *Kitab Kuning* 'canon' is concerned with social matters. A distinction was normally made between the religious books dealing with Islamic law, biographies of the Prophet Muhammad, *Tasawuf*, morality and the interpretation of the Qur'an and the Sunnah, and those dealing with the so-called instrumental sciences such as astronomy, biology, mathematics and logic.

Many of these texts were written by leading Arabic or Middle Eastern figures in the twelfth and thirteenth centuries and earlier. Some of the writers, however, were Malay and Javanese. The texts that related to Islamic jurisprudence and the interpretation of the Qur'an and the Sunnah generally came from the so-called Syafi'i school or *mazhab*. Of the four orthodox *mazhab*, the Syafi'i school was the most influential within Indonesia. But there was a general understanding that the work of scholars from any one of the four schools could be profitably studied and often was. Each *pesantren* had its own range of specialist expertise and the *kiai* were known as much for their scholarship in certain texts and disciplines as they were for their personality and other attributes. This was one of the reasons why students typically wandered from *pesantren* to *pesantren* to complete their studies.

What was interesting about the traditionalist approach to *tajdid* or renewal was that it was more diverse and extensive than commonly understood by modernists. Many modernists believed that the traditionalists were opposed to *ijtihad*, or individual interpretations of the Qur'an. To a large extent this is a misunderstanding of traditionalist thought. It is true that many traditionalist or *ulama* were conservative in their approach to *ijtihad*, but it is not true that they were all completely opposed to it. The misunderstanding arose partly as a result of a preference in terminology. Many traditionalist scholars preferred to speak of 'making inferences' rather than 'developing new interpretations', because this suggests a less radical activity. But some scholars, including Abdurrahman's mentor and former Rais Aam of the Syuriah, Achmad Siddiq, spoke openly of the importance of *ijtihad*, as did his brother Mahfudz Siddiq and Wahab Chasbullah before him. Throughout the period of Abdurrahman's leadership *ijtihad* was increasingly discussed; there was a general feeling that it was a topic that could be investigated and debated openly. Younger thinkers, in particular, were keen to discuss approaches to *ijtihad*.

Until the late 1980s the general approach of traditionalist *ulama* was to talk of collective *ijtihad*. By this they meant that religious scholars would get together and discuss critical issues in order to arrive at consensus on a way forward. This approach was shaped by a general understanding that *ijtihad* was most useful and most applicable when it related to new social phenomenon and new issues to which previous generations of scholars had not been exposed; they therefore could not be relied upon for guidance. Consequently, there was much discussion about Islamic approaches to contraception, in vitro fertilisation, the AIDS epidemic, drug-taking, sexual practices and other modern issues. It was generally accepted that elements of these issues were wholly contemporary and unprecedented and therefore that developing an appropriate response to them required fresh initiatives in interpretation of the Qur'an and the Sunnah.

In 1987 Masdar Mas'udi and his colleagues in P3M, together with Abdurrahman, Achmad Siddiq and other progressive thinkers, were instrumental in encouraging a symposium at a *pesantren* in Probolinggo, East Java. This meeting was intended to provide a forum for like-minded *ulama* to get together and engage in collective *ijtihad*. The symposium was described as being a *halakah* meeting. The Arabic word *halakah* means 'circle' and therefore implies discussion. This was intended to invoke earlier efforts at collective *ijtihad* that were called *bahts al-masa'il*, or 'a discussion of books'. As it happened, this *halakah* was the first of a cycle of five major *halakah* marking a new approach to Islamic thought within NU. This development has recently been described in detail by Djohan Effendi, who sees it as playing a central role in driving renewal of thought within NU.[12]

One year later a second *halakah* headed by leading *kiai* from across Java, including Abdurrahman, was held in Semarang in Central Java. The theme was 'epistemology and the nature of traditional knowledge in *pesantren*'. At first glance this might seem like an esoteric topic but it was really a bold choice, for it involved critically examining the very basis of traditionalist knowledge and belief. Another *halakah* was held in Central Java in 1989, which focused on understanding and interpreting the *Kitab Kuning*. One of the main theological innovations of the neo-modernist movement was, as Munawir Sjadzali put it, contextualised *ijtihad*: the development of an appreciation of the need to take into account the historical, social and cultural contexts in which the classical texts of the Qur'an and the Sunnah were written, as well as the current social cultural context in which the principles would be applied. By January 1990 six *halakah* had been held, covering such issues as the cultural interpretation of classical Islamic texts (*Kitab Kuning*) within the context of modern Indonesian society, and the question of adherence to *mazhab* or orthodox jurisprudential schools in a contemporary context. These meetings resulted in the acceptance that NU scholars would be encouraged to use the methodology of the *mazhab* and apply it to new problems. This might not appear like a breakthrough, but in effect it opened the doors for fresh approaches to interpreting the Qur'an and the Sunnah within NU.

Throughout the 1990s the *halakah* meetings continued, effectively giving birth to a new tradition within NU: meeting in *halakah* symposiums to engage in scholarly but robust discussions about key issues, so that the group engaged in critical reinterpretation, or *ijtihad*.

In all these matters it is difficult to quantify or delineate the direct influence of Abdurrahman Wahid. There is no doubt, however, that his leadership afforded a licence for frank and probing discussion and served to inspire many within the organisation who now felt that they could openly discuss and talk about critical new ideas. The effect on younger thinkers in particular was remarkable.

ABDURRAHMAN AND RENEWAL

Throughout its early history NU and the *pesantren*-based traditionalists continued to produce a steady stream of interesting *ulama*, although few of them could also be regarded as modern intellectuals. Clearly, men such as Kiai Wahid Hasyim, Kiai Mahfudz Siddiq and Kiai Wahab Chasbullah were significant exceptions in their day, but there were few other traditionalist *ulama* who were as conversant in European languages and ideas. Nor were there many who felt as confident in the elite circles of Jakarta society as did Wahid Hasyim. Is Abdurrahman Wahid, then, like his father before him, simply an interesting exception to the rule, or is there something in his development which indicates that he is part of broader social change? Certainly there was nothing unusual about a *pesantren* graduate being sent to the Middle East to undertake higher studies. What was unusual about Abdurrahman was that he approached his studies in the Middle East in such a way as to also gain a genuine education in Western thought. As we've seen in earlier chapters, this was largely the result of his own initiative and his own strong passion to explore new ideas, whether in religion, social science or literature.

The efflorescence of NGOs established by *pesantren* graduates since the mid-1980s and the bold rethinking of Islamic thought seen in the *halakah* gatherings strongly indicate change. Some identify the cause of change as being Abdurrahman himself, that as chairman he exerted significant influence over NU, particularly in the changing of its intellectual culture. Others contend that, however intellectual Abdurrahman may have been, his influence must be understood as part of a broader social movement. Certainly, looking back from the vantage point of the 21st century it does appear as if Abdurrahman's generation marked a turning-point. His was the first generation of *pesantren* graduates who, through formal or informal education, sought to synthesise traditional Islamic learning with modern Western thought. It is also difficult to conceive of the sort of intellectual vitality, creativity and freedom that flourished in NU under Abdurrahman emerging in anything like the same form or extent without his presence as its leader.

BENNY, TRY AND SOEHARTO'S ISLAMIC TURN

During 1987 Soeharto began to revise his previous antagonism towards political Islam, and the modernists in particular. By 1988, speculation was increasing about the presidential succession. Soeharto, worried about the extent of support within the military for his re-election, began to court other allies. He began to emphasise his 'Muhammadiyah background', pointing out in speeches that he had been a teacher at a Muhammadiyah school and had been raised as an adopted son in a *santri* household.

In 1988 General Benny Murdani was made Minister for Defence, a 'promotion' that effectively diminished his hold on the military by taking him out of the direct chain of command. He had enjoyed a long twilight of power, but his relationship with Soeharto had been on the wane for several years. Benny had angered Soeharto by criticising the corrupt business practices of the avaricious Soeharto children and calling for greater openness in political management. Until Soeharto elevated him out of the post of armed forces commander, the charismatic general had been seen as a kingmaker because of his extensive contacts across the archipelago, and the strong degree of support for him within the armed forces. A protégé of General Ali Murtopo, he rose steadily to power during the 1970s on the basis of on his commanding influence within military intelligence circles, an influence that was to last well into the 1990s. Nevertheless, many modernist Muslims hated Benny because of his involvement in nefarious military intelligence operations carried out at Soeharto's bidding to subdue and intimidate militant Muslims. The most significant incident was the rioting in Tanjung Priok, the impoverished port district of Jakarta, in September 1984. Many believed that the real death toll from military intervention numbered in the hundreds and that Benny's intelligence operatives had engineered the rioting in order to intimidate radical Islamic groups.

Just as the modernists were delighted to see Soeharto break with the Catholic general whom many had regarded as their nemesis, they also welcomed his appointment of General Try Sutrisno to replace Benny as head of ABRI. They were quick to interpret the switch as indicating a sea-change within Indonesia's political elite. The appointment of Try marked the first time ABRI was led by a *santri* Muslim. What was more, where Benny had been a behind-the-scenes shadowy manipulator easily cast as a villain, Try had a friendly personality and boyish good looks that made it easier for his admirers to cast him as a hero of Islam. Whether Try was as intelligent as Benny was quite another matter, but it is likely that his relative naivety and straightforwardness lent him favour in the eyes of Soeharto, who by this stage was increasingly concerned about dissent within the military and challenges to his authority.

In 1989 the regime passed two bills that won considerable praise from conservative Muslims. One involved making family law 'more

Islamic' and strengthening the role of the religious law courts in family law matters. The other opened the way for religious instruction to move into the curriculum of mainstream schools. These and other developments were signs that Soeharto, after having repressed the modernists for the past two decades, was now courting them. He was seeking to shore up his power base by looking for allies outside the armed forces. The question of the presidential succession was now being more or less openly discussed and Soeharto was looking to enlist the support of the modernists in order to check the power of the military.

ABDURRAHMAN AND CONTROVERSY

The end of 1989 marked the end of Abdurrahman's first five-year term as NU chair, and a *muktamar* was planned for November that year to determine NU's leadership team for the next five years. Earlier, it had seemed automatic that Abdurrahman and Achmad Siddiq would be re-elected. Many saw them as a perfect combination. Most of the conservative *ulama* respected Kiai Achmad Siddiq's strict piety and religious learning, while many younger and more progressive *ulama* and most *pesantren* students appreciated his willingness to champion new ideas, just as they welcomed the intellectual vitality and boldness that Abdurrahman brought to the organisation.

Even those who had little interest in such things were glad to see NU begin to reassert its position within Indonesian society. They might not have understood why the world was paying so much attention to their chairman, but they welcomed the attention all the same. After so many years of being regarded as peripheral and unimportant, the sense that NU was once more being taken seriously was in itself appealing. NU branch heads and other leaders welcomed the new sense of dynamism at the top of the organisation, and they were impressed when Abdurrahman came all the way from Jakarta to meet with them. The administration of the organisation might still have been in shambles and its chairman an enigmatic and perplexing figure, but at least there was a sense that the executive chairman and Rais Aam in Jakarta cared about what was happening in their branch.

For others, the changes brought more immediate and tangible benefits. Construction contractors, traders and other businessmen could see the effects of improved relations with the government and more positive community sentiment regarding NU — particularly on the part of the Chinese community — in their cash flows and contract books.

Nevertheless, the final two years of Abdurrahman's first term saw him become an increasingly controversial figure. In particular, his reckless approach to commenting on disputed social and political issues had the effect of annoying, if not alienating, many within NU. But to some extent the controversy was also fuelled by elements close to Soeharto, who wanted to put Abdurrahman on notice that he owed his power to the president and that he should rein in his critical stance against Soeharto.

Paradoxically, whereas some in NU were angry with him because they saw him as being too close to the regime, others thought that he was not close enough. At the time of the 1987 general elections many were outraged that he had been so critical of PPP, and had consequently benefited Soeharto's Golkar. But others, in fact sometimes the same people, saw him as being too antagonistic towards the Soeharto regime in his stance on issues such as the Kedung Ombo dam, and consequently as needlessly endangering NU's good relations with the government.

Politics may have been at the root of anti-Abdurrahman sentiment within NU but it was not the only area in which he could be faulted. Some suggested that he cared more about his inter-faith dialogue initiatives and his friendships with Christians than he did about supporting Islam. At the same time his record as NU's chief executive officer left much to be desired. When he became chairman in 1984 he inherited a ramshackle and broken-down organisation, the reform of which would have challenged even the most skilful manager. Abdurrahman was not the most skilful of managers, and even after five years he had done little to repair the organisational structure within NU. By 1989 it was not at all clear that Abdurrahman would be re-elected.

THE 1989 *MUKTAMAR* - ABDURRAHMAN FACES HIS CRITICS

The venue for both the 1983 *munas* and the 1984 *muktamar* had been Kiai As'ad Syamsul Arifin's *pesantren* in Situbondo in rural East Java. As'ad had his own agenda in promoting reformers, and he had obtained a decided advantage by having both the *munas* and the *muktamar* on his home ground. But by 1989 most of Kiai As'ad's influence had been exhausted; even though he was increasingly outspoken in his criticism of Abdurrahman, he had little means of striking back at the chairman he had helped elect. As'ad let it be known that he wanted the *mukta-*

mar to be held in Situbondo once again, but Abdurrahman and Achmad Siddiq were not at all keen on returning there. Instead they lobbied for Krapyak, and the *pesantren* of Abdurrahman's former teacher Kiai Ali Ma'sum, to be the venue. Both Ali Ma'sum and As'ad were highly respected as founding members of NU, but there was little doubt that it was Kiai Ali Ma'sum who was held in higher esteem because of his scholarship and charismatic authority as a religious teacher. Moreover, Ali Ma'sum was known to be ailing, and it was agreed that holding the *muktamar* at his *pesantren* in Krapyak would be an appropriate way to honour one of NU's last remaining founders.

The Dutch anthropologist and long-time observer of NU, Martin van Bruinessen, witnessed the 1989 *muktamar* and wrote a vivid firsthand account.[13] He explains that the choice of Krapyak gave Abdurrahman and Achmad Siddiq a distinct advantage. Kiai Ali Ma'sum could be relied upon to defend his former student, and this would make it much harder for critics to argue that Abdurrahman didn't have the backing of senior *kiai*. Abdurrahman had fallen out briefly with Kiai Ali Ma'sum over the incident concerning the greetings *selamat pagi* and *assalamu alaykum*. But after Abdurrahman wrote to Kiai Ali Ma'sum asking his forgiveness and apologising for the misunderstanding, he had been quick to forgive him, and their relationship remained strong. Kiai As'ad had also complained about his comments regarding the Islamic greeting but Abdurrahman had not bothered writing to him.

Prior to the 1989 *muktamar* Abdurrahman stepped up the tempo of his visits to *pesantren*. From his first months in office he had made a habit of regularly touring Central and East Java as well as NU branches in South Sumatra, South Sulawesi, Bali, Lombok and elsewhere. Rarely a week went by when he was not on the road, at the very least across town or in the immediate environs of West Java. In the months leading up to the *muktamar* he was busier than ever, and he made a point of focusing on the outer island branches. He was aware of their dissatisfaction with the central leadership of NU and was keen to demonstrate that he was listening to their concerns and sympathetic to their grievances.

In the final days before the *muktamar*, Abdurrahman slipped away quietly on a quick trip to Mecca. Van Bruinessen observes that newspaper reports noted that in Mecca Abdurrahman had called upon the great West Sumatran-born sheik, Muhammad Yasin or 'Syeikh

Minangkabau' as he was sometimes known.¹⁴ Sheikh Muhammad Yasin was regarded by most *kiai* within NU, including the most conservative, as their supreme religious authority. When Abdurrahman was speaking at the *muktamar* he made no mention of his trip to Mecca, much less of his meeting with Sheikh Yasin. He had no need to discuss it because it had already been widely covered in the press. Nor did he have any need to reinforce the impression that Sheik Yasin had given his blessings to Abdurrahman in seeking a second term of office.

Even though, by November 1989, relations between Abdurrahman and President Soeharto were beginning to sour, Soeharto was still keen to seek support within NU for his bid for re-election in 1992. There is good reason to believe that Soeharto was also keen to remind Abdurrahman who held ultimate power in Indonesia; for that reason he was probably not unhappy that Abdurrahman was facing fierce criticism at the *muktamar*, even if he did not actively back Abdurrahman's critics. Ironically, some of the covert opposition to Abdurrahman's bid for re-election appears to have arisen precisely because of concern that Abdurrahman was too much in favour with Soeharto. The American anthropologist and scholar of Indonesian Islam, Robert Hefner, argues that Benny Murdani 'secretly supported those opposing Wahid's re-election, on the grounds that Wahid was too close to Soeharto. These were the years, of course, when Murdani was locked in a bitter struggle with the president, and Soeharto's triumph was not yet assured'.¹⁵

So it seems that the 1989 NU national congress was not simply the private affair of a rustic, rural-based religious organisation. The election of the leaders of one of the few mass national organisations outside the direct control of the Soeharto regime was not something that anyone in the ruling elite took lightly. Consequently, NU's 1989 *muktamar* was a grand affair. The organising committee had received considerable amounts of sponsorship and assistance from a variety of business and community sources as well as from the president himself. President Soeharto was there to open the congress. This was significant in itself, but even more significant was the symbolism of his method.

A large traditional drum, or *bedung*, of the kind used to announce the call to prayers in rural mosques, was placed in the centre of the stage. It was made known that this particular *bedung*, which was exceptionally large and well made, had belonged to the family in which Soeharto had been raised as an adopted son. The drum was much better than the one the *pesantren* itself owned. When the time came to formally open proceedings, Soeharto stepped up to the *bedung*, seized the padded mallet, and struck the drum with the distinctive rhythm that only somebody who had been raised in a religious home could have learned. The effect was not wasted; the audience erupted into cheers and applause, together with choruses of prayers and thanks to God. Now at last, it seemed, Indonesia had a president who was taking Islam and NU seriously.

The importance of the *muktamar* was signalled not only by President Soeharto officiating at the opening, but also by the attendance of high-level government ministers. Interior Minister Rudini, the Secretary of State Moerdiono, Minister for Defence Benny Murdani and Armed Forces Chief Try Sutrisno all gave long speeches. Several days earlier Vice-President Soedharmono had opened a pre-*muktamar* congress for NU-affiliated *tarekat*, or traditional Sufi brotherhoods, and the NU sister organisation responsible for co-ordinating *tarekat* affairs. Since his demise as chairman of NU, Idham Chalid had spent his time leading the *tarekat* union. The symbolism of the vice-president opening the much smaller *tarekat* was also significant. All of these senior ministers had vested interests in the outcome of the *muktamar*, but three in particular were keen to see their men go forward. Rudini, Benny and Try were known to be backing certain candidates.

As the first *santri* Muslim ever to command the armed forces, Try's address was greeted with loud applause and clapping of hands. His speech did not disappoint; it was appropriately peppered with Arabic phrases and quotations from the Qur'an and the *hadith*. (As Try finished speaking, the assembly spontaneously broke into a rousing recital of the *Shalawal Badar*, a martial prayer sung before going into battle, much as stirring Christian hymns are sung by Welsh football fans before a rugby match. As the assembly broke into the *Shalawal Badar* hundreds surged forward to embrace Try or to shake his hand.)

When given a chance to speak on the second day of the *muktamar*, the regional representatives were reminded that it was to be a forum for serious discussion and not a speech-giving contest. Van Bruinessen observes, however, that the majority of speakers gave long addresses rich with rhetorical flourishes in an attempt to impress the crowd. Perhaps surprisingly, many of them were greeted with boos and jeers, and young men yelled out comments like 'Hey, it's not supposed to be a Friday sermon' and 'Get to the point'. Many young people within NU had become fanatical supporters of Abdurrahman and his fellow reformers, and they appeared to sense, in many of these long-winded speeches, unfair, or empty, criticism of Abdurrahman.[16]

The young reformists and supporters of Abdurrahman had formulated a position paper to be put forward to the assembly at a special session held for NGOs and development activists within NU. The initial draft, however, was regarded as too provocative, so Abdurrahman and others toned it down. Nevertheless, the substantive points of 'working for the benefit of community' and 'avoiding social harm' remained hidden among traditional-sounding phrases. When accepted and passed, this paper committed the new leadership of NU to initiate the points listed, which included direct foreign funding of *pesantren*-based community development projects and the development of a community banking network. This gave the green light for community development activists to pursue foreign support for their programs and to encourage local *kiai* to be co-operative.

Amidst the normal rumblings about the central board in Jakarta not paying attention to rural concerns and their problems, there were accusations that Abdurrahman had sympathies with Shiite Islam and that he supported the ideas of those influenced by medieval Mu'tazilite rationalist philosophy. These criticisms were not without foundation. Abdurrahman was never a crypto-Shiite but he was sympathetic to the small group of Indonesian intellectuals who emerged in the late 1980s, the most prominent of whom was Jalaluddin Rakhmat, who had become Shiites or at least were exploring Shiite thought. Abdurrahman even went as far as allowing the Shiites to use 'his mosque' in Ciganjur (built in front of his plot of land as part of Soeharto's large-scale mosque building program that commenced in the late 1980s). There were at least four reasons why Abdurrahman was supportive of the Shiites. Firstly, he is inclined by nature to help persecuted and downtrodden minorities. Secondly, and related to this, he is against anything that impinges on freedom of belief and freedom of conscience. Thirdly, he sees Shia scholarship, with its ongoing tradition of *ijtihad* and its openness to metaphysical speculation, as representing a rich vein of learning that can be profitably mined by all Islamic intellectuals. Finally, he argues that many aspects of NU worship (*ibadah*) and approaches to mysticism (*Tasawuf*) have their origin in Persian Shia Islam, and that NU scholars should understand Shia Islam if only in order to understand Sunni Indonesian Islamic traditionalism. Moreover, Abdurrahman is also an admirer of Mu'tazilite rationalist philosophy; even if he is critical of the Mu'tazilite philosophers on some points, there is little doubt that their rationalism does influence his thinking. He was also criticised for arguing in his writings that Indonesian Islam should become more Indonesian and less Arab.

One of the substantive points of criticism was his promotion of the *halakah* discussion groups. These upset many of the older conservative *kiai*, particularly those who felt that their traditional authority would be undermined by questioning the *Kitab Kuning*. In the past it had been the *kiai* who had taught the *Kitab Kuning* and young *santri* who sat listening and memorising the texts. Authority rested with the *kiai* and the texts and none with the young students. Now the old *kiai* felt that, with the younger men critically discussing the *Kitab Kuning*, there would be an erosion of authority and respect for the older generation and for the traditions.

When finally, at the conclusion of the congress, Abdurrahman was given an opportunity to reply to his critics, he responded coolly and rationally. He did not seek to evade the criticism that had been brought against him, acknowledging that in many ways he had failed to achieve what he had promised five years earlier. To some extent, he suggested, this was because he had been given a leadership team that was deeply divided and in some cases strongly antagonistic towards him. He did not mention any names, nor did he have to; everyone knew he was referring to his Secretary-General and other appointees of Kiai As'ad. He also, quite realistically, acknowledged that he was not a good administrator and that the process of reforming the central administrative structure of NU had been beyond his capacity to achieve in the first term. In responding to criticisms about his openness to Mu'tazilah-like rationality and the Indonesianisation of Indonesian Islam, he was frank and bold, just as he was in talking about the critical re-examination of the *Kitab Kuning* discussion groups. He put before the assembly his opinion that they had no choice but to wrestle with these issues if NU was to find a place in the modern world. To fail to do so, he suggested, was to risk further stagnation and the eventual collapse of both the institutions and the traditions of which NU was so proud. Abdurrahman argued that the *pesantren* could no longer rely upon rote learning and the uncritical acceptance of the classical texts. Young people naturally wanted to do more than that, and if their needs were not addressed they would go elsewhere.

Van Bruinessen recounts that Abdurrahman's address was peppered with witty references and good humour, so that even though he was often critical, the assembly became increasingly responsive and appreciative. He spoke of NU as being like a car in which some passengers were constantly trying to step on the brake pedal. If the car was to continue motoring forward, he argued, then somebody had to step on the accelerator. That, he said, was his task and it was one that he was not shying away from. It was a brilliant speech, so rhetorically well constructed, skilfully delivered and cleverly leavened with humour and good grace that few could argue against it. Abdurrahman stepped down from the podium to rousing applause.

When the time came for choosing the national leadership team for the next five years, Abdurrahman and Siddiq both faced fierce competition led by As'ad Arifin Syamsul, Idham Chalid and Yusuf Hasyim. If their supporters were to be believed, Abdurrahman and Siddiq were deeply unpopular and the voting would be close run. The reality proved otherwise. In the contest for Rais Aam, Achmad Siddiq defeated Idham Chalid by 188 votes to 116. Abdurrahman's main competitor for the post of Ketua Umum was his uncle, Yusuf Hasyim. But in the end Yusuf Hasyim failed to gain the requisite 40 branch votes needed to contest the post and Abdurrahman was returned unopposed by acclamation from the floor.

The *muktamar* had been a testing time for Abdurrahman, but in the end he had come through strengthened in his position. He now had a leadership team more of his own choosing, and his authority within the organisation was strongly reinforced by the testing of his position at Krapyak. Moreover, the agreements that were passed on the floor of the assembly strongly supported his initiatives, particularly in the area of community development.

The 1990s began with Abdurrahman looking and feeling very comfortable. He now had a central board at both Syuriah and Tanfidziyah levels that he could rely upon and was surrounded by like-minded progressives in official positions so that he could count on his orders being followed through. Evidence of the degree of support for the organisation within broader Indonesian society was seen in the opening of a small-scale credit branch and a bank branch in the industrial town of Sidoarjo, outside Surabaya. For many years Abdurrahman had dreamt of establishing a small-scale rural banking network, along the lines of Bangladesh's Grameen Bank, to provide credit to those with whom conventional banks would not deal. The bank was backed by the Chinese-owned Bank Summa and offered conventional interest-bearing accounts. Abdurrahman and fellow progressives rejected the opinion of many conservative Muslims that modern bank interest was equivalent to *riba*, usury, something that was prohibited in the Qur'an.

Abdurrahman had been consistently outspoken in his defence of Indonesian Chinese and Indonesian Christians, both Protestant and Catholic, and as a result many Indonesian Chinese were prepared to support his initiatives. Many observers at the time praised the alliance between NU and Bank Summa. Former Minister for Religious Affairs Munawir Sjadzali declared warmly, 'It's something that should have been done much earlier'. Echoing those thoughts, Dorodjatun Kuntjorojakti, Dean of the School of Economics at the University of Indonesia, stated: 'The NU-Summa venture is a magnificent idea. I wish that they had done it fifteen years ago.'[17] Soeharto said nothing publicly about the deal, but according to senior government officials he was deeply unhappy about it. Apparently it troubled him to see the Chinese Christian Soeryadjaya family, who owned Bank Summa, developing a close relationship with the traditional Muslim community, just as it had troubled him to see NU, under Abdurrahman, spreading its social role and influence.

DIABETES AND LOSS OF EYESIGHT

Physically Abdurrahman appeared to be in robust good health with seemingly endless energy. He was travelling constantly both around Jakarta and across Central and East Java and not infrequently internationally, to speak at conferences and seminars. He was probably thirty kilograms overweight, sufficient to make certain things, such as kneeling in prayer, somewhat uncomfortable, but this did not seem to have any great effect on his health. Nevertheless, he was, by this stage, already feeling the effects of Type II diabetes, although he remarked little on it. Indeed, the diabetes was unremarkable because most of his peers in Jakarta, men in their fifties in stressful positions, carrying more weight than they should and getting less exercise than they needed, suffered from a similar condition. Tragically for Abdurrahman, however, the disease was already beginning to make inroads on his eyesight. He had already effectively lost the sight in his left eye after his scooter accident in 1978 when the retina failed to re-adhere. Now his right eye was gradually losing vision through the effects of diabetes and glaucoma. By the time of his fiftieth birthday the glaucoma had begun to cloud his peripheral vision.

For a man who loved reading as much as he did, this was a worrying development, though he showed no signs of trying to prevent its progress by changing his lifestyle. One indication that he may have been concerned about his health was his frequent remark that his father and grandfather had died young and he expected that he might not live long either. The comment was generally made, not so much as a reflection on impending mortality, as an explanation of his bold, even reckless, approach to political engagement. Abdurrahman threw himself enthusiastically into every aspect of his position, with the significant exception of administration and general management.

He had come through the 1989 *muktamar*, surviving considerable pressure from Soeharto and indeed improving and strengthening his position; the outcome had left him optimistic. The dark clouds gathering on the horizon in the form of mounting opposition from Soeharto did not seem to him a cause for concern, but rather a challenge and a spur to action.

EIGHT

PUSHING THE LIMITS, 1990-1994

THE LIMITS OF OPENNESS

By the late 1980s President Soeharto's grip on power was being questioned more openly than at any time since the Malari riots of 1974. The image of the avuncular leader whose sage visage endlessly graced the nightly television news was being challenged. The sober 'Father of Development' who unfailingly delivered wise speeches, the patient adviser to peasant farmers who tirelessly stood in the paddy fields talking to the little people, was being asked to listen. In some ways he was the victim of his own success. Two decades of steady growth had created so many islands of wealth in a sea of poverty that people in every corner of Indonesian society could see before them the evidence that life could be very much better than their experience of it. Few of the nation's then 180 million citizens lived in booming Jakarta, but the steadily rising levels of literacy and general education, coupled with the rapid expansion of both print and electronic media, informed even simple peasants in remote villages that the elite in Jakarta lived in a very different world to their own.

By the late 1980s many of Soeharto's most trusted advisers were no longer by his side. Ali Murtopo had died of a heart attack in 1984, others had retired and others still, such as Benny Murdani, had fallen out with 'the old man' — as the Jakarta elite had taken to calling him.

Abdurrahman continued to enjoy positive relations with the increasingly taciturn president, but it was an uncomfortable relationship. Benny's estrangement from Soeharto meant that Abdurrahman lost his most powerful point of contact with the mind of the president. At the same time, Abdurrahman's activism and outspokenness in civil society meant that Soeharto saw him as troublesome and unreliable. In particular, with the question of succession now preoccupying the Jakarta elite, Abdurrahman's pointed refusal to publicly endorse Soeharto's candidature for the presidency in the lead-up to the general elections and ensuing five-yearly sessions of the MPR was an irritant to a leader accustomed to having his will prevail. Consequently, there was little surprise in 1988 that Abdurrahman was not invited to sit in the assembly for a second time.

ICMI: SOEHARTO'S ISLAMIC TURN IS INSTITUTIONALISED

Shortly after his seventieth birthday in the middle of 1991, President Soeharto travelled to Mecca to make the *haj* pilgrimage. This was the first time that he had done so. Until then Soeharto had been understood to be an *abangan* Muslim — not irreligious, but more inclined to mystical Javanese beliefs than orthodox Islam. When Soeharto returned from the *haj*, in addition to the title Haji he adopted the name Muhammad as an indication that he was applying himself more seriously to the task of being a Muslim. Many commentators accepted the claim that as Soeharto was growing older he was naturally becoming more religious. After all, many people in Indonesia become more pious as they approach the end of their life. Other, more cynical, observers suggested that Soeharto's completion of the pilgrimage was a political move designed to convey to conservative *santri* Muslims that he was now someone they could trust and work with. As the decade progressed, it became increasingly clear that this second interpretation was closer to the truth. Soeharto was, after all, a cynical political operator par excellence — it was no accident that his grip on power was without effective challenge for over three decades.

In fact, several years before Haji Muhammad Soeharto returned from Mecca there had already been indications that he was toying with the idea of co-opting conservative Muslims to balance the power of the military. Following the 1987 general elections Soeharto began to change his approach to dealing with conservative Muslims. In the run-up to the 1982 general elections Soeharto's regime had sought to intimidate those campaigning for PPP and had intervened heavily in the party to emasculate NU's political strength. Then in 1983–84 Soeharto had upset Muslim groups with his insistence that Pancasila become the *asas tunggal*, or sole basis, of all organisations, even religious ones. It was also assumed that Soeharto had ordered Benny Murdani and his military intelligence operatives to violently repress Islamist study cells in Tanjung Priok in September 1984. At the same time it was clear that he had ordered Benny to be supportive of NU's new liberal leadership aspirants, Achmad Siddiq and Abdurrahman Wahid, and that he was generally supportive of liberal Muslim figures. In 1986, for example, Nurcholish Madjid, having returned from PhD studies under Fazlur Rahman at the University of Chicago several months earlier, encountered little trouble in establishing his socio-educational NGO called Paramadina, designed to promote a sophisticated and tolerant understanding of Islam among middle-class Jakarta's increasing numbers of 'new-*santri*'.[1] By 1988, however, when Soeharto sought the input of Islamic intellectuals into proposed new laws (to be passed the following year) dealing with Islamic law courts and Islamic education, he snubbed Abdurrahman and NU and turned instead to conservative intellectuals opposed to Abdurrahman and his liberal approach to Islamic thought.[2] Worse was to come.

In October 1990 something happened that served as an ominous warning that a serious shift in the regime's policy towards Islam had occurred. It involved the popular magazine *Monitor*. This magazine had links with the elite broadsheets, *Kompas* and *The Jakarta Post* through its Catholic Chinese backers. *Monitor* had run an opinion poll asking readers to indicate who they felt to be the most important people who had ever lived. Perhaps it was not surprising that President Soeharto polled number one. What was of concern to *santri* Muslims, however, was that the Prophet Muhammad came in at number eleven, behind not just the president but also Arswendo, the Catholic editor of *Monitor*. The provocative poll produced a sizable jump in circulation for *Monitor*, and Arswendo initially regarded it as a marketing triumph. He quickly revised this opinion when an angry mob turned up at the office of the *Monitor*, stoned the windows, and called for Arswendo's arrest. Arswendo was subsequently charged, taken to court and sentenced to five years' jail (of which he served four years) and Harmoko, Minister for Information and one of Soeharto's most sycophantic loyalists, withdrew *Monitor*'s licence to publish. Neither the unrestrained mob nor the hefty jail sentence for Arswendo would have occurred without Soeharto's express approval, though there was also no doubt that Arswendo had violated a taboo and caused genuine offence. Even liberal figures such as Nurcholish lamented Arswendo's callous indifference to *santri* opinion and his cynical, commercial disregard for religious feelings for something as trivial as an attempt to improve a magazine's circulation.[3]

One of the few public figures who spoke out in defence of Arswendo was Abdurrahman. Arswendo, he wrote, had been foolish and wrong in running his poll, but the appropriate response was not to arrest or jail him, but simply to boycott his magazine. After all, if Indonesia was serious about free speech it was difficult to put forward a compelling argument for the jailing of a magazine editor for what appeared to have been essentially a non-malicious error of judgment, albeit an irresponsible and indulgent one. Abdurrahman also expressed his disappointment with Nurcholish and other liberals for not defending more vigorously the principles of free speech. Abdurrahman had taken a similar stance the year before when he had spoken out against the *fatwa* declared in Iran against Salman Rushdie following the publication of his novel *Satanic Verses* (an act of bravery that provided further ammunition for his critics opposing his re-election at the *muktamar* at the end of the year).

Final proof of a sea-change in Soeharto's approach to conservative Islam came in December 1990 when the Indonesian Association of Muslim Intellectuals (ICMI) was launched. Five years earlier it would have been hard to imagine such an organisation being formed. This association promised to be a nation-wide network linking all university-educated Muslims, or at least those active in public life. It styled itself as being non-political, and no doubt some of those behind it hoped that it would remain so, but from the very outset it was enmeshed in politics. In the months prior to its official launch Soeharto had made clear his willingness to sponsor the organisation. As a result ICMI, from its birth, became closely identified with Soeharto's Golkar. Not only did Soeharto back it with considerable financial support; he also appointed his own protégé and senior minister, B. J. Habibie, to be its official chairman.

Conservative *santri* were delighted with Soeharto's support for ICMI. Many of the leading lights involved in the push to establish ICMI had been active in Masyumi or had actively worked for the rebirth of Masyumi and had experienced decades of discouragement as the Soeharto regime actively worked against political Islam. Now former enemies of the state were being welcomed into its very bosom. The president's sudden 'conversion' to their cause seemed like an answer to their prayers.[4]

The emergence of ICMI with the full support of the president had alarmed Abdurrahman and others, such as Djohan Effendi, who sensed that Soeharto planned to use conservative *santri* to back him in his re-election bid. During 1991 people within the ICMI camp made repeated approaches to Abdurrahman, urging him and other NU leaders to join the organisation. Some did join, but the majority declined, following the example of Abdurrahman, who was outspoken in his criticism of ICMI. Abdurrahman was concerned that the very formation of an elitist association of Islamic intellectuals encouraged sectarian sentiment and would therefore play into the hands of the conservatives. He also argued that Soeharto was cynically manipulating religious sentiment for his own purposes, with the potential that things might develop in a way that even Soeharto could not manage. At best, he argued, the composition of ICMI's leadership made it unlikely that ICMI would be able to effect genuine reform: 'There are so many more career bureaucrats in ICMI than there are activists that expecting change to emerge from within these circles is like expecting that roosters will lay eggs.'[5] A year later, in December 1994, he explained:

> I have said that the majority of ICMI's members are good people, I take my hat off to them for their aspirations. Unfortunately, at a certain level, there are some members of ICMI who are sectarian. I have said that from the beginning. Why do I say this? So that they will understand [he draws out the word for emphasis]. So that they will take the appropriate steps to correct for this.[6]

What worried critics of ICMI such as Abdurrahman was not its moderate intellectuals and activists, many of whom harboured reformist ideas, or its Habibite technocrats, or even its regimist opportunists. Rather, it was the small but significant core of radical Islamists who, after so many years out in the cold, were now in ICMI being warmly embraced by the regime. After decades of antagonism, Soeharto, it appeared, was finally holding out an olive branch to the Masyumi hard-liners.

Although militant fundamentalism, until recently, had been largely unknown in Indonesian Islam, its more moderate cousin, Islamism, made substantial advances through Dewan Dakwah and similar bodies. For many years Islamism of the Dewan Dakwah variety lacked significant drawing power in Indonesian society. Nevertheless, it did serve to blunt the edge of Islamic modernism as a progressive movement of thought. The effects of this sort of conservative thought extended well beyond the bounds of those who were formally members of Dewan Dakwah. It resulted in the emergence from within Muhammadiyah of a conservative right wing that was increasingly sympathetic to Islamist ideas. During the second half of the 1990s Amien Rais, as chairman of Muhammadiyah, remained close to many Islamist figures, giving them a voice that they would not have had otherwise.

FORUM DEMOKRASI

Following the *Monitor* affair and the launch of ICMI, Abdurrahman and some like-minded friends concerned about the rising tide of sectarianism decided it was time to form an organisation to speak out in defence of pluralism and democracy. Early in 1991 forty-five intellectuals drawn from across the religious and social communities of Indonesia launched an organisation they called Forum Demokrasi. The group chose Abdurrahman as its leader and spokesman because it calculated that his prominence and influence would draw attention to the small group and give it credibility, and because his mass base in NU made it difficult for the regime to silence him. The Forum Demokrasi intellectuals were careful to point out that they were not campaigning on a party-political basis, nor did they expect to directly influence the political processes. Rather, Abdurrahman explained, Forum Demokrasi was established to provide a countervailing force to institutions such as ICMI which were encouraging sectarian thinking. Forum Demokrasi, he said, was campaigning against the political exploitation of sectarian sentiment. In the 1950s most major parties were formed along religious or ideological lines, and for a long while it was assumed that this was the natural course of political development. Such 'confessional politics', he argued, was inherently sectarian and unhealthy and against democracy.

Writing shortly after the formation of Forum Demokrasi, Abdurrahman explained why he saw the establishment of democracy as being so important: 'Unfortunately, the issue of sectarianism is addressed as if it were the central issue. It is as if it were the cause not the effect. In fact the core of the problem is the lack of democracy and freedom.'[7]

The Forum Demokrasi group was only small, and most of its members were not high-profile figures. Few of them were from NU, indeed few of them were Muslims — many were Catholic or Protestant Christians, and some had socialist activist backgrounds. Two of the key figures were Marsillam Simanjuntak, an outspoken social activist, and Bondan Gunawan, an *abangan* Javanese also active in civil society. Some within NU were critical of Abdurrahman for associating with such elements, arguing that if he wanted to form a ginger group 'he should have looked within his own organisation for support'. But Abdurrahman had always enjoyed a wide circle of friends drawn from across religious communities and intellectual circles. His association with Forum Demokrasi and its eclectic membership was deliberate. He wanted to convey the message that there were other bases apart from religion and ethnicity on which to organise politically.

Ironically, the more the regime expressed disaffection with Forum Demokrasi, the more popular it became and the more media coverage it received. For a group with such a small membership and so little in the way of formal activities, or even carefully worked out position statements, Forum Demokrasi cut quite a profile. As the June 1992 general elections approached, the regime became increasingly agitated by the mere existence of Forum Demokrasi and even small-scale Forum meetings were broken up — generally on the grounds that the organisers did not possess 'the appropriate permits'.

In February 1992 the Forum issued a statement setting forth its policy position. American political scientist Douglas Ramage observed:

> Two points in the six-point statement are noteworthy. In addition to reiterating its commitment to democracy, the Forum noted its concern that people in 'dominant positions resorted to violence to resolve problems'. The Forum also stated that it 'views the succession issue as an important matter which is inextricably linked to the democratization process'. The Forum added that it was prepared to give 'special attention' to the problem of succession as one of its 'short-term programs'.[8]

Not surprisingly, both the military and the president were concerned about Forum Demokrasi and Abdurrahman's involvement in it.

Without Abdurrahman as its leader, it would have been relatively easy to silence the Forum — even easier than the silencing of prominent retirees in the Petition of Fifty a decade earlier. With Abdurrahman, and NU's tens of millions, linked to the Forum, it was not so easy for the regime to take action against the small group, especially when Abdurrahman was wielding Pancasila as both a sword and a shield. Forum Demokrasi's February statement was a severe irritation to the military, which resented the assertion that there was a need to make changes to Indonesia's 'Pancasila Democracy', an assertion made all the more galling by Abdurrahman's use of Pancasila to justify his call for change.

THE GREAT ASSEMBLY (*RAPAT AKBAR*)

On 1 March 1992 Abdurrahman called a *Rapat Akbar* (literally a great assembly) to celebrate the sixty-sixth anniversary of the founding of NU. He explained to the media that the rally was part of his campaign to steer Indonesian politics aware from sectarianism in the face of strong pressure from Soeharto to do the reverse. The ostensible aims of a *Rapat Akbar* were to declare NU's loyalty to the Pancasila in the form of an *ikrar*, or declaration, and to state NU's support for a violence-free general election later that year and a successful meeting of the MPR early the following year. Abdurrahman had consulted few of his colleagues in organising the rally, a move typical of his style. Since the death of Kiai Achmad Siddiq in 1991, he had run NU almost as a one-man show, especially when it came to such political actions.

Abdurrahman had been facing serious pressure from Soeharto's camp to have NU declare its support for Soeharto's next term of presidency. Abdurrahman's controversial activities, including his outspoken statements in his engagement in inter-faith dialogue and promotion of reform of Islamic thought, had earned him many enemies within NU. Many questioned the extent to which he still had the backing of the organisation. Abdurrahman declared that the *Rapat Akbar* would be an occasion when more than one million people would turn up to demonstrate their support for NU's acceptance of Pancasila. It would be evidence of the organisation's overwhelming endorsement of his moderate and tolerant approach to engagement of Islam in modern society. As it turned out, only a fraction of that number attended the rally at the Senayan sports stadium in central Jakarta. The all-important licence to hold the *Rapat Akbar* was issued only a day before the assembly was to be held. Soeharto was reluctant to issue a direct ban on the NU assembly, which after all was being promoted as a show of support for Pancasila. But to have a million or more people meeting in the national capital at the invitation of Abdurrahman was intolerable. Acting under direct instructions from the president, the police intervened to stop NU members from boarding buses in East Java, and in Jakarta they turned back busloads of NU members seeking to enter the city. Even so, the appearance of between 150 000 and 200 000 NU members made it the biggest non-governmental rally in twenty-five years.[9]

Abdurrahman declared the rally a modest success, even though the numbers were nothing like those he had been seeking. He explained that this was due to the actions of the security forces in preventing thousands of NU members from attending. Angry with Soeharto for sabotaging the rally, Abdurrahman sat down later that day and drafted a letter. In it Abdurrahman told Soeharto that the *Rapat Akbar* had achieved its internal goals: to celebrate sixty-six years of NU; to confirm NU's commitment to Pancasila and the constitution of 1945; and to affirm its support for peaceful general elections and for a incident-free MPR session.[10] He went on to add that, although the three internal goals had been achieved, the external goals had not. NU had not been given an opportunity to demonstrate mass support for a vision of Indonesian Islam characterised by openness, fairness and tolerance. To have done this, he explained, they needed to have between one and two million people there, and he believed that many had been blocked from attending by Soeharto's intervention. As a consequence, Abdurrahman argued, there remained a threat to the perpetuity of Pancasila and the Republic of Indonesia:

> By preventing Nahdlatul Ulama from obtaining conclusive legitimacy for its views, the responsibility for orientating Indonesia's religious movement now moves to the government. If the government fails, then within ten years the strength of those who don't accept the national ideology will grow, and they will threaten the Republic of Indonesia and Pancasila ... What is now happening in Algeria will happen again here ... and, if the trend continues, an Islamic state will replace the state we have now.[11]

It is hard to think of anyone else who could have written to the Indonesian president so frankly and boldly. Whether this was sheer recklessness or moral courage is a matter of dispute (there is good reason to say that, reckless or not, Abdurrahman was extraordinarily courageous in the way that he consistently challenged Soeharto); but there is no doubt that the mass backing of NU gave Abdurrahman significant leverage, which he employed when he felt the need to drive home the point. Almost anyone else would have been very smartly crushed for such impertinence; it was difficult, however, to turn openly on the leader of NU.

PUSHING THE LIMITS

In the wake of Forum Demokrasi's February position statement and NU's *Rapat Akbar*, Soeharto decided that it was time for Abdurrahman to be reined in. In March Soeharto dispatched his son-in-law Prabowo Subianto to take a message to Abdurrahman, inviting him to meet with Prabowo at his battalion headquarters outside Jakarta. Prabowo warned him to stay out of politics — or else endorse Soeharto's next term. Abdurrahman's simultaneous leadership of two politically significant bodies — NU with its tens of millions of members and Forum Demokrasi with its bold agenda calling for change — irritated the military. Prabowo put it this way:

> Gus Dur, we can understand you leading NU and we can understand you being interested in Forum Demokrasi, what concerns us is that you should do both. We think it would be better if you chose one or the other rather than trying to lead both this NGO group and NU. Why don't you consider resigning?

Abdurrahman instantly replied, 'I would be glad to resign. Forum Demokrasi, its values and commitment to promoting democracy mean more to me than even NU and so it's simple, I'll resign from NU and concentrate on Forum Demokrasi'. Several days later the reply came back to Abdurrahman. 'Just forget it. You can stay on with both organisations. Don't worry about it any more.'[12]

The military was concerned that if Abdurrahman should suddenly leave NU, the next chairman might be much less open to negotiation and discussion. They knew Abdurrahman to be a moderate committed to maintaining communal harmony. He was frequently called upon to intervene in communal disputes. It was not uncommon for a military vehicle to arrive in the middle of the night at his house in Ciganjur and for Abdurrahman to be driven to an airfield and flown to East Java, Sumatra, or wherever there was unrest, in order to negotiate with the community groups. Many within the military appreciated his desire to talk through differences to achieve peace and maintain stability. Abdurrahman was well aware of the desire of certain officers to use him and found it to be an irksome relationship. Although he and his military contacts held very different political outlooks, they shared a common desire to prevent social instability and unrest.

Another thing these senior officers appreciated was Abdurrahman's opposition to the political exploitation of Islamic sentiment. What they feared most of all, at least now that the great bogey of Communism was gone, was political Islam, and the launching of ICMI had made them anxious. This was no doubt what had been intended. As the military felt themselves being played off against conservative political Muslims, they increasingly looked to moderate figures such Abdurrahman to support their position. Abdurrahman, by this stage, had a good working relationship not just with Benny Murdani but also with several other key figures. Privately he expressed extreme distaste for their violence and 'their bloody hands' as he put it, but he also acknowledged that it was necessary to have good contacts in the military. 'It is better,' he would state, 'for them to come and talk to me before they take action than simply to start shooting. At least if they include us in discussions we have a chance of avoiding conflict.' He explained his position in terms of his pastoral care for over 30 million people: 'Whatever else happens my priority is to keep these people from trouble and to try and turn their enemies away from hurting them.'[13]

The next month, in April 1992, Forum Demokrasi organised a *Halal bi Halal*, a meeting to mark the end of Ramadan. It was broken up by police, drawing incredulous responses even from some Golkar politicians.[14] A week later Abdurrahman was stopped by police when he tried to address a PPP rally. Sudomo, the powerful Co-ordinating Minister for Political and Security Affairs, announced that Soeharto had asked him to 'monitor' the Forum's activities.[15]

When interviewed by Ramage in June that year, Abdurrahman said: 'Nahdlatul Ulama is in a very good position as the anchor of politics in Indonesia; PPP, PDI and Golkar all need us, and the Armed Forces needs us; nearly everyone needs us because of our mass base, which we utilise very prudently.'[16] In later interviews with Ramage he went on to say:

> Without it [Pancasila] we will cease to be a state ... Pancasila is a set of principles and it will live forever. It is the idea of the state that we should have, that we strive for. In this Pancasila I'll defend with my own life. Regardless of its being castrated by the Armed Forces or its being manipulated by the Muslims, or misused by both.[17]

Abdurrahman was similarly feisty and outspoken when interviewed by Adam Schwarz in late 1991 and early 1992:

> We have to have a socio-economic transformation as a first step in a long-term process of democratisation. That's why I am working to create an awareness of democracy within Nahdlatul Ulama. I'm convinced that the silent majority in Indonesia is pluralistic in attitude. If we can get the government to loosen its grip on society, Indonesians will take it in their hands to counteract the sectarians and maintain the unity of the nation ... Given time and legitimacy [for the neo-modernist approach], we can make Islam a positive force in Indonesia.[18]

Articulating his vision for the development of Muslim society and Indonesia more broadly, Abdurrahman was openly critical of Soeharto's ploy of using ICMI for short-term advantage:

> For Soeharto, ICMI is a short-term marriage of convenience. He thinks he can control [ICMI modernists] if they go too far. I'm afraid the strategy will backfire ... Moderate Muslims will win if the system is free but the problem is that Soeharto is giving help to the militants ... We need to develop a full religious tolerance based on freedom of faith. Instead Soeharto is giving an opening to a certain group of Muslims, most especially to the militants who propose Islam as the solution to all the problems of modernisation.
>
> Abdurrahman was given to frank commentary. His critics tended to dismiss his outspokenness as sheer recklessness, and sometimes they were right. Behind his cavalier façade, however, a shrewd political mind was constantly calculating just how far he could push the limits. Abdurrahman wanted to send a message to Soeharto and, knowing that many in the military shared his concerns, he reasoned that he could safely decry the foolishness, as he saw it, of giving hardline Islamists sanctuary within ICMI. Even so, he almost went too

far in his comments to Schwarz in March 1992, published in *A Nation in Waiting* in mid-1994: 'In an interview in March 1992, Wahid was no less forthcoming when I asked him why he thought his views were being disregarded by Soeharto. Two reasons, he said, stupidity, and because Soeharto does not want to see anyone he doesn't control grow strong.'[19]

If Abdurrahman was outspoken in his criticism of ICMI and certain ICMI intellectuals he labelled as sectarian, they for their part were no less forceful in their criticism of him. Amien Rais said to Schwarz in 1992: 'I fail to understand why Wahid thinks the way that he does. Wahid is not only exaggerating differences among Muslims but he is distorting our positions and sowing disinformation ... I believe in Islam and democracy too, a democracy that allows freedom of religion, press and speech.'[20] Similarly, ICMI activist and well-known conservative Sri Bintang Pamungkas commented to Schwarz, 'Why should minorities be in more need of protection than the majority? The suggestion that Muslims are opposed to Pancasila is created by those who do not want Muslims to be great.'[21]

Late in 1992, as if to confirm Abdurrahman's warnings about increasing sectarian tensions, there was a spate of church burnings in East Java and North Sumatra. Abdurrahman was called upon by Benny Murdani to intervene and mediate between communities in the troubled district. Ironically, although it would appear that such incidents were often instigated or engineered by hard-line elements in the military, other military officers respected the consistency of Abdurrahman's position and appreciated his intervention in time of need.

Abdurrahman saw his working relationship with Benny and Try as useful. He argued that it was better for himself as leader of NU to be kept in the loop than out of it. At the very least, his links with them often enabled him to secure the safety of his members when a confrontation with the military was brewing. Nevertheless, Abdurrahman privately abhorred both Benny and Try for their penchant for cold-blooded violence. One occasion on which he was unable to help his NU members occurred in Lampung in 1989. Much like the Tanjung Priok incident in 1984, when perhaps hundreds of alleged Islamist extremists were killed at the apparent instigation of Benny, the 1989 Lampung 'incident' saw at least a hundred villagers killed. The village that was attacked had been accused of harbouring Islamist extremists; it later became clear that the real issue was land reform. When the military, on Try's orders, laid siege to the village, the menfolk escaped into the surrounding jungle; the military unmercifully attacked the women and children who were left behind. Most of the villagers were NU members. Such incidents did not stop Abdurrahman from maintaining his connection with both Try and Benny, but they weighed heavily on his mind.[22]

THE JUNE 1992 ELECTIONS AND SOEHARTO'S NEW CABINET

Abdurrahman was not the only one who felt the pressure from Soeharto in the lead-up to the sitting of MPR in March 1993. By then PPP had become stagnant and no longer presented a significant challenge to Soeharto's authority. In the 1982 general elections PPP had polled 28 per cent. Two years later NU withdrew itself from the party, and in the next election in 1987 the party polled just 16 per cent. Despite extensive campaigning in the 1992 elections, PPP polled just over 17 per cent, a disappointingly modest increase. Morale was at an all-time low; even those within the PPP jokingly referred to it as 'not united, not a development and not a party'.[23] At the same time Islamist conservatives who had previously gone beyond PPP to express their frustration with the Soeharto regime were now being accommodated within ICMI.

The only serious element opposing Soeharto in Indonesian society now, apart from Abdurrahman and NU, was PDI. Soeharto was concerned that Abdurrahman might move towards an alliance with PDI. Abdurrahman had withdrawn NU support from PPP and declared his opposition to sectarian or professional parties in general, so there was reason to believe that he might attempt to direct NU support to PDI. In fact, in the 1992 elections, Abdurrahman had gone out of his way to lower tensions with the government by directing national support towards Golkar. At the time many were critical of him, arguing that he was seeking to spoil the position of PPP out of spite, or in order to prove his own position right. Others, however, interpreted the move as being a political ploy to take pressure off himself just when it was reaching a peak. In any case, following the 1992 elections PDI remained strong and Soeharto continued to be concerned about the possibility of an alliance between NU and PDI.

In October 1992 the three political parties met to prepare the agenda for the MPR session which was to be held the following March.

PDI activists were exerting strong pressure on party leadership to push for reforms. As a result the party decided not to nominate its presidential candidate until after its January 1993 national congress, even though all the other MPR factions had already nominated Soeharto.

Soeryadi, leader of PDI, was under enormous pressure from both sides. This intensified when Guruh Soekarnoputra, son of the late president and a popular party campaigner, offered himself as an alternative presidential candidate. On 14 January, at the conclusion of the party congress, Soeryadi announced that the party would be officially nominating Soeharto. Many observers claimed that Soeryadi had come under intense pressure from the regime, particularly by way of key military figures. In July 1993 when, under pressure from ABRI, another party congress was held to elect a new chairman, Soeryadi's expected nomination as chairman was blocked and an interim leadership established.[24]

Several months later, at a second congress in December 1993, there was a surprise: Megawati Soekarnoputri, an older sister of Guruh, was elected as the party rode on a surge of Sukarno nostalgia. By this time Sukarnoism had become a codeword for democratic reform.[25] The government and the military were caught offside. Having ousted Soeryadi, they now had somebody much less to their liking. Initially the government refused to acknowledge Megawati, but by the end of the month conceded it had no choice but to deal with her. Even so, having acknowledged her, the government manipulated the formation of Megawati's board in order to weaken her position.

Across town a similar tussle for reform was going on within Golkar, where Soeharto, until the late 1980s, had been seen by many as a popular and respected president. By the 1990s many former supporters and close colleagues of Soeharto were speaking out against him, arguing that Golkar needed to be reformed in order to act as a viable political force and corrective influence upon the government. It generally was not Soeharto himself but his children and their increasing prominence in business activities which angered people. Soeharto was criticised for being indulgent and blind to the ways in which his children's unfettered ambitions were undoing years of hard work. At the same time, reformists such as Akbar Tandjung and Marzuki Darusman argued that an increasingly well-informed society was now expecting more from its political leaders than had been delivered in the past, and that Golkar needed to be transformed into a proper modern political party with all that that entailed.

One of the aims of the reformers had been to have former Vice-President Sudharmono elected as party chairman. At the Golkar congress in October 1992 they were blocked by ABRI hard-liners, who pushed instead for a Soeharto loyalist, Harmoko, to be elected, along with a new 45-member executive packed with friends, relatives and other loyalists, including Soeharto's daughter Tutut as vice-chairman and son Bambang as treasurer. 'It's nepotism on a grand scale,' said Marzuki 'It's simply no longer realistic to expect Golkar to ever be independent of Soeharto.'[26]

On 17 March 1993, following the sitting of the MPR, a new cabinet was formed and Soeharto was sworn in for his sixth term as president. Somewhat surprisingly, very few ICMI activists had been rewarded with positions in Soeharto's new cabinet and, despite intensive campaigning and lobbying by many within ICMI, Habibie had not become vice-president. Instead Soeharto swore in Try Sutrisno as his new vice-president. Some thought that Soeharto might have intended to appoint former Vice-President Sudharmono to a second term. However, Sudharmono was unpopular with many within ABRI (his military background was as a legal officer and he had no combat experience); he was not considered to be a good ally in cabinet for ABRI. Many interpreted Try's appointment as having been forced by Benny Murdani, while others argued that Soeharto had possibly been intending to appoint Try as vice-president all along.

Soeharto also appointed Faisal Tanjung, who was known as one of the 'green generals' with Islamist sympathies, as the new military commander. Faisal Tanjung's appointment was well accepted by Islamist conservatives within ICMI. The elevation of General Faisal Tanjung to head the armed forces was not good news for Abdurrahman, although Try Sutrisno's promotion to the vice-presidency, despite his popularity with conservative Muslims, did not present a problem. Try, who like most vice-presidents before him, was a former personal adjutant of Soeharto, had close relations with Benny, and Benny maintained good relations with Abdurrahman. In 1988 Try had replaced Benny as head of the armed forces when Benny was effectively demoted to become Minister for Defence. In 1993 Benny was dropped from the cabinet line-up altogether — a final confirmation of his fall from grace with Soeharto. Nevertheless, Benny was far from having lost all influence and was still widely regarded as a kingmaker. His years of service in Indonesian military intelligence had secured for him numerous supporters and friends throughout the military. He was to repeatedly use these to good advantage, even when he had entered into a period of silent opposition to Soeharto.

A COMPLEX RELATIONSHIP

Following his re-election in March 1993 to his sixth term as president, Soeharto seemed more relaxed and political tensions began to ease. Confident once more, Soeharto decided to experiment again with *keterbukaan*, or 'openness'. As before, the new openness was met with a wave of student and worker protests and expressions of dissidence, and Soeharto quickly reassessed his strategy.

At the best of times Soeharto was disinclined to overlook or forget challenges to his authority. And with protests increasing as quickly as he relaxed his tight controls, Soeharto was not about to ease up his pressure on Abdurrahman. The president made it clear that he was determined to ensure that Abdurrahman would not be re-elected, or given any major position of authority within NU, even though Abdurrahman had already indicated that he did not intend to seek re-election as chairman of NU at the coming 1994 *muktamar*.[27]

Abdurrahman's relationship with Soeharto had always been complex. In this relationship, as in many others, Soeharto typically played a double game. As he was with many who challenged his authority, Soeharto was polite to Abdurrahman while at the same time working to undermine his position.

Early in their relationship Soeharto came to the conclusion that if he could not easily intimidate Abdurrahman into doing what he wanted him to do, he might be able to buy his support, or at least get him to tone down his critical line. In 1992 Abdurrahman's new house in Ciganjur was completed. Years earlier the opportunity had arisen for Abdurrahman to buy a plot large enough to build, not just a house, but also a *pesantren* complex. It had been his dream to settle his family into Ciganjur, and when he stepped down from NU, to run a *pesantren*. He poured all of his savings and his inheritance into the purchase of the land, but even that had been insufficient; he had then been forced to rely upon the good graces of his brothers and sisters to assist him in the project. They generously gave him much of their share of their inheritance to help purchase the land in Ciganjur and to assist Abdurrahman and Nuriyah to move into their own home. Building the house had been a difficult process. As chairman of NU Abdurrahman did not draw a salary or stipend so, apart from his inheritance from his mother and the generosity of his siblings, he had relied upon gifts from a wide range of friends and well-wishers. This was not considered unusual as it was typical for *pesantren* to be built, at least in part, on the basis of goodwill gifts from well-to-do members of society.

As work on Abdurrahman's house progressed, he reached a stage where he had completely exhausted all of his resources. Soeharto, who had Abdurrahman closely monitored and was aware of the situation, intervened and offered a gift of money to help complete the project. In the end Soeharto eventually contributed about one-third of the costs of the building project, allowing the house to be finished and for work on the *pesantren* to be started.[28] In the late 1980s, even before the house was built, Soeharto, who was in the midst of a massive program of mosque-building across the nation, arranged for a new mosque to be built in Ciganjur in Abdurrahman's *pesantren* complex. As a result a modern mosque of moderate size was built in the centre of the compound, right in front of Abdurrahman's house.[29] A small plaque inside the mosque acknowledges that it is one of the hundreds built as part of the government mosque-building program. No doubt Soeharto had hoped that these acts of generosity might at least buy a modicum of support from Abdurrahman. Soeharto was to be bitterly disappointed.

A RUDE INTERRUPTION

By 1993 things seemed to have settled down a bit for Abdurrahman and Nuriyah. They had moved into their new home in Ciganjur and were enjoying the new setting. Soeharto's renewed promotion of 'openness' suggested that he had become more relaxed following his March re-election. Abdurrahman was also feeling more relaxed and positive about the future. He looked forward to 1995 when he could step down from NU and retire to his *pesantren*. For the eight years that he had led NU he'd had little time for writing and he was looking forward to the opportunity of becoming a public intellectual again.

But something happened that year to disturb Abdurrahman's sense of normality and confidence in the future. Abdurrahman's wife and his mother were travelling in a mini-van along one of Jakarta's toll roads when suddenly, without any warning, the mini-van swerved across the road and toppled over, rolling several times. A tyre on the mini-van had blown out and caused the vehicle to lurch violently out of control. Outside peak hours, traffic on Jakarta's tollways travels at close to one hundred kilometres an hour. The mini-van had been travelling at around this speed when it had rolled, and the damage to the lightly built vehicle was horrendous. Abdurrahman's mother was badly bruised but appeared to have escaped with a broken leg and some other minor injuries. Nuriyah, however, had suffered serious spinal trauma and required weeks of hospitalisation, followed by what proved to be years of therapy. Her doctors said that she would most likely spend the rest of her life in a wheelchair and would never be able to walk again. Abdurrahman was badly shaken. Ironically, Nuriyah had always been worried about his health and Abdurrahman had never given much thought to hers, which until the accident had always been good. Now her future — their future — appeared uncertain.

In 1994 Abdurrahman's mother passed away. She had never really recovered from injuries sustained in the accident the previous year. In particular, some minor wounds failed to heal because they had become infected and proved unresponsive to antibiotics. Her passing affected Abdurrahman almost as much as Nuriyah's injuries had. Abdurrahman had always listened to his mother and respected her. She, along with Nuriyah, had been a mainstay in his life; now she was gone, and Nuriyah was undergoing a long and painful course of therapy. Abdurrahman was devastated.

More controversy erupted when Abdurrahman announced his support for the previous secretary-general of PPP, Matori Abdul Djalil, to become the new PPP chair. Abdurrahman was opposed in this view by both his uncle Yusuf Hasyim and Idham Chalid, NU's former chair. Compounding matters was the news that Abdurrahman had been chosen to become an international president of an NGO based in New York, the World Conference on Religion and Peace. This appointment received surprisingly wide coverage in the Indonesian press, and many people were openly critical of his association with such an organisation.

Abdurrahman's interest in inter-faith dialogue continued unabated throughout his tenure at the helm of NU. In the late 1980s and early 1990s he sought out opportunities for exchange and dialogue between Indonesia's faith communities and leaders of religious communities around the world. He saw these exchanges as part of the process of educating Indonesian society about modernity and democracy, as well as part of his mission as leader of NU to set an example of how Muslim society should develop. He was proud that Islam in Indonesia was, on the whole, more liberal and tolerant than many other expressions of

Islam around the world. When travelling abroad he was keen to encourage greater interest in and more sympathetic understanding of Islam generally, also seeking to encourage fellow Muslim leaders to engage in dialogue. In Indonesia his greatest ally was his close friend Djohan Effendi. Djohan had continued working on inter-faith dialogue ever since his student days in the early 1970s, and the two frequently collaborated on projects.

Abdurrahman was widely respected for his liberal ideas and his championing of tolerance. In 1993 he received an invitation to go to Manila in August to receive an award recognising his contribution to inter-faith understanding. This was hardly the first award he had been given, but it pleased him more than any that he had received so far. The award that he was invited to the Philippines to receive was the Ramon Magsaysay Award, widely regarded as being 'Asia's Nobel Prize'. The citation recognised his contribution for 'guiding Southeast Asia's largest Muslim organisation as a force for religious tolerance, fair economic development and democracy'.

If Abdurrahman's efforts to promote understanding between religious communities earned him praise from some quarters, it also earned him condemnation from others. Many conservative Muslims viewed his eagerness to engage in dialogue with other faith communities as a sign that his commitment to Islam was suspect. Even before he became chairman of NU in 1984, Abdurrahman was regarded by many as excessively liberal and insufficiently concerned with defending Islam. For his critics, his activities since becoming chairman only proved that their initial suspicions about him were well founded. In the 1990s his constant criticism of Islamists within ICMI, his warnings about the danger of linking sectarian sentiment with party politics, and his public association with non-Muslims through Forum Demokrasi only confirmed for many that he was not a true friend of Islam.

Further fuelling controversy was Abdurrahman's acceptance of an invitation to visit Israel in October 1994 to witness the signing of Israel's new peace treaty with Jordan. After visiting Jerusalem and touring Israel, accompanied by Djohan Effendi, he returned home and recommended to the government that it should investigate opening diplomatic ties with Israel. The condemnation from Islamist conservatives was predictable; perhaps just as predictable was the flurry of criticism that came from conservative elements within NU such as Idham Chalid and Yusuf Hasyim. Abdurrahman seemed to completely disregard such criticism, even though he was to report to his members in the *muktamar* in November that year. Some friends and admirers spoke warmly of his boldness while others, including many friends, declared him to be hopelessly reckless.

ABDURRAHMAN FACES RE-ELECTION

Abdurrahman faced considerable uncertainty and unrest when he returned from Israel. Megawati and PDI were being squeezed harder as the regime feared more than ever that NU would link up with PDI. It was clear that Soeharto was personally worried that Abdurrahman would attempt to stand for a third five-year term at the head of NU, and that he intended to make sure that this could not happen.

Abdurrahman had talked casually about the possibility of retiring from the Tanfidziyah and taking up a position on the Syuriah. In October he floated an idea for abolishing the Tanfidziyah and bringing all NU control under the one Syuriah; however, this proposal did not get far.[30] He argued that there was a danger that political interests would once again hijack NU, only this time they would be interests aligned with the regime. Soeharto was angry with Abdurrahman for discouraging NU members from becoming active within ICMI. Through ICMI the president had successfully co-opted his most militant critics and won over almost half of the Muslim *umat*. It irritated him immensely that one man should be able to stymie his best efforts to win over all of the *umat*.

Abdurrahman was, of course, aware of this. He also knew that Soeharto would probably be forced to step aside within the coming five years and that his demotion would precipitate a turbulent political transition. Consequently, when Abdurrahman announced, only weeks before the November *muktamar*, that he had changed his mind and would stand for a third term, few were surprised. He sought to justify his eleventh-hour about-face by saying that he was concerned about what might happen to NU in the prevailing political climate and about the impending end of the Soeharto regime. 'There are stormy waters ahead,' he reasoned, 'and more than ever NU needed a seasoned captain at the wheel.'

While many welcomed his change of mind, others, for various reasons, were critical of his decision to stand again. PPP activists and politicians within NU felt that, for no good reason, Abdurrahman had thrown away the opportunity for NU to be a potent political force. Many were also critical of his management style and pointed to the raft of projects that had foundered during his tenure. These included a pineapple cannery, a tapioca plant, a freshwater fish farm, and lastly and most importantly the joint venture between NU and the Bank Summa.[31] When the latter was launched Abdurrahman had spoken in grandiose terms of having two thousand branches by the end of the decade. By 1994 there were only twelve, although, given the rustic nature of NU, the venture might still be regarded as a moderate success.

In late 1991 Abdurrahman's venture in promoting the alliance between the Chinese-backed banks and NU had begun to go awry. Finally, in late 1992, Bank Summa was forced to close, declaring it had problems with mismanagement at the head office. In April 1993 Bank Summa's shares were purchased by the financial body behind the Surabaya daily newspaper *Jawa Pos*. Abdurrahman claimed that in March of that year he had been told by former Minister for Finance Johannes Sumarlin that Soeharto had instructed the Finance Ministry 'to place obstacles in the path of NU–Summa banks'. Most observers of the time were quick to blame the failure of Abdurrahman's somewhat grandiose, if laudable, scheme on traditional NU mismanagement. No doubt that was a key element in the bank's failure, but it also seems plausible that the bank was actively undermined by the Soeharto government.[32] Even so, the takeover of the Bank Summa's shareholding by the *Jawa Pos* group had been reasonably successful and to have established twelve functioning branches was not a bad achievement, especially given NU's poor record of economic management. It might seem unfair to lay the blame for the failure of the other projects at Abdurrahman's feet, but as NU's chief executive officer he should, at least, have observed stricter oversight of such ventures. His failure to do so suggested that he was not a gifted or conscientious administrator.

One of the main reasons given for criticising Abdurrahman's leadership of the organisation was that he had frequently placed the organisation on a collision course with the Soeharto regime. Through his civil society activities, which had exploited his mass base within NU, he had risked making the organisation an enemy of the state. Many questioned the wisdom of Abdurrahman's political manoeuvrings and outspoken criticism of the regime.

Despite all this criticism, it appeared that the majority of the organisation still supported him. Certainly most of the young people, both the younger *kiai* and their students, seemed to be firmly on his side. They contended that, for all his failings, he had brought new life to the organisation. Under Abdurrahman the NU once again had become a force both in religious and civil society. Without him, they argued, it would have continued to sink into stagnation, decline and eventual death. Few wanted to go back to the NU of Idham Chalid. Under Abdurrahman the organisation may not have been managed well, but at least it was no longer moribund or divided. Many of the young people felt that the reform of religious thought and practice that Abdurrahman had encouraged was one of his greatest contributions. They were concerned that if he was not re-elected such reforms might be brought to a halt even before they were fully in place.

Abdurrahman's strongest opposition seemed likely to come from outside the organisation. In principle, his re-election was an internal affair; in practice, it seemed likely that the government and the military would seek to play a major role. After all, in every other comparable large organisation or political party, the government had always been able to get its way. Initially, it appeared as if the regime would leave NU to sort matters out for itself. Initial statements by the government suggested that there might even be moderate support for Abdurrahman. State Secretary Moerdiono, for example, privately assured NU leaders that the president had no objections to Abdurrahman's re-election and would not interfere with *muktamar* proceedings.

An anti-Abdurrahman campaign, however, quickly picked up pace in the weeks prior to the *muktamar*. It became known as the ABG campaign, the initials standing for *asal bukan Gus Dur*, literally, 'so long as it's not Gus Dur'. One of the key figures behind the campaign was Lieutenant-General Hartono, head of the influential ABRI Social and Political Affairs Section. He was joined in his opposition to Abdurrahman by Golkar chairman, Harmoko; the Minister for Religious Affairs, Tamizi Tahir; and B. J. Habibie. There were also clear signs that Soeharto's eldest daughter, Tutut, was one of the driving forces behind the effort to topple Abdurrahman. For his part, Abdurrahman was cautious in identifying those behind the ABG campaign. Publicly, he blamed ICMI, causing some to dismiss his comments as simply more 'ICMI bashing'. When speaking in private, however, his analysis was more sharply drawn. He identified links between certain elements and individuals in ICMI, such as Adi Sasono, Din Syamsuddin and Amir Santosa, and ABRI's so-called green generals, namely Feisal Tanjung, Hartono, Syarwan Hamid and Prabowo Subianto, working together with Tutut. Hefner observes:

In public comments after the congress, Wahid blamed ICMI for the campaign against him. In private he was more specific, saying Din Syamsuddin and Amir Santosa (both of the CPDS) had joined forces with Adi Sasono in the campaign to unseat him. Although he was well aware of the support provided by Feisal Tanjung, Hartono and Mbak Tutut to Hasan's initiative, Wahid made a point of *not* mentioning their participation. To attack Mbak Tutut would invite the wrath of the president. To attack Feisal or Hartono would violate the armed forces' first commandment: that no matter how great the tensions between its various factions, military laundry should never be aired in public. Wahid's identification of ICMI as the force behind the campaign to allowed him to fend off his attackers without degrading his relationship with the president or alienating fence-sitting members of the armed forces.[33]

Three alternative candidates were put forward by Abdurrahman's critics: former NU board member Fahmi Saifuddin, Chalid Mawardi and Abu Hasan. Unlike the first two Abu Hasan was relatively unknown in NU, although he had already established a reputation as a generous donor and patron. He was a wealthy entrepreneur from Jambi, Sumatra, who had business links with the president's family through shipping, construction and trade. It seemed likely that his strongest support would come from the outer island branches where such patronage was always appreciated. During the course of the *muktamar* the other two opponents dropped away and Abu Hasan emerged as the prime contender. Although, in certain respects an unlikely choice for NU chairman (he had, for example, none of Abdurrahman's religious qualifications), it seemed that he had some backing in the government and military. Hundreds of thousands of dollars, perhaps more, appeared to be spread around in support of his campaign.

Was Soeharto playing his usual double game? He had given positive indications through Moerdiono that he was supporting Abdurrahman; however, he also seemed to be actively engineering a campaign against him. The real situation became much clearer when, as usual, Soeharto was invited to open the *muktamar* and give the initial speech. Significantly, this time Abdurrahman was placed three rows from the front and was not greeted formally by Soeharto. Although clearly a deliberate snub, it was publicly dismissed as an oversight. Almost half of the time at the *muktamar* was taken up with addresses from ministers and armed forces personnel. General Faisal Tanjung, the armed forces commander, addressed the assembly along with ten government ministers. The meeting was finally closed by Vice-President Try Sutrisno. By this time the delegates were heartily sick of speeches from ministers, and Try received none of the rapturous welcome of five years earlier.

This *muktamar* in Cipasung, outside the West Java town of Tasikmalaya, was a busy affair. As usual there were sideshows and stalls along the main arena, while most of the meetings took place under a large canvas pavilion erected in the central courtyard of the *pesantren*. This time, however, the heavy military presence made a marked difference. At least fifteen hundred personnel in uniform were deployed, along with more than one hundred intelligence officers posted to monitor affairs.

Tension rose markedly towards the final day when voting on the chairmanship was due. Participants attending on that day had to pass through a military check before entering the *muktamar* grounds. Once inside they were virtually sealed in, as the grounds were surrounded by soldiers and armoured personnel carriers. Ministers and ABRI officials came and left by military helicopter. On the final night of the *muktamar*, Abdurrahman jokingly thanked the army for lending extra troops to Banser, the uniformed 'troops' of NU's youth wing Ansor. It appeared that many of the fit young men patrolling the *muktamar* grounds in Ansor uniform were in fact ABRI personnel.

The 'anyone but Gus Dur' forces pulled out all stops. Many NU branches, particularly those from the outer islands which made up the great majority of branches, were offered significant financial inducements to support Abu Hasan. These were especially effective because a large proportion of the board members from outer island branches were government servants who could be easily intimidated by the threat of sacking or demotion. Attempts were also made to control the media, with newspapers favourable to Abdurrahman blocked from entering Cipasung and the *muktamar* grounds. There were also many incidents of misreporting and misquoting of NU supporters by newspapers like *Republika*, the daily run by ICMI.

As was expected, Abdurrahman was cross-examined about his support for controversial policies and issues such as his recent visit to Israel. With characteristic eloquence he defended his position and appeared to have generally won over the majority of his critics. This time, however, he was much less ebullient than normal. Gone were most of his witty asides, replaced with a much more sober and serious demeanour. As the level of opposition to him became clear, so the level of tension increased. In particular the young NU members began to worry desperately about the future of the organisation without Abdurrahman at the helm. A mood of depression descended upon many as they considered it inevitable that Abdurrahman's re-election would be blocked by the efforts of the regime.

In the initial round of voting Abdurrahman received 157 votes, Abu Hasan 136, Fahmi Saifuddin 17 and Chalid Mawardi 6. This brought Abu Hasan within striking distance of Abdurrahman. It seemed almost inevitable that Chalid Mawardi's six votes would go to Abu Hasan, so everything hinged on the seventeen delegates who had initially supported Fahmi Saifuddin. Abdurrahman's supporters were in disarray. They had initially expected stiff opposition but nevertheless predicted that he would gain 65 per cent of the vote; instead, he had not even achieved 50 per cent in the first round. Old *kiai* broke down and cried while the young men paced nervously. Some of the senior *kiai* closest to Abdurrahman retired to quietly pray for God's intervention. It was well past midnight before counting had begun; it did not conclude until three hours later.

Everything hinged on these final few hours of the *muktamar*. If Abu Hasan was victorious it seemed likely that the government would have its own way with NU and intellectual vitality would be quashed. For the younger people, this vote represented a make-or-break point. If Abdurrahman lost, they would turn their backs on the organisation and channel their energies elsewhere. Many argued that without Abdurrahman there was no future for NU.

The final voting took place in the large main assembly hall that, on this final evening, was jam-packed. The atmosphere was charged. Throughout the early hours of Tuesday morning no one knew what to expect; and by 3 am, as the final vote counting approached an end, the tension was palpable.

A crowd of anxious young members gathered outside the door to the main auditorium listening to the vote counting over the loud-speaker. It appeared that anything was possible if the vote went against Abdurrahman. The compound was surrounded by ABRI personnel and armoured troop carriers. It would be difficult for Abdurrahman's supporters to leave the compound, and the prospect of conflict erupting within it seemed all too real.

Finally, the result was announced. Abdurrahman had gained 174 votes against Abu Hasan's 142 votes. A wave of euphoria broke over the assembly. In the crowd outside the assembly hall young men erupted into spontaneous yelping and cheers of relief. Dozens formed a circle, rushing round and round and calling out in English, 'Soeharto has to go, Soeharto has to go'.

This page intentionally left blank

PART 5

POLITICS, REFORM AND THE PRESIDENCY

This page intentionally left blank

NINE

CONTENDING WITH SOEHARTO, 1994-1998

THE ANTI-GUS DUR CAMPAIGN COLLAPSES

Abdurrahman emerged, triumphant but hardly unscathed, from NU's *muktamar* in November 1994, although Soeharto's regime had mounted strong, intimidating opposition to his re-election as chairman. Abdurrahman declared he had won 'a victory over money, slander and intimidation'. Although this assessment is rather melodramatic, it's hard to argue with. He had achieved something unprecedented in Soeharto's New Order. He stood up to the full might of Soeharto and his regime and prevailed despite their best efforts to thwart him.

It was, of course, not clear-cut. Things never were in Soeharto's New Order. The regime was obliged to use restraint, or at least work indirectly, in its efforts to block Abdurrahman, for fear of a backlash from NU's masses. At a person-to-person level, Soeharto's snubbing of Abdurrahman at the opening ceremony of the *muktamar* was nothing compared with his cool demeanour towards Abdurrahman for two years after the *muktamar* that made it clear he was unhappy with Abdurrahman's victory. Although he met with several individual leaders, Soeharto refused to meet with the new NU board and especially with its chairman.[1]

In the final days of the *muktamar*, the anti-Abdurrahman forces had channelled all of their energies through Abu Hasan (after the other 'anyone but Gus Dur' candidates had dropped out of contention). After the elections Abu Hasan was encouraged to persist in his opposition to Abdurrahman. His first move was to claim that he had the right to the deputy's position on the central board. After all, he argued, he had garnered 45 per cent of the votes, and there was a tradition within NU that the loser got a consolation prize in the form of the deputy's position. Abdurrahman refused Abu Hasan outright, even though Abu Hasan had been correct in pointing to the NU tradition of being gracious in defeat and accommodating opponents.[2] The nature of Abu Hasan's opposition made it almost certain that, given half a chance, he and his appointees would move to destabilise the central board.

Evidence of the continuing antagonism came during the following months with efforts to try to organise an extraordinary *muktamar*. Ultimately this initiative failed because the new constitution stipulated that to call an extraordinary *muktamar* the support of 200 out of 306 branches was required. At the same time, Abu Hasan pursued a strategy of running a rival NU central board which included many of the figures from the old 'Cipete group' close to former NU chairman Idham Chalid.[3] This group received considerable backing from Abdurrahman's opponents in the army and government as well as from ICMI, but ultimately it failed. In the traditional world of NU the rival board had neither constitutional nor cultural authority, and only a group of long-time enemies of Abdurrahman took it seriously. Finally in desperation, in late 1995, Abu Hasan attempted to sue Abdurrahman. This bid failed and ultimately Abu Hasan was bankrupted. Much of the money that had been poured into his campaign had come from his own pocket. His contract with anti-Abdurrahman figures within ABRI, such as General Hartono, was based on an understanding that he would be repaid handsomely for his campaign against Abdurrahman. When he sought payment, however, his ABRI backers refused to reimburse him, arguing that he had been contracted to defeat Abdurrahman and, having failed, deserved no payment whatsoever.

Several years later a demoralised and broken Abu Hasan sought and received reconciliation with Abdurrahman, following which Abu Hasan accompanied Abdurrahman on a tour of several NU districts and appeared on stage with him at NU rallies. Abdurrahman explained that he was happy to reconcile with Abu Hasan because this was the culturally proper way of handling such disputes in NU; what is more, he argued, Abu Hasan had merely been used as a pawn by others. Even though the reconciliation did not prove long-lived, Abdurrahman's acceptance of Abu Hasan's request for forgiveness was approved by the senior *kiai* and the NU members, who saw it as further proof of Abdurrahman's standing as a religious leader.

Although Abu Hasan eventually dropped his campaign against Abdurrahman, others continued to attack him at every opportunity. Leading them was Abdurrahman's uncle, Yusuf Hasyim, together with former NU chairman Idham Chalid. In September 1995 Yusuf Hasyim formed the Forum for the Sons and Daughters of NU Founders. This oddly named organisation was intended to make the most of the authority that Yusuf Hasyim and his friends had on the basis of their blood links with the founding generation of NU. As an anti-Abdurrahman vehicle, however, it ultimately failed. Just like the alternative NU central board, no one took it seriously, despite support from certain figures within ICMI and the army, including General Hartono.

Abdurrahman was unfazed by the continuing opposition to him and correctly judged that it would soon dissipate of its own accord. Some interpreted this as justified confidence, some as arrogance; others, in accordance with traditional Javanese understandings of power, saw it as a sign of strength.

THE ANTI-MEGAWATI CAMPAIGN BEGINS

Throughout 1995 and into 1996 Abdurrahman worked closely with Megawati, and she became dependent upon him for guidance and encouragement. Megawati had found herself thrown into the leadership of the PDI quite unexpectedly and was uncertain how to marshal and channel the considerable support that she was receiving. Although Megawati was not a *santri* Muslim, her *abangan* mystical outlook overlapped Abdurrahman's Sufistic approach to the unseen world. Where many modernists such as Amien Rais could never feel comfortable with the religiosity of *abangan* Javanese such as Megawati, Abdurrahman and many of his fellow traditionalists found it easy to establish a point of contact.

Megawati was not an intellectual and had no thought-out political platform or clearly articulated political vision, but she intuitively pursued a path which she saw as supporting her father's ideals. Abdurrahman arguably had a much stronger grasp of Sukarno's political philosophy than did Megawati, something which she not only understood but also respected. He rejected Sukarno's leftist excesses, as he saw them, but clung to the core elements of his philosophy: deep concern for the *rakyat*, or the ordinary people; nationalism inspired by the desire to transform society that it might become both richer and fairer; and the dream of building an Indonesia that was at once united and comfortable with its plural nature.

Abdurrahman was, in most respects, much less romantic than Sukarno and certainly more cynical about the practical working out of Marxist thought than Sukarno had been, but he shared the former president's passion for building a just society in which wealth was distributed equitably. Megawati regularly consulted with Abdurrahman and he counselled her on the necessity of thinking strategically in confronting the Soeharto regime. He argued that it was vital to recognise when to push forward and when to pull back. By late 1995, however, serious differences had began to emerge between the two. Megawati, excited by the possibilities latent in PDI's passionate millions, was keen to maintain pressure on Soeharto. To her, and to many in her party, this was more than simply a matter of politics. It was bound up with her desire to avenge her father's suffering at the hands of Soeharto and his New Order regime. As a young woman she had seen her father die a broken man — a sad shell of the larger-than-life extrovert who had enthralled the nation for decades, a prisoner in his own house. Abdurrahman, however, was urging restraint and warning Megawati about the threat of a violent crackdown by the military. Abdurrahman's contacts within the military were more extensive than Megawati's and he was receiving feedback that hard-line elements in the military would eventually strike back if Megawati continued to allow herself to be presented as an immediate threat to Soeharto.

It had never, of course, been Soeharto's intention for Megawati to become leader of PDI. Ironically, it was because Soeharto considered the former leader Soeryadi to be too outspoken that he had ordered his ousting in 1993, thus opening the way for Megawati's ascent.[4] Although Megawati was deeply introverted and hardly charismatic, it quickly became clear that she was a popular leader with tremendous drawing power for PDI. Much as he had done with Abdurrahman over the previous three years, Soeharto sought to undermine Megawati by using assorted opportunists, pro-Habibie military officers and elements of ICMI to engineer dissent within her organisation and slander and intimidation from without. Throughout 1994 she was made to contend with rebel local PDI branches, many of which were controlled by the military and stacked with their appointees. Provincial governors — most notably in East Java, a heartland of both PDI and NU support — went so far as to deny her permission to address PDI rallies on the pretext that she had to first 'reconcile' with her 'critics'. The regime was working behind the scenes to orchestrate events that made reconciliation virtually impossible, while all the time government officials presented themselves as neutral arbitrators in 'internal party affairs'.[5] Matters came to a head in late December 1994 when a 'Reshuffled National PDI Executive' was formed in competition with PDI's official national board, much as Abu Hasan's NU Central Co-ordinating Executive was established to rival the official NU Board of Management. In itself this rival board was unable to dislodge Megawati from the leadership, but it did allow the regime to claim that Megawati was incapable of uniting her party's 'factions'.

In 1995 the leadership of the rival PDI board embarked on an extensive smear campaign designed to weaken Megawati's credibility and suggest that Megawati's supporters had ties with the Communist Party. Although the attacks, which continued through 1995 and into 1996, failed to dislodge Megawati, they did seriously hinder her program of reform within the party, preventing her from removing Soeharto loyalists planted in the party over many years.

The regime's efforts to discredit Megawati and Abdurrahman were bitter and nasty but there were, nevertheless, some funny moments, at least from Abdurrahman's point of view. He likes to tell of a rally in 1995 at which General Syarwan Hamid was present. At one point, in a botched attempt at intimidation, Syarwan got up to address the audience. 'I am deeply worried about this apparent alliance with Gus Dur and Megawati,' he said. 'It is not a good thing at all, it's bad for society — it's destabilising and destructive. They think that they are in the Philippines — it is as if Megawati is Corry Aquino and Gus Dur is Cardinal Sin — who do these people think they are!' To which Abdurrahman replied: 'Well, Syarwan, if Mbak Mega is Corry Aquino and I am Cardinal Jamie Sin, then who is Ferdinand Marcos?!' At which point Syarwan got up to leave the auditorium and the audience began chiming in: 'Ya Wan, Wan, who is Ferdinand Marcos Wan!'[6]

When it became clear that the campaign against Megawati was not as effective as had been hoped, Golkar undertook secret polling to assess the extent to which Megawati represented a significant threat in the upcoming general elections scheduled for early 1997. Golkar and ICMI strategists were horrified to learn that Megawati's PDI enjoyed greater popularity among voters in Central and East Java than did Soeharto's Golkar.[7] It appeared that the regime's heavy-handed attempts to destroy Megawati had only made her stronger. Stoic but quietly confident in the face of a barrage of slander and intimidation, the 'non-politician' leader of PDI was fast becoming a hero in the eyes of many ordinary Indonesians. Worried by Megawati's unexpected climb in popularity, Soeharto ordered that the campaign against her be intensified; henceforth it would be handled directly by General Feisal Tandjung and General Syarwan Hamid rather than by ICMI operatives such as Din Syamsuddin and Amir Santosa and their colleagues in Golkar's Research and Development Bureau.

Informed of the intensification of efforts to oust Megawati, Abdurrahman counselled a strategic retreat. Now was the time, he argued, for Megawati to lie low for a while. In particular it was important, he advised, that she announce publicly that she would not allow herself to be nominated as a presidential candidate to symbolically challenge Soeharto at the 1997 elections, as some were urging her to do. Abdurrahman's call for restraint was at odds with popular sentiment. By early 1996 there was growing public excitement about the potential of a partnership between Megawati and Abdurrahman. Many felt it obvious that the combination of her millions of supporters in the PDI and his millions in NU would give them the numbers to topple Soeharto. Young Indonesians, in particular, were keen to confront the regime, and they saw in Abdurrahman and Megawati the natural leaders of the reform movement.

At this point in time most modernist Muslims felt that their political voice was increasingly heard, either through PPP or through ICMI. Those involved with ICMI generally had little immediate incentive to speak out against Soeharto as it seemed that his regime was finally giving them a voice in the running of the country. Consequently, the only senior national figures speaking out for reform were the leaders of NU and PDI, along with Amien Rais; the latter, despite his senior position within ICMI and his friendships with hardline Islamists, was much more of a reformist than most of his colleagues in the senior echelons of ICMI.

MOUNTING UNEASE

By early 1996 there were ominous signs of impending trouble, especially after April when Ibu Tien, Soeharto's wife of more than forty years, died suddenly. Soeharto had depended heavily upon Tien's counsel. She was perhaps the one person he really trusted and to whom he consistently turned for advice. A naturally reclusive and distant man, he had few friends with whom he was really close, and the loss of his intimate friend and confidant seemed to destabilise him. In the weeks that followed many commented that the man who had once been a master strategist and astute manipulator of politics and power was showing signs of having lost his normally sound judgment. The sense of unease that prevailed in Indonesia turned to panic several months later when Soeharto was suddenly rushed to a health spa in Germany for medical treatment, accompanied by his extended family. The public relations of his sudden illness and evacuation to Germany was badly handled. Ministers and senior government officials squabbled in public over what was to be said about his illness. The markets were shaken up, as was the international community. As it happened, the health alarm turned out to be a false one. His problem was merely kidney stones, and he returned home later that month seemingly in fine health. Even so, to a jittery community, he seemed a changed man; when he began to move decisively against Megawati, it was difficult to know how things would turn out.

Soeharto was deeply troubled by the alliance between Abdurrahman and Megawati, in particular by their appeal among young Indonesians. He was well aware that in the following year's elections a further 20 million voters, or 20 per cent of the total voting population, would be added to the electoral roll. Indeed 60 per cent of Indonesians at that time had been born after Soeharto had come to power, and knew no other president. They had not experienced the tremendous instability of the mid-1960s, or the horrors of the Communist pogrom that followed the alleged coup of October 1965. Where older Indonesians were naturally reluctant to risk confrontation which could result in the polarisation of society, many young Indonesians, particularly students, wanted change and seemed to have little regard for the risks involved.

Soeharto's sudden flight to Germany, conspicuously accompanied by most of his immediate relatives, pushed the succession issue to the top of the agenda. Most commentators now expected that he would begin a seventh term in 1998 following elections in 1997, but would not, in all likelihood, complete it. One way or another, Indonesia seemed set for change.

In June the government ordered PDI to hold a special congress. Along with Feisal Tandjung and Syarwan Hamid, several other hard-line generals seemed to be involved, including the president's son-in-law, Prabowo Subianto. Hefner asserts that other players, contributing much of the financial support required to hold the Medan congress, were Yusuf Wanandi of the Center for Strategic and International Studies (CSIS) and senior ICMI leader Adi Sasono. Allegedly Yusuf Wanandi was keen to regain Soeharto's favour, and Adi Sasono, who had solid credentials as a community development activist, was brought in to win over PDI's Muslim members.[8] The intention in calling the congress was clear, especially after it was announced that neither Megawati nor her supporters would be allowed to participate. Soeharto and the hard-liners had had enough of Megawati leading PDI and thought that it was time for her to go. As was expected, Megawati was rolled at the congress and former PDI leader Soeryadi installed in her place. Megawati was further humiliated by being ordered to make her peace with Soeryadi and accept what happened. Not surprisingly, her supporters were furious; almost immediately hundreds of young supporters gathered at the Menteng headquarters of the party to protest.

The confident tone of Megawati's supporters soon produced a carnival atmosphere at the protest, although around the edges there were daily clashes with security forces as tension steadily increased. Each day, students at the party headquarters would hold 'freedom forums' during which they talked about the need for democratic change and freedom of speech.[9] Initially the government responded by trying to quash the media coverage, but Soeharto's handling of the whole affair seemed much less calm and astute than it had been in the past.

The Soeharto regime was, of course, by no means unaccustomed to manipulating political processes in mass organisations and parties. It had for many years exerted a controlling influence within PPP and, prior to Megawati's emergence, had little to fear from PDI. The June special congress of PDI achieved for Soeharto the objective that he had failed to obtain in the NU *muktamar* in 1994, namely the toppling of a populist opponent from the leadership of their organisation. In time, however, it proved to be a pyrrhic victory. Soeharto had made a martyr of Megawati.

When the government's campaign to limit the media damage relating to the students' demonstration appeared to be failing, preparations were made for the use of force in removing the protesters. At 5.30 on the morning of 27 July several hundred Soeryadi supporters, accompanied by what appeared to be groups of *preman* (hoodlums or gangsters), gathered outside the PDI headquarters. With the support of the police and the military, they stormed the building and drove out the Megawati loyalists. The whole event was captured on television and broadcast live to the nation. Almost spontaneously Jakarta erupted into two days of rioting, the worst that had been seem in the national capital in decades. The government immediately blamed the radical Peoples Democratic Party (Partai Demokrasi Rakyat — PRD), which they said represented 'the new Communists'. An unknown number of people were killed and 124 Megawati loyalists arrested.

Abdurrahman had been urging Megawati to back off and avoid confrontation before the inevitable occurred. 'What point is there,' he asked, 'in pushing the regime so hard that it fights back with bloody violence and we're no further advanced in our cause? Better to beat a strategic retreat and live to fight another day.' Abdurrahman was right, but only partly so.

Not content with ousting Megawati from the leadership of her party, Soeharto was determined to besmirch her reputation and create suspicion about the motives of those supporting her. Working through their partners in ICMI's right wing, Soeharto's green generals set about turning conservative Muslim opinion against Megawati and her 'Communist–PRD' supporters. True to form, Nurcholish Madjid called for calm; he bravely dismissed talk of a 'Communist threat' as being 'old language' and insisted that it was the state's failure to permit the peaceful expression of dissenting political views that lead directly to confrontations such as the one that occurred on 27 July.[10] Nevertheless, even moderates within Muhammadiyah, who were generally disgusted at the regime's efforts to use religion to stir up emotions, were caught up in the mounting hysteria about the 'threat from the left'. Amien Rais, who was now chairman of Muhammadiyah and who, despite his senior position within ICMI, had for some years now been outspoken in his criticism of Soeharto, was goaded into intemperate commentary, saying of the Megawati supporters who had occupied the Jakarta headquarter of PDI: 'The discovery of Molotov cocktails, explosives, and gasoline shows that there probably was an intention to destabilise the country in a dangerous way.'[11] Hard-line Islamists, such as Ahmad Sumargono, leader of KISDI (the Committee for World Islamic Solidarity, the radical Islamist group born out of Dewan Dakwah), and Hussein Umar from Dewan Dakwah, had no hesitation in condemning the violence as being the work of the Indonesian Communist Party (PKI), although the party had been comprehensively destroyed three decades before.[12]

On 11 August, a fortnight after the attack on Megawati's supporters, around 40 000 Muslims attended a rally in Jakarta's Senayan stadium to show their support for the government's stance. Even then, the regime did not relent, and all Muslim organisations faced strong pressure to make public statements supporting the government's position.[13] NU was one of the few large Muslim organisations not to yield, but the organisation and its members paid a high price in loss of government business contracts and intimidation by the security apparatus. Abdurrahman was accused of sympathising with PRD and the Communists; his enemies within ICMI, Dewan Dakwah and KISDI revived their campaign of propaganda against him, alleging that he was lax in his personal devotions and pro-Christian. Incredibly, he was accused of having links with both Iraq's socialist Baath party and Israel's Mossad!

COMMUNAL CONFLICT

Megawati's people were crushed but, in time, that suffering was to produce something that even the military regime of Soeharto could not stop. In the weeks after the July rioting, students and workers around the country launched campaigns of their own. Most of them were small-scale but together they represented a significant phenomenon, one that suggested that even the New Order regime was limited in the extent to which it was able to control society. Controlling isolated groups of reformist protesters was one thing, but controlling an entire society that was unravelling at the edges was quite another. And, unfortunately, it was not just protesting students that the nation had to worry about.

Indonesia had long prided itself on being a plural nation in which diverse ethnic groups and religious communities lived side-by-side, mostly without significant incidents or problems. It was commonly said that Indonesian culture was essentially tolerant and easy-going. By the mid-1990s this was beginning to change. The awful events of the mid-1960s were a reminder that no society is ever completely free from the threat of communal violence, however much the preceding decades might have given grounds for hope. Thirty years later it was beginning to look as if Indonesia might once again descend into sectarian violence.

In October 1996 anti-Christian and anti-Chinese rioting broke out in the East Java town of Situbondo. The rioting apparently followed the trial of a man charged with blaspheming the Prophet Muhammad. In the violence that ensued, twenty churches were burned, along with scores of Chinese shops, and at least five people killed. Anecdotal accounts suggested that there was much more to this violence than disputes about the outcome of a court trial and differences between religious communities. Many local people reported seeing 'muscular young men with short haircuts' speaking with 'out-of-town' accents asking for directions. Most people assumed that provocateurs from outside of the town had played a decisive role in instigating violence.

Abdurrahman suspected that the incident had been *direkayasa*, or 'engineered' — a previously rare verb which, along with the noun *provokator*, was to become widely used in the ensuing years. He had been warned by contacts in the military intelligence community in August and September that the regime was planning a new round of attacks against him. This time, it was said, an incident would be provoked in order to discredit him by showing him as unable to control the Muslim community.[14] Situbondo, a modest town located towards the eastern extremity of Java and an easy day's sailing south of the island of Madura across the shallow straits, was an ideal location to embarrass the liberal chairman of NU. Along with a significant Christian minority, it is also home to tens of thousands of Madurese settlers, who, like most of their fellow Madurese in Madura and scattered in settlements around East Java and Kalimantan, are simple, hardy folk — poor, ill-educated, and with a reputation for a feisty direct manner and for being easily provoked. The Madurese, though regarded as less tolerant and easy-going than the people of East Java, are also loyal members of NU.

When Abdurrahman went public with his suspicions about the Situbondo violence, he was scoffed at by his critics in Jakarta but not by the majority of people in East Java, who were firmly convinced that the violence had not been spontaneous. Opinion among foreign observers was divided; many were uncomfortable with anything that smacked of conspiracy theory. But many seasoned observers, familiar with the tactics of Indonesian military intelligence operations, took seriously the eyewitness accounts of provocateurs instigating the violence. Hefner, for example, notes:

> Reports from the shattered town — confirmed by journalists who visited Situbondo — indicated that most of the rioters were not local people but provocateurs ferried in aboard three trucks from outside town. In crisp black ninja uniforms the rioters moved around town unimpeded for four hours before security officials finally appeared. Their leaders blew whistles directing their troops to their targets: a truck dispensed gasoline for petrol bombs. By the time the police arrived, the rioters had moved on to neighboring towns, where they carried out a similarly well-planned program of terror against Christian churches and schools.[15]

Shortly after the violence broke out, the military flew Abdurrahman to Situbondo, a town that was the site of several large *pesantren* located deep in the heart of traditional Muslim territory. Shaken by what he saw in Situbondo, he made an emotional apology to the Christian communities there, expressing regret that some of the people who were involved in the violence had links with NU. Abdurrahman encouraged the Christian and Muslim communities there to be more diligent about communicating with each other, to pay more attention to relations between leaders. He later remarked to Christian and Muslim leaders in Situbondo, 'You have lost some beautiful churches but you gain something much more precious and that is the relationship that you now have between each other'. Catholic priest and social activist Romo Mangunwijaya later said that it was only with the Situbondo church burnings that the church really began to appreciate the need for inter-faith dialogue and the importance of building good inter-communal relations. 'Prior to that,' he said, 'only a handful of activists in the church had been calling for this.'[16] Having witnessed both large-scale violence and the potential for restoring relations through dialogue, the church hierarchy was now awake to the need for better relations between communities.

It is difficult to assess definitively the extent to which the Situbondo violence was orchestrated, but many analysts are persuaded by strong anecdotal evidence that there was a significant level of provocation from external forces and that the provocateurs were probably linked with the right-wing, hard-line generals who themselves were aligned with Islamist extremists. Looking back, the events in Situbondo were a sign of things to come.

A STRATEGIC RETREAT

Abdurrahman had managed to stand up to intense pressure from the Soeharto regime for the two years that followed his re-election to the chair of NU in November 1994. By late 1996, however, he became increasingly concerned about the level of tension building in Indonesian society and the extreme measures the Soeharto forces would use to get their way. Moreover, the campaign against the NU membership had intensified. It was not simply a matter of NU businessmen being cut out of government contracts or local leaders being questioned and intimidated by the military. It was reported that several NU youth arrested in conjunction with the Situbondo violence were tortured by the military. One youth was apparently tortured so severely that he died while in detention. Graphic details of his suffering at the hands of 'Christian officers' were revealed in interviews with him secretly taped in prison.[17]

The violent attack on Megawati's supports of 27 July had shaken Abdurrahman to the core, but it was only after the Situbondo riots that he realised that he had no choice but to negotiate a truce with Soeharto. Abdurrahman secretly made contact with Soeharto via State Secretary Moerdiono and negotiated a meeting. On 2 November 1996 Abdurrahman was attending a national meeting of Rabitah Ma'ahid Islamiyah (RMI), one of NU's daughter organisations, at a *pesantren* in Probolinggo, East Java. Unannounced, the president appeared at the entrance to the meeting hall. Abdurrahman, who was already standing there, reached out his hand to Soeharto and drew him to his side. Soeharto responded warmly and the two walked hand-in-hand to the front of the hall. The next day Abdurrahman announced that NU accepted the fact that Soeharto would serve another term as president.[18] Many within NU were delighted that the cold war with the president had finally ended, but most of Abdurrahman's friends in the democracy movement were shocked and upset. More was to come.

Several days later Abu Hasan, the bitter rival who, at the regime's behest, had spearheaded the campaign against Abdurrahman two years earlier, met with Abdurrahman to ask his forgiveness, as we have seen. This was followed two weeks later by a meeting in Situbondo between Abdurrahman and General Hartono, the general who had masterminded Abu Hasan's campaign and was known to work closely with Tutut, Soeharto's eldest daughter and presidential aspirant. The handsome, independent-minded Madurese general was known as one of the green generals but he, like Tutut, disliked Habibie and did not trust fellow green generals Prabowo Subianto and Feisal Tandjung.

Tutut had apparently wanted to accompany her father to Probolinggo on 2 November but had been blocked by Abdurrahman. Even though she had worked closely with Hartono in trying to defeat Abdurrahman two years earlier, she was now keen to reconcile with him. Her enthusiasm for rapprochement was driven by her ambition to prove herself to her father as a worthy heir to the presidency. She knew that to secure her father's backing for some future transfer of power she had first to demonstrate that she could gain the support of the masses. In recent years she had made a show of her interest in Islam. She always appeared in public with her hair wrapped in a scarf and dressed modestly in traditional *santri* outfits. The surest way for her to demonstrate to her father that she had the necessary modicum of public support to lead the nation was to secure the backing the Islamic masses. Were she close to Habibie and Amien Rais, then ICMI and Muhammadiyah would have provided all that she was looking for. Unfortunately for her presidential ambitions, however, she loathed Habibie and consequently was unlikely to have much luck with Amien either, who in any case was becoming increasingly strident in his criticism of the president and his children. Consequently, having failed to destroy Abdurrahman in 1994, she now felt compelled to court his support in 1996.

In most respects, in late 1996 Abdurrahman was the most vulnerable he had ever been. He well understood Tutut's dilemma, however, and in his dealings with her negotiated from a position of strength. Having shaken hands with Soeharto, then Abu Hasan, and then Hartono, he was ready to meet with Tutut. But first he wanted to secure some concessions. Hartono and Tutut had been generous patrons to the Centre for Policy and Development Studies (CPDS) the group of regimist intellectuals in ICMI led by Din Syamsuddin and Amir Santosa. CPDS saw itself as a successor to the Centre for Strategic and International Studies (CSIS), which had long since fallen out of favour with Soeharto. It was locked in a bitter struggle with another ICMI thinktank, the Centre for Information and Development Studies (CIDES), led by Habibie's lieutenant Adi Sasono. Both CIDES and CPDS had been involved in the campaigns against Abdurrahman in

1994 and Megawati in 1996, but Abdurrahman believed that CPDS was the more guilty of the pair. He demanded that Hartono and Tutut drop their support for CPDS and call off the CPDS attacks on himself, Megawati and NU. They obliged, as did also Amir Santosa, and CPDS dropped its campaigns. But the other green generals, Prabowo, Feisal Tanjung and Syarwan Hamid, who were close to Habibie and did not have any interest in furthering Tutut's presidential ambitions, did not want to make peace with Abdurrahman. They immediately established yet another thinktank — the Institute for Policy Studies (IPS) — and appointed Din Syamsuddin and Fadli Zon as its directors. Not only had Abdurrahman successfully negotiated a truce with the regime: he had also split the Islamist camp.[19]

With Megawati denied any role in PDI, and PPP dominated by regimist career politicians, Abdurrahman could see no point in fighting Golkar at the May 1997 elections. He also said that, given Soeharto's state of mind, unless Golkar polled extremely well, civil society groups would face another round of repression. He also, of course, had personal reasons for not wanting either of the pseudo-opposition parties to poll well in 1997. With Soeharto's treatment of Megawati reducing the vote for PDI, it stood to reason that PPP should pick up a big windfall in May. If this were to happen it would convey the impression that Indonesians were endorsing the actions of the regimists and Islamists linked to PPP. At the same time, Abdurrahman felt that he still needed to work hard to ensure that the ceasefire that he and NU were enjoying with Soeharto did not quickly collapse. He was by now convinced that Soeharto was unstable and dangerous and liable to overreact to signs of dissent. For all of these reasons Abdurrahman agreed to accompany Tutut at several NU rallies during the election campaign. At the rallies he explained that he 'wanted to formally introduce Mbak Tutut to the people of NU because she was somebody whom they ought to get to know'. 'She was already an important person and may well become even more important in future' he explained.

Privately he explained his actions by saying 'It's better that Golkar has a good win in the 1997 elections, because if the numbers drop too much then Soeharto might panic and lash out again. In any case,' he continued, 'we're going to be stuck with Soeharto for some years yet, so now is not the time to push for change — we'd best retreat and consolidate.' He also said that he recognised that he had no choice but to bargain for peace. It was, he said, not just a question of his own safety and security: it was a question of the welfare of tens of millions of his followers. Many of the students and young people, both within and without NU, were shattered by his apparent willingness to 'make a deal with the regime'. At the time, however, he argued he had no choice and that he had driven a very good bargain.

RAPPROCHEMENT WITH AMIEN

Abdurrahman's rapprochement with Soeharto gave him and NU some valuable breathing space. It also happened to precede another rapprochement, which was to prove equally important. On 1 December, a couple of weeks after his much observed handshake with Soeharto, Abdurrahman met with Amien Rais at the Sunda Kelapa mosque in Menteng, Central Jakarta. It was a historic public meeting in which leading modernists and traditionalists came together in a very public fashion. It was thought that if Amien and Abdurrahman could work together, they would generate tremendous leverage to push for change.

One of Soeharto's main objectives with ICMI had been to drive a wedge between the modernists and the traditionalists and thereby prevent them from joining forces against him. In the early 1990s Amien, who was by nature outspoken, had not been highly critical of Soeharto. His position on ICMI's board of experts more or less guaranteed his acquiescence. But as he started to become increasingly critical of the regime, many began to see the possibility of his joining Abdurrahman and Megawati as a third figure to lead the reform movement. The willingness of Amien and Abdurrahman to meet publicly indicated, at least, the possibility of their collaboration. At the time of their meeting Nurcholish Madjid commented, 'The two of them both share the same concern regarding justice and both cannot stand to see people who have pretensions about power'. The road ahead for Abdurrahman and Amien was, of course, bound to be rocky, but at least a beginning had been made.

MORE COMMUNAL VIOLENCE

While some good resulted from the horrible violence in Situbondo, in that the communities there began, for the first time, to get to know each other and establish good relations, the violence unfortunately did not stop. In December that year similar violence broke out in Tasikmalaya, West Java, near the location of NU's 1994 congress. Ten churches were burnt down along with numerous Chinese shops, houses, and Christian schools. At least four people were killed, with blame attributed to the local NU community. Local NU members claimed that they had been deliberately framed and that the violence had, in fact, been instigated by people from out of town. There was an eerie parallel to what had happened two months earlier in East Java.

Abdurrahman lashed out at ICMI and the Islamic right and was quoted in the media as saying that he knew who was involved. He stopped just short of naming names, but he did say that he thought one of the figures behind the violence was a man with the initials A.S. There was no doubt that he was referring to Adi Sasono. Naturally Adi Sasono and his colleagues in ICMI denied their involvement, and the evidence against them remained inconclusive. Nevertheless, they faced a burden of suspicion. There was evidence to suggest that members of the Islamic right, including some elements in ICMI, had been involved in earlier confrontations. Moreover, it appeared that they had been involved in the 'anti-Gus Dur' push at the time of NU's 1994 *muktamar*.

One figure frequently mentioned in speculation about involvement of the political elite in instigating the violence was Soeharto's own son-in-law, General Prabowo Subianto. Abdurrahman frequently claimed to have evidence linking Prabowo with the Islamic right and with ICMI figures like Adi Sasono. His failure to produce this evidence for public scrutiny was seen by his critics as proof that he was simply speaking out of his own prejudices. Others, particularly his supporters within NU, said that it was understandable that he couldn't divulge his sources. Few doubted that one of Abdurrahman's key sources of information was Benny Murdani.

After graduating from the military academy in 1972, Prabowo had served with the Army Special Forces (Kopassus) up until 1986, and then with the Army Strategic Reserve (Kostrad) and finally had been put in charge of Army Special Forces. He had served three terms of duty in East Timor and some there regarded him as being 'a borderline psychopath'. In East Timor he had worked with militia groups, training and financing many militia members. It was in East Timor that Prabowo, previously a Benny Murdani protégé, fell out with Benny. In the mid-1980s Benny recalled him from active service in East Timor, claiming that he was out of control. Since that time Prabowo came to hate Benny with a vengeance.

There is clear evidence linking Prabowo with KISDI and other groups from the Islamic right, and he was very open about his support for conservative Islamists. Ironically, Prabowo came to replace Benny as one of the key figures in military intelligence command. Many suggested that it was Prabowo's intelligence people who were behind the storming of the PDI headquarters in July 1996 and spreading the campaign, in August, against the so-called new Communist People's Democratic Party (PRD). When the Army Special Forces were placed under his command, Prabowo moved, with his father-in-law's permission, to increase the size of the force from three to six thousand troops. This prompted Murdani to say that 'Prabowo was trying to make the Special Forces into the Iraqi Secret Service'.

Whatever the truth behind Prabowo's involvement in inter-communal riots and unrest, it was clear that ABRI, under its new commander General Feisal Tandjung, was now dominated by so-called green officers, who were seen to champion Islamic interests. The 'red-and-white' secular-nationalist officers, who for decades had been fearful of militant Islam, had been marginalised. None of this, of course, was accidental. It can be largely explained in terms of Soeharto's deliberate manipulation of army command structures, playing off the green officers against the red-and-white ones in order to prevent them uniting and challenging his authority. This plan dovetailed neatly with Soeharto's promotion of radical Islamists more generally and with his sponsorship of ICMI.

SOEHARTO LOSES THE MANDATE OF HEAVEN

In traditional Southeast Asian literature the state of the natural environment is often said to be linked to the authority of the ruler. Consequently, failure in the natural environment, an imbalance or series of disasters, suggests that there is a problem with the leader. This is certainly the way that many Indonesians interpreted the disasters that befell them in 1997. Indonesia was in the grip of its worst drought since independence. Failure of rain resulted in extensive crop losses and in some parts of the country, where ordinarily people seldom knew hunger, thousands were forced to go without food. The lack of rain not only destroyed crops but also had a disastrous effect on the forest burn-offs that normally signalled the beginning of the dry season. Forests are burnt both by small-scale slash and burn agriculturalists and by large plantation companies clearing land. In the midst of the drought these burn-offs resulted in choking pollution; most drifted northwards to Singapore and Malaysia but some also blanketed parts of Sumatra and Kalimantan.

At the same time Soeharto appeared to be acting more and more irrationally. Technocrats and former loyal ministers began to say that he was refusing to listen to advice, or discuss issues, even with those whom he trusted most. Further adding to Soeharto's woes was Amien Rais. Early in 1997 Amien Rais had spoken out over the Freeport copper mine in Irian Jaya, arguing that '90 per cent of profits in the mine were expatriated and the remaining 10 per cent went largely to one family'. Soeharto was furious. If there was one taboo in Soeharto's Indonesia it was to point the finger at the 'first family', particularly if you were a member of his favoured elite. Immediately after Amien's outburst, Soeharto called Habibie into his office and lectured him, saying, 'Amien is making subversive statements and is now more dangerous than Abdurrahman Wahid'. Habibie then confronted Amien and repeated the treatment he had from Soeharto. Amien was unfazed. He simply packed his bags and left ICMI.

Unfortunately for Soeharto, this left Amien Rais chairman of Muhammadiyah, but outside ICMI and free of any need for self-censorship. Amien Rais had been elected to the chair of Muhammadiyah in 1995; if he had previously been reluctant to speak out too strongly, he now felt no compulsion about speaking his mind. Soeharto had made for himself a particularly vexatious enemy.

ABDURRAHMAN CONSOLIDATES

At that time Abdurrahman and NU were enjoying a period of peace with the regime. It now appeared to Soeharto that modernists such as Amien Rais were more difficult to deal with than the generally quiescent traditionalists. In any case NU was left largely alone. This didn't automatically secure popular support for Abdurrahman. Some members, including many young reformists who were previously his strongest supporters, thought he had sold out to the regime.

Nevertheless, at the *munas*, or congress of *ulama*, called in November 1987 on the island of Lombok, it was clear that Abdurrahman had strengthened his position within the organisation. While many at the *munas* were outspokenly critical of him and demanded an explanation of his reconciliation with Soeharto and his backing of Golkar during the 1997 campaign, most accepted his explanation and indicated their support for him. The end of the congress saw the *ulama* formally endorse a number of the initiatives and positions being pushed by the liberal reformists close to Abdurrahman, and it seemed that he had once more consolidated his position within NU.

At this time many external observers had been inclined to write Abdurrahman off. He was nearing the end of three five-year terms at the helm of NU, and some argued that he had little to show for it. The organisation seemed no better run or managed than when he had first taken charge. Moreover, his dalliance with civil society and his challenges to Soeharto seemed to have occupied most of his energy and time, leaving little to contribute to day-to-day management within the organisation. The Lombok *munas*, however, suggested that many were more generous in their interpretation of Abdurrahman's performance.

Unlike most previous *munas* or *muktamar*, this congress was a quiet affair. Only one government minister addressed the NU masses, the Minister for Religious Affairs, Tamizi Tahir. Even this was significant because Tamizi in the past had been critical of Abdurrahman and now seemed much quieter. No other ministers attended, the NU leadership explained, because most were busy preparing for the March 1998 session of the MPR. After the last *muktamar*, in which half the time had been taken up with lengthy speeches from ministers, few seemed to mind the lack of government presence. This congress was a welcome change: an air of peace and tranquillity characterised the meeting.

When the *munas* concluded, four main achievements were evident. Firstly, it was clear that the progressive line supported by Abdurrahman had been successful in the face of opposition from conservative and reactionary elements. This was particularly evident during the discussions about the role of women. After some long and heated discussions, the reformists gained the upper hand. Secondly, there was general support for the leadership of the younger *ulama* who had been encouraged by Abdurrahman. Thirdly, after some debate regarding Abdurrahman's reconciliation with Soeharto, it was generally agreed that he had done the right thing. And finally, the overall mood of the *munas* suggested that Abdurrahman's authority and leadership in the organisation were stronger than ever.

REFORMIST STRATEGIES

While Abdurrahman had been quietly consolidating his position and avoiding antagonising the regime, Amien had been on the move. Previously closely associated with the Islamic right conservative elements, he consciously made a move to the centre of the political stage. By August 1997 he was calling for reform and was one of the first major public figures to speak out about the need for Soeharto to resign. At the time his erstwhile colleague, Adi Sasono, dismissed Amien as a foolish romantic. This may have been partly because KISDI and hard-liners such as Ahmad Soemargono and Fadli Zon continued to support Soeharto, backed by General Feisal Tandjung and encouraged by Prabowo. Even so, they also continued to maintain links with Amien.

On the other side Wiranto sent messages of support to Abdurrahman. Wiranto was generally associated with the red-and-white nationalist faction within the military and was worried about the increasing strength of the green generals, particularly General Prabowo.

Abdurrahman was pressed to consolidate the push for reform by joining with Amien and Megawati to call for Soeharto to resign. When asked, Abdurrahman explained that he was indeed of the same mind as Amien and Megawati but there was no formal alliance. On one occasion in December 1997 when asked about the alliance, he explained that he had recently been approached by a senior general who had asked, 'What about the relationship with Amien and Megawati?' To which Abdurrahman replied, 'We work together, we have a similar vision'. 'Yes but is there a formal alliance?' 'No we have no formal alliance.' 'Well that's a good thing because if it were formalised I would have to crush it.'

Of course this may simply have be a convenient pretext for Abdurrahman to avoid having to work closely with Amien, with whom he had a long and rocky relationship. But there is also good reason to believe that a formal alliance between the three main protagonists for reform would indeed have been crushed by the military, very likely by the green faction.

Abdurrahman argued at the time that the reformists had no choice but to be patient because Soeharto was not set to resign in the near future. 'There is no point in pushing,' he argued, 'until the time is ripe, and now is not the time.' In this at least, he turned out to be wrong. Unbeknownst to Abdurrahman and in fact to most observers, Indonesia was in the initial stages of what was to prove a truly major crisis.

KRISMON (KRISIS MONETER)

The crisis was triggered by the floating of the Thai baht on 2 July 1997.[20] No sooner had the baht been floated than it sank. By August Thailand had turned to the International Monetary Fund (IMF) for help and received a $17 billion bailout. At the time Indonesia appeared to be fine; few were worried about it succumbing to Thailand's problems, arguing that the underlying structure of the Indonesian economy was much more robust than that of the Thai economy. This was the view of many expert economists, but no one could have been more wrong.

On 14 August Indonesia removed the trading band that kept the rupiah at around Rp2400 to the US dollar. The rupiah immediately began to sink but not nearly as fast as the Thai baht had done. Analysts remained confident. Just two months later, however, Indonesia, like Thailand before it, had been forced to turn to the IMF for help. By the end of October the IMF had promised a $43 billion bailout. At the same time the United States began to worry about a contagion effect and was talking about a 'regional crisis'. Worried by what it saw, the United States contributed $3 billion directly to Indonesia.

As part of a crisis management plan, Bank Indonesia (BI), the central bank, closed down sixteen defunct banks. This unfortunately provoked a run on the remaining banks and at the same time BI raised interest rates from 18 to 70 per cent.

On 9 December Soeharto suddenly cancelled a planned trip to an ASEAN meeting in Kuala Lumpur, Malaysia, and the market really began to panic. Then, on 6 January 1998, Soeharto unveiled a new budget that was judged to be wildly unrealistic. Panicked investors began to sell off rupiah holdings, and in a period of five days the rupiah dropped half its value. A mood of panic settled over Indonesia and scores of Jakartans rushed the supermarkets to buy up rice, oil and canned goods, and hoarded food. By 15 January the IMF came up with a second package. This, however, was immediately undermined by Soeharto and his family. Finally, in what seemed to be a calculated piece of stupidity, Soeharto announced that Habibie would be the next vice-president and would be sworn in in March. Many officers within ABRI had no admiration for Habibie, but General Feisal Tandjung and General Prabowo openly backed him. On 22 January the rupiah collapsed to 17 000 per US dollar.

Many analysts, at the time and since, blamed the IMF for the sudden worsening of Indonesia's financial crisis. The IMF may have been partly responsible — indeed, it acknowledged that it had miscalculated in its initial response to the crisis — but there is good reason to point the finger at the first family. Indeed, looking back, the crisis, although sudden, had been a long time building. Ever since the 1993 cabinet the influence of the technocrats who had done so much to make 'the Indonesian miracle' had been in decline. Soeharto's children, and even his grandchildren, became increasingly avaricious. A pattern emerged in the 1990s where the children would demand to be given 10 or 15 per cent equity as a kind of licence fee in any major new project. At the same time the World Bank acknowledged that Indonesian corruption was among the worst in the world. At least 20 to 30 per cent of all grant money from the bank was siphoned off.

Once the IMF could begin its planned rescue package, its reform initiatives were resisted at every turn, first by Soeharto and then by his children; where they could not deny outright, they sought to undermine. For all this, Soeharto failed to see the need to change anything. In the past he had always been able to outsmart his opponents even in the midst of crisis. This time he was badly out of touch.

By this stage Amien was speaking out more stridently than ever against Soeharto and calling for his immediate resignation. He asked Abdurrahman and Megawati to join him in a common front against Soeharto but Abdurrahman declined, saying that ABRI sources had warned him off, and that bloody confrontation would certainly result if they were to openly form a front against Soeharto. Privately, he said that he believed that Prabowo and his thugs along with the Islamist radicals 'were capable of anything'.

ABDURRAHMAN'S PERSONAL CRISIS

The fall of Soeharto in May 1998 caught most people, including Abdurrahman, by surprise. In hindsight it all seems so obvious. Soeharto had failed to respond not just to the financial crisis of late 1997 and 1998, but also to years of nepotism and a hollowing out of his administration, so that when it finally came under pressure it collapsed. But even in mid-January most people did not believe that Soeharto was going any time soon. The students were on the street anxious for change. Amien Rais was leading them on, anger and frustration was rising, but Soeharto had toughed out challenges in the past and it seemed possible he might tough this one out as well. Abdurrahman said that it was not clear how long Soeharto would last but it might be much longer than anyone thought.

Everyone looked to Abdurrahman and Megawati to join the fray, sensing that if they did there would be an irresistible force for change. Both of them hung back, Abdurrahman arguing that it was still too early to push and that elements in the military were actively looking for opportunities for confrontation, even engineering such opportunities.

The attention of millions was focused on Abdurrahman, waiting for him to indicate when they should move.

Abdurrahman seemed as relaxed and confident as ever, but trouble came suddenly upon him from a quite unexpected quarter. On the evening of 19 January his youngest brother Hasyim had been waiting for him at his office when he had began to feel alarmed. Abdurrahman had gone to the bathroom across the corridor from his office at the NU headquarters; a long time had passed and he had still not emerged. Finally, feeling that he could wait no longer, Hasyim and others pushed the door down and found Abdurrahman collapsed on the floor. His brother Umar, a medical doctor, was called and he was rushed to hospital.

Umar began calling friends, and later that evening Indonesia's best neurosurgeons gathered to talk with Umar at the hospital. It seemed almost certain that Abdurrahman was going to die. His blood pressure had soared to near fatal levels, and his heartbeat and other vital signs indicated that he was a hair's breadth from death. The diagnosis was made that he had suffered a major stroke. The only possible way to deal with it was risky emergency surgery and the insertion of a 'shunt', a plastic tube to drain fluid from his cranial cavity. But surgery that night was impossible; his vital signs indicated that any attempt to operate would kill him. They decided to wait until the morning. When the morning came, Umar asked the neurosurgeons to operate. They protested that it was still too risky and the patient would die on the operating table. Umar responded by saying: 'We owe it to him to give him a chance. My brother is somebody who often makes surprising recoveries from difficult situations. We've at least got to give him the chance; we should go ahead and open him up.' As the team gathered in the operating theatre, everyone felt a sense of impending doom, almost certain that Abdurrahman would not come out of the theatre alive. But against all expectations, the operation went well. Within hours he was making a modest recovery

The next day he was able to talk to visitors and appeared to have come through the stroke and the brain surgery virtually unscathed. But obviously he was left in a very weakened condition. Almost the entire *Who's Who* of Indonesian elite society visited his hospital room. The guest book records a most unusual collection of names: every faction, every side of politics, every religious community from every level of society. Everyone had their own reasons for worrying that he might die. For some it was concern about the instability that might follow. Even conservative generals regarded Abdurrahman as an known quantity, somebody who was a voice for moderation, somebody who controlled the masses, not just within NU but beyond. For others he was a hero or a close friend.

Ordinarily everyone has something to say about Abdurrahman: even his close friends are not afraid to speak critically of him. But for a week all his annoying foibles and faults seemed to be forgotten; quite apart from political calculations, there was a genuine sense of mourning and concern.

In the first few weeks it was still not clear whether he would recover and if so, how much. But he didn't show any anxiety, and within weeks, much sooner than expected, he was at home. Over the next couple of months he steadily regained much of his strength. Initially he saw visitors mostly in his bedroom at the front of the house. Some of his doctors would rather he didn't have too many guests, arguing that he needed to preserve his strength. After a while, however, they relented, conceding that he needed at least some visitors if he was to find the strength that he needed to recover.

Even when flat on his back fighting for his life, Abdurrahman remained a thorough extrovert, and without human company he soon became morose. Before long a steady stream of visitors made their way to his house in Ciganjur and sat by his bedside, exchanging jokes and keeping him informed about what was happening. Those who could not visit phoned instead, and it seemed as if the phone beside his bed was seldom idle for more than a couple of minutes. Nevertheless, in the eyes of the general public, Abdurrahman was off the scene. After years of featuring almost daily in the newspapers, he had disappeared overnight.

BLAME THE CHINESE

Out on the streets the activity that had begun at the time of Abdurrahman's stroke had picked up pace. University students throughout the country and all the major cities had left their campuses and were holding protests in the streets. Most of these protests went without violence, but there was a sense of uncertainty about what might happen if confrontation should occur between students and troops.

Further adding to this uncertainty was an outbreak of sudden episodes of violence in small towns in Central and East Java, mostly directed against the ethnic Chinese.[21] Many believed the violence was deliberately engineered and that behind it lay provocateurs with connections to Prabowo and his Army Special Forces personnel.

In Jakarta the elite began to turn on Chinese business leaders. In February prominent Chinese businessman Sofyan Wanandi was accused of being behind a plot with PDI to disrupt the upcoming MPR in March. Prabowo's colleague and close friend Syafrie Syamsuddin interrogated Sofyan for several hours, wanting to know the details of an alleged bomb plot in which Sofyan was said to be involved. It was clear from the start that the whole thing was a fabrication. There was no bomb plot and there was no reason to suspect Sofyan, but he was one of Indonesia's leading Chinese. he was linked to CSIS through his brother Jusuf who was the centre's director. CSIS in turn was closely linked with Murdani, who for some years had made his office in its building and was known as one of its major backers.

Less than twelve months earlier, Abdurrahman had joined the board of CSIS. It was considered a bold and provocative move. A decade and a half before, CSIS had been close to Soeharto. Gradually the technocrats had lost influence, ranks closed around the family, ICMI became the president's main political vehicle for social engagement, and CSIS was marginalised, along with Benny Murdani. Following Sofyan's interrogation, CSIS was targeted by Muslim extremist protesters. They crowded around the central Jakarta office holding up placards emblazoned with slogans like 'CSIS is a parasite' and 'Sofyan Wanandi is a traitor'. There was strong evidence to suggest that not only Prabowo but also Soeharto himself was behind the framing of Sofyan Wanandi.[22]

SOEHARTO FUMBLES

In the lead-up to the March session of the MPR, Wiranto was made head of the armed forces and Prabowo was promoted to the rank of three-star general in command of the Army Strategic Reserve. The Army Special Forces that he had led was taken over by a close friend, General Muchdi Purwoprandjono. Soeharto's moves seemed to be calculated to appease extremist Muslim elements. If so, the strategy worked. Islamist activist Fadli Zon said, 'Muslims are very happy with ABRI now. Prabowo, Syafrie and Muchdi are all sincere and close to the people. We don't know yet about Wiranto, he never shows his sincerity to people'.

By placing Prabowo in charge of the 27 000 strong Army Strategic Reserve and surrounding him with close friends linked to Islamist extremists, Soeharto was aiming to split the military. At the same time the replacement of Feisal Tandjung by Wiranto as head of the armed forces placed the secular-nationalist, red-and-white camp opposite the green faction, and power was evenly balanced in the military. Playing groups off one against another was a tactic Soeharto had used many times in his thirty-two years of rule, and there seemed to be no reason for this reshuffle except that he wanted to set both camps against each other while securing support from the Islamists.

When Soeharto announced his new cabinet in March, it was met with cries of disbelief. The cabinet, in the eyes of most commentators, was completely unrealistic and blatantly provocative, a line-up of Soeharto's old friends, cronies, loyalists and family members. His eldest daughter, Tutut, was given a post, as was his old golfing buddy and business partner Bob Hasan, the timber tycoon. Bob Hasan's Chinese ethnicity meant nothing to the Chinese community, who regarded him as a traitor to his own people.

Not only did the new cabinet alarm the financial markets: it further antagonised the students. It now seemed impossible to believe that Soeharto was in any sense committed to moving towards reform or change. He seemed to be turning his back upon the whole *reformasi* push and instead seeking to tough things out by surrounding himself with loyalists. From his bed at home in Ciganjur, Abdurrahman urged the students to show restraint. He argued that there was every reason to believe that Soeharto was now at his belligerent worst. Moreover, with Prabowo in charge of the Army Strategic Reserve and Muslim extremist green generals in other key positions, there was, he argued, a high likelihood that the hard-liners were spoiling for a fight.

On 11 March, the day that Soeharto was sworn in for his seventh term, 25 000 students demonstrated at Gadjah Mada University in Yogyakarta; both modernist Muslim and traditionalist NU students took part. Calls continued to come for Amien and Abdurrahman to join forces. Abdurrahman kept urging restraint. Tension mounted throughout March and April, but Soeharto was still very much in control. Then on 4 May that control began to disintegrate. That day he announced a reduction of subsidies on fuel that would cause a 70 per cent price hike for petrol, in line with IMF prescriptions. The announcement met a violence response. Large-scale riots broke out in

Medan, North Sumatra, and students began flooding into the streets throughout Java. Once again Amien urged the students to action but Abdurrahman continued to call for restraint, being more fearful than ever that a bloody confrontation was looming.

Then on 9 May Soeharto, who seemed by this stage to be completely out of touch with popular sentiment, left the country on a trip to Cairo for an economic summit. In his absence the students began to gather in even larger numbers. On 12 May, six thousand students at the prestigious private Trisakti University in Jakarta marched on the parliament complex, located several kilometres south of their campus along the toll road. Afterwards they were returning to the campus and most were inside the university grounds when six students were shot from a pedestrian overpass that crossed the toll road in front of the Trisakti campus. Four were fatally wounded. Witnesses who saw the snipers, including an international television crew that filmed the incident, said that they were wearing uniforms of the Mobile Brigade Police. The police chief, however, said his men were armed only with rubber bullets.

Later forensic analysis revealed that the students had been killed with fire from Steyr rifles. These were high-powered rifles possessed only by a handful of uniformed police units. Many pointed the finger towards Prabowo or the Army Special Forces units. Over time evidence accumulated to suggest that it was not the police but soldiers in police uniforms who fired the shots. The attack seemed carefully calculated to provoke a response.[23]

On 13 May a funeral was held for the Trisakti students. Following the service the mood turned ugly, and rioting and looting broke out on a large-scale throughout Jakarta and Solo. The rioting was worst in Chinatown and in areas with clusters of Chinese-owned shops and houses. Soon 150 000 foreigners and ethnic Chinese had fled Jakarta. Thousands of shops and houses were destroyed and another 1200 people killed. Reports began coming in of scores of Chinese women being raped by gangs of paramilitary thugs.

In hindsight it seems strange that Soeharto should have chosen to attend an economic summit in Cairo at that time. It was a curious time to be leaving the country. Clearly Soeharto himself did not feel under any immediate threat, and he perhaps had good reason for confidence. Soeharto had weathered numerous storms in the past and come through, not only unscathed but strengthened. He had also survived severe economic crises, although nothing on the scale of the one then besetting Indonesia, and the associated bouts of communal unrest.

Abdurrahman, similarly, had no sense that Soeharto's demise was imminent. On the contrary, he believed that the ageing president would continue to fight hard once cornered, and that his departure might be some years off. Consequently, Abdurrahman continued to urge his people to show restraint and avoid placing themselves in the path of the military. In early May leading figures in the military seemed likewise to have been persuaded that Soeharto would tough out the current challenge and emerge victorious to continue as president.

Ironically, Soeharto himself planted the seeds of his demise by falling back upon his old tactic of dividing the military in order to control it. He had set up evenly matched power blocs between Prabowo and his Islamic extremist friends on the one hand and Wiranto and his moderate secular Javanese allies on the other.

PRABOWO?

At the time of the riots of mid-May, there was widespread speculation that Prabowo was orchestrating much of the violence. Although much of the evidence is anecdotal, it seems highly likely that somebody in ABRI was instrumental in engineering the mob attacks on shopping centres and the burning of these centres and of Chinese shop-houses. One of the common features mentioned in eyewitness accounts is the involvement of well-built young men with hair cropped short, acting with the quiet determination and discipline of well-trained military squads. At the least, the leaders of the gangs appeared to be military officers out of uniform. In some cases it was claimed that the fires themselves were started with accelerants in a professional fashion.

It was also clear that, along with these military or paramilitary elements, there were large numbers of so-called *preman* or semi-organised criminal thugs. It was well known that Prabowo and other ABRI officials had trained such *preman* for use in privately controlled militia while on duty in East Timor. In many ways what was happening in Jakarta and Solo in May 1998 mirrored the same kind of military-organised terrorising of a civilian population that had occurred for many years in operational zones such as East Timor and Aceh.

One of the most damning pieces of circumstantial evidence against Prabowo was that when General Wiranto ordered Prabowo's colleague and close friend Syafrie to get his men back on the streets on 13 May, nothing happened. Syafrie was in charge of the Jakarta garrison and his men should have been intervening in the rioting hot spots. Some eyewitness accounts claim that there was radio contact between Syafrie's men and the paramilitary gangs seen to be leading the worst of the violence.

At the same time neither Kopassus nor Kostrad seemed to be responding to stop the violence. Vice-President Habibie's aides claimed that throughout 13 May the vice-president's communication system was consistently jammed. On 14 May Wiranto ordered in troops from Central and East Java but they did not arrive until the following day. By that afternoon, exasperated by Syafrie's inaction, he finally confronted him and demanded that Syafrie get his men onto the street. Late that day they appeared and began to take control. It appears that Syafrie, under intense pressure from Wiranto, finally succumbed and decided to support Wiranto and effectively turn on his friend Prabowo. The failure of Syafrie's troops to take to the streets is one of a most damning pieces of circumstantial evidence against Prabowo and Syafrie; it shows at the very least a failure to intervene to stem the violence.

SOEHARTO'S DENOUEMENT

Late on the evening of 14 May a new organisation, styling itself Majelis Amanat Rakyat, or the Council of the People's Trust, called for Soeharto to step down. It was headed by Amien Rais and several other outspoken intellectuals. None of this was surprising, but it was noteworthy that well-known economist Sumitro Djojohadikusumo was named on the membership list of Majelis Amanat Rakyat. Sumitro is Prabowo's father. Prabowo's scheme appeared to be running into serious trouble. Not only had he lost the support of his friend Syafrie, but even his own father appeared to be calling for Soeharto's resignation.

At almost the same moment, Nurcholish Madjid presented a bold paper demanding political reform, at the army headquarters in South Jakarta. In it he called for an election to be held before January 1999, to be followed three months later by a special session of the MPR to appoint a new government. He also argued that Soeharto should apologise for his failings and especially for his corrupt gains and make restitution with his nation by returning his ill-gotten wealth. Leading reformist General Susilo Bambang Yudhoyono supported Nurcholish's paper, although he did caution that the last section calling for a public apology from Soeharto and remittal of money should probably be dropped.

The violence of 13 and 14 May appears to have galvanised opposition to Soeharto and strengthened the hand of those calling for his immediate resignation. If the violence was in part the work of Prabowo and his colleagues — presumably designed to strengthen Prabowo's standing in the eyes of Soeharto against his arch-rival Wiranto, and to prove the necessity of a military response — then Prabowo's military adventurism had been counter-productive. Rather than strengthening Soeharto's position, he had dealt it a fatal blow.

From Cairo, Soeharto made it clear that he was extremely displeased with Prabowo's purported behaviour. Early on the morning of the 15 May Prabowo headed south with a small convoy of military vehicles towards Ciganjur and the home of Abdurrahman Wahid. He arrived around 2 am and was ushered into Abdurrahman's bedroom at the front of the house. He knelt at the foot of the bed and began to massage Abdurrahman's feet. Prabowo was known to be a skilful masseur and Abdurrahman had benefited from massages, though never from such a masseur, as part of his post-stroke therapy. Nevertheless, when Abdurrahman awoke to find Prabowo and his personal guard at the end of his bed one can assume it must have come as a fright. Indeed, anyone who was visited by Prabowo at such an hour immediately in the wake of the violence of 13 and 14 May could be forgiven for becoming rather agitated.

Prabowo immediately launched into a cry of despair, designed to convince Abdurrahman that he was the victim of slander and was not involved in the violence despite all of the damning stories already circulating the city. 'Look what's happened to our city, what's going on, what's happening to us, Gus?' Abdurrahman, only moments before awakened from his slumber, instantly replied, 'That's what happens when people can't control themselves' (*Begitulah kalau orang nggak bisa menahan diri*). The Indonesian phrase was suitably ambiguous: 'people' could refer to Prabowo himself or the masses of the city. Evidently Prabowo had come to Ciganjur hoping for sympathy from Abdurrahman or at least hoping that Abdurrahman could be turned against his old rival Amien Rais. He left Ciganjur, however, with no such assurance.

Hours later Soeharto flew into Jakarta, having cut short his visit when he heard of the violence of 13 and 14 May. As his plane approached Jakarta, he witnessed the city literally smouldering. Thick palls of smoke continued to rise from Chinatown in the north and from scattered shopping malls all around the city.

Throughout his stay in Cairo, Soeharto had been briefed almost hourly by Wiranto. Wiranto had of course informed him of the stories circulating about Prabowo's involvement. Soeharto rebuked Prabowo and commanded him to 'stick to the chain of command'. Aware that the crisis was now much more severe than he had first thought, Soeharto hurriedly cancelled the earlier cuts to fuel subsidies.

On Saturday, 16 May, Nurcholish held a press conference. He had been invited to present his paper to Soeharto's Cabinet Secretary on Monday. But prior to that he and Amien Rais made a television address together, urging restraint from the students. Later that Saturday Nurcholish and Amien met with Soeharto's Cabinet Secretary, only to be interrupted when an agitated Prabowo burst into the meeting. He was furious at the demands that Soeharto hand over his wealth and suggested that Nurcholish and Amien should call for Habibie to be made president. Nurcholish responded that ABRI would not support Habibie's nomination. Prabowo replied, 'Don't worry about that. I will protect Habibie', and he went on to suggest that he, Prabowo, should replace Wiranto in order give him more power to protect Habibie.[24]

That Saturday evening ABRI spokesman Brigadier-General Mokodongan read a formal press statement, welcoming the earlier statement by NU that called upon Soeharto to step down, or *lengser keprabon* to use the language of Javanese kings. Prabowo rushed off to Soeharto with the press release. Soeharto, visibly agitated, called in Wiranto to explain. Wiranto ducked for cover and suggested that it had all been a misunderstanding.

That same Saturday afternoon Soeharto had received a delegation from the parliament to which he declared that he intended to re-establish the notorious Army Security Command, Kopkamtib, abolished in 1988. Over the course of the weekend he made three decrees to this effect, but Wiranto refused to endorse the plan. Soeharto also declared that he was cancelling the fuel price hikes and now formally promised to reshuffle his cabinet. It was all too late, however; the tide of events was moving against him. On Sunday, 17 May, General Bambang Yudhoyono met with Amien at the Muhammadiyah headquarters in central Jakarta. Later that day Nurcholish went public with his proposals that Soeharto step down and that fresh elections be held. The next day ICMI joined in and declared that it too wanted Soeharto to step down. Finally on Monday evening even Harmoko, known as one of Soeharto's most loyal and certainly most self-serving senior ministers, and at the time serving as the Speaker of the House, issued a press statement in which he said that Soeharto now faced an ultimatum: 'He must resign by Friday.' Even old sycophants like Harmoko could see that the army was turning against Soeharto.

By Monday, Soeharto, uncharacteristically, was beginning to panic. He called General Subagyo in and offered him the post of Commander of Kopkamtib. Evidently Soeharto, even at the eleventh hour, was hoping that he might subvert the tide of sentiment running against him within the military by splitting ABRI. Subagyo, reportedly close to tears, refused. An hour later Wiranto met with Soeharto, and then, whether having been told by Subagyo or by Soeharto himself about the Kopkamtib offer, proceeded immediately to the military headquarters for an emergency leadership meeting. On Monday evening Soeharto asked Nurcholish to meet him at the Presidential Palace. Nurcholish, characteristically without guile, stated his position plainly: 'The people's understanding of reform is that they want you to resign.' Soeharto responded by saying 'I don't have a problem with that. I already hinted at that in Cairo'. Soeharto promised to resign as soon as possible but gave no timeline.[25]

He said that, before announcing this on the following day, he wanted to meet with leaders from the Muslim community. Nine leaders were chosen in discussion with Nurcholish. Soeharto was emphatic about his desire that Abdurrahman should be among them, despite his ill-health and the need to bring him by wheelchair from his sickbed. Nurcholish tactfully suggested that Amien also should be among those in the delegation. Soeharto emphatically rejected the inclusion of Amien, perhaps because he was angry with him and perhaps because he was hopeful of splitting the Muslim opposition.

On Tuesday, 19 May, the nine Islamic leaders — four from NU and five from Muhammadiyah — were ushered into Soeharto's office. Clearly Soeharto's efforts to split the Muslim opposition had not worked. Earlier Nurcholish had met with Amien at the home of Malik Fadjar to discuss the meeting. As a consequence the nine presented a united front. All refused to join Soeharto's reform committee or accept places in his proposed cabinet reshuffle. Nurcholish once again addressed Soeharto with polite frankness: 'You have to end your presidency gracefully and honourably, not in a Latin American way. Not a repeat of our 1965–66 experience.'[26] The meeting with the Islamic leaders was supposed to have lasted thirty minutes; it stretched to two hours. Throughout it Soeharto appeared relaxed and confident. He listened politely to what Nurcholish and others had to say to him, but drew the line firmly at apologising or returning money to the state.

In response to pleas for his immediate resignation, Soeharto replied that for him to step aside now would mean the elevation of Habibie to the presidency, and 'there is a question of whether he was capable'. Later Soeharto repeated to the media his misgivings about Habibie not being up to the task. Soeharto pleaded with the nine leaders to at least show him a modicum of support. When they refused to join either his reform committee or his reshuffled cabinet, he asked them to stand behind him while he read his reform agenda proposal to the nation on a live television broadcast. Recognising that this would suggest their endorsement, they refused.

Amien Rais was critical of Abdurrahman's performance in the meeting. Abdurrahman let Nurcholish do much of the talking, and when the issue of Soeharto's resignation came up he joked about whether they were really calling Soeharto to resign. Amien described Abdurrahman's behaviour at the time as sycophantic. Abdurrahman himself explained it in cultural terms. Now that the knife had been thrust deftly into Soeharto's side, there was no need to twist it for it to accomplish its work. A display of graceful civility, he argued, was appropriate under the circumstances. But this was not the only thing on Abdurrahman's mind. He continued to be anxious that Soeharto might renege on his promise to step aside and was worried that even at this point that Soeharto might decide to 'go out fighting', in which case bloody confrontation was likely.

Abdurrahman later explained that in a private conversation with Soeharto that morning the president had said that his long-standing anxiety about right-wing Muslim extremism had proved to be well founded, and that he was now deeply concerned about the forces that he had unleashed with ICMI and his support for the Islamists. It seems likely that even now Soeharto was still attempting to split the *umat* and turn Abdurrahman against Amien Rais.

When Habibie heard about Soeharto's statement later that Tuesday, he was furious. Until this point he'd been unwavering in his loyalty to

Soeharto. Soeharto's public questioning of Habibie's competency to succeed him wounded him deeply and galvanised him into action. Habibie immediately sat down to draft a four-page handwritten proposal calling for Soeharto's resignation. Soeharto, not surprisingly, rejected Habibie's proposal and personally apologised to him for his remarks of the previous day.

At the same time Abdurrahman called upon the students to stop protesting and to get off the streets. Soeharto, he argued, should be given a chance to implement his promise. Amien was furious, but Abdurrahman privately argued that it was still too dangerous to continue pushing Soeharto publicly, and that the students risked a bloody backlash if Soeharto decided to tough it out rather than going through with his promise of resignation. At the time long-term Forum Demokrasi colleague and good friend Marsillam Simanjuntak said Wahid had 'no faith in the students who are most effective agents of change. He abandoned his chance to play a key role of history'.

Amien responded by threatening to bring one million people onto the streets the next day, Wednesday, 20 May. Only at the last moment did he back down, and only then after receiving a personal message from General Kivlan Zein, a close associate of Prabowo, warning him that there would be indeed a bloody confrontation if he went ahead with his demonstration.[27]

That Wednesday dawned with the city in a state of high military alert. Significantly, it was the marines who were visible on the streets. They were well known for their moderation and for their loyalty to Wiranto. The presence of the marines strongly suggested that Prabowo's push for confrontation was failing and Wiranto's more moderate approach was succeeding. The students were disappointed that the rally had been called off but remained relaxed and could be seen chatting and joking with the marines. For the time being they were persuaded that it was worth waiting to see what Soeharto did next. Meanwhile Soeharto was desperately trying to put together a reform committee. He once again approached moderates such as Nurcholish Madjid, but they all repeatedly refused to join.

By Wednesday even Soeharto's most conservative and loyal backers sensed that the tide was running against the president and were looking desperately for the chance to jump ship. One dramatic development occurred when Ginanjar Kartasasmita, one of Soeharto's loyalist-technocrats and his trusted Minister for Economics gathered together with thirteen fellow cabinet members and issued a joint statement announcing their immediate resignation from the Soeharto cabinet. That evening Soeharto met with Habibie and talked over the possibility of handing power to Habibie. Soeharto offered to resign in favour of Habibie, with the proviso that he be allowed to select Habibie's new cabinet. Habibie refused. Annoyed with Soeharto's public shaming of him the previous day, Habibie was now resolute in his stance towards his former mentor.

Harmoko sent word from the parliament explaining that impeachment proceedings would commence on Friday, 22 May, if Soeharto had not stepped down before then. At eleven o'clock that night Soeharto's personal secretary handed to his boss a copy of the letter from Ginanjar announcing the resignation of fourteen cabinet members. Soeharto turned to him and asked how the list of prospective members for the new reform cabinet was going. 'Who do we have?' The secretary replied: 'We have you and me.' 'Is there no one else?' 'No, just us.'[28] Soeharto recognised that his position was now beyond saving. He phoned Habibie and asked him to begin work on his acceptance speech for the following morning. A ceremony would be held, he said, at nine o'clock in which he would hand over power to Habibie. Habibie's close aides worked through the early hours of the morning, hastily crafting Habibie's acceptance speech.

At the ceremony the following morning Soeharto spoke little; he simply asked for forgiveness for his mistakes and announced his immediate resignation, ceding power to his vice-president.

He left the room without speaking with either Habibie or Wiranto. Wiranto in his speech pledged to support both Habibie as the new president and to protect Soeharto as the respected former president. In theory, Soeharto's New Order was over.

TEN

ISLAM, POLITICS AND ELECTIONS, 1998-1999

CALM AFTER THE STORM

It was finally over. After decades of waiting, this was to be Indonesia's new beginning. But no one could be sure of what was to come. On Friday, 22 May 1998, the people of Indonesia woke to their first day in three decades without President Soeharto.

The parliament building was still occupied by students; it was not clear whether they would be forcefully removed by the military or would accept Soeharto's resignation as sufficient cause to move on. Detachments of marines set up on the corners of the city's major thoroughfares seemed strangely comforting. After all, the marines were supposed to be the good guys; in the previous weeks it had been they who had protected the students.

Ironically, the city hotels were as lively as the streets were desolate. Thousands of Chinese had flown out of Jakarta for temporary safe haven in Singapore, Perth and Sydney, but many more remained in Jakarta. They camped in the major city hotels, trusting that the madness that had threatened their homes would not now engulf these bastions of civility.

A visit to Glodok, Jakarta's Chinatown, made it abundantly clear why so many Chinese huddled in hotels fearing for their lives. Here and in other Chinese districts across the city, department stores and entire shopping malls were gutted by fire. People walked around picking through the ashes, their faces revealing the shock that they felt even one week after the nightmare of 13 and 14 May. Locals warned against entering the gutted shopping malls, explaining that not only were the burnt-out structures unsafe, but also among the ash lay scores of charred bodies. The stories circulating Jakarta hinted at the grim horror of the week before. In many of the shopping malls, it was said, children just out from school had joined the looters on 13 May. In some cases the entrances of the buildings had been locked and the looters were chased back upstairs by gunfire as the buildings were set alight. Horrifying stories circulated of mass rapes and unimaginable brutality. The suggestion that the violence had been, at least in part, planned and directed made it all the more awful. In whatever manner it had occurred, it was clear that something evil had happened in the city. And yet, barely a week later, there seemed to be a sense of hopefulness in the air. After so many years Soeharto had gone. Most Indonesians had not even been born when he had come to power.

Early the next morning the normally bustling city was eerily quiet. The trip south from the city centre to Ciganjur, and the home of Abdurrahman, normally takes the best part of an hour. On this surreal Saturday it took little more than twenty minutes.

ON THE SIDELINES

Located at the front of Abdurrahman's house, opening off the front room, was a modest sitting room flanked by a small bedroom that, in another house, might have been the servant's quarters. The stacks of CDs, an eclectic collection of Beethoven, Mozart, *dangdut* and rock and roll, testified that it was now Abdurrahman's room. Abdurrahman had made considerable progress in his recovery but was still frustrated by his loss of sight. Although he appeared to be as sharp as ever, he explained that the effects of the stroke were a continuing source of irritation. Whenever he tried to sit up for more than a few minutes, he was overwhelmed by nausea, made worse by difficulties in maintaining his balance. Compounding these difficulties was a lack of energy and overpowering lethargy. 'It's not so bad when I'm lying down,' he explained. 'It's just when I sit up or try to walk. It's okay in short bursts, but I can't go through the day like I used to.' The most obvious change was the fifteen or more kilograms of weight that he had lost, a change which, if anything, made him look fitter and more healthy. These things aside, talking to him as he lay on his bed he seemed little changed. The sparkling wit, often droll and ironic, remained as lively as ever, and there seemed no significant change in his personality.

When asked how he felt about the fall of Soeharto and the prospects for democracy, he exclaimed, 'I'm torn between despair and hope'. Months earlier he had said that he thought the prospects for democratic change were fifty-fifty; now he was more optimistic but still somewhat apprehensive. 'There is still the real chance of confrontation,' he explained. 'The military is edgy and they'll get nervous if large crowds gather, and once they start shooting who knows what will happen?'

On the previous evening a confrontation had taken place at the parliament building. The pro-*reformasi* students gathered there had been confronted, not by the military, but by busloads of Islamic extremists. Some appeared to be linked to Pemuda Pancasila, the militia semi-officially established by Soeharto and often used for political intimidation and crowd control. Fortunately, the marines had intervened and bussed out the protesting students before major confrontation could take place. The incident suggested that an uneasy truce existed between rival factions in the military and competing political blocs.

Over the past several days Prabowo Subianto had twice confronted Habibie, once on the Thursday that Soeharto resigned and again the following day, hoping to somehow rescue his career and establish his position. Finally, in desperation, he had gone to his father-in-law, only to be rebuked by Soeharto and Tutut who accused him of causing too much trouble and failing to defend Soeharto. Prabowo exclaimed that he was flabbergasted that he, 'the loyal son, was now the one who was banished'. Tensions between troops loyal to Prabowo and those loyal to Wiranto had risen sharply. When it was clear that Prabowo's confrontation had badly backfired, Wiranto's hand had been strengthened and he had moved quickly to clean out Prabowo's men from the chain of command. However, Wiranto's power was still far from absolute. This was demonstrated when his move to appoint a new head of the Army Strategic Reserve (Kostrad) had to be reversed within hours of being announced because the appointee was a Christian and unacceptable to the Islamic conservatives who supported Habibie.

Abdurrahman was surprisingly sanguine about Habibie's appointment as interim president. 'There really is no alternative,' he explained. 'There has to be some sort of interim arrangement, and the military will be most comfortable with what they feel to be in accordance with the constitution. The important thing is to move towards elections.' As always, Abdurrahman argued in favour of evolutionary rather than revolutionary change, and continued to call for restraint. His apparent quiescence was an ongoing source of disappointment to the students. They felt, reasonably enough, that it was their presence on the street that had given the final push to Soeharto, and Abdurrahman's reluctance either to back them directly, or to encourage Megawati to join them in their protests, was both inexplicable and regrettable. Student anger and disappointment with the Habibie interim government was understandable. After all, Habibie's cabinet consisted of twenty-one members directly from Soeharto's previous governments and fifteen new members, many of whom were Habibie loyalists from ICMI. It hardly seemed to be the stuff of which reformation was made.

Shortly after the swearing-in of the new cabinet on Saturday morning, Abdurrahman was visited by his old friend Djohan Effendi and their mutual friend Malik Fadjar. Malik Fadjar arrived in his old Corolla and was dressed in casual clothes, although he had been sworn in as the new Minister for Religious Affairs only an hour or so earlier. Malik had been pressured into accepting his post by friends who argued that it was necessary to have the Department of Religious Affairs controlled by a moderate Islamic intellectual. His own affiliation was with Muhammadiyah and not NU, which made him uneasy about taking the job. NU had traditionally regarded the Department of Religious Affairs as its own territory, and he feared that Abdurrahman might not welcome his appointment. He need not have worried. 'The main thing you have to work for is to avoid communal violence and elements that want to use religion for political purposes,' Abdurrahman explained. Malik's nodding assent suggested quiet relief.

Over the next few days Abdurrahman had a steady stream of visitors and it seemed he regained a little more energy with each new wave of guests. A week or so later President Habibie himself came, asking for Abdurrahman's blessing. Habibie seemed appreciative that Abdurrahman did not side with the students in pressing for immediate change but accepted the need for a staged transition. Abdurrahman, however, was not entirely uncritical of Habibie's new administration. In particular he spoke out against half a dozen or so cabinet ministers whom he accused of being anti-Chinese. He mentioned in particular Adi Sasono. Abdurrahman felt that Adi Sasono and other conservative intellectuals within the ICMI were linked to some of the violent confrontations witnessed around the city. He was also fearful that, as new political parties were established over the coming months, militant Islamists would not hesitate to manipulate sectarian sentiment for party-political purposes.

ABDURRAHMAN'S ANXIETIES

Wiranto, now simultaneously commander-in-chief of the armed forces and Minister for Defence in the Habibie administration, seemed to share Abdurrahman's concerns about militant Islamists. Nevertheless, Abdurrahman was reluctant to trust Wiranto too much. He continued to voice his apprehension about the potential for violence, saying that if political reform failed ABRI had 'the potential to turn into a brutal repressive apparatus along the lines of the Myanmar military'. There was, he felt, a danger that Wiranto might even use the threat posed by militant Islamists, alongside the increasingly outspoken demands of the students, as a justification for imposing stricter controls. Fortunately, the military's reputation and morale were at an all-time low and there was little will to deal harshly with social protest.

In June Habibie moved to sack the incumbent Attorney-General and replace him with Andi Ghalib, a serving military officer. Most people interpreted the change as a move to protect Soeharto, and indirectly Habibie, from too vigorous an investigation. This cynicism later appeared to be justified as Andi Ghalib's prosecution of the Soeharto case failed to go anywhere.

Privately Abdurrahman was extremely critical of Soeharto, in particular of his manipulation of religious and communal sentiment to bolster his own regime. He interpreted many of the problems that Indonesia now faced as the direct result of Soeharto's self-serving adventures in playing off elements in society against each other. Nevertheless, Abdurrahman was reluctant to give too high a priority to the prosecution of Soeharto. 'Soeharto still has too much power,' he explained, 'and at the very least there are many who acted in Soeharto's name, or think they are serving Soeharto, who will not hesitate to act harshly if they see the prosecution against Soeharto proceeding too rapidly.' He was worried that student concern with prosecution of Soeharto might become a dangerous obsession that could end up playing into the hands of reactionary elements of the military. 'The military is now too demoralised to do anything,' he suggested, 'but in time they will become increasingly dangerous. It's important we don't press too hard too fast.'

While some of his fellow reformers, not least Megawati Soekarnoputri, understood Abdurrahman's cautious stance, most saw it as evidence of weakness. For many, Abdurrahman had begun to lose his touch in politics and public life ever since his victory at the NU congress in November 1994. Certainly, his third term as chairman of NU was marked by a seeming inattentiveness to day-to-day administration and organisation. What really upset many of his former supporters, however, was his failure to add to the momentum of the *reformasi* push. Many interpreted his stroke in late January 1998 as a sign that the time had come for Abdurrahman to fade from the public scene. If they had been disappointed by his reluctance to join Amien in pushing for change in late 1997, they were fed up with his continued 'inaction' in the weeks following Soeharto's fall. The stroke, they argued, had changed him. The Abdurrahman of old was a jovial, relaxed, easy-going man; after his stroke, many asserted, he was irritable, grumpy and lacked the focus and intellectual clarity that he had earlier been renowned for. Those close to him, however, found him little changed apart from his obvious physical infirmities. Certainly his quick wit and mental agility had not left him, nor did he appear to have any trouble with his memory. He was obviously frustrated by his position but seldom voiced his frustration, much less grumbled about it. The only thing that he really complained about was not being allowed to eat the things that he wanted to.[1]

PKB AND NU

By the middle of June it became increasingly clear that new political parties, whether permitted by changed legislation or not, would quickly emerge of their own accord. Many groups within NU competed for Abdurrahman's patronage. At first Abdurrahman expressed grave concern at the fact that NU groups wanted to form an NU political party because it seemed to suggest a linking of party politics and religion. By July his attitude had begun to soften: by then there seemed little doubt that some sort of NU party would emerge, with or without his blessing. If he was to make a serious contribution to politics, it would have to be channelled through a party that drew upon NU's large membership.

Some saw this as another warning sign of egocentric behaviour. Was Abdurrahman seriously egocentric? Was his ego so large that it dominated his political and public behaviour? It's difficult to answer such questions with any degree of objectivity. His personal style continued to be modest and self-effacing and his humour self-deprecating. But there was no doubt that Abdurrahman's extroverted nature thrived on public attention. His enduring sense of 'manifest destiny' made it natural, in his mind, that he should welcome the opportunities that providence delivered him in order that he might play out his role in history.

In the turmoil that followed the collapse of the Soeharto regime, it was understandable that Habibie's new administration was slow in pushing through legislation permitting the formation of political parties. Ever since 1973, when the existing ten parties were compacted into just three, it had been illegal to form a new political party. In the euphoria following Soeharto's fall, when all attention was focused on the hope of fresh elections, illegality was no longer a barrier to the formation of new parties.

Throughout June Abdurrahman remained uncertain about which course to take. He was greatly worried that in the post-Soeharto vacuum Golkar was well positioned to regroup and mount a professional campaign for the elections. It was clear that Golkar carried a lot of baggage from its long association with Soeharto, but it was also clear that it possessed an unparalleled nationwide grassroots network with enormous cash reserves. Golkar was not expected to gain a majority in its own right, but there were worrying signs that PPP would be willing to form a coalition with Golkar. Together these two large parties might get the critical numbers they needed to form government, especially if joined by some of the numerous new Islamist parties. Not one of these new parties was expected to win a large share of the vote, but if grouped together, working in conjunction with Golkar and PPP, they might well form government.

In July, when a Golkar national congress was held, a fierce contest emerged between the two camps. Habibie's ultimately won through, with their candidate Akbar Tandjung becoming party chairman. This strengthened the impression that Golkar was a political force to reckon with. Akbar Tandjung was a formidable politician and had a reputation as a reformer even during the Soeharto period. His former role in the leadership of the Association of Muslim Students (Himpunan Mahasiswa Islam — HMI) confirmed his appeal in the eyes of many modernist Muslims. At first it seemed as if Akbar Tandjung had no hope of winning the Golkar chair. His main rival Edi Sudrajat was strongly backed by General Try Sutrisno; the army continued to play a large role in Golkar and was able to organise considerable voting strength. In the end it was Try's public boasting that he was acting on Soeharto's behalf that served to swing support behind Akbar Tandjung. That, and Habibie's threat to sack Wiranto unless he backed Akbar. In any case the ascension of Akbar confirmed the view that the 'new' Golkar, now styling itself as a reformist party, would not be easily defeated, even if its stocks in post-Soeharto Indonesia had sunk to an all-time low.

Abdurrahman had begun to publicly endorse the idea of a NU party. To defeat Golkar, he explained, he would have to lead a party that exploited NU's mass following. He and his colleagues in the central leadership team of NU nominated as the party of their choice the National Awakening Party (Partai Kebangkitan Bangsa — PKB). Abdurrahman took no formal leadership position in the party. Instead, Matori Abdul Djalil, a political veteran with many years of experience in PPP, was chosen as leader. Abdurrahman's de facto role in PKB as its spiritual head was still a source of embarrassment for him. He sought to counter this, and to assuage his own conscience, by strongly arguing that PKB should be non-sectarian, open to everyone, and that it should be concerned about representing all sections of society. Nevertheless, it was clear that as a party it relied almost entirely upon the members of NU. In justifying his apparent reversal of principle, Abdurrahman argued that NU had no choice if it were to defeat Golkar. This was, he argued, an 'emergency situation' in which emergency measures were required.

AMIEN AND PAN

Meanwhile Amien Rais was engaged in a personal struggle of his own. His political experience and natural affections inclined him towards PPP. By mid-July, he had, in fact, already formally signed a letter promising to accept the offer extended to him to become the chair of PPP. He was increasingly aware, however, that he could play a much larger role in Indonesian society, as a reformist statesman representing all sections of society. This second choice was emotionally and politically more risky than the first. It also ultimately proved to be more enticing. At the eleventh hour, just before he was to announce that he was taking up the chair of the United Development Party, he was persuaded by an old friend and moderate Muslim intellectual, Syafi'i Anwar, to join forces with the new National Mandate Party (Partai Amanat Nasional — PAN). PAN had been put together by a group of largely Muhammadiyah and modernist figures who had a vision of building an inclusive non-sectarian party along the lines of Megawati's PDI and Abdurrahman's PKB. Their initial policy drafts and formulations showed greater sophistication and understanding than found in any other party. The party's direction was unambiguously reformist and democratic. It opposed sectarianism and championed the development of a modern secular state that was home to all people, groups and faiths.

The chief obstacle for the new party was that it had no historical roots. Golkar, PPP and PDI could all claim to be old parties, and certainly they already had a claim on voting preferences. Even PKB, with its association with NU, had an established voter base. Some of the visionaries behind the formation of PAN spoke hopefully of it getting 90 per cent of the modernist vote. In reality it was difficult to see this ever being possible, given that many modernists would continue to vote for the parties that they has always voted for, either PPP or Golkar, and that many others might support the new Islamist parties claiming to represent the spirit of Masyumi. What PAN desperately needed was somebody with an established national profile who could guarantee them national attention and credibility. The appointment of Amien Rais promised precisely that, although given Amien's record of associating with the Islamic right, it also meant having to work even harder to convince voters that PAN was non-sectarian.

Many of the key figures behind the new PAN had previously been involved with ICMI. One example was Syafi'i Anwar, who was also editor-in-chief of the weekly investigative news magazine *Ummat*, which was self-consciously targeting the so-called new *santri* urban modernist community. But figures like Syafi'i Anwar represented the liberal and progressive wing of ICMI. Another major figure backing the new party, although not formally a member of its leadership, was veteran journalist and editor Gunawan Mohammad. Gunawan explained his support for PAN on the grounds that Indonesia needed a modern, non-sectarian, democratic party such as PAN to work alongside Megawati's PDI and Abdurrahman's PKB. This would bring together the three key reform figures, Amien Rais, Abdurrahman Wahid and Megawati Soekarnoputri. It could also bring together the major groupings of Indonesian society: traditionalist Muslims, modernist Muslims and *abangan* and non-Muslim nationalists. The growing strength of the new Islamist parties and the professionalism shown within Golkar, along with the undoubted strength still evident in PPP, made it all the more important that this three-cornered coalition be worked out. Without it there was a danger that Golkar would cling on to power. Nevertheless many analysts argued that a partnership between modernists and traditionalists would be fundamentally unworkable, given the mutual antagonism between Amien Rais and Abdurrahman Wahid, together with the many entrenched social, cultural and historical differences between Muhammadiyah and NU.

Throughout the second half of 1998 Abdurrahman refused to assent to the formalising of a coalition. Nevertheless, he and Amien continued to meet, and relations between the two steadily improved, assisted by intermediaries such as Syafi'i Anwar. Over the previous eighteen months Syafi'i had developed a friendship with Abdurrahman, enabling him to serve as a bridge to moderates within ICMI . He and other like-minded colleagues in ICMI and Muhammadiyah had long been working to bring Amien and Abdurrahman together. By August there were signs that some sort of partnership was, indeed, possible. As chair of PAN, Amien had begun to speak out in support of secular nationalism, democracy and reform. He even went as far as repudiating his earlier anti-Chinese and anti-Christian statements, saying that he had been mistaken in promoting such a narrow understanding of Islam.

HABIBIE UNDER PRESSURE

President Habibie continued to baffle observers. Confounding the low expectations held for his administration, he instituted a series of reforms that were hard to argue with. From the beginning there was greater media freedom under Habibie than had ever existed under Soeharto, albeit still incomplete and subject to a certain degree of manipulation. But Habibie himself seemed to act without any political instincts whatsoever. For example, when awarding Indonesia's highest honours in August he gave several to close associates and family members and presented the highest honour to his own wife.

More consequential was the military honour council which convened, that same month, to hear evidence regarding Prabowo Subianto's alleged involvement in the abduction and torture of pro-democracy activists earlier that year. The honour council decided to discharge Prabowo from active duty. Nevertheless, he was allowed to receive full pension benefits and was permitted to leave the country and relocate to Jordan. Many questioned why Wiranto didn't push ahead with a full court-martial, since there seemed to be ample evidence to justify one. Perhaps two factors held him back from doing this: fear of what Prabowo would divulge and fear of a Muslim extremist backlash. Evidence for the latter was to come at the November MPR session, when over 100 000 'civil militiamen' were organised to protect the meeting. The militiamen who roamed the streets of Jakarta largely unchecked, menacingly armed with sharpened bamboo sticks, were apparently organised by General Feisal Tandjung and General Kivlan Zein, both linked with the Islamic right. It was assumed that their objective was to protect Habibie from student groups and others demanding his resignation. Although their stated aim was to maintain the peace, they so irritated citizens that many of them were set upon and attacked.

By October Habibie was feeling increasingly uncomfortable. Not only was the *reformasi* movement outspoken in its criticism of him; it was also able to draw huge numbers. Evidence of this came in October when Megawati's National Democratic Party, now known as the Indonesian Democratic Party of Struggle (Partai Demokrasi Indonesia — Perjuangan, to distinguish itself from the old Indonesian Democratic Party) held its national congress on the island of Bali. In an impressive display of strength the new party was able to attract more than 100 000 supporters to its first congress. Equally impressive was Megawati's rousing speech on the final day. Carefully scripted, it presented the impressive policy platform that had been put together by her key advisers. Mochtar Buchori, the secretary-general of PDI-P, presciently stated that even in the most pessimistic scenario the party could expect to gain a quarter of the votes, and it might gain as much as 40 per cent.

One thing that Habibie didn't need to fear, however, was a call from Abdurrahman or his close friend and ally Megawati for his immediate resignation. To the continued disappointment of the people, Abdurrahman and Megawati argued for moderation and patience, saying that the focus should be on the 1999 election. Organising an election, preparing the parties and campaigning, they pointed out, would require many months of work, so there was little point in toppling Habibie at the moment. So long as Habibie continued to move towards holding a free and fair election in 1999, they argued, he should be given a chance to fulfil his mandate as interim president.

THE CIGANJUR MEETING

By November the university students, who represented the flesh and bone of the *reformasi* movement, were growing impatient with their reluctant heroes, Amien, Megawati and Abdurrahman. Finally, they decided to take matters into their own hands. On 10 November, the day that the four-day Special Session of the MPR began, they arranged a meeting to which the three reformists were summoned. Out of consideration for Abdurrahman's health the venue chosen was his home in Ciganjur. For good measure, also in attendance was the Sultan of Yogyakarta, who had been quietly supportive of the students active in the *reformasi* movement in his university town.

The four senior reformers issued an eight-point statement. Nothing in it was particularly new, and much of it failed to meet the expectations of the students. The four were prepared, for example, to allow the military six years to fully withdraw from the DPR and a direct role in politics. They urged Habibie not to allow fresh elections to be delayed any longer than was strictly necessary, but recognised the legitimacy of his transitional government. Much more important than the statement, however, was the agreement of the four leaders, arguably Indonesia's most popular reformers, to meet together. It was not exactly a coalition, or even a partnership, but it was a beginning.

MORE VIOLENCE

Abdurrahman was still concerned about the possibility of violent confrontation. Many critics, and indeed many supporters, of Abdurrahman continued to argue that he was being dramatic and that now was the time for him to add to, rather than to detract from, the momentum for reformation. On Friday, 13 November, the final day of the MPR session, a violent confrontation took place at the Semanggi flyover in central Jakarta. Whether out of panic at being confronted by an enormous crowd of potentially angry students, or acting at the instigation of some who wanted to send a warning to the reform movements, police and troops opened fire on a large crowd of students, wounding hundreds and killing fifteen. That day quickly became known as Black Friday. It was an ominous warning that, even with

Soeharto gone, there were limits to the pace of reform: the military remained a force to be reckoned with.

By the time the special session of the MPR was over, the students had distilled their demands down to two. Firstly, there should be an independent investigation into the wealth of Soeharto and his family; and secondly, there should be an immediate end to the military's role in politics. The students had been scathing of the MPR because the majority of its members were long-time associates of Soeharto hand-picked for their loyalty. Abdurrahman and others argued that there was no other constitutional way of proceeding with reform save that the Assembly met. In particular, it was vital that the Assembly pass the legislation for holding an election in 1999. When pressured by the students to support their demands, Abdurrahman grew irritated. 'There was no question of the need to investigate Soeharto's wealth,' he said, 'but we must be realistic in our expectations and methods.' Similarly, he argued that the immediate removal of the military from politics was too much to expect. It was better to work on a six-year plan that began with them playing a much reduced role in the MPR and ended with them eventually withdrawing from politics altogether. He pointed to Black Friday as evidence of the need for moderation.

If the students were angry with Abdurrahman at the time of the MPR meeting in November, they became furious through December and January, when he not only failed to support their call for immediate prosecution of Soeharto, but took the unorthodox step of repeatedly meeting with the former president at his home. Abdurrahman justified his actions by saying that there was a need to negotiate with elements of the former regime to stop the violence that was breaking out all over Indonesia.

Throughout the second half of 1998 a particularly cruel and bizarre form of violence had been occurring in Banyuwangi, East Java. Over two hundred people were killed, it was said, by black-clad assassins who came to be styled as *ninja*. Initially it appeared that the killings were an attempt to eliminate practitioners of black magic believed to be powerful and behind all sorts of misadventure and misfortune. Over time, however, many NU members, including some *ulama*, were killed, raising doubts that this was simply a settling of local issues relating to black magic. Anecdotal accounts spoke of small, well-organised bands of individuals who appeared to be trained militiamen, and of carefully co-ordinated attacks. Abdurrahman immediately pointed the finger at elements of the former regime loyal to Soeharto. It was likely, he said, that people acting for Soeharto, or in Soeharto's name, were involved in the Banyuwangi killings in an effort to provoke and foment violence. Abdurrahman travelled to the area and argued passionately against a response to the violence. 'These killings,' he said, 'are the work of *agents provocateurs* who want us to lose our temper and strike back, thereby plunging the community into violence. Consequently, this is precisely what we must not do.' Abdurrahman's moral leadership was sufficient to limit the extent of retribution, but he was not able to stop vigilante-style executions of alleged assassins who were caught and often killed by locals before the police could intervene. Nevertheless, widespread communal violence did not occur and it seems likely that it was the discipline of the NU community that limited the potential damage.

East Java is the heartland of both NU (and by extension, PKB) and PDI-P. If the Banyuwangi killings were, in fact, the work of *agents provocateurs* then it is probable that the intention was to set *santri* against *abangan*, or in other words, Abdurrahman's supporters against Megawati's supporters. [2]

Because he felt that it was likely that Soeharto, directly or indirectly, was involved with the violence, Abdurrahman felt that the only way to bring it to an end was to confront Soeharto and ask him to call his people off. Amidst much controversy, this is precisely what he did. He was also hoping that Soeharto, now an old man in broken health, might come to a point of repentance and voluntarily hand over much of his wealth. The examples of Ferdinand Marcos in the Philippines and the Shah of Iran suggested that seeking the return of wealth through legal measures was unlikely to be successful. Instead, suggested Abdurrahman, 'If we can get Soeharto to willingly hand over his wealth, or at least a significant portion of it, we could at least get something back. In any case Soeharto is simply too dangerous for us to move against him without fear of grave repercussions'. Some understood Abdurrahman's reason for negotiating with Soeharto, others accepted it out of respect for Abdurrahman, but many rejected it. For many, it was the final blow to their steadily diminished respect for Abdurrahman as a reformist leader.

It seems likely that Abdurrahman's involvement in urging restraint in Banyuwangi was significant in limiting violence in the district following the so-called *ninja* killings. Unfortunately, he had no similar role to play in another outbreak of violence that started in North Jakarta on

22 November. On that day a gathering of several hundred Muslims was informed that Christian youths had been seen throwing stones at a nearby mosque. The crowd ran wild, bursting into nearby churches, pulling up pews and setting them alight. They also went looking for the Ambonese Christian youths who had allegedly thrown the stones. When they caught those they considered responsible, they paraded them through the streets and then beat them to death. By the end of the second day, at least ten Christians were dead and a similar number of churches destroyed.

Several days later the inevitable retaliation occurred, this time not in North Jakarta but in West Timor. Christians went on a rampage, destroying dozens of Muslim houses and mosques, burning them to the ground and turning on Muslim transmigrants from Sulawesi. Given the tensions between rival street gangs in North Jakarta, in which Ambonese youths played the key role, it is possible that the whole incident was simply a boiling over of frustration and tensions between rival groups. As usual, there were accounts of young men looking like soldiers out of uniform throwing stones at mosques and precipitating the violence. Abdurrahman again voiced his concerns about what was going on and the need for moderation in the face of a deliberate attempt to provoke retaliation.

During December the violence appeared to have calmed down. But on 19 January 1999 a petty dispute in the eastern province of Maluku erupted into incessant, large-scale violence. The violence that began in Ambon that day between Christians and Muslims appears to have started with a minor dispute between a Christian mini-bus driver and a Muslim passenger. Some saw a link, however, with the earlier violence in North Jakarta and suggested that there were attempts to provoke violence. Whatever the case, the violence increased at a horrifying pace and continued through the course of the year. Shortly after the violence broke out, a Muslim labour activist and assistant to Adi Sasono, Eggy Sudjana, urged Java-based Muslims to get together and act against those who were persecuting Muslims. He said, 'that they should launch a *jihad* since more and more Muslims are being shot down'. Whether the conflict was deliberately provoked or simply a spontaneous expression of frustration, its potential to erupt into a major conflagration was all too clear. It seemed as if Abdurrahman's nightmare of sectarian violence was becoming real. Hefner observes that Adi Sasono, who was now serving in Habibie's cabinet as Minister for Co-operatives, made no attempt to rebuke his friend and confidant, Eggy Sudjana, and that weeks later he was rewarded for his 'discretion' by receiving the endorsement of KISDI in his campaign for the presidency.[3]

Ambon was not the only focus of violence. In late 1998 the situation in Aceh once again began to deteriorate. In August 1998 General Wiranto visited Aceh and publicly apologised for the military's past violation of human rights and pledged to reduce the number of troops deployed in the province. But Acehenese activists, outraged by years of violent abuse, and now able for the first time to talk openly about the terror that had been visited upon them, showed foreign and local journalists numerous sites of suspected mass graves. Witnesses who had escaped the violence came forward with tales of kidnappings and torture at the hands of the soldiers. Human rights groups estimated that at least two thousand people had been killed. The military acknowledged that many civilians had died but gave the conservative number of seven hundred. They also asserted that 111 soldiers had been killed. Matters took a turn for the worse in December 1998, when rebels linked to the Aceh Freedom Movement dragged seven soldiers off a bus and killed them. The new year started with ethnic and communal violence raging out of control in Aceh and Ambon. Abdurrahman was concerned that the political race for the 1999 elections would exacerbate sectarian conflict and also that evidence of the military's involvement in the violence demonstrated that there were limits to the pace of reform that the military would accept.

Compounding Indonesia's many difficulties was the dire state of the economy. The year 1998 had begun with the rupiah collapsing and, although it eventually recovered somewhat, continued to be of concern. By the close of the year the economy had contracted by 14 per cent and was expected to shrink by as much as 4 per cent in 1999. Unemployment was at an all-time high. According to some estimates as many as a hundred million people were living in abject poverty. One measure of this was the fall in per capita income to US$400 in 1998 from a little over US$1000 two years earlier, a 60 per cent drop. The economic crisis meant that there were millions of young men angry and disappointed. The fall of Soeharto had not brought about the sudden reversal of fortunes that had been hoped for, and they wanted to see the new government take practical measures to return jobs. Conditions were ripe for the recruiting of militiamen and the spontaneous emergence of gangs of disgruntled youth.

In January 1999 another development occurred, which alarmed Abdurrahman because of its potential to produce a violent response from the Indonesian military and their militia. That month the Australian government changed its official stance on East Timor. It had previously been one of the few nations to recognise Indonesia's annexation of East Timor and its inclusion as the Republic's twenty-seventh province. This had always sat uneasily on the Australian conscience on both sides of politics. In January conservative Prime Minister John Howard and his Foreign Minister Alexander Downer made the surprising move of writing to President Habibie to explain that, although Australia continued to recognise East Timor as part of Indonesia, it urged Jakarta to move towards holding a genuine act of self-determination as quickly as possible. Few in Canberra anticipated the outcome of that simple letter. When it arrived, Habibie was annoyed by the intervention in Indonesian affairs, particularly at a time when he felt the nation was facing so many other problems. On 27 January he announced that he was committed to offering 'greater autonomy' to East Timor and that he would hold a referendum offering a choice to the East Timorese. (It was commonly understood that if the East Timorese chose to reject the offer of 'greater autonomy' they would be setting out on a course for independence.) What surprised everyone about Habibie's response was that he pledged to have the issue resolved by the end of the year.

Abdurrahman voiced his alarm at Habibie's haste to 'be rid of the East Timor problem'. 'To hold a referendum in East Timor before Indonesia had a chance of installing a new government,' he argued, 'was foolhardy.' While Abdurrahman had long been committed to the struggle for greater human rights, he had not been active regarding East Timor. He regarded East Timor as a problem only soluble with the fall of Soeharto and the dismantling of his military-backed authoritarian regime. Like most intellectuals in Jakarta, he was not as well informed about what was taking place in East Timor as he might have been. Thanks to the military, the news that reached Jakarta was limited and distorted. Nevertheless, he knew that certain officers treated the province as their personal fiefdom and were accustomed to ruling with cruelty and violence. Not only did they plunder significant economic wealth from the benighted province; as a zone of operational duty it also provided an opportunity for the advancement of many military careers. Moreover, Abdurrahman was well aware of the reputation of former commanders in East Timor, such as Prabowo Subianto, for training and recruiting of militiamen and of their appalling human rights violations. He was worried that a move towards a referendum before reform had taken hold in Indonesia would both annoy the Indonesian military and provide an irresistible opportunity to wreak mayhem on the people of East Timor.

GUS DUR FOR PRESIDENT?

From the foundation of the party in July 1998 many within PKB held the hope that Abdurrahman would become president. At the very least they reserved the right to nominate him as their presidential candidate, but then most parties nominated their own people as presidential candidates regardless of their prospects for victory. On 7 February 1999, party chairman Matori announced that the party would nominate Abdurrahman and spoke optimistically of the prospects of the party gaining as much as 30 per cent of the vote. Few political observers, however, held strong hope for the possibility of Abdurrahman's election because they did not expect that the party could do much more than draw the votes of a proportion of NU members.

In March 1999 Abdurrahman alarmed supporters and enraged his critics once again. While on a visit to Singapore he said that there was a problem with Megawati's candidature for the presidency. He explained that many conservative *kiai* and other Muslim leaders felt uncertain about her, and that many cited her gender as the reason for questioning her suitability for the presidency. Certainly many did question Megawati's suitability for the presidency although it had more to do with her own personal attributes than her gender. Why then did Abdurrahman raise the issue? Some suggested it was a deliberate attempt to stymie Megawati's advance and was therefore a premeditated act of betrayal. Others interpreted it as 'kite flying': he was seeking to draw out a response as to where people stood on the issue. He denied that he was against Megawati's candidature on the grounds of her gender and said that he thought those conservative *kiai* were clearly wrong to hold such a view.

Even if Abdurrahman was not intending to undermine Megawati's position, there is no denying that his comments about her in public were frequently offensive. For example, on a number of occasions he said words to the effect that she was 'honest but stupid'. In private Abdurrahman often spoke of Megawati with great affection and respect, so it is difficult to account for his cavalier attitude to her in public. For her part, Megawati was understandably offended by Abdurrahman's comments and their friendship began to show signs of stress.

Why then make such statements? Perhaps it can be explained on the basis of his habit of thinking aloud; sometimes he simply made a gaffe while talking without stopping to think about what he is saying. Perhaps another factor was his blindness. On more than one occasion his comments have gone to air when he didn't even realise that a camera was pointed at him and was recording. Not one of these explanations, however, is entirely satisfactory in explaining his comments about Megawati. Whatever his intention, those statements did have the effect of stigmatising her candidature. It is possible that Abdurrahman did have genuine concerns about conservative sentiment within NU circles. His uncle Yusuf Hasyim and Idham Chalid, the former chairman of NU (Abdurrahman's long-time nemesis) had both become involved with small parties claiming to represent NU (and freely using NU symbols). Both of these men were seeking to garner the support, not just of traditional enemies of Abdurrahman, but of conservative elements who were worried about Abdurrahman's possible alliance with Megawati and Amien Rais.

Besides these tensions between PKB and the various other parties that contended for support from NU members, such as the NU Party and the Awakening of the Ummat Party, there were also considerable tensions between PKB members and those supporting PPP. Many NU *kiai* had continued to be active in PPP long after NU officially withdrew from the party in 1994. NU's policy under Abdurrahman had been to allow involvement in any political party that individuals chose, with the proviso that NU office-bearers could not simultaneously hold office in a political party. The creation of PKB came with the expectation that many of those who had previously belonged to PPP would return to support the party endorsed by NU's central board. One example of such a shift was Khofifah Indar Parawansa, an impressively outspoken member of DPR for PPP, who emerged in the post-Soeharto era to play a leading role within PKB.

Bad blood remained between elements of PKB and PPP in certain districts. One such location was the town of Jepara, near Semarang in Central Java. On 30 April a clash broke out that quickly became violent and resulted in the death of five people, with six others sustaining serious injuries. Also destroyed in the violence were two houses, fourteen cars and six motorbikes. A week after the outbreak Abdurrahman flew to Jepara in order to hold a large rally, much to the consternation of local officials who were worried that the violence would recur. The rally fortunately proved uneventful. Abdurrahman appealed to NU members to remain calm and to forgive those who hurt them, saying 'PKB members must remain calm and at peace. Some of our people were killed, but we forgive them'. He explained that in the current murky circumstances it was often impossible to know whether people wearing certain uniforms or insignia were genuine members of the party or group that they appeared to represent, or were planted there for the purpose of provoking violence. For this reason, he argued, it was vital that NU members resist all attempts to incite them to violence. Fortunately the incident in Jepara proved the worst of such clashes, but discontent between the PPP supporters and PKB supporters continued to simmer throughout the campaign.

By late March Abdurrahman's recovery was largely complete. He still suffered somewhat from nausea and lethargy, but otherwise there was surprisingly little sign that, just fourteen months earlier, he had nearly died from a massive stroke. True enough, to those who did not know him he looked like a tired old man, a clumsy invalid unable to function without his ever-attendant helpers. To those who knew him better, however, and especially to those who were with him daily, he had almost returned to his former self. It had been many years since Abdurrahman had looked the picture of health, but anyone who had ever travelled with him could testify to the stubborn bull-like energy that lay behind his chubby, world-worn appearance. Ill-accustomed to blindness, Abdurrahman looked more clumsy than ever, but by May his robust stamina had returned. When he spoke at rallies in early and mid-April he addressed the crowds seated in a large armchair. By the end of month he began to stand, often speaking for more than an hour at a time.

TEAM GUS DUR

By this point poor health was no longer a serious impediment to a vigorous campaign by Abdurrahman. His main impediment was the same one that had dogged him throughout his career: a shortage of human and other resources, exacerbated by his poor administrative ability. Throughout his chairmanship of NU Abdurrahman had typically acted as a one-man show. It was not that he couldn't get along with people or build alliances; in fact, when he put his mind to it he could be an extraordinarily skilful and inspirational leader. It was more that, for a variety of reasons, not least being lack of human resources, he was accustomed to working alone. This may have served him reasonably well in leading a cultural and social movement such as NU, but it was not a good basis for campaigning for the presidency.

Despite his annoying foibles, Abdurrahman inspired great loyalty and deep affection in those around him. For the 1999 campaign season he received help from several individuals whose contribution was decisive. The first was Alwi Shihab, an old friend of Abdurrahman's from their student days in Cairo. In recent years they had seen little of each other, largely because Alwi had spent more than a decade studying and teaching in the United States. Alwi had a PhD in Islamic studies from Ain Shams University, Egypt, and a second PhD in religious studies from Temple University in the United States. He then taught at Hartford seminary and at Harvard University Divinity School. He had returned to Indonesia in 1998, intending to make a brief visit but, as the PKB machine gathered momentum, he decided to put aside a couple of months to see what sort of contribution he could make. By early 1999 Alwi's original plans of taking several months off to help out at home had gone out the window. It was largely through Alwi's intervention that Abdurrahman was able to achieve harmonious relations with Amien Rais and to build up good relations with leading modernists, including many ICMI moderates.

A second person who made a decisive difference to the campaign was Ratih Hardjono. Ratih had been, for many years, a correspondent for *Kompas*, the Catholic-owned national newspaper. She had worked mostly as a foreign correspondent based in Sydney and Melbourne. Early in 1999 she decided to take leave without pay for several months in order to return to Jakarta and help Abdurrahman in his campaign. She had known Abdurrahman and his family for many years and had been instrumental in arranging therapy for Nuriyah in Australia following her car accident of 1993. Abdurrahman and Nuriyah frequently stayed at her home in Sydney and she had proved herself a generous and loyal friend. When Abdurrahman lost his eyesight in January 1998, Ratih swung into action to organise the purchase of a reading machine to enable him to continue reading with the help of a voice synthesiser and scanner. The project was ultimately unsuccessful, even though Ratih was able to purchase the machine and transport it to his house, simply because Abdurrahman was still in a state of denial about his blindness. Psychologically, he was not ready to learn the coping skills that those who have accepted their loss finally come to learn. Despite a long friendship with Abdurrahman's family and being related to Abdurrahman through her father, Ratih was largely unfamiliar with the culture of traditional Islam and NU. Culturally she was much influenced by her father, who followed *Kejawaen* or Javanese mysticism, and by her Australian-born mother, who was Catholic.

Intense and passionate by nature, Ratih brought to Abdurrahman's campaign a degree of managerial rigour and discipline that had, until her arrival, been completely foreign to him. Not only did she arrange travel and press engagements and solicit funds for the campaign, but she was also a gatekeeper protecting Abdurrahman from a press keen to capture a quick quote on which to build a controversial story. For this reason many were fearful of Ratih and her often fiery outbursts, but there was no question of her loyalty to Abdurrahman.

In day-to-day arrangements Ratih worked closely with Abdurrahman's second daughter Yenny, who had known her for many years. Together the two women organised Abdurrahman's life. Nuriyah was occasionally able to join him on his expeditions in the country, but her need to use a wheelchair to cover more than the shortest of distances made it hard for her to join his small, poorly equipped entourage, as did the rigorous and unrelenting nature of his travel regime.

By this point Al Zastrow, Abdurrahman's personal assistant since the time of his stroke, had passed the baton to another young *pesantren* graduate, Munib. Quiet and unassuming, Munib's personal style was very different from that of the flamboyant Zastrow, who had become something of a media personality, but Munib proved no less effective in attending to the day-to-day needs of his near-blind master.

The small band that assembled for most of Abdurrahman's campaign trips was woefully inadequate and, by any measure, inexperienced. It was also grossly under-resourced. Frequently it was not known if funds were available for a trip until hours before, though they could always rely on local *pesantren* and friends for hospitality. Despite the ramshackle nature of the campaign team, its members were almost invariably in good spirits and engaged in constant banter. Although no one thought it likely that Abdurrahman would become president, they were well aware that it was not beyond the bounds of possibility. The sheer ludicrousness of the notion struck everyone as ironic and amusing. No president or prime minister from a democracy of any size could have achieved office with the sort of minimalist campaign that backed this candidate for the presidency of the world's third-largest democracy.

Of all the campaign team, Abdurrahman was always the one who possessed the most energy and seemed least affected by the rigours of travel. He explained that he welcomed travel precisely because it afforded some opportunities to rest. It was easy for him to switch off for five or fifty minutes when travelling in a car or plane, and it seemed entirely probable that he did get more rest while on the road than when at home. More importantly, though, he was clearly re-energised by speaking to people around the country, whether they were ageing *kiai*, party faithful, Chinese businessmen, or other friends. It seems likely that the adrenaline rush of the campaign served to consolidate Abdurrahman's final recovery.

Despite the less than polished nature of Abdurrahman's personal campaign team, his appearances were invariably dramatic affairs. Police escorts would guide the ad hoc convoy in from the airport to the site of the rally. Many of the rallies were very large, involving tens of thousands of people, and as the campaign progressed it become increasingly common to see PKB supporters mingling and working alongside PDI-P supporters. One of the key elements providing practical assistance on the ground was NU's youth wing Ansor. Members of Ansor are organised into uniformed troops known as Banser — a kind of Boy Scouts movement replete with black, military-style uniforms. Some find these Banser troops intimidating, but for the most part the Banser are more like overgrown Boy Scouts than militiamen. It was evident when Banser troops lined up to welcome Abdurrahman to a rally that they took great pride in the uniforms, which were mostly paid for through their own savings, and that they were serious about doing their job. It was equally obvious that, despite their paramilitary appearance, theirs was for the most part an amateurish and innocent enthusiasm. For all of their attempts at seriousness when arrayed in uniform, they tended to make a comic assembly. It was not uncommon at the rallies to hear a cry to march left and see the group break off in two directions, both unsure which was left. All of this added a carnival air to the campaign process. On the one hand the whole campaign was deadly serious, but on the other the amateurish and limited nature of some contributions could not help but raise a smile.

The first big rally of the PKB campaign was held on 9 April in

Jombang. It was preceded by a lesser rally in the town of Mojokerto, half an hour south of Jombang. Ratih had been travelling with the team for only a few weeks and was still trying desperately to consolidate an element of professionalism in the campaign. Having covered many political campaigns as a journalist, Ratih was aware of the importance of projecting the correct image; she saw it as a high priority that, as far as possible, Abdurrahman's presentation should be polished. Part of this was preventing him from speaking off-the-cuff in a provocative fashion, but a large part was simply a matter of grooming. One small ploy to improve his appearance was to fit him out with a smart pair of gold-rimmed spectacles. They were no help at all in enabling him to see, but they did give him a more dignified appearance.[4]

A dignified appearance was precisely what Abdurrahman's dress sense did not convey. Abdurrahman had never been a snappy dresser, being deeply averse to pretension and to deliberate display and, it must be said, lacking any innate sense of what makes for good presentation. Alwi is exactly the opposite, immaculately turned out and dressed correctly for every occasion whether formal or informal. If some of Alwi's sartorial elegance, if not urbane demeanour, could be transposed onto Abdurrahman, it was felt he would be better understood both by domestic and international journalists. After all, how can anyone take seriously the spiritual leader of a major party and possible future president, who goes around in a bright red Hawaian shirt with curry stains down the front?

SHIFTING ALLIANCES

While Abdurrahman was out on the campaign trail, Alwi was working hard to improve relations between modernists and traditionalists. He was helped in this by a growing friendship between Ansor leader Saifullah Yusuf (Abdurrahman's nephew and also a PDI-P candidate) and Imam Ardyaquttni, leader of the Muhammadiyah youth group. Throughout the campaign period these two young leaders arranged for Muhammadiyah youth and Ansor to meet in a series of public seminars and meetings, and by mid-May there was a real sense that many modernists and traditionalists could work together. It even appeared that personal relations between Amien and Abdurrahman were steadily becoming more intimate and warm.

The day 17 May was to prove a turning-point in the campaign. In many ways it was a typical day of campaigning with Abdurrahman: an early-morning start driving to the port of Merak on the western end of Java to board a ferry to Sumatra, and then another two hours of driving eastwards across the coastal hills of Lampung to the site of the day's rally. As usual the rally was preceded by a lunch at the home of a *kiai* and a series of private meetings with local elders. Once the rally concluded, a high-speed convoy led by a police escort rushed back through the hilly terrain of southern Sumatra to the ferry port and then by high-speed hydrofoil to Java and by road back to Jakarta. For most people this would be more than enough work for one day. For Abdurrahman it was but half a day's work — the other half was to come that evening. Attending a book launch at a city hotel and having a polite dinner with intellectuals was but an intermission. The focus of the day was the press conference that was planned for 10:30 that evening between Amien Rais, Megawati Soekarnoputri and Abdurrahman Wahid to announce the formation of a common front between their three parties to work together to overcome Golkar.[5]

It was not until half an hour or so after midnight that news came back to the hundreds of journalists jammed into Alwi's suburban home that the press conference was about to begin. Into the room minutes later came a relaxed Abdurrahman and Amien, looking more than ever like old friends, but there was no sign of Megawati. A whispered comment from Yenny made it clear that the evening had not gone very well at Megawati's house. Abdurrahman quickly offered an apology on Megawati's behalf, explaining that she was due to travel to Sumatra tomorrow. He had suggested, he said, that she get an early night and that he and Amien could handle the press conference alone. Relations between Amien and Abdurrahman were clearly much better because they both talked enthusiastically about the possibility of presenting a common front against Golkar along with Megawati and her party. No one was using the word coalition — it was felt that such a formal political arrangement could not be worked out until after the election — but it was clear that there was a real possibility of secular nationalists, traditionalist Muslims and modernist Muslims working side-by-side against Golkar and its partners.

That meeting on 17 May was to prove ominous. Relations between the modernists and traditionalists continued to improve during the period of the campaign, due to the efforts of Alwi and others and also to Abdurrahman's realistic acceptance of the need to restore relations with Amien. But relations between Abdurrahman and Megawati went from bad to worse. An increasing frostiness came into their personal relationship and throughout the rest of the campaign period there were few occasions when they talked at any length about serious matters. One of the main reasons, evidently, why Megawati had not been keen to attend the press conference at Alwi's house on 17 May was that she was distrustful of Amien.

A MOST UNUSUAL CAMPAIGN

There was no doubt that Abdurrahman was engaged in a serious political campaign to raise support for PKB, and to an extent for the alliance between himself, Megawati and Amien, but there were many aspects of his campaign that did not add up. It was not just the amateurishness and the limited resources, it was also a matter of his choice of venues. Abdurrahman travelled relentlessly across Java, where PKB stood to make good gains. He also, however, visited a number of other places where it seemed most unlikely there was anything to be gained from campaigning.

One such trip occurred in May when he made a visit to Banda Aceh, the capital of the province of Aceh on the northern tip of Sumatra. There are very few members of NU in Aceh, even though the dominant expression of Islam in Acehenese has many parallels with the traditional Islam found in NU and rural Java. Abdurrahman had good relations with the *ulama* in Aceh and was keen to strengthen them, but there was no serious expectation that a large number of their supporters would vote for PKB. Instead, they were inclined to give their votes to PPP, which had long been their custom. One of the major obstacles to voting for PKB was its Javanese base. For understandable reasons, the Acehenese were suspicious of anything coming out of Java. Nevertheless, Abdurrahman was well received by the *ulama* and it was clear that there was a genuine rapport with the religious leadership in Aceh. The same could not be said for many of the students. While many students admired him as a reformist who had stood up to Soeharto, others were just as critical of him and, given his Javanese origins, suspicious of his intentions.

One of the central points of the campaign was to have been an address to students in a large sports stadium in Banda Aceh. As we approached the hall it was clear that the atmosphere was tense. A handful of youths were in a highly emotional state, waving placards and shouting abuse at Abdurrahman as his small entourage entered the guest room. The next half an hour was spent in the guest room beside the main auditorium evaluating whether or not to proceed with the meeting as planned. Eventually it was decided to go ahead, but Abdurrahman, Yenny and Ratih were heavily jostled as they made their way through the crowd to the podium. From there it seemed that the vast majority of the several thousand students who were gathered there were keen to listen, but several hundred, congregated in one corner of the room, were clearly angry and upset. This group waved large placards with slogans written both in Indonesian and in English of a nature rarely seen at gatherings where Abdurrahman was speaking. One placard consisted simply of the name 'Dur Rahman' across which was stamped a large footprint. Another placard read 'Abdurrahman is an evil spirit in a human body'. Clearly there were some people in the room who were not happy with his visit.

Almost as soon as he began speaking, he was met with sharp heckling from the quarter of the room where the angry placards were evident. Other students tried to stop the hecklers; they argued that Abdurrahman should be given a chance to speak since he had been invited to come. About twenty minutes into the proceedings, things suddenly went badly wrong. A surge of angry students broke through the ranks and surrounded the podium. Fajrul Falaak tried valiantly to negotiate a discussion with them, and for a while it appeared that this was working. What wrecked everything was Abdurrahman's response. For perhaps half an hour he had been trying to negotiate with and respond to the students, but as they surged forward he lost his cool. As the shouting students came on three sides to within a metre of the platform, Abdurrahman began to shout back, saying 'You invited me here. If you want me to speak, give me a chance — if not I'll go'. When the heckling failed to stop, he abruptly got up and made for the exit. As a result the main rally planned for later that afternoon was also called off.

Later that afternoon Abdurrahman contacted the student leaders to say that he would like to meet with them and explain his position. A meeting took place in the early hours of the following morning; he apologised for his outburst, explaining the circumstances for his frustration. That evening he also met with key *ulama* and members of the media, but it was clear that there was little to be gained from prolonging the visit in Aceh. The rally planned for the next day, a combined rally between members of PDI-P and PKB in Medan, 500 kilometres to the south, went rather better, but there was no hiding the sense of disappointment that the visit to Aceh had gone so badly wrong.

A similarly 'non-political' visit occurred after campaigning had officially closed on the Friday before the polls on Monday, 7 June. It took place on the Sunday at Pontianak, West Kalimantan, not far from the region of Sambas which had seen much violent fighting between Dayak and Madurese transmigrants. Like the trip to Banda Aceh, this was a genuine, if perhaps naive, attempt by Abdurrahman to meet with community leaders and persuade them to be patient in the face of enormous pressure. The meeting in Pontianak took the form of a post-lunch address to a large gathering of community leaders. Heads of the various churches, local Muslim leaders, leaders of Dayak communities and Madurese communities all gathered. Both Abdurrahman and Alwi addressed the meeting and both were in excellent form, speaking passionately of the need for tolerance, and for the disengaging of religious sentiment from politics.

EXTRAVAGANT OPTIMISM

Abdurrahman finished the campaign in high spirits. He told journalists that he thought that PKB would get more than 30 per cent of the national vote — perhaps even 40 per cent. There was little basis, of course, for these wildly optimistic forecasts. His reckless predictions can perhaps best be seen as 'locker-room talk', a deliberate boosting of sentiment to maintain team morale ahead of a tough game. Realistically it seemed that PKB would be doing well to get as much as 16 to 18 per cent of the vote, and that was only possible if it succeeded in gaining the votes of almost everyone involved with NU — which was not likely, given that many had maintained strong links to PPP. In the two elections after NU broke with PPP, the latter's vote had dropped to around 12 per cent. Unless PKB was successful in attracting non-NU voters in large numbers — which hardly seemed likely in 1999 — it was itself heading for a share of the national vote of about 12 per cent.

Abdurrahman was not the only one making wildly optimistic poll predictions. PPP leader Hamzah Haz, when questioned several weeks before the election, had said that he thought that his party could get 22 per cent of the vote.[6] Similarly Amien Rais, and many within the PAN, spoke confidently of getting 90 per cent of all modernist votes and maybe as much as 30 to 40 per cent of the total. Although speculation within PDI-P was much more modest, some voices still spoke confidently of achieving a bare majority. Given that no free and fair election had been held since 1955, there was no simple yardstick to direct expectations about polling results, and consequently the wild speculations about possible outcomes were understandable in the circumstances. Even Golkar officials spoke bravely of securing 40 per cent of the total vote, although in many areas in Java it was hard to imagine more than a handful of votes going to the party of the despised former president. In the outer islands, however, the story was different, for in many areas outside Java the economic crisis had hardly touched people's welfare. Given their long experience of prosperity under Golkar, it seemed likely that many would to continue to vote for the party that had so consistently delivered for them.

THE VOTE IS IN

Polling day, 7 June, dawned unusually bright and sunny in Jakarta, a city that on most days was grey and overcast. Abdurrahman woke early and voted at his local polling booth in Ciganjur before proceeding as usual to the NU headquarters in central Jakarta. Over lunch he was expansive and optimistic, not just about the prospects for PKB but also for the election generally. As usual though, his optimism was tinged with a streak of sober realism about the prospects for defeating Golkar.

In many districts the whole community come out to gather around the polling booth and a festive atmosphere prevailed. Everywhere one went there seemed immense optimism and sheer joy at being able to vote. This euphoria continued well after voting closed. It was generally agreed that the vote had been surprisingly free and fair. However, the excruciatingly slow rate at which results were collated over the following days steadily dampened that earlier sense of optimism.

Public scrutiny of vote counting took place in the Media Centre at the Hyatt Aryaduta hotel in central Jakarta. With the assistance of various foreign governments, the Committee for Elections had organised, not just a room filled with computers for the use of journalists, but also an information-rich website where one could track counting moment by moment. In the first few days after voting closed, many foreign correspondents along with other observers gathered at the Hyatt Aryaduta in the early hours of the morning, expecting at any moment a sudden surge of results that would confirm the overall pattern of voting. The surge never came: the results trickled in at a painfully slow pace over several weeks.

Most major political parties and many of the smaller parties had set up their offices with banks of computers to monitor the results on the internet site. At the headquarters of NU, however, not a single computer was to be seen, let alone one with an internet connection. Indeed, it was difficult to find even a functioning typewriter. For those gathered in the 'characterful' but decrepit rooms of the NU national headquarters to assess the progress of PKB, the best information was gained by crossing to an adjoining building where a television set was tuned to the Indosiar private channel, on which the election results were periodically updated on a ticker-tape display running across the bottom of the screen. Moreover, in discussions about the meaning of results, it was clear that no one at NU's National Headquarters completely understood exactly how vote counting and allocation of seats would occur. This was not so surprising given the extraordinarily complex methods for seat allocations and vote counting.

Whereas the minor Islamist parties had signed a formal 'Stembus Accord' to pool their results, and so maximise their total number of seats, the idea had not even been raised in PKB, largely because no one really understood how such an accord would work. As a result, when the votes began to trickle in, party supporters were not only disappointed with the percentage of the total vote won, they were even more disappointed with the number of seats. Although PKB did well in Central and East Java, it made few gains outside this heartland, and as a result there was a discrepancy between the number of its votes and the number of its seats.

At the end of counting, PKB had secured a disappointing 12.4 per cent of the total vote. Even more disappointing was the result secured by PAN, which managed only a little over 7 per cent. Golkar was still able to retain 22 per cent, which, given the way in which the electoral system favoured outer-islands seats, was perhaps to be expected. Many were surprised by PPP's result, as much as 10 per cent of the vote, but then the party did consistently well in outer-island areas and had many loyal supporters, who for decades had been in the habit of voting for the official Islamic party. Not surprisingly, PDI-P did best of all, gaining almost 34 per cent — in line with some of the more sober predictions of its leaders — and it also did well in the total number of seats that it secured. It soon became clear that the PKB would be a junior member of any coalition with Megawati's party.

THE EMERGENCE OF THE CENTRAL AXIS

For weeks Amien Rais was so crestfallen at the result gained by PAN that he largely withdrew from political negotiations, but by the end of June he was talking again with Abdurrahman about the best way to work together. At the same time relations with Megawati continued to deteriorate. When the results became clear, Megawati said that the best that PKB could expect in her new government was 'one cabinet position — no more than that'. This deeply disappointed many PKB members who had hoped for at least two or three cabinet places.

Megawati's coolness extended to her demeanour towards Abdurrahman. On several occasions in late June and early July when Abdurrahman had visited Megawati, as a sign of her displeasure she kept him downstairs in a waiting room for an hour or more — on one occasion as long as two hours. Megawati was understandably thrilled with the result of her party and took it as given that she would now ride this wave of success to the presidency.

On 17 May, several days after the meeting between Abdurrahman and Amien Rais to announce to the press the formation of their three-cornered common front with Megawati, Amien had held another meeting of no less consequence. He met with leaders of PPP and the Justice Party (Partai Keadilan — PK) to explore the possibility of forming a common grouping of Islamic parties. Many observers wondered whether Amien was not simply reverting to his old habits of aligning himself with sectarian forces. By early July it was clear that what had begun with that meeting had potentially much broader ramifications. At about this time there was talk of a third force in Indonesian politics that balanced Golkar and its coalition members against Megawati's PDI-P. This third force was dubbed the *poros tengah*, or central axis, group.

Initially no one was sure what to make of this group, but by late June it was being treated as a credible third power bloc and the press was referring to it with capital letters. It had earlier been assumed that after the poll the balance of power would be divided evenly between a 'reformist' push led by PDI-P and the PKB, and a so-called 'status quo' coalition led by Golkar and PPP along with the smaller Islamist parties. Now the Central Axis led by Amien appeared to offer the potential of drawing PPP, the Crescent Star Party (Partai Bulan Bintang — PBB) and PK away from an otherwise inevitable coalition with Golkar.

At about the same time, Amien, in the name of the Central Axis, began to float the idea of nominating Abdurrahman as the presidential candidate. The nomination was explained in terms of seeking to balance the power of Megawati's camp against Habibie's camp and possibly providing an alternative candidate should a deadlock emerge between the two. Abdurrahman, whose relationship with Megawati was at this stage showing little sign of recovery, was increasingly criticised for his failure to work harder on the relationship. When he accepted, without comment, the proposed nomination of himself as alternative presidential candidate, many were incensed. It seemed to be the ultimate betrayal of Megawati.

Others argued that what Abdurrahman was doing was a clever ploy to draw away potential coalition partners from Golkar and towards a reformist push. Habibie's long sponsorship of ICMI, it was argued, gave him the advantage when it came to drawing in parties like PK and PPP. It was to remain unclear, right up to the eve of the presidential election, exactly what Abdurrahman's strategy was. Privately, Abdurrahman said that he was willing to make a run for the presidency if Megawati failed to become serious about uniting a coalition around her party. This placed the leadership of PKB in a difficult position. Officially Megawati remained their nominated candidate; unofficially many party leaders acknowledged that if Abdurrahman were serious about running for the presidency then his followers in NU, in other words the members of PKB, would be obliged to support his bid.

By the end of the first week in July Abdurrahman and Amien Rais were speaking openly about the possibility of a second Ciganjur meeting, dubbed Ciganjur Two. What they meant by this was obvious. They would seek to restore their three-cornered coalition with Megawati and start this off with a public meeting with her.

In early July, Alissa, the eldest daughter of Abdurrahman and Nuriyah, was married. The traditional three-day Javanese wedding ceremony was held at the family home in Ciganjur. Significantly, Megawati attended on every day and played a key role in certain ceremonial aspects of the wedding. On Sunday, 4 July, a public reception was held for the wedding. Over three thousand guests attended the grand ceremony held at a reception house in central Jakarta.

Abdurrahman had worked hard to maintain a working relationship with Habibie. He regularly called upon him at his home in central Jakarta to discuss his plans and he visited him ahead of the wedding to explain his desire for a second Ciganjur meeting. When asked why he bothered to liaise with Habibie, Abdurrahman explained that it was proper in a democracy to keep a head of state informed and that this was the best way of avoiding suspicion and misunderstanding. Habibie appeared to have genuine respect and affection for Abdurrahman and made a generous donation to the cost of the wedding. The downside of Habibie's contribution to the wedding was the presence of over four hundred security personnel who exhaustively swept the site for bombs and explosives ahead of the ceremony and maintained a heavy presence throughout Habibie's visit. It is significant that, although both Habibie and Megawati visited that night, they carefully timed their visits not to overlap. The reception served as a reminder of Abdurrahman's power within Jakarta society and showed that no one was ready to discount his influence.

As July drew to a close, the much-awaited second Ciganjur meeting failed to materialise. On one occasion it was cancelled at the last minute because it was said Amien had to accompany his mother to the hospital. At the same time Abdurrahman was working hard to try and rebuild the relationship with Megawati. By way of an olive branch he extended an invitation to join him on a visit to East Java to pray at the tombs of both their fathers. Megawati declined the invitation, or at least deferred taking it up, and continued to be cool towards Abdurrahman. At the same time Amien had become outspoken in this support for Abdurrahman's nomination as alternative candidate for the presidency, saying: 'There should be an alternative figure, not just Megawati or Habibie's groups. The nation's children should not be led to believe there is no other presidential candidate in the country.' When questioned about the nomination, Abdurrahman said:

> It is important to me as it is the first time the Islam-based parties have agreed to choose a person like me. It carries an important meaning. But, I've made my choice. I am supporting Mega although it is not final. As a good citizen and a good Muslim I'll always abide by the ruling of the house, no matter who would be elected.[7]

A SERIOUS CANDIDATE?

In his public statements Abdurrahman was careful to maintain a degree of ambiguity about his position on nomination for president. By early August he was on record as saying that he accepted the willingness of the Central Axis forces to nominate him but that he personally continued to support Megawati. Privately, he was much more frank. He explained that if Megawati failed to put together a credible coalition force and to take seriously the need to lobby and build up understanding among different political factions, he was prepared to oppose her openly. 'If I contest her,' he explained, 'then I will do it seriously. If she wins, good, then she will have learnt some important lessons about democracy. If I win then that's fine also. Either way, once the contest starts I'll be serious.'[8]

As is often the case with Abdurrahman, it was never possible to tell exactly how much he was joking and how much he was serious. There seemed no question that a resolve was forming in his mind to make a serious bid for the presidency, nor was there any question that he believed in his heart that he could win. It also seemed to be the case, however, that Abdurrahman and perhaps even Amien Rais were still waiting for some response from Megawati and still held out the hope that she might make a serious effort to build a coalition. Abdurrahman felt that if Megawati failed to seriously consider the interests of Muslims then, even if she were successful in forming a government, it would create a serious social and political liability in terms of anger and upset on the part of those who felt excluded.

On 22 July, after a two-hour meeting with Habibie, Abdurrahman responded to the waiting press by saying, 'Mr Amien Rais supports me. I support Megawati. Mega had better say that she will support Amien. That is much better than just making a lot of noise'.[9] Amien expressed similar sentiment when interviewed the same day: 'As a friend and colleague, I would have greater hope if Megawati could come into public sight more often to speak about her ideas. That is much better than to stay quiet.' In explaining his support for Abdurrahman, Amien said, 'Out of talks I've made regularly, it appears that Gus Dur is trustworthy and could tackle objections significantly. Resistance against Gus Dur is minimal'. He explained that minority groups, the military and the international community would be willing to embrace Abdurrahman. He went on to explain, 'Out of that though, Gus Dur is still the strongest candidate of the middle faction. But we're still waiting for Megawati, Akbar Tandjung, and the possible reaction of Habibie'.

FRUSTRATION, DEPRESSION AND EAST TIMOR

Shortly after this Abdurrahman left for an international tour. His primary destination was Salt Lake City, Utah, where he had an appointment at the Mormon General Hospital. He was desperately hoping that doctors there would be able to restore his eyesight. His choice of the Mormon hospital seemed odd, given that presumably he could have chosen any hospital in the world. In fact an American businessman, who happened to be a Mormon, had offered to pay for his treatment. In the end there was no hospital in the world that could restore Abdurrahman's eyesight. He left for America, as always on such trips, full of hopes that just one more operation would be required to make a significant difference. The doctors made some small corrections to his eyelid so that his eye presented itself better but could do nothing for his sight. Too many of the vital capillary and nerve connections had been lost.

Abdurrahman is seldom melancholy or morose, but after the doctors' failure he returned home more depressed than he had been in many years. Perhaps his mood was also the product of the physical strain he had placed himself under throughout the campaign period. His ongoing poor relationship with Megawati, although he was quite prepared to use it for political advantage, troubled him. The impending referendum in East Timor also troubled him. He was deeply worried that a referendum at the end of August 1999 would provoke a vicious response from sections of the Indonesian military and the militia. He believed it would have been much fairer and safer to wait, perhaps for several years, until there was a stable democratic government in Jakarta.

When conditions continued to deteriorate and violence broke out, Abdurrahman was upset by what he understood to be the response of the international community and particularly Australia. He was quoted on several occasions in the media making strong statements against Australia, or more specifically, against the conservative government of John Howard. He felt that the attitude of the Australian government was overbearing and arrogant and had failed completely to show sympathy or understanding of the plight of reformists like himself. Indonesia, he argued, was in the midst of tremendous upheaval and at a critical point in transition, yet there seemed to be no recognition of what Indonesia was going through, or the inability to control forces on the ground in East Timor.

At that time some of Abdurrahman's statements were extreme, but it seemed to be the season for extreme statements, most of which were later regretted by both sides. Abdurrahman's depression and ill-temper continued through September, as did his anger towards what he saw as the patronising attitude of Australia regarding Indonesia and the disastrous violence in East Timor. Making matters worse was

Abdurrahman's serious underestimation of the anti-Indonesian sentiment within East Timor. In the months leading up to the poll he had spoken with concern over the potential for violence because he believed that both sides would be fairly evenly balanced. As it turned out, an overwhelming number, almost 80 per cent, of East Timorese voters had voted against accepting the autonomy package offered to them by the Indonesian Republic. The result caught Abdurrahman off-guard and probably contributed to his intemperate tone reported in the media.[10]

At the same time that Abdurrahman was struggling with coming to terms with what was happening in East Timor, Yenny was witnessing it firsthand. When the election campaign in Indonesia finished in June, Yenny returned to her work as an assistant journalist with the *Sydney Morning Herald* and the *Age*. In mid-August she flew to East Timor with the papers' foreign correspondent Lindsay Murdoch and reported from there until being evacuated to Jakarta in a TNI C130 transport aircraft in early September. It was a formative time for Yenny, and her experiences there were later to have a great impact on her father and his understanding of what had really happened in East Timor. Unusually for someone of her age and without formal training in journalism, she was encouraged to file her own copy. Together with her colleagues she was later given the Walkley Award, Australia's equivalent of a Pulitzer Prize, for her reporting from East Timor. One of the many things she witnessed was the fatal shooting of an East Timorese by an Indonesian policeman. After spending a week at home in Ciganjur, she boarded an aircraft chartered by Reuters and flew back to Dili in mid-September. There she was one of fewer than a dozen Indonesian journalists permitted to stay in East Timor at a time when TNI was refusing to allow foreign journalists to return. Living in the TNI headquarters in Dili and surviving on limited military rations for a week before the Australian-led UN peace-keeping Interfet forces landed in East Timor on 20 September, she reported on the post-ballot violence perpetrated by TNI and its militia following the 30 August vote. Before she left at the end of the month, she witnessed atrocities the like of which she could not previously have imagined. In particular the death of fellow journalist Sander Thoenes left her very shaken. She had become close to Thoenes and was with him shortly before he was last seen alive, catching a ride on the back of a motorbike.

After returning from East Timor Yenny talked to her father about what she had seen. Her account of her experiences had a profound impact on Abdurrahman and strengthened his resolve over the months that followed to push for the reform of the military.

By mid-September Abdurrahman seemed over the worst of his depression and ill-temper and was beginning to be more upbeat about his political circumstances and the prospects for reform in the nation. He had recently made the long-awaited East Java tour with Megawati to pray at the tombs of their fathers. It had marked a degree of reconciliation, though not a deep healing of the relationship. Megawati had slept during most of the journey, and when they had talked it had been mostly small talk. It seemed there was little chance of a turnaround in their relationship yet.

Abdurrahman was now resolved to contest the presidency and run a serious campaign against Megawati. It seemed to many there was every chance that he would crash and end up with nothing to show for his efforts and with little public recognition for his contribution to reform. Others around him were also worried although Alwi, ever cheerful and optimistic, seemed rather more confident.

Several days later, on 7 October, the reform faction made up of Central Axis elements and PKB nominated Abdurrahman as their presidential candidate. The reform faction was an alliance of PAN and PK, and the fact that it was joined now by the PKB was a sign of how seriously Abdurrahman's candidature was being taken. Even at this stage, however, it was not clear that Abdurrahman was really going to formally become a candidate for the presidency. Alwi explained it as being dependent upon gaining the approval of senior NU *kiai*. The senior *kiai* were due to gather with Abdurrahman just days before the vote-counting later that month. 'PKB as well as NU will abide by the words of holy wise men and this applies to Gus Dur as well. At the last moment the holy men will give their approval or not. That's what I meant by at the last moment,' explained Alwi.[11]

A SURPRISING TURN

When given a chance to respond to initial criticism of his accountability speech, Habibie had replied with a surprisingly confident speech in which he completely failed to acknowledge genuine concern about his performance. That night, Tuesday, 19 October, the vote was to be taken on whether his accountability speech was to be accepted or rejected. While the constitutional ramifications of the vote were uncertain, it was generally understood that the result would be a powerful indication of whether Habibie was to be supported or rejected. If Habibie failed to win majority support, it was likely that he would back down from the campaign.

The large assembly hall was packed with people, not only in the body of the hall, but also on the large back balcony and the two side balconies, which were filled with dozens of journalists jostling for position. As the count began, the mood was electric. There was a sense that maybe the expected support for Habibie would not materialise. By rights Golkar had the numbers to carry Habibie through. But as the counting proceeded, it quickly became clear that Habibie's victory was by no means assured; in fact, it soon became apparent that Habibie was in trouble. Evidently Akbar Tandjung's 'White Golkar' faction had decided to vote as a bloc against Habibie. The final vote made it clear: Habibie had been rolled. The pressure was on him to withdraw from the presidency, so it came down to Abdurrahman or Megawati. There was genuine shock, and also excitement and elation. The vote of no-confidence in Habibie now made it possible for Akbar Tandjung to be nominated in Habibie's place. Indeed there was considerable pressure on Akbar to accept Golkar's nomination. In the early hours of the morning of Wednesday, 20 October, Habibie had withdrawn himself from the race, explaining that he did not have the support even of his own party. Hours later, under pressure, Akbar yielded and accepted the Golkar nomination before rejecting it again early the following morning.

It was a long night. Abdurrahman did not get to sleep until napping briefly at 6.30 in the morning. Outside, the large sitting room of his hotel suite was packed with friends, relatives and supporters, some of them very recent. Alwi was clearly elated and confident about the result the day would bring. Next to Alwi sat Abdurrahman's brother Solahuddin, who had actively supported one of the small alternative NU parties and then in mid-1999 had switched to Golkar and become part of Habibie's so-called 'success team'. His presence in Abdurrahman's suite was a sign that he now judged his older brother to be the only viable candidate. This made sense when it was explained that Akbar had withdrawn his candidacy earlier that morning, and the contest for the presidency was now a two-person race. Shortly before 8 am Alwi's mobile phone rang. It was Akbar Tandjung. Akbar explained that there was now no question that his 'White Golkar' faction would back Abdurrahman. 'In that case,' responded Alwi, 'you had better come across and tell him yourself.' Five minutes later, Akbar was at the door.

From Abdurrahman's point of view, it had all gone perfectly to plan. As the vote count wound into its second half several hours later that day, Abdurrahman pulled ahead of Megawati and went on to a resounding victory. He clearly had received the support of the Central Axis and Akbar Tandjung's faction of Golkar. As he was guided to the podium by adjutants on both sides, looking clumsy and out of place, the international media announced to the world the news that Indonesia was now to be led by 'a frail, half-blind Muslim cleric'.

Megawati was clearly shaken by the result but was nevertheless polite in her congratulations to Abdurrahman. Even so, that night her supporters were anything but sanguine about the outcome. In the early evening the tens of thousands of youthful PDI-P faithful gathered in the city centre had begun to celebrate with exuberant jubilation, mistakenly believing that the vote had gone in Megawati's favour. When the error was realised things began to turn nasty in central Jakarta. Cars were overturned and burned; on Bali, where Megawati's part-Balinese ancestry contributed to her massive support, violence broke out on a large scale. That Wednesday evening it seemed that the country might quickly spiral out of control. Even Megawati, who ordinarily proved herself surprisingly capable of controlling her people, now seemed unable to bring herself to say the words to call them back off the streets.

Everything now hinged on the vice-presidency. In the early hours of Thursday morning several figures came forth vying for the second most powerful position in post-Soeharto Indonesia. General Wiranto ardently believed that he could win the vice-presidency and that he had every right to do so. Only desperate last-minute negotiations persuaded him that it was neither in his, nor the nation's, interests to oppose Megawati for the vice-presidency. Persuading Megawati, however, to contest the position was no easy job. Early in the day she indicated that she would only be willing to run for the position if she could be voted in by acclamation. She couldn't risk, she said, being rejected a second time. In the end she was persuaded that, as the leader of PDI-P, arriving at the vice-presidency by means of anything less than an open contest for the position would undermine the party's credibility. Alwi and others persuaded her that running for the position against PPP leader Hamzah Haz was the best way to ensure, not only that she became vice-president, but also that it was seen to be a fair contest.

Sitting on the steps of the parliamentary building during the recess before the final counting of votes, Alwi looked a little nervous. When congratulated on his success in negotiations over the previous twenty-four hours he responded by holding up crossed fingers and saying, 'Let's hope it works'. Prompted for an explanation, he confessed that that they were fairly confident that they had the numbers against Hamzah Haz but they couldn't be sure until the votes was counted.

When the recess was over, the atmosphere back in the assembly hall was tense. Early in the counting it appeared as if Hamzah Haz might indeed take the vice-presidency. Everyone was well aware of the implication. If Hamzah Haz — no friend of Abdurrahman but associated with NU and traditional Islam — were to become vice-president, not only would Megawati's supporters be outraged but so too would many other sections of society. In the end the numbers began to come in on Megawati's side and she surged to a comfortable victory. All around the room there was a genuine sense of relief. Across the nation people came to terms with the fact that the new vice-president and president represented perhaps the best combination imaginable. Few had predicted the outcome even a few days before, but it now seemed to be almost unbelievably good.

ELEVEN

A BRIEF HONEYMOON, 1999-2000

WHY BECOME PRESIDENT?

In the lead-up to the presidential election almost all of Abdurrahman's close friends and relatives expressed two reasons for grave concerns about the prospect that he would become president. Firstly, Indonesia's fourth president would have to manage a difficult and turbulent transition, which would certainly include concerted efforts by elements of the former regime to block and, if possible, topple him. At the same time the economy was in tatters, social cohesion was beginning to break down, and people's expectations about democracy were grossly inflated. Consequently, the new president would be roundly criticised and his work little appreciated. The second reason for their concern was that Abdurrahman was an eccentric and maverick leader. Although he was a visionary who could inspire and lead as few others could, his idiosyncratic approach to management was certain to draw criticism. In ordinary circumstances it would have made little sense to promote his candidature for the presidency. However, under the circumstances that prevailed in Indonesia at the time, there was reason to believe that negotiating the transition to democracy would require just such an approach. Abdurrahman was one of very few people who had gone head-to-head with Soeharto for more than a decade and had consistently come out on top, or at least been able to beat a strategic retreat and live to fight another day.

A COMPROMISED CABINET

Following the election of Megawati to the vice-presidency on Thursday, 21 October, Abdurrahman spent all of Friday and the weekend on what he termed 'cattle trading' (*dagang sapi*). In the run-up to the election he had talked about the necessity of forming a 'national unity' cabinet composed of members from across the political spectrum. That idea would have worked, had he been given free rein to choose his cabinet ministers. The reality was that almost all his cabinet ministers were imposed upon him.

On Monday morning he spoke hopefully about the cabinet he was planning, reeling off the names of those he considered the best of its twenty-five members. Between Monday morning and the public announcement of the cabinet at noon the next day, it had grown by ten members, most of whom were people Abdurrahman had not chosen. By the time of the announcement the cabinet had grown into an unwieldy amalgam of political interests and personalities, deeply compromised by the inclusion of political elements that were not merely diverse but mutually antagonistic. In theory a measure of accountability and discipline was to be achieved through Akbar, Megawati and Amien agreeing to act as guarantors for the members of their party selected for cabinet positions. Even in a mature democracy, this arrangement would have presented many challenges. In Indonesia, where 'democracy' had arrived not so much through the slow evolution of civil society but through the sudden collapse of a decadent and decayed regime, it was naive to expect that regime apparatchiks reborn overnight as democrats would exhibit the selflessness, maturity and professionalism needed to make such an unlikely union work.

Nevertheless, the cabinet was not wholly bereft of potentially good ministers. It benefited from the inclusion of people such as former Human Rights Commission chairman Marzuki Darusman as Attorney-General, and PDI-P's Kwik Kian Gie, a professional economist, and Laksamana Sukardi, a respected banker. The inclusion of PKB's Alwi Shihab as Minister for Foreign Affairs and Khofifah as Minister for Women's Affairs also appeared promising. But this bloated cabinet of thirty-five was also saddled with soiled hangovers from the *ancien regime* and unknowns of uncertain competency.

The live television announcement of the new cabinet line-up was a revealing event in itself. Abdurrahman began by saying that Megawati would read out the list, since he was obviously unable to do it himself. He then added, 'I probably shouldn't call the vice-president *Mbak* (sister) Mega, but I will, just as everyone will probably keep on calling me Gus Dur, which is what I want them to do, because that's how we know each other and that's the style we should keep'. He then handed over to Megawati, who seemed to make heavy going of the straightforward task of reading the list of names. Afterwards Abdurrahman did something that would have been unimaginable during the Soeharto period. He said simply, 'Are there any questions?' And then he launched into a spontaneous press conference. It was evident right from the start that this was going to be a very different government both in content and in style.

A VERY DIFFERENT STYLE

Abdurrahman returned to Ciganjur on Friday. This time, of course, he rode in a large black armour-plated Mercedes that rocketed south at the head of an alarmingly fast motorcade. Abdurrahman's return as president was greeted enthusiastically by the thousands of locals who lined the streets. There he announced that he was going to follow a pattern of returning to Ciganjur once a month to say his Friday prayers in the mosque and then have a question-and-answer session with the people. He would do the same thing once a month at the palace mosque, and twice a month he would travel to other mosques in Jakarta or elsewhere in Indonesia. He was to make frequent use of the Ciganjur home as a low-key venue for meeting with people outside the formal setting of the palace. Over the following months he held numerous meetings with students and religious leaders from Aceh both at the Merdeka palace and at Ciganjur. Ciganjur was also the place where he often spoke, in private, with friends, business people and political associates.

The family had intended to settle into the Merdeka Palace, formerly the Dutch Governor's residence, which had been used by Sukarno as both official residence and as a second office. Preparations took several weeks because the palace had stood largely unused for so long. Soeharto had used it only for occasional state functions and had never slept in it, except once a year. (Even then, it is doubtful he was actually able to sleep. Soeharto would spend part of the eve of Independence Day on 17 August in the palace, but it was clear that he was not at home there and feared its ghosts, both figurative and literal.)

Before Abdurrahman's family could move into the palace, they were stopped on the doorstep and told of the need to negotiate with the spiritual occupants of the palace. Those who believed in such things needed little persuading that the palace was haunted. One reminder of this was a room off the main hall; the light was always on there but it was entered only once a year, on 17 August, to remove the original national flag from the display casket in the centre of the room, which stood between large bronze reliefs of founding fathers Sukarno and Hatta. Shortly after moving in, Abdurrahman commented matter-of-factly that the room was believed to be occupied by an invisible presence. Abdurrahman set up his office on the other side of the main hall, in the room that Sukarno had used as an office, asking Megawati to help him reassemble it just as it had been during her father's time. Megawati arranged for Sukarno's old library to be reinstated and the office set up in the kind of gentlemen's den style that her father preferred. It was clear that Abdurrahman felt at home working in Sukarno's old office. For day-to-day meetings Abdurrahman met with official guests at Bina Graha, the venue for cabinet meetings and other official functions located about three hundred metres from the Merdeka Palace. Bina Graha has a heavy feel, to the point of being oppressive, as have most of the Soviet-style buildings in the compound of the State Secretariat (Sekretariat Negara — SekNeg) that ring the palace complex.

From the beginning of his presidency, Abdurrahman's days were filled with official engagements, in addition to a heavy schedule of unofficial meetings and discussions in the late afternoons and evenings. He made it clear from the outset that he wanted a very different style of presidency. In fact, left to his own devices Abdurrahman would have done away with protocol arrangements altogether. Fortunately he was not left to his own devices: it soon become clear that protocol intervention was essential, not just for his personal security, but also to make his schedule functional.

A WELL-TRAVELLED PRESIDENT

In November Abdurrahman left for his first major overseas trip. Like his other overseas trips, this one was organised around a few key meetings that had been set well in advance, together with state visits to fill the itinerary. He had agreed in 1997 to give a speech at the international congress of the World Conference of Religion and Peace, which was holding its five-yearly meeting in November 1999 in Amman, Jordan. He was also keen to return to Salt Lake City, still hopeful that some sort of surgical intervention might help his eyesight. This last quest, a product of his continuing denial about his permanent blindness, was a driving factor in several international visits the following year.

Around his itinerary to Amman and Salt Lake City he arranged a quick tour of the ASEAN states to introduce himself and his new government to his neighbours, capped with visits to Tokyo and Washington, DC. One reason that he wanted to keep his appointment in Amman was personal. For a number of years he had been convinced that until Indonesia ratified and formalised relations with the State of Israel, Indonesian Muslims would continue to fight an imaginary enemy. He believed that for Indonesia to mature as a nation it must face up to such imagined enemies and replace suspicion with friendship and dialogue. Within days of being sworn in as president, he called a meeting of Arab ambassadors and affirmed to them his ongoing concern for the cause of the Palestinians. This was a pre-emptive move to ward off suspicions because he planned to work towards establishing full diplomatic relations with Israel as quickly as possible. The appointment of Alwi Shihab, an ethnic Arab, as Minister for Foreign Affairs was another important move to build confidence in his administration in the region. While on the way to Jordan Abdurrahman made a point of visiting Kuwait and Qatar; in Amman he met with King Abdullah and his brother Crown Prince Hussein and also with Yasser Arafat, who made the trip across the Jordan valley to speak with him. Abdurrahman had earlier been keen to meet with the Prime Minister of Israel, Ehud Barak, and had spoken with some excitement of the possibility of such a meeting. At the last minute this visit was cancelled. Abdurrahman initially said he thought that a secret visit by Barak to Amman might have been impolite to his Jordanian hosts, an explanation which made little sense in the context of Israeli–Jordanian relations at the time. The real reason appears to be that he had come under increasing pressure from right-wing Islamist elements at home and felt the need to back off until times were more opportune.

Contrary to conventional protocol, Abdurrahman often made use of meetings overseas to raise issues connected with domestic politics. Like

Soeharto he travelled with a full entourage of journalists, but unlike Soeharto he regularly gave both formal and informal press conferences. At one of these he raised the issue of KKN (Korupsi, Kolusi and Nepotism) or corruption, collusion and nepotism, one of the buzz phrases of the reform movement encapsulating the central sins of the former regime. In Salt Lake City he alluded to suspicions that three of his ministers were involved in KKN. One week later the Welfare Minister and chair of PPP, Hamzah Haz, suddenly resigned. Hamzah Haz denied that there was any link between his resignation and Abdurrahman's statement; even though Abdurrahman spoke no further about it, most observers were convinced that there was a connection.

Abdurrahman's second major overseas trip, in mid-December, was to Beijing. This was also a crucial visit for the new president who, throughout his public career, had made such an emphasis of defending Indonesian Chinese. As with all of his visits as president, there was also an issue of economic concern. He hoped that by visiting Beijing he would be sending a positive signal, not just to mainland Chinese but also to the Chinese throughout Southeast Asia, that his was a Chinese-friendly government.

As a gesture of goodwill, the Chinese premier offered to send leading eye specialists to Jakarta to work with Abdurrahman to restore as much sight as possible. A team of medical professors arrived later that month and set to work on Abdurrahman with a regime of acupuncture and Chinese medicinal herbs in an attempt to improve blood circulation to his right eye.

MAKING A START ON REFORM

One of Abdurrahman's first presidential concerns was to build a team of people whom he trusted to oversee the process of reform and the management of government. A first official act was to abolish two government departments. He closed down the Ministry for Information, arguing that it did more harm than good, both because of its Stalinist approach to the control of information and because of its entrenched practice of extorting money from media outlets. His second, and perhaps more surprising, act was to close down the Department of Welfare, arguing that the scale of corruption and entrenched practices of extortion were such that the department was beyond reform and that its activities should be carried out by other departments. These closures were controversial, the second much more than the first, and made him unpopular in certain circles. Nevertheless, many analysts welcomed the changes and argued that it was difficult to see what else he could have done. Although constrained by the need to work with his coalition partners where he could, he downsized departments and set in process reforms to gradually bring them into line. He moved quickly to try to reduce the powers of the State Secretariat, infamous during the Soeharto period for acting as the government public service within a public service and controlling aspects of governance far outside its ostensible brief. The new Minister for Religious Affairs was a competent and trusted NU academic, formally the rector of the NU University in Malang. Abdurrahman had high expectations of him, being convinced that the Department of Religious Affairs needed to radically rethink how it went about its business. He declared that matters such as the arrangement of *haj* pilgrimage, one of many activities of the department seen as corrupt, be handed over to the private sector. Abdurrahman believed that the department's sole role should be assisting religious communities, rather than intervening in religious affairs. He even proposed that the religious communities should, as soon as possible, manage their own affairs and that the Department of Religious Affairs need not keep such close tabs on certain day-to-day matters. Not surprisingly, Abdurrahman's reforms ruffled feathers.

On 25 December he called into his office at Istana Merdeka Bondan Gunawan and Marsillam Simanjuntak, two old friends from Forum Demokrasi. During a leisurely, frank conversation, he explained that he wanted them to come and work for him as presidential secretaries. He told Marsillam that he wanted him as Cabinet Secretary and that he wanted to create a new secretariat, under Bondan, overseeing the function of the government. 'I want you to ride shotgun over this new cabinet. I want you to tell me when they're out of line. I want you to report to me when things are not being done. I need you as part of a feedback and control mechanism to try and make this cabinet work.'

Outside the office, Marsillam threw up his hands in desperation. 'I don't want to do to this,' he said. 'This cabinet is too much of a compromise and his bringing me in here is too much too soon.' Nevertheless, several weeks later Bondan and Marsillam were sworn in. Friends in the reform movement had persuaded Marsillam that there was more to be gained from working within the government than from standing outside and criticising. Marsillam, in particular, was to prove an invaluable aid in Abdurrahman's attempts to gain control of an unwieldy and seemingly unworkable government.

ACEH AND PAPUA

The list of things to be done and problems to be solved was overwhelming. One was the heading off of the separatist movement in Irian Jaya while encouraging indigenous leaders there to enter into dialogue with the new government. Another was to break the cycle of violence in Aceh.

As president, Abdurrahman continued to meet with Acehenese community leaders in an attempt to negotiate a settlement. Unfortunately for the new president, and tragically for the people of Aceh, Abdurrahman found it no easier to achieve progress in Aceh after becoming president than before. Having lost control of East Timor, and scores of lucrative businesses, TNI was in no mood to lose Aceh, whether to separatists or to a reformist president. Resolving separatist conflicts in any part of the world is never easy; it is especially difficult during the transition from military-backed authoritarianism to full democracy. Although he talked optimistically about quickly finding a solution in Aceh, Abdurrahman knew in his heart that he was facing a long and difficult process. His first priority was to try to persuade the Acehenese to trust him and to give him time.

Faced with demands for a referendum to be held within weeks, Abdurrahman stalled for time. In doing so he fell into a pattern of behaviour that was to bedevil his presidency. As he had learned to do under Soeharto, Abdurrahman, now president himself, dodged and weaved; his behaviour and statements were driven more by the ad hoc demands of tactical manoeuvring for short-term survival than by strategic planning for the long term. At the same time, he repeatedly failed to explain what he was doing. He fudged the issue and spoke of his support for an eventual referendum. Privately, he explained that what he had in mind was a referendum not about independence but about forms of autonomy. His motive was to try to pull the Acehenese back from the brink of all-out conflict with the Indonesian military. Unfortunately, his well-intentioned dancing around the issues only served to undermine his credibility. Nevertheless, he was able to keep alive the ideal of a negotiated settlement at the same time as frustrating TNI's desire to launch a large-scale 'military solution'. None of this saved the dozens being killed each week, but it may well have prevented many more being tortured and killed.

Abdurrahman had more success in Irian Jaya, in large measure because the situation there was not yet as bad as in Aceh. In Irian Jaya the separatist movement was neither as organised nor as radicalised as in Aceh, and the mere fact that an Indonesian president was willing to talk with them seriously about their aspirations was enough to encourage a cessation of violence.

On the evening of 30 December Abdurrahman travelled to Jayapura, the capital of Irian Jaya, where he met with community leaders from across Irian Jaya. The meeting had a shaky beginning, with the leaders complaining that they had to queue for an hour or more to get through the security to come to the meeting to which they had been formally invited and even then, there was little chance of dialogue. Nevertheless it was a symbolic start. When he had landed in Jayapura earlier that day, Abdurrahman had been greeted by a noisy demonstration with protesters waving the banned Morning Star flag and demanding independence. The protests continued in one form or another throughout the trip. The president's willingness to receive such protests, to acknowledge the need for dialogue, and to talk frankly about past abuses, went a long way to convince the leaders of Irian Jaya that he was serious about making changes. That evening he explained that 'Irian' was derived from an Arabic word meaning 'naked' and was an offensive way of describing the people of the province. Henceforth they were to be known by their own chosen name, 'Papua'. The presidential declaration 'this was the name that should be henceforth used' was well received on that last evening of the twentieth century, even if it was to take a long time before the new name officially passed through parliament. Abdurrahman explained to the gathering that he was prepared to talk about anything; the important thing was to negotiate, to dialogue. The only condition was that there was to be no violence in support of political ambitions. It was clear that he did not want Papua to break away from Indonesia. Nevertheless, he said that independence was one of the allowable topics, arguing that it was only through communication that progress could be made. The next morning the president's group was up early to greet the new dawn high above Jayapura, welcoming the new millennium with a tangible sense of optimism about the new Indonesia.

Returning to Jakarta, Abdurrahman set about dealing with the Indonesian Bank Restructuring Agency (IBRA). He moved decisively to replace its head, once again amidst much controversy. He argued that the previous head had been too close to the former regime and was not pushing for reforms as quickly and decisively as was required. Many argued that his intervention represented political interference.

Later that month Abdurrahman travelled to Davos, Switzerland, to attend the World Economic Forum. On the way he took the opportunity to visit Saudi Arabia, hoping to secure greater financial support for Indonesia's economic recovery and also to explain his handling of the situation in Aceh. The following month Abdurrahman set out on his first major European trip. He travelled to London, Paris, Amsterdam, Berlin and Rome, returning home via New Delhi, Seoul, Bangkok and Brunei. The purpose of his trip, he explained, was to try to secure support within Europe, both economically and politically, for the reforms to be undertaken in Indonesia. As with most of Abdurrahman's trips, the schedule was exhausting for all except Abdurrahman. He was well received in the major capitals of Europe although it was less clear whether the economic side of the program was successful. Nevertheless, he built on the success of his November visit to the United States and encouraged Western nations to take seriously his commitment to the building of a new Indonesia. He felt that his visits on the way home to New Delhi and Seoul were particularly important because — idealistically, and perhaps naively — he intended to complement continued support from Europe and the Unites States with fresh ties to New Delhi and Beijing. It also looked increasingly possible that Seoul might provide a source of future investment capital. Abdurrahman received a warm welcome in both India and South Korea and came home pleased with what had been achieved.

DEALING WITH WIRANTO

It seemed that something else had also been achieved during Abdurrahman's visit that was not apparent at that time. When in Europe Abdurrahman had commented on domestic affairs and the prospects for the reform of the military, he had particularly singled out Feisal Tanjung and Wiranto as being the source of various difficulties representing obstacles to reform. He suggested that Feisal Tanjung had been behind the July 1996 attack on Megawati's supporters in central Jakarta, and that he was asking Wiranto to step aside. Back in Jakarta, Defence Minister Susilo Bambang Yudhoyono conveyed this message to Wiranto, but they agreed to leave it to Abdurrahman to work out matters directly with Wiranto upon his return.

Many commentators thought that Abdurrahman's long-distance handling of his tussle with Wiranto was particularly unusual, if not foolhardy, and that his reference to Feisal Tanjung while in the midst of an overseas visit was inexplicable. But Abdurrahman had not been nearly so gauche as he appeared. In criticising Feisal Tanjung, he was flying a kite. In the past Feisal had had many supporters in the military who were quick to defend him. The extent to which the military defended Feisal against Abdurrahman's criticisms would be a measure of the degree of support for the reform process within the military. As it turned out, no one came out in defence of Feisal Tanjung. This gave Abdurrahman confidence to proceed with his reforms. Another exercise in kite-flying was his reference to a meeting of senior generals with Wiranto. He did cite the wrong location for the meeting, whether deliberately or because he was misinformed, but he was on target about the existence and nature of the meeting. His intent in referring to the meeting ahead of his return to Jakarta was to flush out a response. Wiranto had, in fact, met with other senior generals, and there was good reason to believe that he was plotting to defend his position against Abdurrahman.

When Abdurrahman landed in Jakarta early on the morning of Sunday, 13 February, Wiranto met him at the airport, keen to persuade Abdurrahman to be patient and wait before demanding his resignation. Wiranto pleaded with Abdurrahman for more time, saying that it was not just for himself, but also for his family, as they would be devastated if he was suddenly forced to resign. Abdurrahman backed off and indicated to Wiranto that he would be prepared to wait for his resignation. When he arrived back at the palace, however, Abdurrahman called in several aides and asked them to investigate what Wiranto had been up to during his absence and to report back to him that afternoon. He then went to bed and caught up on few hours of sleep. When he woke, Marsillam told him that they had ascertained that over the past few weeks Wiranto had been meeting with Habibie and several senior generals and power-brokers in a manner that strongly suggested that he was plotting against Abdurrahman. Marsillam was emphatic in his advice. 'You must grasp the nettle.' Abdurrahman asked for Wiranto to be brought to his office. When Wiranto arrived he explained to him that he was asking for his immediate resignation. Wiranto was shocked; he had apparently been gloating around town about his victory. There was little that Wiranto could do, at least in the short term.

So, after a tense stand-off, Abdurrahman had won his confrontation with Wiranto. Many analysts had predicted that it would be extremely difficult, if not impossible, to force Wiranto out of power without provoking an immediate backlash from the military. In the end, however, no one rushed to Wiranto's defence, and over the following week he was left with the slightly comic recourse of appearing on a series of television talk shows. Several of these interviews were embarrassingly lengthy, with the dapper general using PowerPoint demonstrations and narrated video clips to convince viewers of his loyal service to the military and the nation, including his intervention to deliver peace and reconciliation in East Timor. Just up from the parliament building a large banner was stretched across Jalan Jenderal Gatot Subroto, the main highway leading out of Jakarta, proclaiming: 'For the good of the nation, Indonesians should all support Gus Dur, Megawati and Wiranto.' It was generally assumed that Wiranto had spent a large amount of money on this campaign (even though he claimed to be a poor retired soldier and attributed his hours of airtime to enlightened television executives). If that were the case, it would seem that the money was largely wasted. In the months that followed, Wiranto turned to more insidious ways of reasserting his influence but, in the short term, Abdurrahman had won a decisive victory.

A BRIEF SEASON IN THE SUN

In many ways this time was the high point of Abdurrahman's presidency. When he came to power there had been much scepticism about his ability to serve as an effective president. Certainly his election had come as a surprise to almost everyone, although within weeks things had settled down and many previously critical commentators observed that the combination of Gus Dur and Mega did in fact seem to be an ideal partnership. By March Abdurrahman seemed to have proved himself worthy of his election to the presidency. He remained, of course, a highly unusual president, but then these were highly unusual times. With the uneventful sacking of Wiranto hard on the heels of a successful European tour, many people became outspoken in their praise for Abdurrahman. Although critical of his methods, including his long-distance confrontation with Wiranto, many were prepared to believe that he was indeed a masterful political operator who might yet be able to lead Indonesia through a difficult transition.

Further confirmation of Abdurrahman's credentials and capacity as a reformist leader came in early March when he made a one-day visit to East Timor. In Dili he was greeted warmly by Xanana Gusmao and Jose Ramos-Horta. Indeed the people of Dili, with the exception of a handful of demonstrators, welcomed the Indonesian president with great warmth. When Abdurrahman addressed a large crowd gathered on the foreshore in Dili, he was joined at the rostrum by Xanana Gusmao. Xanana's presence beside Abdurrahman spoke volumes about the warmth between the two men and also seemed to be a deliberate action by Xanana to protect his friend against any act of violence by those who might feel tempted to strike out in anger at Indonesia. Abdurrahman spoke eloquently and powerfully about his personal regret and sorrow for all the wrongs and violence that had occurred in East Timor, and he apologised on behalf of his nation for the wrong it had inflicted. In his visit to Dili, Abdurrahman went further than had been expected. When he went on to explain the need for Indonesia and East Timor to form a good relationship and work together as friends, his comments were warmly received and accepted as genuine. On the way home he stopped in Kupang, where he addressed gatherings in refugee camps and later spoke to community leaders. Returning to Jakarta that night, it really seemed as if Abdurrahman's presidency was on track to produce good results.

In April Abdurrahman was travelling again. This time the main attraction was the International Meeting of the Group of 77, the spiritual successor to the Non-Aligned Movement which Sukarno had championed half a century before. The location for the meeting was Havana, Cuba. Not surprisingly, the Americans counselled him against attending the conference. Abdurrahman had initially thought of travelling on to Washington at the conclusion of the conference, but abandoned the idea when it received a frosty response from the State Department. Although the US government was very encouraged by Abdurrahman's presidency and keen to be as supportive as possible, they considered his visit to Havana to be pushing things too far. Abdurrahman was in no mind to accept such intervention. The Havana meeting was important, he argued, because the Group of 77 nations represented the overwhelming majority of the planet's population. For the leader of a large developing nation such as Indonesia not to be involved in such a gathering was, he felt, plainly wrong. For his troubles Abdurrahman was rewarded by a warm reception in Cuba, including a surprise visit by President Fidel Castro to his hotel room. Castro singled him out for a visit because, he said, he was keen to meet personally with Indonesia's surprising new president.

On the way to Havana, Abdurrahman had stopped off in Johannesburg. He had for years been a great admirer of Nelson Mandela and had some time earlier secured his promise to support a proposed Truth and Reconciliation Commission in Indonesia. After the conference in Havana Abdurrahman travelled on to Mexico City before returning home via Hong Kong, where he lobbied for investment interest in Indonesia.

The president had good reason to try and drum up investment interest in Indonesia. The national debt stood at US$134 billion or 83 per cent of its gross domestic product. Fortunately for Indonesia, and for Abdurrahman, in that month the Paris Club of nineteen sovereign creditors agreed to reschedule the US$5.8 billion foreign debt, extending terms to between eleven and twenty years. (The London Club of private creditors followed suit with similar terms for a further US$340 million which otherwise would have fallen due around March 2002). At the same time the World Bank and the Asian Development Bank were lending considerable support to Indonesia. Even so, Abdurrahman had been increasingly criticised for his failure to intervene more decisively in the application of economic policy.

Part of the problem seemed to be the structure of Abdurrahman's economic team: there was no clear delineation of responsibilities and duties between the four different government ministers whose portfolios were concerned with economic affairs. At the same time Abdurrahman appeared personally uninterested in economics. He denied this, claiming to be passionately concerned with economic issues, but there was no doubt that the minutiae of the discussions bored him.

By this stage he had allowed such a heavy daily schedule to develop that he was clearly running low on sleep. In late February things became so bad that one Thursday morning he woke feeling so off-colour that he cancelled his walk after only half a lap of the palace compound.[1]

His doctors diagnosed a mild case of flu and immediately sent him off to bed to rest. His schedule cancelled, he slept for several hours. During the day word spread around town that he had suffered some sort of stroke, or other major reversal of health, and the markets panicked. Of course, no such thing had happened, but the incident highlighted the nervous nature of the financial markets in Indonesia.

THE PRESSURE MOUNTS

Abdurrahman's forced rest also revealed just how hard he was driving himself, and also how poorly his public relations were managed. By then everyone in his team was tired. Munib looked exhausted, and Yenny was also feeling the strain both emotionally and physically. She carried a particularly heavy load as a stand-in first lady, personal assistant and confidante. Because Abdurrahman could not read himself, either Yenny or Munib had to read out documents that were presented to him through the day, as well as excerpts from the daily newspapers.

When Abdurrahman became president he had made Ratih his presidential secretary. The job was not a blessing. Ratih's experience showed the multifarious obstacles to reforming the bureaucracy that existed after four decades of authoritarian rule. From the outset it was clear that she would have to reinvent the entire office. Even though she nominally had a large team of people working under her, only a handful were able or willing to make a significant contribution. Her office was located within the State Secretariat and here she met considerable resistance, at a variety of levels, as she attempted to reform the function of presidential secretary. No doubt, this resistance was partly a response to Ratih's somewhat abrasive and direct style. But she was in a difficult situation. She was not welcome as an outsider to the State Secretariat, and many forces were positively opposed to the sort of reforms Abdurrahman was trying to institute.[2]

Ratih had achieved various reforms during the political campaign of 1999; in 2000 she tried to change the way in which Abdurrahman functioned as president. Journalists accustomed to easy access to Abdurrahman became annoyed as she imposed a regime of press conferences and tried to discipline press contact. Although such innovations were unpopular, it was clear that, had she not done this, Abdurrahman would have been even more worn down by impromptu interviews. It was also clear that he was vulnerable to underhand tactics by the less scrupulous members of the media keen to get a good quote. By this stage Abdurrahman's political enemies, including elements aligned with the former regime, were manipulating the media on a grand scale through money and intimidation.

By this stage the political pressure against Abdurrahman had become intense. While Wiranto's initial doubtful media apologies following his sacking were ineffectual, there was reason to believe that he might apply himself to some more serious ways of getting back at Abdurrahman. It now appeared that there were two camps opposing Abdurrahman: one keen to pressure him into backing off in corruption investigations and prosecutions, and the other intent upon causing enough unrest to undermine the credibility of his government. By now the communal conflict that had started in Ambon in South Maluku had spread to North Maluku and the island of Halamera. Until early March it had appeared as if the situation in Maluku might have begun to recover, but the spread of the conflict marked a downward spiral.

In late February Ratih decided that she had had enough. The job had proved immensely stressful and remarkably thankless. At the best of times Ratih is highly strung and passionate about whatever she is doing, sometimes to the extent of appearing melodramatic. These extraordinarily stressful circumstances in which she found herself created unendurable pressure. Because she took every aspect of the job seriously, and probably took upon herself more than was expected, she found that it was not possible for her to switch off and let things flow over her. In March she announced that she was tendering her resignation.

REGIME CHANGE AND FALSE EXPECTATIONS

The pressure against Abdurrahman was considerable by late March. The media, which had never been particularly sympathetic towards him, was becoming increasingly hostile. There were several reasons for this; one was that his eccentric style frequently damaged his credibility. Paradoxically, at his best he could be a masterful communicator but at worst he often miscommunicated so badly that he undermined his own position. His habit of thinking aloud was made worse by his blindness; as mentioned, he was unable to judge the context in which he was talking because he could not see who was in the room or monitor reactions to what he said. This tended to work against him with the press.

A more serious reason for increasing frustration with his leadership was that expectations of his presidency had been grossly inflated. The nation, including professionals in Jakarta who should have known better, looked to Abdurrahman to solve the economic crisis, mend communal relations, reform the military, reform the civil service, reform and reinvent the traditional legal system, and they felt that it could and should all be accomplished in the first six or twelve months of his presidency. It was an impossible set of expectations.

A third, and perhaps more significant, factor was that Abdurrahman's presidency was subject to the contingencies of regime change. This he understood well, but few around him acknowledged it in the media, either domestic or international. He often spoke about fighting 'dark forces' aligned with the former regime, forces loyal to Soeharto, Wiranto and other, often competing, elements of the *ancien regime*. His talk was often dismissed as wild speculation that was dangerously beholden to conspiracy theory. The more cynical of his critics rejected it as escapism, as shifting the blame, even though the record of the Soeharto regime was well known. It was no secret that the military had engaged in systematic terrorism against its own citizens in provinces such as East Timor, Papua and Aceh. Even in Jakarta and Yogyakarta students had often 'disappeared' Latin American-style, and torture was a routine technique. More insidious was the use of psychological warfare techniques and intense intelligence surveillance. There was no reason to believe that any of this suddenly stopped when Soeharto stepped down. Rather, there was every reason to believe that Soeharto, and those loyal to him or to their own interests, would make use of such methods to destabilise the new government.

Several tactics were used against Abdurrahman in an attempt to undermine his legitimacy and pressure him into backing off, or perhaps even to step down. One of the more common tactics was to subvert the media. This was relatively easy because of an entrenched culture of encouraging and rewarding journalists with money-filled envelopes. To some extent this was an understandable cultural practice. The paying of travel expenses, or per diems, was understandable in a context in which journalistic salaries were low and journalists had a real need of supplementation. In the Soeharto era almost every profession — except perhaps the elite end of town, the private sector — suffered such low rates of remuneration that people had to top up their salaries through other means. For civil servants this often involved some form of corruption or bribery. Similarly, the police and the military often took part in business activities, legitimate and illegitimate. University lecturers were obliged to find other jobs to make ends meet, and journalists understandably were happy to take contributions of cash. By the first few months of 2000 this 'envelope' culture was showing up in the Indonesian press, and the profoundly distorted reports were repeated in the international media.

SACKING LAKSAMANA: A FATAL ERROR

Amid all this pressure, Abdurrahman began to make errors of judgment. On 24 April he made what was probably his most significant mistake. Under pressure to reform his economic team, he sacked the Industry and Trade Minister, Yusuf Kalla of the Golkar party, and the State Enterprises Minister, Laksamana Sukardi. In a closed session with members of parliament, he said that he was sacking Yusuf Kalla because of allegations of KKN and that he was sacking Laksamana Sukardi because of his inability to work with his team members and also because Abdurrahman was unhappy with his appointments to the state offices. Unfortunately, the media reported him as saying that both Yusuf Kalla and Laksamana were tainted with corruption. While he has denied that he ever said this (it was a closed-door session so no journalists were present to verify the story), the story quickly spread. This was particularly unfortunate because Laksamana Sukardi was a favourite protégé and associate of Megawati and a key figure within PDI-P. He was regarded, in fact, as the party's bright shining star because of his unparalleled record as a professional banker and his reputation for integrity and professionalism.

Ironically, it was, in part, his professionalism and integrity that got him into trouble. Laksamana had been dogged in his pursuit of corruption, even when this pursuit went outside the bounds of his portfolio. Abdurrahman tried on a number of occasions to restrain him in his pursuit of certain figures because of the political consequences of continuing. Laksamana however, was used to operating alone rather than as part of a team and was not easily reined in. His single-minded approach meant that he fell out with a number of his colleagues. In particular he was actively undermined by Abdurrahman's old friend from his days in the leadership of NU, Rozi Munir, who was himself keen to have Laksamana's job — which in due course he obtained, albeit not for very long. Sadly, for Abdurrahman it was a case of 'With friends like these, who needs enemies?'

Were it a singular case it would have been bad enough; the tragedy was that it marked a pattern of behaviour by many within NU and PKB, which served to spoil whatever good work was being done by others in both organisations. NU, like most manifestations of traditional Southeast Asian society, was strongly coloured by patron–client relations. And when NU 'came into power', many saw an opportunity to milk their position for all it was worth. Some, no doubt, had relatively good intentions and looked to pick up money for productive projects. Others were more concerned with filling PKB's war-chest in preparation for the next election. Many others, however, seem to have been largely self-serving and greedy, and unconcerned about the damage that their avaricious behaviour was inflicting on NU, PKB and Abdurrahman's presidency.

In their defence — though it is a pretty poor defence — it should be recognised that corruption within NU and PKB was mostly amateurish and small-scale in comparison with what was occurring in the other large parties. Unfortunately, the damage inflicted by the self-serving behaviour of individuals such as Rozi was extensive precisely because it struck at the Achilles' heel of the Wahid presidency — the fragility of the relationship between Abdurrahman and Megawati and between PKB and PDI-P.

Laksamana's demise was not, however, entirely the fault of Abdurrahman's self-serving 'friend'. At the same time that he was under attack from Rozi, Laksamana's position was also being white-anted by fellow PDI-P minister Kwik Kian Gie. Between them, Kwik and Rozi made sure that Abdurrahman was subject to a constant stream of bitchy complaints about Laksamana.

One of the people that Laksamana fell out with was more than just another aggrieved colleague: Taufik Kiemas, husband of Megawati and senior backroom powerbroker within the party. Some of Laksamana's corruption inquiries crossed over the business interests of Taufik. The relationship between Taufik and Megawati was thought to be rocky, and in a significant power struggle inside the party, Laksamana became a victim of factional politics. Not that this excuses Abdurrahman's error of judgment in sacking Laksamana. Abdurrahman had failed to consult with Megawati, and when she heard the news she reportedly broke down in tears and immediately flew to Singapore to recover.

THE END OF THE HONEYMOON

The sacking of Laksamana was to prove a turning-point in the first period of Abdurrahman's government. It was a move that he quickly regretted, but the circumstances and the pressure under which he had made the error were not widely understood. It could hardly have been said that Abdurrahman was enjoying a honeymoon period — he had had a turbulent reception ever since becoming president — but up to that point he had benefited from the goodwill of many senior intellectuals and media figures who admired his idealism and vision. With the sacking of Laksamana, the honeymoon, such as it was, was over.

Weeks later another scandal broke which was to gravely damage Abdurrahman. In January he had asked the State Logistics Agency (Bulog) for information about its cash reserves. It was common for such agencies to hold significant reserves, and Abdurrahman was finding it difficult to get even small amounts of cash to carry out projects. He was keen to send money to Aceh to help community welfare programs to reinforce his moves to negotiate peace in the troubled province. He recognised that the community had many concrete needs and had been badly treated during the Soeharto regime, not just in terms of military terrorism, but also in terms of basic infrastructure in health, education and transport. When no money seemed available through any of the regular government accounts, he explored the possibility of borrowing from the cash reserves of a government agency such as Bulog. This was a typical technique, used for decades under Soeharto and continued under Habibie. He was quickly informed, however, that he would first need to consult parliament; he therefore decided against it, feeling it to be too time-consuming and politically difficult.

In early May, Abdurrahman heard, via people working at Bulog, that a significant sum of money, almost US$4 million, had gone missing from its cash reserve account; the person to whom it had allegedly been handed was Suwando, the former masseur of Soeharto, and for a period, also of Abdurrahman. Apparently Suwando had approached Bulog and said that he was collecting the money because the president had sent him as personal envoy. Most of the money was recovered within months, although Suwando himself went into hiding. There was no suggestion of any link between Abdurrahman or his family with Suwando. Nevertheless, Abdurrahman's political enemies insinuated that Abdurrahman had been involved in the scam and the resulting scandal was immensely damaging to Abdurrahman.

At around the same time another scandal broke. When Abdurrahman had trouble securing liquid funds to use in Aceh, he sought the help of foreign countries to invest in the province. In late February he visited Brunei and spoke with its sultan about his concern for what was happening in Aceh. The Sultan of Brunei gave Abdurrahman a personal donation of US $2 million . From the sultan's point of view it was small change, and he stipulated that he did not want his gift to be made public. He said that he had entrusted the money to Abdurrahman as a *ulama* and religious man and was confident that he would use it well as he saw fit. Abdurrahman failed to declare the money and lodge it in a formal government account partly, he said, because the Sultan of Brunei had asked for it to be kept confidential and partly because he didn't trust those who had access to such government accounts.

After the sacking of Laksamana this represented a second major error of judgment. Although few believed that Abdurrahman was guilty of personal corruption, it certainly looked foolish and unprofessional. The sacking of Laksamana, the $4 million taken from Bulog by Suwando (which became known as the Bulogate scandal) and now the gift from Brunei (which was quickly dubbed Bruneigate), weighed heavily upon Abdurrahman's reputation.

Abdurrahman was also coming under increasing pressure from his political opponents, many of whom fought behind the scenes. Also, as the pressure through prosecution from the Attorney-General's office intensified on Soeharto and his family, there were signs that his sympathisers and cronies were fighting back.

ISLAMIST RADICALISM AND LASKAR JIHAD

In April a troubling phenomenon emerged which Abdurrahman seemed powerless to stop. Earlier in the year Jakarta had been rocked by a series of rallies calling for a peace in Ambon and Maluku, and blaming the government and the Christian communities for failing to work for peace. These rallies were organised by the Islamic right, and there were strong indications suggestions that they were funded by Abdurrahman's political opponents. By April the phenomenon had been transformed into a more sinister and threatening one where thousands of so-called Laskar Jihad, or holy war warriors, were trained in a camp in Bogor just outside Jakarta. For months the camp in Bogor remained free of intervention or censure from the military or the police. The three thousand or so young men, mostly from rural Java, who were in training in the camp held a series of rallies in Jakarta itself. At some of these rallies they were seen parading around the city centre with swords and other sharp weapons without being challenged by either the police or the military. Abdurrahman was initially reluctant to crack down too heavily on the demonstrators for fear of a violent confrontation.

At one point angry Laskar Jihad members stormed the presidential compound and demanded an audience with Abdurrahman. He received them but was so incensed by their militant accusations of a Christian and PDI-P conspiracy in Maluku that he threw them out of the palace. A variety of groups aligned with the Islamic right were daily protesting against Abdurrahman's presidency, claiming that he failed to defend Islam and was callously unconcerned about Muslim deaths in Maluku.

The situation took a further turn for the worse when the Laskar Jihad troops declared they were ready to set sail from Surabaya for Maluku. Abdurrahman gave orders to the police and the military, and particularly the navy, to block their departure. Initially they were able to do this, but in the end the Laskar Jihad forces landed in Maluku. Although they landed unarmed, they were soon equipped with weapons, including military-issue assault rifles and other army weapons. In June and July there were reports that these Laskar Jihad troops were involved in attacks on Christian villages that had resulted in hundreds of deaths. Abdurrahman was exasperated; he gave orders for the military to stop these troops, but elements of the military were not only turning a blind eye to the Laskar Jihad, it would seem that they were actually providing them with weapons.

By mid-July the Minister for Defence, Juwono Sudarsono, went public and blamed sections of the military for helping the Laskar Jihad and for also acting in the conflict in Maluku, particularly in Halamera and Ambon. There had always been a suspicion that the troops had become partisan as they became caught up in the violence. To counter this, Abdurrahman appointed a new commander for the region, a respected and experienced Balinese Hindu officer, and set in process a rotation of all fourteen hundred military officers serving in the region. On 26 June he declared a civil state of emergency in Maluku that gave authority to impose nightly curfews and to check people for weapons. He was reluctant to go for a full-blown military solution because he believed that this approach had failed in the past; also, he did not completely trust sections of the military. By mid-July there was talk, even at the level of Defence Minister, about the involvement of figures like Wiranto and elements aligned with the former regime. The violence in Maluku, which had previously appeared to be winding down, had built up in intensity with the arrival of the last Laskar Jihad troops from May onwards. Abdurrahman's failure to bring about a cessation of the violence in the province was used as another reason to argue that he was failing as president.

ECONOMIC CRISIS AND UNCHECKED CORRUPTION

Abdurrahman was also facing increasingly sharp criticism for his 'failure to fix the economy'. Even members of his own economic team and former allies such as Jusuf Wanandi, director of CSIS, were now openly critical of him. Key economic advisers revealed that occasionally during lengthy meetings, Abdurrahman appeared to nap when economic matters where being discussed. They accused him of being uninterested in economics.

This criticism seems unfair; both his private conversations with cabinet ministers and other advisers and his public addresses showed that he was passionately concerned about economic recovery and also concerned that such a recovery help those most in need. Nor was he a complete dilettante in the field, for in big-picture terms he has a well-thought-out position. Faced with the array of problems that have been besetting Indonesia, it has not always been clear what he could or should do. The problem was not so much to find a solution that was technically advisable, but to find one that would work politically.

Many of his economic advisers were keen for him to prosecute corruption and immediately crack down on those accused of it. Abdurrahman has been reluctant to move too quickly in this direction for several reasons. One was that the legal system was inadequate for the task and Marzuki Darusman, as Attorney-General, was already overloaded. Secondly, Abdurrahman was persuaded by lobbyists that many of these businessmen, while undeniably corrupt, held the key to economic recovery in the short to medium term; even if they would have to face justice later, their help was needed immediately to restart the economy. He explained that to prosecute the head of the giant conglomerate Texmaco, for example, would have been to risk the economic failure of the whole conglomerate.

Thirdly, Abdurrahman was under pressure to abandon his prosecution of anti-corruption cases of these and other elements who had strong connections with the former regime. Given the difficult circumstances under which he worked, he felt that there was a limit to how far he could press such cases, and some degree of compromise was involved in a real political solution, at least during the transitional period that he was overseeing.

There was another not readily understood reason for Abdurrahman's difficulties. Between Abdurrahman and most of his key advisers there was a significant cultural gap. He was unconvinced that neo-liberal economic theories held all the answers for Indonesia's economic recovery. Many of his advisers believed that if market forces were respected and their models applied rigorously, recovery would surely follow. Abdurrahman was sceptical and deeply worried about the social cost of the cures being pushed by many of his economic team. He was under enormous pressure and faced expectations that he could not possibly meet.

A PRESIDENCY ADRIFT?

In mid-June Abdurrahman left on another overseas trip. He was, by this stage, being widely criticised for travelling so frequently. In one sense he was following his life-long pattern of frequent travel and regular consultation with people around the country and around the world. But there was another factor driving Abdurrahman's travel that was not readily understood at the time. His June trip — to Tokyo, Salt Lake City, St Louis, Washington, Paris, Teheran, Islamabad and Cairo — was probably primarily driven by his desire to return to Salt Lake City. Despite a gloomy prognosis from medical specialists there, he continued to cling to the hope that his eyesight might be restored. The course of acupuncture and Chinese medicinal herbs he had received from the team of high-ranking Chinese doctors during February and March had been partially effective, but Abdurrahman's basic problem was that he was psychologically in denial about his blindness. This, according to experts in such matters, was not unusual; but Abdurrahman was president of the world's third-largest democracy in the midst of an enormously difficult change of regime. Unfortunately, as long as he was in denial he was unable to learn coping mechanisms for living without sight.

In Paris Abdurrahman had a more happy event. He had been invited to Paris by the Sorbonne University to receive an honorary doctorate. He was enormously proud and grateful for this award, having been a lover of French literature and culture all of his adult life. He greatly valued the honour and appeared genuinely moved during the award ceremony.

On this overseas tour he spoke to Indonesian student groups and others about his plans to reshuffle his cabinet. Amien Rais, among others, was critical of Abdurrahman and questioned what a reshuffle would achieve. On 17 June Amien said, 'Gus Dur has not yet shown his leadership'. Abdurrahman's brother, Hasyim, defended him by saying that lawmakers were exerting pressure to extract privileges from the government. 'Most members of the parliament are extortionists,' he said. Whatever the case, when Abdurrahman returned home in late June he retracted his earlier statement about the reshuffle. Privately, though, he confided that he was looking to reshuffle the cabinet towards the end of the year, after the MPR session in August. He also spoke about the possibility of moving towards the appointment of a 'first minister' system, in which a first minister would complement the president by running the day-to-day administration. 'It could be in some ways,' he said, 'like the French system where there is a strong president and also a strong prime minister.' He had in mind names of those who might do this job; he saw the need for somebody with a strong record as a reformist who would also be able to negotiate with elements of the former regime, particularly the military.

By late June Abdurrahman had reached an all-time low in the eyes of both the domestic and international media. *Time* magazine and *Asiaweek* ran cover stories in which they spoke of a president all at sea and unable to act decisively. The 7 July issue of *Asiaweek* had Abdurrahman on the cover, his image manipulated by the artist to show a man looking morose and lost. Across the bottom left-hand corner of the cover in yellow type was 'Adrift: Inside Abdurrahman Wahid's Sinking Indonesian Presidency'. The Asian issue of *Time* for 3 July also had Abdurrahman on the cover; the image was more complimentary but the headline was even worse than that of *Asiaweek*. It had in bold red letters 'Wahid's Woes' with the sub-heading 'Visionary one moment, vague the next, Indonesia's President may be losing control of his crippled country'. In these and other stories he was written off as a man out of his depth, as an amusing and genial eccentric who had lost his way in a task that was too big for him. His failed management was explained in terms of his background in the *pesantren* and his inability to apply an appropriate management style to the presidency. His statements about the campaign to topple him or undermine his leadership were treated cynically as an excuse for failure to perform. The critical line by many economists was that he had failed to give sufficient attention to the economy. This became a leading element in foreign reporting at the time, as did the various scandals like Bulogate and Bruneigate. There was also the short-term appointment of his youngest brother, Hasyim, to a consultative post with IBRA — apparently without Abdurrahman's knowledge. (Hasyim had welcomed this because he saw himself acting as a debt collector, working with people he understood well and who, he claimed, would not respond to polite requests to return money.) Such scandals made the Abdurrahman Wahid presidency look hopeless. As if this was not enough, the escalation of violence in Maluku and the steady decline of the Indonesian rupiah confirmed the picture. By mid-July the rupiah was bumping towards 10 000 to the US dollar and showing no sign of recovery.

There were signs, however, that some of Abdurrahman's peers understood his predicament. On Saturday, 1 July, he flew to Bali to attend the final session of a four-day conference that had been convened to discuss his presidency and the situation facing the nation. He listened politely as prominent social commentator Wimar Witoeloar read out the findings of the gathering. Those assembled were the cream of the Indonesian intelligentsia, leading figures from the media and from academia, over two hundred influential social commentators and opinion leaders. Encouragingly for Abdurrahman, their conclusion, although critical, was not entirely damning; there were signs that they understood his predicament and recognised the context of regime change in which he had to work. As a report card though, the message was very clear: 'Could do better!'

In conversation on the way to the Bali meeting it seemed an encouraging sign that Abdurrahman was sanguine about his friends' motives in calling this conference to assess his presidency. The three leading figures behind the conference were Wimar Witoelar, Nurcholish Madjid and Emil Salim. 'These people are all good people. They're very sincere in what they do and in their intentions,' Abdurrahman explained. 'Maybe I won't agree with what they have to say, but I respect their right to say it and I'm absolutely confident they mean well.'

HEADED FOR IMPEACHMENT?

By then there was considerable speculation that Abdurrahman might be toppled in the annual session of the MPR in August, which was essentially an extension of the DPR. The exact powers of the MPR were unclear. Under Soeharto the MPR existed only to rubber-stamp the president's re-election when it met once every five years following the general elections. In 1998 it had played a more decisive role with a special meeting to pass the necessary legislation required for the 1999 elections, and again on 19 October 1999 when it rejected the accountability speech by incumbent President B. J. Habibie — a critical factor in his decision not to contest the presidency. In theory, the MPR could impeach the president, but most commentators agreed that this was only realistic and legal if the president could be shown to be guilty of gross impropriety. In practice, it seemed unlikely that the MPR would go so far. There was another significant reason why such a step seemed unlikely, although it still remained a possibility. If Abdurrahman were toppled, another president would have to be appointed. A reliable opinion poll taken in mid-July showed that 83 per cent of the population could not conceive of a better president than Abdurrahman, given the available alternatives.

Abdurrahman felt that, by late June, he had the clear support of Akbar Tandjung from Golkar, of Amien Rais from PAN, and of Megawati. Nevertheless, his relationship with Megawati remained troubled. She was still hurt about Laksamana's sacking. In mid-July there were attempts to organise a 'Ciganjur Group' meeting of the four political leaders. Shortly before a meeting scheduled for Wednesday, 12 July, however, Megawati sent word that she would not attend. Instead, she went to the cinema with Laksamana. This was a deliberate snub by Megawati, who was hurt that Abdurrahman had not consulted her sufficiently in the previous months. Other attempts to organise a meeting also failed. Nevertheless, there were good reasons to expect that, when pushed, Megawati would continue to support Abdurrahman, at least in the short term.

The first major hurdle he had to face was a meeting, not with the MPR but with members of parliament. He had been summoned to explain his actions in the sacking of Yusuf Kalla and Laksamana Sukardi. Although it was not expected that they could do more than severely reprimand him, nevertheless, there was an element of great uncertainty about the whole process because there was considerable evidence that many members of parliament were not responding to party discipline. Some were guilty of grandstanding, or trying to launch their own political careers, by making a name for themselves in parliament. Others appeared to be following a political agenda which was not the party's. Some, for example, spoke out wildly in the commission sessions about the possibility of foreign powers conspiring to undermine regional security in Indonesia. There was a suggestion made by some members of parliament that Australia and America were behind the violence in Maluku or that they wanted to see Irian Jaya break away from the republic.

In late February Ratih, Yenny and Marsillam had been separately summoned to explain to a parliamentary commission allegations against them of covering up for the president and exercising undue influence. They gave sterling performances and easily outshone their critics; nevertheless the charges that were raised were disturbing. Ratih was accused of being an Australian spy — a ludicrous charge, given her well-established dislike of the Howard government. Clearly many such allegations were being put forward by 'loose cannons' within parliament. But the existence of such 'loose cannons' made the 20 July meeting between the president and the parliament all the more important.

Even Abdurrahman's greatest admirers recognised that changes were needed. The expectation was that, once he got through the MPR session, Abdurrahman would act to reshuffle his cabinet and possibly appoint a first minister. Abdurrahman's openness to the appointment of a first minister showed that he was aware of the limitations of his own personal abilities.[3] Indeed by late June Abdurrahman was well aware of the need to make changes. He was no administrator and found little joy in the minutiae of day-to-day governance. The idea of delegating the tasks that bored and frustrated him began to appeal more and more. In theory, of course, the vice-president was the natural choice for such a position. It's debatable whether Abdurrahman ever really gave Megawati a fair chance to step into the role. Certainly his critics, and especially her friends, argue that she was never given a real opportunity. Abdurrahman, however, points to many occasions when Megawati could have done more but failed to seize the opportunity.

There seemed little doubt that Abdurrahman needed help to run his administration. Wimar Witoelar, who was often critical in his analysis but nevertheless admired the president, put it this way:

> I don't think there's anyone in Indonesian history who is as enlightened as he is in ideas of diversity, pluralism, ethnic tolerance, religious understanding, and human rights. If he were not the president, he could get a Nobel Prize for his thoughts. But being president, he has got to manage, he has to watch the budget, he has to know which account to put his money in, and he's flunking in all these day-to-day government matters, but the man is a very, very good person.

AN APPOINTMENT WITH PARLIAMENT

In early July Abdurrahman announced that he was prepared to speak to the parliament on 20 July. By setting this date for his interpellation (an appearance before parliament to justify controversial behaviour) only days before parliament went into recess, he hoped to minimise the chance for them to do damage. Nevertheless, as the day drew near it was clear that the next few weeks were going to be difficult for him. Abdurrahman explained that, if all went well in the MPR session, he intended to announce his new cabinet by the end of August. There was a chance he would come out stronger than ever with a trimmed, loyal cabinet behind him and the interpellation and the MPR response to his accountability speech resolved. However, there was also a good chance that things might get worse. Impeachment seemed unlikely — the Bulogate and Bruneigate affairs provided little justification for such action. His sacking of two cabinet ministers could not be construed as a gross abuse of his position. Even so, anything was possible.

Abdurrahman had been working hard on his relationship with Megawati but she remained diffident, and he was uncertain about how secure their friendship was. One of the biggest obstacles seemed to be people close to her who were counselling her not to trust him. Tragically, Abdurrahman did much himself to damage his relationship with Megawati by allowing his frustration with her to well up in his off-the-cuff remarks about her. Abdurrahman seemed not to realise that virtually everything he said, whatever the forum and whether he liked it or not, was on the record. He frequently joked about Megawati in a way that was bound to aggrieve her when his comments found their way back to her, as they invariably did. In this, as in so many aspects of his presidency, Abdurrahman played directly into the hands of his opponents.

Even so, Megawati had not yet given up hope in Abdurrahman. On Tuesday, 18 July, she urged her supporters to go easy on Gus Dur, saying: 'I ask PDI Perjuangan members at the house to behave properly and normally during the hearing.' Many within PDI-P were still intensely angry over the sacking of Laksamana and also the suggestion that Abdurrahman had accused him of being corrupt. The depth of feeling against Abdurrahman was made plain when 332 members of the 500-member parliament signed a petition calling for the interpellation.

By then the text of his speech for Thursday, 20 July, had already been crafted. Most of the work had been done by his Cabinet Secretary, Marsillam Simanjuntak, but the time and direction were set by Abdurrahman. If the members of parliament were angry with him, the feeling was mutual. He felt strongly that the use of interpellation over his dismissal of two cabinet ministers was inappropriate and could only be explained in the context of a political push to topple him, or at least undermine his authority. Consequently, the text of his interpellation speech was angry. Although it had a scholarly tone and the main point of the argument was objectively true, it left a negative impression. The night before the speech was to be read, Abdurrahman got cold feet. He had been pleading with Megawati to read the speech as was expected, but she refused, unhappy with the content. As the text of the speech had already gone to the House, it was not possible to cancel it.

On Thursday morning it was agreed that Djohan Effendi, as State Secretary, would read the speech. There was no prospect now of a last-minute reprieve from Megawati. Abdurrahman sat motionless on the podium in the parliamentary building, subjected to several hours of harsh criticism and tough questioning from the floor. Later many expressed sympathy for his position; it is probable that if his response had been more neutral and not so defensive and angry, he might well have won the day. However, when Djohan read the seventeen-page speech prepared by Marsillam any sympathy for Abdurrahman evaporated. The text was a new defence of the president's right to hire and fire cabinet ministers, combined with sharp criticism of the House for seeking to manipulate the interpellation process for party-political purposes.

That night Djohan described reading the speech as one of the most difficult things he had ever done. It was completely at odds with Djohan's outlook and disposition; he felt deeply that the appropriate response would have been to simply ask for forgiveness from the House. Djohan urged Abdurrahman to think carefully about his written response to the House the following day. That evening Djohan and others set to work drafting a conciliatory letter asking for the understanding and forbearance of the members of parliament and promising more thorough explanations of actions in the future. All through Friday, Djohan and colleagues worked on the response. When Abdurrahman rang Akbar Tandjung (chairman of the House) and asked for an extension of the five o'clock deadline, it was granted.

When the letter was finally couriered to the parliamentary offices it was examined and received well. Over the weekend three petitions were circulated among members of parliament. The largest, with 252 signatures, said, 'We accept the President's apology but insist that he give an open explanation for firing two economic ministers'. The following Monday Akbar Tandjung formally announced that the House was deferring its response to the interpellation, along with further investigation into Bulogate and Bruneigate, ahead of its recess for the annual MPR session. For the time being, at least, it looked as if Abdurrahman was safe.

Over the following week Abdurrahman met several times with Megawati and with Akbar Tandjung and other leading figures in the MPR. He felt confident that he had their understanding and that he would be given more time for his government to prove itself. In all likelihood none of the power-brokers really wanted to topple him during the August 2000 annual session. Megawati, who was the person most likely to replace him, was apprehensive about receiving a poisoned chalice. Moreover, she knew that, if PDI-P sided with Golkar to bring down the president, there was every likelihood that she would experience a similar fate before twelve months were out. If Akbar Tandjung were made vice-president, it would be easy for Golkar to push for Megawati's resignation as president and precipitate the automatic ascension of Akbar Tandjung. Similarly, both Amien and Akbar probably recognised that, for now, there was no better choice than Abdurrahman and that their own ambitions would be better served if they were patient. Nothing, however, was certain.

A TIMELY MEETING

One encouraging development occurred on Tuesday, 1 August, when Akbar Tandjung, Megawati and Amien Rais agreed to meet with Abdurrahman and the Sultan of Yogyakarta at his palace. Ostensibly the occasion was to celebrate the sultan's birthday. In the Javanese calendar this particular birthday was an important one and the sultan explained it was for this reason that he was inviting the nation's leaders to his home. There is no doubt that the main aim of the meeting was to try to consolidate consensus among the four leading political figures ahead of the annual MPR session and to communicate that consensus to the public.

Abdurrahman flew down to Yogyakarta early on Tuesday morning and drove straight to the Yogyakarta palace. There he met Akbar

Tandjung and Megawati. Curiously, Amien was nowhere to be seen, even though it was known that he had flown in the previous evening. At noon the party moved a short distance down the road to the *kraton* or Sultan's Palace. An enormous crowd of waiting media was gathered outside the gates as Abdurrahman's party entered the palace compound. The sultan had chosen the so-called Yellow Building as the site for the meeting. The five leaders were to meet in the back room of the Yellow Building, a seldom-used venue and one regarded as being of great spiritual importance. They were to be seated around a table used by the sultan's great-grandfather. Shortly after arriving, Abdurrahman, Megawati, Akbar and the sultan together cut the top off the yellow rice cone traditionally prepared for such occasions. Each received a portion and ate together, a powerful symbol of consensus. Amien had not arrived when the four retired to the special meeting room at the back of the Yellow Building. Half an hour later he turned up looking anxious and stern, and went straight into the meeting without comment.

While the five were meeting, news came through of a bomb explosion in central Jakarta apparently involving the Philippines ambassador. There was confusion as to who was behind it and exactly where it had occurred, but it seemed likely that it was connected with Muslim separatist activity in Mindanao in the south of the Philippines. While there was no concrete evidence for this, circumstances encouraged everyone to hope that that was the answer. The prospect of the bombing having a local cause was a frightening one with the annual session of the MPR only days away. An hour later the doors of the Yellow Building opened and Amien came out, mumbled a brief greeting to those waiting outside, and walked briskly out of the palace compound. About twenty minutes later Megawati appeared, looking relaxed but saying little as she walked to the gates of the *kraton*. The short conference was over. It was not until half an hour later that Abdurrahman, Akbar and the Sultan appeared together, walked leisurely to the gates and paused momentarily to speak to the assembled media. There had early been an expectation that the five would appear together (as they had in Ciganjur in November 1998) at the *kraton* gates to explain their position to the assembled media, but with Amien and Mega leaving separately this was not to be.

Abdurrahman later explained that the sultan had told him that the historic meeting room would be the site of a spiritual contest and the order in which individuals left would suggest something of their power. Clearly, he said, Amien and Megawati had been overpowered. Inside the *kraton*'s Yellow Building Amien and Megawati as individuals may have been overpowered, but what it meant in Jakarta's parliamentary building was something else altogether.

The problem wasn't so much with Amien or Megawati; rather, it lay with those around them. Megawati had been increasingly influenced by strong personalities who had only recently joined the party. Chief among them was Arifin Panigoro, previously an active Golkar politician and known to be a close friend of Ginanjar Kartasasmita. Ginanjar had been a long-serving minister under Soeharto, regarded as one of Soeharto's brightest and most able ministers. He was also said to have been one of the most corrupt. American academic Jeffrey Winters accused him of having strong links with the Freeport mine in Papua, and some believed he had much to hide. Many observers saw links, not just to Ginanjar and Arifin Panigoro, but also to Fuad Bawazier, director of taxation and Minister for Finance in Soeharto's last cabinet. Fuad was one of Indonesia's wealthiest businessmen; since the fall of Soeharto he had built up strong ties with Amien Rais. Perhaps because of his Arab ancestry it seemed natural for Fuad to support Amien's new party; in any case, he came to be one of PAN's leading financial backers. By August 2000 Fuad seemed to have established enormous influence both over Amien and his party. He managed to secure a position for himself as head of the Reform Faction in the MPR, representing PAN and Islamist parties such as PBB and PK.

FACING THE MPR

Although they met every two or three days and talked on the phone every day, the relationship between Abdurrahman and Megawati remained troubled. Apart from Megawati's own personal grounds for annoyance, another destabilising factor was a clique of personalities within Megawati's party who were determined to turn her against Abdurrahman. Even without such factors, however, the relationship had always been a fraught one. Although there was genuine affection between the two, communication had never been ideal. Since the middle of 1999 their meetings had mostly consisted of small talk. Either Megawati did not know how to make her point to Abdurrahman or she was uncertain about what she wanted; matters of substance were seldom raised in their meetings. Consequently, although things had been going reasonably well during July, on the eve of the MPR session Megawati was still reluctant to read the presidential address.

When the MPR assembled on the morning of 7 August, many of his supporters were fearful that that Abdurrahman might repeat his interpellation performance. Instead, he delivered a conciliatory, exquisitely judged and unscripted speech and then handed over to Marsillam Simanjuntak, who read the carefully crafted presidential progress report. The latter was solid, and consequently in places difficult to digest, but the overall tone was contrite and polite. It was exactly the sort of speech that should have been delivered to parliament in July.

Many of the details of the progress report were in a series of appendixes attached to the speech. These had been distributed to all members of the House, but when the members came to make their response the following day it was obvious that few had read them. Critics pointed out that the progress report skipped many of the details, that it was too broad-brush and visionary in nature. However, it was unlikely that more could have been included in the body of the report and, in any case, the appendixes addressed most of the issues raised.

The mood in Jakarta changed as soon as the speech was delivered. Suddenly the hope of many observers that somehow the beleaguered president would manage to turn things around seemed realistic. He seemed to have learnt some important lessons from the experience of interpellation and was trying hard not to repeat his mistakes at this more important annual session of the MPR. The next day the eleven factions in the MPR were allotted half an hour each to make their responses. Half a dozen factions were scheduled to present the reports in the afternoon, with the remaining five to be delivered after a two-hour evening meal break.

Just as the presidential progress report had been some months in preparation, it is likely that the critical responses to it had been largely crafted in the weeks leading up to the Assembly. Consequently, the speeches were expected to be largely critical, referring to the points raised earlier in the interpellation. The first three or four faction responses were surprisingly positive. The faction representing PPP, for example, was critical, as expected, but also acknowledged the tone of contrition in the president's speech on the previous day. Similarly, the faction representing the armed forces and the police made a number of predictable criticisms, particularly regarding Abdurrahman's handling of secessionist movements and communal violence. But the overall tone of the response was much more positive than had been expected. So too was the case with the other reports up to the time when the final response before the evening meal break was to be delivered.

The last report that afternoon was by the Reform Faction. It was said, with good evidence, that the entire speech had been scripted by Fuad Bawazier. Over the previous two weeks Fuad had invested considerable time and energy, and very likely other resources, in engaging with the media in an angry campaign against the president. Fuad did not however, read the speech to the Assembly. Instead it was read by a young woman dressed in traditional Islamic *jilbab* (head scarf) who spoke with a firm but pious tone of voice.

From the outset the speech was sharply critical. It was said later that many members of the Reform Faction were embarrassed by the angry tone of the speech. The criticism had become increasingly personal during the latter section and accused Abdurrahman of being a hypocrite, failing to live up to his title of Kiai Haji as well as failing as a religious leader to fulfil the hopes of the people. The final part of the speech was peppered with texts from the Qur'an and the Hadith referring to tyranny and injustice and accused the president of the worst hypocrisy and betrayal of his own principles. By the time the speech came to its angry close, with the speaker virtually yelling, there was a deep sense of disquiet in the Assembly.

The rest of the faction responses that evening followed a predictably critical line and harangued the president for having failed to turn Indonesia around over the previous two months. In particular, the Reform Faction response appeared to have overplayed its hand by being too personally critical, but the subsequent responses, though less personal, were also considered to have been unreasonable and unrealistic in their tone. Taken together, the eleven speeches blamed the president for almost every mishap and tragedy that had befallen Indonesia over the previous year. The following morning most commentators agreed that the criticisms had gone well beyond what was reasonable. Some pointed out that the president alone was not responsible for the economic team; others like Kwik Kian Gie and PDI-P also bore some responsibility, and yet none of this was acknowledged.

The next morning Abdurrahman rose at four o'clock as usual and went for an early-morning walk. He was in good spirits and joked about the events of the previous day. The anger and sadness that had been evident the previous evening had been replaced by his usual nonchalance and quiet confidence. The previous day he had, unusually, taken a nap in his hotel suite, from 10 am until 1 pm, a clear sign of the emotional pressure upon him. He had also met with media and with other senior colleagues that afternoon and had clearly been anxious about the speeches that were to come. Now, he felt that the worst was over; whatever happened, things were going to turn for the better. Throughout the day politicians and others came and went from his suite as final adjustments were made to the speech for that evening. The president's speech on Wednesday evening was to be a reply to the responses to his Monday accountability speech. In the previous session of the MPR it was in this speech in particular that former President B.J. Habibie failed to make a sufficient response to the criticisms levelled against him. The fact that Habibie then lost the accountability vote was a reminder of how important it was to get this final speech right.

One of the most surprising elements about the previous night's speech, and no doubt the one that had been the focus of all the discussions and comings and goings from the presidential suite over the previous two days, was a reference to the delegation of daily tasks to the vice-president. Throughout the eleven faction responses on Tuesday, the theme of the president's inability to handle day-to-day administration — partly because of his blindness and poor health, and partly because of his personality — was constantly brought up. In his Monday speech Abdurrahman had mentioned that in his new cabinet, which was to be formed after the annual session was concluded, he wanted to hand a lot of day-to-day authority over to a senior minister. Most of the eleven factional speeches on Tuesday picked up this point, with many arguing strongly that any significant delegation of duties should be to the vice-president, rather than a third party. Ironically, most of the seven hundred members of the House, including many within her own party, would ordinarily have been critical of Megawati's ability to handle day-to-day management and sceptical about her capacity to do a better job than Abdurrahman. The next day, however, in all the speeches, she was portrayed as the natural and rightful heir who would of course be able to make up for the shortcomings of the president.

Many of the factional responses that day alluded to the need to divide the president's authority between the vice-president and the president, some even going as far as to say that the president should henceforth be a symbolic figure like a university chancellor, with the real power being wielded by the vice-president. There was a suggestion that such a major shift should be spelt out in a resolution in the annual session.

Consequently, when Abdurrahman himself referred to the handing of duties to the vice-president, it caught everyone by surprise. This was the last thing they thought that he would do, given that it had been the major thrust of substantive attacks upon his authority the previous day. Not surprisingly then, Thursday, 10 August, saw most of the domestic and international media in Jakarta in a whirl.

Few understood exactly what the president had meant the previous night. To those close to him, however, it was perfectly clear. The words of his speech had been chosen carefully. They spoke of delegating daily tasks to the vice-president. There was no mention of sharing authority. It was also spelt out that the vice-president would work closely with two senior ministers who would be styled as co-ordinating ministers and together these three would report to the president. While it was not exactly Abdurrahman's 'plan A', it seemed clear all the same that 'plan B' was not substantially different from his original plan. Given Megawati's personality and abilities, it was clear that the work would be carried by the two co-ordinating ministers. There did not seem to be a major shift involved at all, since a month earlier Abdurrahman had spoken privately of the need to involve her on a daily basis in consultation with these senior ministers and to draw her more into day-to-day tasks, like running cabinet meetings.

Nevertheless, there was great confusion in the media. Some spoke erroneously of the president delegating authority to the vice-president; some saw it is a dangerous move against the presidential nature of the Indonesian constitution; others welcomed the shift with glee, interpreting it to be a final collapse of Abdurrahman's authority. On Thursday morning, Abdurrahman flew to Bandung to address an assembly at the Institute of Technology and then flew northeast to Banjarmasin in Central Kalimantan. At both venues he hinted at his intentions in the previous night's speech stressing that he was not speaking about the diminution of presidential authority, which, he pointed out, was against the Indonesian Constitution. By the close of Thursday the picture seemed a little clearer.

The question now on everyone's mind was not whether the president would be impeached, but whether his enemies within the Assembly would move to formalise the delegation of tasks to the vice-president via an official recommendation ratified by the Assembly. If this arrangement were formalised by the Assembly it would not automatically block Abdurrahman's plans, but it would narrow the space in which he had to work. If, however, he succeeded in spelling out the task-sharing with a presidential decree, rather than with a MPR decree, then it was likely that he would lose very little authority and the decree could not be used against him in six to twelve months' time. There was a real danger that the Assembly's decree might have been malevolently crafted in such a way as to serve as a constitutional trap for the president, particularly if Megawati failed to live up to the expectations of such a decree and the blame for her performance could then be sheeted home to the president.

Most of the Assembly members were staying in five-star accommodation at the Hilton or at the Hotel Mulia close to the parliamentary complex. Abdurrahman preferred to sleep at home in his usual bedroom in the palace. At Megawati's request, however, he shifted to the Hilton on Friday night and stayed there throughout the weekend. Megawati had argued that it was important for them to be in constant contact, and with rooms on the same floor it was easy for her and others to drop by and talk with him. It was to be a busy weekend with numerous discussions.

The following day the eleven MPR factions were scheduled to present their replies to the president's response. Much of the negativity of the previous Tuesday was absent; most factions welcomed the president's contrition and willingness to learn from past mistakes. Predictably, although some of the more critical factions, like the Reform Faction and Golkar, said that the president was on notice, most of the heat seemed to have gone out of the previous week's criticism. That evening Abdurrahman sat in his suite joking with old friends Djohan Effendi, Mohamad Sobary and Marsillam Simanjuntak and was in good spirits.

Marsillam read him the text of the next day's State of the Nation speech. It was solid but lacked the grace and eloquence of the first speech. As Marsillam was going over the text a final time, news came through that Megawati was also rehearsing the speech. She had previously indicated that she was not willing to read the State of the Nation speech, but now it appeared that she would, and she did so the following morning. The language of the address was unfortunately overly bureaucratic, and in tone reminiscent of speeches from the previous era, but the substance was regarded as being credible. It spoke of modest plans for the following twelve months and a vision for the nation's recovery. It was well received. No doubt that was partly because, as originally planned, it was the vice-president who read it.

There was a sense now that the worst was over. The MPR session was scheduled to conclude on Friday, but a technical possibility remained that it could be extended, if need be, into the following week. The warm response to Megawati's delivery of the State of the Nation speech suggested that there would be no further developments at the annual Assembly, and it was unlikely that an Assembly decree regarding the delegation of tasks between vice-president and president would be tabled.

OPTIMISM RETURNS

The next day, Thursday, 17 August, was a historic one, for it was Indonesia's National Day. For weeks extensive preparations had been made around the city and especially in the Presidential Palace gardens, where great podiums had been constructed and the garden decked out in all manner of lights and other curious structures. Also, a vast temporary veranda had been built onto the section of the palace facing back towards the Monas square. The scale of these preparations for a one-day celebration seemed amazing, but members of the presidential staff pointed out that the National Day had been celebrated with even more fervour under Soeharto and that the most amazing celebrations had been held the previous year under President Habibie. Some lamented the fact that Abdurrahman, concerned about the nation's economic position and the cost of such preparations, had asked for a relatively low-key celebration. Even so, there was a festive and colourful mood throughout the day at the Presidential Palace, and in the evening when ambassadors and dignitaries dined with the president inside the palace, thousands joined in the feast outside in the gardens.

One significant difference between this celebration and those of the previous three decades was that half of the invited guests were ordinary people. People from every region of Indonesia had been invited to attend, with every local agency being asked to send a couple of guests. Consequently, much like the Lebaran (the fast-breaking day at the beginning of the year) when the palace had been opened to members of the public, there was a curious atmosphere around the grounds as ambassadors and cabinet ministers were joined by citizens from every walk of life. No doubt the fact that the annual MPR session had gone far better than anyone had dared hope led to the relaxed and joyous atmosphere that pervaded the palace grounds that day.

Friday, 18 August, saw the closing session of the annual Assembly. Only days before it had looked as if the Assembly might end with a bang, but it was ending with a whimper. As chairman Amien Rais read a short speech, there were a few moments of prayer and then, with a tap of the gavel, the MPR was declared closed until the following year.

ASSEMBLING A NEW CABINET

The sound of Amien Rais' gavel on the heavy wooden desk at the front of the parliamentary Assembly signalled freedom for Abdurrahman Wahid. Barring disasters, he would not face the Assembly for another twelve months, and he now had a chance to go ahead and put together a cabinet of his own choice. To have come through the Assembly as well as he did exceeded the expectations of most observers. By its close Abdurrahman, though chastened, had strengthened his position. All he had to do now was put together a credible cabinet, while reinforcing the coalition relationship between his and Megawati's party, and he would have the basis of a strong government for at least twelve months. Few things with Abdurrahman, however, are ever entirely straightforward.

Shortly after the close of the annual session Abdurrahman flew to Yogyakarta. There it was planned to hold a special ceremony involving a *ruwetan*, a special *wayang kulit* performance intended to secure blessing. The *ruwetan* had been scheduled to be held several weeks earlier ahead of the MPR session but for various political reasons it had been postponed. Many non-Javanese and many modernist Muslims in Java would be inclined to dismiss the *ruwetan* as fairly inconsequential. For those who believed, however, such things were of great importance. The *ruwetan* went on late at night on the campus of the University of Yogyakarta. Abdurrahman sat with his family and the Sultan of Yogyakarta, together with a number of leading intellectuals from across the country. The *ruwetan wayang kulit* ceremony involves a ritual bathing much like a traditional Javanese wedding. This baptism can be done directly on the person for whom the *ruwetan* is being held, as a way of conferring blessing, or by proxy. In this case it was by proxy. Eleven people, mostly academics and intellectuals, were to participate in the ceremony as proxies for Abdurrahman. The ceremony concluded at around 1 am, when the eleven were richly sprinkled with flower-scented water. Even those who do not believe in the power of such rituals to ward off ill recognised that it was significant that the Sultan of Yogyakarta, a charismatic and popular social leader, had organised this *ruwetan* on the president's behalf. It was perhaps also significant that Megawati did not join in the ceremony.

Abdurrahman returned to Jakarta early Saturday morning and spent the next two days in discussion and deliberation about the formation of a cabinet. It might have been thought that he had worked out the cabinet well in advance but there was little sign that this was the case. Indeed, even a week before he had been revising the number of ministries and working out exactly how to reduce thirty-five posts to twenty-three. Some aspects had clearly been on his mind for a long time, even before the involvement of Bambang Yudhoyono and Rizal Ramli had been thought through. Similarly, the decision to keep many of his existing ministers who had proved trustworthy and competent was fairly straightforward, although some only had their fate assured at the last moment.

Most observers, particularly his supporters, expected that he would work closely with Megawati in forming the new cabinet. The pair did meet over several days and had a number of conversations about the cabinet line-up. Nevertheless Abdurrahman said that he found it difficult to work out exactly what it was that she wanted from the cabinet. Many from Megawati's side would say that she experienced difficulty in persuading the president what she wanted. Some indication of improved relations came on Sunday when a celebratory dinner was held in Alwi Shihab's home to give thanks for the fact that the annual session had gone well. Not only did Megawati attend looking relaxed, but she sat next to Abdurrahman and Amien Rais. She even went so far as to make an impromptu speech, which for Megawati was a strong indication that she was feeling comfortable.

If a good credible cabinet could now be secured, the future looked bright for both of them. Given that the efforts of Abdurrahman's enemies to turn Megawati against him had largely come to nought, it was likely that they would now have a period of relative peace in which to get on with their work. There still remained, however, the question of economic recovery. An even more important challenge was the reining in of inter-communal violence that had broken out across the country.

For some time Abdurrahman had been planning to travel to the regional city of Poso in Central Sulawesi. Although they had received relatively little attention in the national media, developments in Poso showed eerie similarities with the outbreak of violence some distance to the east in the island city of Ambon. Violence had first broken out in

Poso late in 1998. It is difficult to be sure of all the reasons involved, but socio-economic differences and the influx of economic migrants were contributing factors. The initial violence, however, arose out of an apparently trivial incident between youths, much as it had in Ambon.

In April 2000 the violence had flared up again, taking on a religious colour as inhabitants of Poso and surrounding villages aligned themselves according to their faith. Numerous churches were destroyed and Christian homes attacked. The following month a third wave occurred, which appeared to be Christian revenge on those who had attacked them in April.

The government formally acknowledged that over two hundred people had died in the violence, although some NGOs argue that it may have been as many as five times that number. Some 23 000 refugees fled the area. At one point Poso was 90 per cent empty, with around 5000 homes destroyed. Knowing these facts, however, was little preparation for the impact of arriving in Poso.

The drive in from the airport revealed scenes of destruction much like those to be found in Dili. The devastation seemed almost total. Most of the timber homes had been burnt to the ground, leaving only stumps. Where homes had been made of brick, only the walls were left standing, on which, more often than not, graffiti had been scrawled in charcoal.

As the presidential convoy passed a cluster of burned-out houses just outside the airport, there was time to read an ugly message scored across one home saying 'Thanks for your work now just wait for payment'. Almost every home had similar graffiti often expressing the same black humour. At the traditional ceremony in Poso that Abdurrahman had come to witness, various communities pledged their commitment to work together to solve the violence, and to cement this declaration a large bull's head was buried. Ominously, even as the declaration was being read out it was met by loud jeering from off to one side of the assembly.

The visit was a reminder of the sort of challenges facing Abdurrahman. How many more Posos would there be? How many more Ambons? The violence appeared to have come out of nowhere and yet escalated into a firestorm that was now hard to extinguish. Few expected that the declaration that day would give any more than temporary respite. The real solution involved much more difficult measures.

When he returned home, Abdurrahman had still not finalised his cabinet line-up. The previous day he had cancelled all meetings to concentrate on the new cabinet and he seemed wearied by the task. Relations with Megawati appeared good but nevertheless remained uncertain.

The next day, Wednesday, 23 August, Abdurrahman decided to make his cabinet announcement that afternoon. He was due to travel to Bandung on Thursday and then Surabaya on Friday; consequently he had to make the announcement either on Wednesday afternoon or on Saturday. Megawati, being cautious, and not yet entirely comfortable with the composition of the new cabinet, wanted the announcement delayed until Saturday. Abdurrahman, however, opted to push ahead on Wednesday, catching both the domestic and international media off guard. This, possibly, was a mistake.

Perhaps one of the reasons why Abdurrahman decided to push ahead in announcing the cabinet, despite Megawati's clear preference for delay, was his concern about last-minute pressure and political lobbying, of the sort which had contributed greatly to the bloating of the numbers of the previous cabinet in the twenty-four hours preceding the announcement. At around three o'clock on Wednesday, Megawati arrived at the palace and went to speak to Abdurrahman in his office, the room used by her late father when he was president. By this stage a large media throng had assembled at the front of the palace awaiting a press conference, although it appears many were caught off guard by the rapidity of developments. At 4.15 pm Megawati left. The atmosphere was tense. It seemed that Abdurrahman had a good cabinet line up, but the big uncertainty was Megawati's reaction. When Abdurrahman left his office and walked around the front of the palace to face the media throng, the glaring absence of Megawati was immediately interpreted as a bad sign. At short notice Marsillam was drafted to read the new cabinet list as Megawati left for home. Megawati had felt uncomfortable about pressing ahead with the announcement and explained that she was not ready to make a public appearance; she said that she needed to go home and bathe and change before she faced the media.

Marsillam read out the list of names. The cabinet was not what had been expected. Besides the president and vice-president, there were twenty-three names. Fifteen of them were members of the previous cabinet, and with one or two exceptions most of these were predictable;

eight of them were new. As many analysts later agreed, it was a solid selection. Abdurrahman had said that 60 per cent of the ministers in his new cabinet would be non-party political professionals, and that appeared to be the case. Eleven of them had PhDs.

None of the new ministers had strong political affiliations. Mohammad Mahfud, the new Minister for Defence, a Madurese constitutional law expert from Yogyakarta, had loose connections with PPP; the new Minister for Culture and Tourism was a member of Megawati's party, as was Bungaran Saragih, the new Minister for Agriculture and Forestry. The initial impression was that Megawati had no members in the cabinet. Abdurrahman later explained that, apart from the two ministers just mentioned, Megawati had specifically expressed her wish for Agum Gumelar to remain as Minister for Transportation and Telecommunications, evidently because she still believed that he had helped her in her initial to bid to become head of PDI-P; she had also requested that Sonny Keraf remain as Minister for the Environment. However, the perception was that PDI-P had missed out badly. Later it also became evident that this cabinet was distinguished by the elimination of Golkar. All these details were overshadowed by Megawati's absence when the cabinet was announced, which was interpreted as a sign of disapproval, and by surprise at the appointment of the Finance Minister, Prijadi.

Most agreed that the appointment of General Susilo Bambang Yudhoyono as Co-ordinating Minister for Political Security and Social Affairs was a sensible move. Slightly more contentious was the appointment of Rizal Ramli as Co-ordinating Minister for the Economy, but he also was regarded as credible. The choice of Mahfud as Minister for Defence was much more criticised on the grounds that it seemed strange to give that portfolio to someone with no defence experience and whose expertise lay in legal reform. Abdurrahman explained that this was exactly the reason for the appointment, because he felt the main challenge facing the military and police was legal reforms and sorting out 'the mare's nest of tangled' legal jurisdictions. He intended, he said, for the new minister to work side-by-side with the Justice Minister Yusril Ihza Mahendra in resolving many of the complicated legal issues.

This contentious approach in itself could have been accepted, but the choice of Prijadi Praptosuhadjo gave rise to the call that this was a crony cabinet. Prijadi had failed the test set by Bank Indonesia to determine whether he was a 'fit and proper' candidate for a post at the head of the People's Bank of Indonesia (Bank Rakyat Indonesia — BRI), where he had spent his career working in the area of rural finance. Many commentators returned to this point in the days that followed. Fuad Bawazier, for example, said at a major seminar in Jakarta that he was worried that a man 'so lacking in integrity' was Finance Minister. Abdurrahman explained that he'd known Priyadi for sixteen years and was confident that there was no question of his integrity. Instead, Abdurrahman said, he'd been the victim of political infighting in the central bank led by Bank Indonesia governor Syahril Sabirin and his colleagues, all them Soeharto appointees. Abdurrahman had clearly expected that the new cabinet would be well received. It was, after all, solid and professional, if lacking in some of the big-name stars of the previous cabinet, but a cloud hung over it because of the appointment of Priyadi and Mafud and because of the perception that Megawati was unhappy with the new line-up.

Having almost miraculously escaped the traps set for him in the annual session, it seemed to be a small matter for Abdurrahman to go ahead and appoint a cabinet that was met with broad approval. Instead he took a high-risk option, choosing people he felt would work as a team and would be personally loyal to himself. The previous cabinet had worked poorly, largely because of political infighting, but also because of contests of egos among the stars who occupied some of the top positions. If Abdurrahman had chosen a popular figure such as Feisal Basri or Sri Mulyani as Economics Minister and included several of Megawati's senior party officials, then the cabinet would have been well received. Instead, it was interpreted as a gamble. Compounding matters was the impromptu press conference which followed the announcement. When asked why Megawati was not there, Abdurrahman joked that she had said she wanted to take a bath. Instead the rupiah took a bath as the currency tumbled by 5 per cent. Was Abdurrahman being courageous, wily, wilful or just plain reckless? As with so many questions about Abdurrahman, the right answer appears to be all of the above.

TWELVE

REGIME CHANGE AND THE FIGHT FOR SURVIVAL, 1999-2001

GETTING OFF TO A BAD START

In many respects Abdurrahman's new cabinet was a step in the right direction. Few disagreed that a reshuffle was required, because the first cabinet had performed poorly. And while there was debate about one or two of the new cabinet ministers, notably Finance Minister Prijadi and Minister for Defence Muhammad Mahfud, once things had settled down there was general agreement that it was a competent and professional cabinet, albeit one largely of the president's own choosing. The problem was not so much the outcome as the process, or rather, the perception of the process. H.S. Dillon, adviser to both President Wahid and Vice-President Megawati, commented in response to a question from *The Jakarta Post* in early September about how he viewed the genesis of the cabinet: 'Gus Dur possesses superior intelligence. He could have finessed it, and got what he wanted without ruffling any feathers. Such rash behaviour does not bode well for the legacy of a great visionary, a true democrat and a real humanist.'[1]

For the president's political opponents, however, the perception that he had ridden roughshod over Megawati was not necessarily a source of genuine personal concern. Golkar, in particular, saw itself as being in a win-win situation. If the president failed, it would be to their benefit. If he succeeded, they were in any case in no position to move into power ahead of the 2004 elections, needing at least that period of time to begin the process of rehabilitating their reputation. Parliamentary speaker and Golkar chairman Akbar Tandjung put it this way: 'If the Cabinet fails to perform well, the Peoples Consultative Assembly will be firm in evaluating the government in the next annual session.'²

The other controversial aspect of the new cabinet following the August 2000 MPR session was that the president had agreed to hand over much of the day-to-day administration of government to his vice-president. In its 1 September issue *The Jakarta Post* noted:

> Following a statement before the Peoples Consultative Assembly earlier this month President Abdurrahman Wahid issued a decree authorising Megawati to run the daily technical affairs of government. However the stipulations contained in Decree No. 121 give little executive power to the Vice President other than as an administrator of the Cabinet.
>
> As if further emphasising the overlying authority of the President, the decree also instructs Megawati to employ the services of the State Secretariat's office and other presidential aides to assist her.
>
> Only if necessary can she seek assistance of her own vice presidential secretariat staff, the decree stipulates.³

The precise details of the agreement to hand over administration to Megawati were to be all-important because the perception that Abdurrahman had failed to live up to his end of the bargain became entrenched over the following months. In fact, days after she become president Megawati herself testified a little less then twelve months later in an interview with *Time* magazine that:

> It is important to manage this transition smoothly. I have already been part of the government as Vice President. After I was given more responsibility for the handling of daily affairs through last year's Presidential Decree 212, I feel that I have gained much experience in administrative affairs. ...
>
> Time: Will you delegate authority to your Vice President under an arrangement similar to when you were Vice President?
>
> Megawati: There are already regulations which state that the Vice

President is supposed to be the President's assistant. But there will be a difference. The last yearly session of the People's Consultative Assembly resulted in a presidential decree that handed more responsibility to the Vice President because of Gus Dur's shortcomings. However, we agreed in the Special Session, that that decree is going to be revoked and those tasks are going to be returned to the hands of the President.[4]

Even though *The Jakarta Post*, for example, had stressed the limited nature of the transfer when reporting on it at the beginning of September 2000, it later opined that the president had reneged on the deal. In fact, the problem was that the deal was flawed in the first place. It was also unclear how far the vice president availed herself of the opportunity to play a greater role in day-to-day government. Certainly, Abdurrahman made matters worse by succumbing to a temptation to micro-manage, thereby reinforcing the perception that he was not prepared to share power. Whatever the case, the arrangement agreed to after the August session ultimately proved unsatisfactory on all sides.

ONGOING SECTARIAN VIOLENCE

From the first days of the Wahid presidency it was clear that one other major challenge facing democratic Indonesia was the resolution of sectarian and communal conflict. This conflict was to prove a major line of attack against the embattled president over the coming months. After all, his critics observed, the president had spent the whole of his public career campaigning against sectarian violence, so why was he incapable of resolving it now that he was president? Abdurrahman for his part was deeply disturbed by the ongoing conflict whether in Maluku, Kalimantan, Sulawesi or back home in Java. He was concerned because of a genuine, deeply felt aversion to such divisions. He was also frustrated as a political leader because of his conviction that the conflict was, at least in some cases, artificially engineered as part of a cynical campaign to discredit his administration.

In Jakarta there were some expressions of sectarianism which were disturbing but fortunately these had not developed to the point of serious bloodshed. This was the case with groups such as the Defenders of Islam Front (Front Pembela Islam — FPI), whose regular attacks on cafés and bars in Jakarta often caused considerable damage to property but seldom resulted in serious injury or loss of life.

This sort of moral vigilantism took a worrying turn in mid-October 2000, when dozens of men clad in green military-style uniforms burst into several international hotels in the city of Surakarta in central Java; they demanded that the hotel management bring out any American guests so that they could be 'rounded up and expelled from the country'. The US State Department was alarmed enough to issue a travel advisory warning for Americans travelling to Indonesia.

While the activity of groups such as FPI in Jakarta and other cities on Java was essentially symbolic, the violence that was occurring in Sulawesi and Maluku was of a different nature altogether. Fortunately, in the city of Poso in Central Sulawesi, the temporary truce that had been negotiated during Abdurrahman's visit continued to hold and a degree of calm began to return to the troubled province. Nevertheless, periodic eruptions of violence continued and most of the tens of thousands of refugees who had been forced to flee their homes — southwards in the case of Christians, northwards in the case of Muslims — were afraid to return home, leaving the city of 400 000 people largely deserted. By this point the total number of internally displaced people in Indonesia was fast approaching one million.

Tragically, the islands of Maluku continued to experience horrific acts of violence. One particularly awful incident occurred in mid-January when hundreds of Christians, including pregnant women and children, were rounded up and barbarically assaulted, being forcibly circumcised as part of their forced conversion to Islam. Besides the psychological trauma of the violent conversion, there were grave concerns about infection because the circumcisions, including female genital mutilation, were performed with unsterilised razors and old knives. Apparently, local Islamic leaders had been obliged to participate in the forced conversion of their Christian neighbours by a group of radical extremists who had come into their village of Kesuai. When the group of 172 Christians were later evacuated to Ambon, these leaders spoke of their trauma and their fear that resistance would have resulted in their immediate execution at the hands of menacing young men wielding large knives and machetes.

LASKAR JIHAD

For some months Abdurrahman had been intensely frustrated by his inability to bring the violence in Maluku to a rapid halt. In September he declared martial law in the region in an effort to clamp down on the free movement of people across the islands. Despite this the violence dragged on; his many critics pointed an accusing finger at him, saying that the endless conflict was proof that he did not have what it took to govern Indonesia at this difficult time. The accusation was particularly galling because Abdurrahman was convinced that the violence in Maluku was not purely organic and spontaneous in nature but was being exacerbated by the presence of external forces such as Laskar Jihad, who were clearly being aided and abetted by military personnel and police on the ground. Groups such as Laskar Jihad must have had some degree of support within the navy; otherwise it is difficult to see how they could have moved around the archipelago so freely.

There was also strong evidence suggesting that Laskar Jihad was financed by some of Abdurrahman's political opponents such as Fuad Bawazier, something that even Fuad Bawazier did not try to deny. Moreover, local military personnel, both active and retired, were taking sides in the violence and in some cases instigating it. Australian-based scholar George Aditjondro identified retired Brigadier-General Rustam Kastor of Ambon as the ideological father of the violence in Maluku. In a book published in 2000, which sold in great numbers not only in Maluku but also in Java and in Sulawesi, Kastor argued that a conspiracy existed involving the separatist group the 'South Maluku Republic' (Republik Maluku Selatan — RMS), the Protestant Church of Maluku (Gereja Protestan Maluku — GPM) and Megawati's PDI-P. Aditjondro notes:

> This is not where Kastor's accusations end. He also accuses Christians of manipulating the student-led Reformasi movement to destroy the Indonesian economy and thereby promote the Republic's disintegration by separating the Christian-dominated provinces in Eastern Indonesia — including East Timor — which would then form a new Christian-dominated country with a fantastic natural resources since it will include West Papua in the current province of Maluku. The first step in this grand scheme is, according to the author, the 'breakaway' of East Timor from Indonesia.[5]

Aditjondro goes on to state: 'Apart from the more ideological inspiration through his book, Kastor has also been personally involved in sending Islamic vigilantes from Java to Maluku. He was one among the six representatives of jihad forces who went to see President

Abdurrahman in Merdeka Palace in Jakarta on Thursday, April 6.' Aditjondro argues that parallels between Laskar Jihad and FPI suggest that military officers such as Wiranto and Djadja Suparman, both recently sacked by Abdurrahman, might be linked with the violence. He also alleges that there are links between Laskar Jihad and the small Islamist Justice Party (Partai Keadilan — PK).

THE BREAKDOWN OF THE MILITARY

Although it is difficult to find conclusive evidence linking groups such as Laskar Jihad to elements of the military in Maluku, it is clear that one of the greatest problems facing Abdurrahman and post-Soeharto Indonesia — perhaps greater even than the problem of communal and sectarian unrest — was the breakdown of the Indonesian military. This was tragically illustrated in early September 2000, when three UN aid workers were stabbed and beaten to death in the town of Atambua in West Timor, close to the border with East Timor. The incident prompted Harold Crouch, long-time observer of the Indonesian military, to say: 'The fragmentation of the Indonesian military has reached the point that they have difficulty controlling the situation in Timor and elsewhere', and 'One likely explanation for what happened on Wednesday in West Timor is that it was all manipulated from Jakarta.'[6] Crouch is normally a conservative commentator not at all given to wild speculation, so it is significant that he was prepared to suggest a military conspiracy. Moreover, Crouch's position was backed up by statement from no less than the Co-ordinating Minister for Political and Social Security Affairs, General Susilo Bambang Yudhoyono, who said, 'I would not rule out the possibility of political motives behind this incident'.[7] A number of other military observers joined in, suggesting that the evidence pointed to a co-ordinated and politically motivated attempt to embarrass the president. This was certainly the way Abdurrahman himself saw it. As it happened, at the time of the killings Abdurrahman was in New York, where he was to address the UN Millennium Summit. Consequently, he suffered the humiliation of having the eyes of an unparalleled assembly of heads of state turn in his direction as UN Secretary-General Kofi Annan expressed the United Nations' remorse and horror at the murder of its three workers in Indonesia. Abdurrahman was convinced that the timing of the killings was not accidental. 'The timing was precisely selected while I was in New York. The purpose was to humiliate me,' he said.[8]

Several days later former Defence Minister Juwono Sudarsono issued a statement warning that militias in West Timor were being funded by elements linked with former President Soeharto.[9] On the same day, a court in Jakarta heard allegations that General Wiranto had ordered the illegal printing of money to pay militias active in Timor at the time of the August 1999 referendum.[10]

On a lighter note — in October the now retired general embarked on a new career as a popular singer. Late that month Wiranto sang before a packed house in a five-star hotel in Jakarta a selection of numbers from his newly released CD titled 'For You, My Indonesia'. The following day, addressing a conference in Jakarta, he spoke, apparently without any trace of irony, about what he saw as 'the subversion of the law in Indonesia by political interests'. Wiranto concluded his address by saying that it was his dream that the legal institutions would be respectful, independent and legitimate so that people were assured of justice, adding: 'I am still doubtful that I will get justice.'[11]

THE SOEHARTOS AND JUSTICE: AN EXPLOSIVE COMBINATION

In mid-September, a day before the trial of former President Soeharto was due to resume, a powerful explosion rocked the Jakarta Stock Exchange. A bomb had exploded in the basement carpark, killing at least fifteen people and injuring more than thirty. Although conclusive evidence was not found, the sort of explosive used and the scale and style of the attack strongly suggested military involvement. It was the latest, and largest, of a series of bombings in the national capital since Abdurrahman had become president. (Apart from the bomb attack that almost claimed the life of the Philippines Ambassador and the attack on the Jakarta Stock Exchange, there had also been an incident at the Attorney-General's Office where a bomb went off in the Attorney-General's private bathroom. Another more powerful device was found before it had a chance to explode. Coincidentally or not, that incident occurred at a time when Tommy Soeharto was under investigation by the Attorney-General's Office.) Political Commentator Wimar Witoelar observed:

> This latest offensive against the Wahid government comes in a sinister double feature with immense public impact: Atambua and now the shaking of the nation's financial centres. This terrorism must stop or the government will lose its hold.

At least, the international community can now see that, as in the Atambua case, the Wahid government in Indonesia's new society are the victims, not the perpetrators, of the violence. This the world must understand before they push this government into a corner.[12]

The next day Defence Minister Mahfud was quoted by Reuters as suggesting that it might be wise to call off the corruption trial against former President Soeharto in order to ensure that further violence did not take place: 'If we keep meddling with this matter we will not have time to take care of other problems because we will continue to be harassed ... more terror will keep coming.'[13] At the same time, Abdurrahman issued a statement suggesting that Tommy Soeharto and his friend Habib Ali Baagil, leader of the FPI, might be linked to the Stock Exchange bombing. Abdurrahman then issued an order to the police chief, Rusdihardjo, to arrest Tommy and take him in for questioning regarding the Stock Exchange bombing. It's not clear what evidence Abdurrahman had, but the order was not entirely surprising, especially since the bombing of the Attorney-General's Office months earlier had been linked to Tommy's personal bodyguards. Habib Ali Baagil immediately retaliated by threatening to sue Abdurrahman for slander and denying any link with the bombing. Akbar Tandjung expressed his regret that the president was so quick to point the finger at Tommy Soeharto and that he had ordered his arrest. Speaking at a seminar in Singapore, Akbar said, 'We are now in the new era where the law is supreme. You cannot arrest somebody if you don't have evidence'.[14]

Further angering his opponents, Abdurrahman sacked national police chief Rusdihardjo when he refused to comply with the request to arrest Tommy Soeharto. In self-defence Abdurrahman argued that the proper process of law had been shown to have failed miserably. He said that the nation was in a Catch-22: unable to get sufficient co-operation from the police and the military to obtain evidence to secure arrests, and unable to arrest people because of deliberate obstruction from the very people who should be obtaining the necessary evidence.

Abdurrahman was convinced that there were links between incidents such as the bombing of the Jakarta Stock Exchange and his efforts to prosecute senior members of the former regime, most especially members of the first family. Early in September while attending the UN Millennium Summit in New York, he had said that if Soeharto was unwilling or unable to appear in court personally he could be tried in absentia. 'If he is summoned [again] but he still does not appear before the court then he must be tried in absentia. That is the plan in my mind and we have decided that as a punishment for him.'[15] Days later, however, lawyers representing the former president defied requests for their client, who they claimed was too ill to answer questions in a court of law, to attend the next session of his corruption trial.

Some weeks later the supreme court sentenced Tommy Soeharto to eighteen months in prison because of his involvement in a US$11 million land-exchange scam with the State Logistics Agency, Bulog. This was not regarded as being in any respect the greatest of Tommy's crimes, but the Attorney-General's Office thought this case offered the best chance of a successful prosecution. This judgment was proved right, but Tommy failed to respond to a summons to arrest him and face imprisonment. In the meantime his lawyers attempted to buy time through legal manoeuvres over claims that proper paperwork had not been served for the arrest. Tommy himself made it clear that he wanted to seek some sort of suspension or annulment of his sentence.

In a move which many thought represented a gross error of judgment, Abdurrahman agreed to meet with Tommy Soeharto at the five-star Borobudur Hotel near the Presidential Palace. The meeting was private but, given the venue, it was hardly secret. The Borobudur Hotel is run by the military as a business venture and is a popular meeting spot for Jakarta's elite. Both Tommy and Abdurrahman were accompanied by modest entourages, which in Abdurrahman's case consisted of a collection of senior *kiai*. When news of the meeting broke, Abdurrahman's opponents seized on the opportunity to suggest that he had tried broker a deal with Tommy. Abdurrahman also said that he had stressed to Tommy that he should accept the modest jail sentence and explained that there was no way in which the state could tolerate his not going to jail. Even so Tommy protested, saying that his life would be in danger if he went to jail and that the only condition on which he would accept sentencing was that his personal bodyguards accompanied him in jail. The next month, his legal avenues exhausted, Tommy simply went to ground and evaded arrest.

PATRIOT GAMES: EURICO GUTERRES ARRESTED

On 23 September, speaking at the installation ceremony of the new national police chief, Abdurrahman described as shocking the news that police had released key suspects in the murder of the three UN aid workers in Atambua. The police explained the release as having occurred because of a technicality. Several days later the notorious former East Timorese militia leader Eurico Guterres was arrested at a Jakarta hotel. Although Guterres was suspected of being involved in the killing of the three UN aid workers, his arrest was for weapons possession charges; these arose from his order to his men to seize weapons which they had only minutes earlier handed over to police, during a visit by Vice-President Megawati to West Timor. The arrest of Guterres was welcomed in the West, and it also elicited surprising expressions of sympathy from the Indonesian elite. Amien Rais immediately spoke out in defence of Guterres, saying 'He is our friend. He's the leader of the pro-integration militia and he lost his homeland. If he's arrested for the sake of the UN, then what a nasty country that makes us'. He later added, 'I think [the arrest] will set a very bad example for our brothers in Irian Jaya and Aceh'.[16]

At the time of Eurico's arrest, Abdurrahman was locked in a struggle with military leadership over a shake-up of senior command positions. On 9 October there was a surprise announcement that the appointment of a new Chief of Staff of Army, Navy and Air Force would be postponed. At the same time a military spokesman announced that reformist generals Agus Wirahadikusumah and Saurip Kadi, who were both known to be close to the president and keen to support him in reforming the military, were being disciplined for 'having breached the code of ethics of the Indonesian army'.[17]

MILITARY SOLUTIONS

One of the main areas of friction between Abdurrahman and senior military personnel was his approach to handling secessionist movements in provinces such as Aceh and Irian Jaya. Abdurrahman's civilian opponents were quick to exploit this area of controversy. In early September unrest erupted in Irian Jaya (parliament had yet to approve Abdurrahman's suggested change of name to Papua) as independence supporters went on a rampage after police cut down flagpoles flying the Morning Star flag. Akbar Tandjung immediately spoke out, saying 'The government must be firm toward groups seeking to encourage separatism. We cannot compromise on such movements'. He went on to say, 'Gus Dur should not allow rebels in Irian Jaya to advance their separatist cause. This is not something we expect from the president. Instead, he should promote unity and development'.[18] On the same day

Megawati spoke out in support of Akbar Tandjung's statement, effectively criticising Abdurrahman's conciliatory approach towards West Papua independence supporters, which allowed them to fly the Morning Star flag provided that it was positioned below the national flag.

The statements by Akbar Tandjung and Megawati cast doubt on the legality of flying the Morning Star flag, and consequently exposed the West Papua activists to rough treatment by the local security personnel. The elders of the Papuan Council Presidium lamented the dual policy coming from Jakarta, blaming uncertainty about such things as permission to fly the flag for various bloody incidents, such as the one in which as many as fifty-eight people were killed in the town of Wamena, 290 kilometres southwest of the capital, Jayapura. Following that incident, Presidium members went to Jakarta to meet with Abdurrahman to talk about ways of resolving the issue.

At the same time as Abdurrahman was struggling to impose a clear policy position in Irian Jaya and seek a compromise between members of the Presidium and the security apparatus, he was having difficulty imposing his will on the military in the troubled province of Aceh. The military commanders were furious with Abdurrahman for persisting in seeking a negotiated solution when they argued that, given free rein, they could quickly resolve the problems with a military operation. Even so, Abdurrahman had more success in prevailing against the military leadership with respect to Aceh than he did with Irian Jaya, possibly because there was a greater degree of sympathy within parliament for the plight of the Acehenese than for the Papuans. In early September he was successful in temporarily extending a three-month humanitarian pause which had been on the point of expiring. Even so, the level of violence in the province suggested that military personnel on the ground were disobeying the presidential order for restraint. In fact, some observers claimed that violence in Aceh was at record levels.

A 'MESSY STATE', AN EMBATTLED PRESIDENT

One month after the August annual session of the MPR any fleeting trace of optimism had been replaced by a return, in double measure, of the gloom that had prevailed in the run-up to the Assembly meeting. The ongoing communal clashes, the spate of bombings and the breakdown of control over the military, as was evidenced by the Atambua incident, and the failure to bring the former first family to heel, combined to paint a picture of an administration, and indeed a nation, hopelessly adrift. In the first week in October, renowned *New York Times* columnist Thomas Friedman visited Indonesia. Writing in the *Times* about his impressions, he had little to say that was positive. Earlier, he observed, it had appeared that Indonesia was one of those promising democratising nations, like Poland, Chile and Hungary, that were emerging from years of military-backed authoritarian rule. Now, he opined, it appeared as if Indonesia had fallen from that hopeful track and become simply a 'messy nation' like Russia. Indonesia and Russia were, he observed 'too big to fail but too messy to work'. That left Indonesia ahead of failed states like Sierra Leone and Liberia, but that was scarcely any consolation for the world's third-largest democracy.

In its editorial of 7 October, *The Jakarta Post* picked up Freidman's theme and declared: 'Although it would be unfair to put the blame entirely on President Abdurrahman Wahid, he has been a determinant in this state of affairs. Likewise, he will be a crucial factor on whether and when Indonesia will move back from being a messy to a democratising state.'

Although a fiercely independent and professional broadsheet such as *The Jakarta Post* still held a glimmer of hope for the Wahid presidency, his political opponents were now ready to pounce on the embattled president. On 18 October Amien Rais was quoted as saying that Abdurrahman 'has lost the plot on how to govern'. He went on to say, by way of suggesting an alternative, that 'Megawati and Akbar have a broad appeal among legislators, unlike Gus Dur who appears to be losing his grip'.[19] Although in the past Amien had been fiercely critical of Soeharto, and by extension Golkar, he had considerable respect for Akbar Tandjung, not least because Akbar had at one stage led HMI. For his part, Akbar, who was probably the nation's most astute and careful politician, made a point of downplaying Amien's suggestion, saying instead that 'If Megawati fails as president, it will also reflect badly with Golkar. It is better for us to remain in opposition until 2004. Golkar's target is for the next general election. Then, we will be there seeking power'. He went on to explain that 'We lost a lot of votes in the last election because we were identified with the Soeharto regime. ... The climate then was not too favourable for us. But in 2004, we will regain lost ground by winning over voters upset with the performance of the PDI-P and the newer political parties'. As a Batak from North Sumatra, Akbar might be expected to speak his mind, but in fact he is exceedingly careful in what he says, weighing each word. On this occasion, however, it appears that he was indeed being perfectly frank. It wasn't that he and Golkar had no interest in toppling the Wahid administration; it was just that, on balance, they had good reasons to be ambivalent. Nevertheless, he was quoted the following day as saying that it would be very hard for the beleaguered president to last until the end of his term, given growing pressures in the MPR to topple him: 'A lot of legislators are increasingly frustrated with Gus Dur's inability to resolve our political and economic problems.'[20]

If Akbar Tandjung was hedging his bets, Amien made it perfectly clear where he stood. Towards the end of October he went on record as saying 'I will pay for my sin by remaining in my position as Speaker of the MPR', when addressing a seminar organised by KAHMI (Korps Alumni HMI), the powerful alumni association of HMI. Amien explained that he was deeply repentant and regretful for having promoted Abdurrahman to the presidency the previous year and spoke of it as 'his sin'. He justified his emotional response by saying 'If Gus Dur continues to be kept as president despite his failure to achieve political and economic stability, there is a risk that Indonesia will break up'.[21]

Fortunately for Abdurrahman, several days later Megawati broke her characteristic silence to lash out at critics of the government. 'To all those critics who frequently say the government is too slow in dealing problems and not carrying out its duty, I want to ask, what have you done besides criticising?' she said, addressing a rally of PDI-P in Surabaya. She added, 'The government's time has been wasted in preparing for the annual session. [We should] minimise the manoeuvring of the political elite and create a working climate which is healthy and calm for the government'.[22]

Further support came from an unexpected quarter when Habil Marati, a parliamentarian from PPP who had been sacked from the parliamentary committee investigating the Bulogate and Bruneigate scandals, spoke out about his frustration with party-political opportunism in the parliament. He declared, 'The Bulogate committee is a huge conspiracy which is actually creating chaotic conditions in order to bring down the president'.[23]

More support was forthcoming from the deputy head of the Supreme Advisory Council, Agus Sudono, who declared in the middle of November that toppling Abdurrahman would not solve the nation's problems, and 'It would make a bad precedent for Indonesian democracy because people would not believe in democracy'. He explained: 'Whoever replaces the current government would also face demands to stand down. Besides, if Gus Dur did stand down, his replacement would not be as good as him.' He went on to explain the reason for his anxiety about the situation: 'As a result, people will suffer. People will suffer the consequences of horizontal conflict.' He concluded: 'If Gus Dur did stand down, is there any guarantee that his replacement would be better? His replacement would probably be forced to stand down. It's a joke. One only takes power for a short period, and then is forced to stand down. We have had this kind of situation during liberal democracy where power shifted so fast.'[24]

At the end of October Megawati appeared still unwilling to move against the president. She explained, 'If I were to choose, I would be happy to remain chairman [of PDI-P], being a vice-president is tough. It turns out that managing the country is no easy job'.[25]

If Megawati was undecided about whether to move against her old friend and snatch the presidency from him, others were not wasting time in seeking to ingratiate themselves with her. The military, in particular, was keen to make an ally of Megawati. It was not so much that they had decided that Abdurrahman would definitely go — though their good relationship with Megawati was a valuable insurance policy should that eventuate — but that by working with Megawati they were able to exercise leverage on Abdurrahman in a way that they had trouble doing directly themselves.

The military was annoyed with Abdurrahman, not just by what they saw as his intransigence in blocking military solutions in Aceh and Irian Jaya, but also by his sympathy for international requests to hold trials for perpetrators of human rights abuses in East Timor.

At the end of December Megawati attended the anniversary celebrations of the army's elite Kostrad unit. Photographs were widely circulated of her dressed in a tailored camouflage uniform, topped off with the green beret of the Kostrad strategic reserve command, riding atop a Scorpion tank at the Kostrad base in Bandung. The military felt comfortable with Megawati, not just because she yielded to their pressure and manipulation but because there was a natural resonance between her conservative nationalist instincts and their desire to maintain the unity of the state. In contrast, the president was described as 'a man not of sound mind and health' because of his clearly irrational objection to solving communal problems by means of force.[26] The military was also angered by the president's tendency to intervene in what they saw as internal military affairs, and to favour reformist officers in routine rotations of the command chain.

AUSTRALIA

Although Abdurrahman was able to resist the pressure from both the legislature and the military, it nevertheless severely limited the options available to him. He could not afford to fight on too many fronts at once. One of the areas that suffered because of the unrelenting pressure from his opponents was his strong desire to rebuild good relations with Australia. Throughout 2000 half a dozen or more tentative dates for a visit to Australia were suggested, but in each case the visit was postponed.

At the beginning of October Abdurrahman was advised not to visit Australia before Prime Minister John Howard first visited Jakarta. Privately he rejected this argument as ridiculous, pointing out that it had been a quarter of a century since an Indonesian president had visited Australia, while Australian prime ministers had visited Indonesia on numerous occasions during that time. Towards the end of the month he was again hopeful of being able to proceed with an Australian visit, only to have to postpone it once again. One month later Foreign Minister Alwi Shihab declared that the president intended to visit Australia and New Zealand sometime towards the end of the year, or early in 2001. Before many days had passed, these plans too were scuttled on the pretext that a visit at that time would coincide with the fasting month of Ramadan. Further tentative plans were made for a visit in February and then finally in April 2001, but these also failed. Unlike previous occasions, planning for the April visit was well advanced and the trip was only cancelled at the eleventh hour.

GROUNDS FOR IMPEACHMENT?

By mid-November anti-Gus Dur activists in parliament were consolidating their numbers in preparation for a final push against the increasingly vulnerable president. Resentful at having been dropped from the cabinet, Kwik Kian Gie organised what he called 'an informal meeting of like-minded parliamentarians'. Remarkably, Kwik's meeting was attended by as many as two hundred of the parliament's five hundred members. The meeting was intended to discuss a broad range of issues, but in the end one issue dominated the conversation of the assembled parliamentarians: how and when the president would be toppled.

By the end of November planning for the move against the president advanced when a group of 151 parliamentarians submitted an official paper to the Speaker, Akbar Tandjung. The paper listed a variety of reasons that the parliamentarians saw as constituting sufficient grounds for impeaching the president. Demonstrating the complex nature of Indonesian politics at the end of the year, the 151 signatories were not all from one or two parties. Instead 47 were PDI-P members, 37 were Golkar members, 22 were PPP members and 34 hailed from the Reform Faction dominated by Amien Rais's PAN. Among their grievances they listed the president's willingness to permit the flying of the Morning Star flag in Irian Jaya, and his proposal to abolish the MPR decree of 1966 that had outlawed the Indonesian Communist Party and its doctrine. They also said that the president was found wanting in his failure to move comprehensively against corruption and nepotism. Added to these issues was dismay at his sudden sacking of the national police chief, Rusdihardjo, and, earlier that year, of Ministers Yusuf Kalla of Golkar and Laksamana Sukardi of PDI-P. They also declared the president's intervention in Bank Indonesia (whose board of governors had been hand-picked by Soeharto) constituted improper interference in the affairs of the bank. Akbar Tandjung was not one of the signatories, but the following day he declared: 'The House will call for a trial of Gus Dur if the investigation by the special committee indicates that the President is allegedly involved in the scandal. And it is legitimate to urge the Assembly to hold a special session if the President is found guilty.'[27]

Although the grievances of individual parliamentarians against the president were multifarious, in the end they decided on the single best mechanism to achieve his downfall: to push ahead with the investigations of the special parliamentary committee (*pansus*) examining the Bulogate and Bruneigate scandals. It was felt that this would provide a suitable trigger for an impeachment, on the grounds that proof of corruption constituted gross violation of the constitution. This was the constitutional requirement for impeaching a sitting president.

When they filed their complaints against the president, the parliamentarians omitted one matter that had drawn fire from his critics. This was Abdurrahman's announcement in October that the government had decided to delay lawsuits against three of its biggest debtors,

Marimutu Sinivasan, Prajogo Pangestu and Syamsul Nursalim. Abdurrahman justified this unorthodox government response by saying that he had been advised that action against these three tycoons might damage Indonesia's economic recovery, so important was their role in Indonesian business. He was not suggesting that they should never be tried for corruption, merely that the trials should be delayed. It appears that he had come to this position as a result of insistent lobbying by businessmen on behalf of the tycoons, and in private he repeated his argument that any move against these men would be risk endangering the economic recovery. 'Marimutu Sinivasan of the Texmaco Group, Prajogo Pangestu of PT Chandra Asri, and Syamsul Nursalim of the Dipasena Group are key figures in encouraging exports. But when the time comes, they will also be brought to court,' he said while visiting South Korea at the end of the month.[28] Sadly, moves such as this further undermined Abdurrahman's credibility. Although there was no evidence that he was motivated by personal gain, his willingness to 'go soft' on some of Indonesia's most notoriously corrupt businessmen made it look as if he were not serious about dealing with corruption.

AN UNCERTAIN NEW YEAR

At the end of 2000, as Indonesia approached the festive season, the mood was anxious. As communities celebrated Christmas, the end of the fasting month and Chinese New Year, important festivals which fell close together, new outbreaks of communal violence were feared. For once, things worked out well, and these three important festivals passed without any large-scale violence.

Nevertheless, a reminder came that anti-peace forces were at work when bombs exploded at churches across the national capital on Christmas Eve, killing fourteen and maiming dozens of people. As with the other major bombings that occurred in Jakarta in 2000, the type of plastic explosive used, and the sophisticated manner in which they were detonated, together pointed strongly to links with the military. Mercifully, the bombings failed to provoke a violent response from the communities involved. They might well have been intended more as a reminder to the government of the power of those behind the bombings than as a catalyst for violence. Certainly, the subsequent failure of the police, once again, to apprehend the masterminds behind the bombings exposed once again the powerlessness of Abdurrahman's government to defend itself against its unseen enemies.

Sadly, the killings continued. In Aceh and in Irian Jaya rumblings of discontent were met with harsh repression by the security apparatus, but at least in Maluku and Sulawesi the much-feared violence didn't erupt. Abdurrahman cancelled all his travel plans throughout the month of Ramadan, as did the rest of his cabinet. By the middle of January those within Abdurrahman's inner circle were beginning to feel a little more relaxed, and even a touch optimistic about events. The optimism was to prove misplaced.

SIGNS OF STRAIN

Throughout this period Abdurrahman had, as ever, projected an image of quiet confidence, but he was clearly feeling the strain. There was no getting away from the fact, too, that everyone around him was preoccupied with the attacks on his government and deeply worried about the future.

Abdurrahman was frustrated with the inaccuracies and editorial bias of much of the media coverage of his government, both domestic and international. Nevertheless, he stuck to his position of refusing to encroach on the freedom of the press. Understandably, this did not stop him from occasionally grumbling about the press coverage. All heads of government, even in stable, mature, democracies, find reason to complain about the media, and few could have more reason to do so than Indonesia's embattled president. He found it particularly galling to be accused of being hostile to the media, pointing out that, even though many stories published about him were patently false and gave strong grounds for legal action, he had refrained for fear of poisoning the media environment and setting a precedent for future intimidatory action.

It needs to be acknowledged that Abdurrahman's eccentric and colourful style made it easy for misunderstandings to occur; statements which were made in jest, or were essentially hyperbolic in nature, were taken too literally. The combination of a hostile media composed of elements that were either opposed to him on ideological grounds, or at least had lost faith in his peculiar cavalier and intemperate style, was frequently disastrous.

One such occasion occurred in the last week of January. Addressing a meeting of university rectors on 27 January, Abdurrahman speculated about the options that would face his government if it continued its downward slide and Indonesia descended into anarchy. If worse came to worst and there was more communal unrest than the security apparatus could handle, and if several provinces simultaneously declared their independence, then his government would have to look at taking drastic action, he told the assembled university leaders. He explained that in a worst-case scenario he might have to think about dissolving parliament and moving directly to fresh elections as a way of breaking the impasse and cooling political tensions. He was thinking aloud, but the mere suggestion that he might dissolve parliament was dynamite.

The meeting was supposed to have been strictly off the record, but as soon as it closed the president's comments were widely reported. Making matters worse, the presidential office botched its response to this public relations disaster. Officials contacted the state news agency Antara and explained that the comments were off the record and had not been intended for circulation. This inept intervention only served to alarm journalists and social commentators, who began to speculate that the president was threatening a return to the dark old days of government intimidation and censorship of the press. The next morning Abdurrahman had a breakfast meeting with the heads of the army, navy and air force to discuss security arrangements ahead of parliament's February sitting, which was scheduled to begin with a vote on issuing a second memorandum of censure to the president. The breakfast crockery had hardly been cleared away when it was being reported that the president had attempted to persuade the leaders of the military to declare martial law. Witnesses to the meeting testify that there had, in fact, been no discussion whatsoever about dissolving parliament and declaring martial law, but Abdurrahman's widely reported comments from the previous day's meeting with university rectors gave life to the rumour.

The tide now turned quickly against the president. Several days later Abdurrahman had a meeting with the head of the state television service, TVRI, to discuss funding and other administrative matters. Following the meeting it was reported that he had requested favourable coverage from TVRI and threatened retaliatory action if he did not receive it. Once again witnesses to the discussion testify that no such threats were made, and that in fact the issue of control over TVRI reporting was never even mentioned.

A SERIOUS BLOW

With the DPR due to commence its next sitting on 1 February following its January recess, tensions were running high: it was widely expected that it would vote to issue a memorandum against the president. Nevertheless, Abdurrahman was quietly confident that the military–police faction (TNI–POLRI) and PDI-P would not move against him. He had received a promise, he said, from Taufik Kiemas, Megawati's husband, that his camp within PDI-P would support him. Similarly, Abdurrahman was confident that the military would not turn against him. As it happened, on 1 February ten of the eleven parliamentary factions voted against him, the only exception being PKB. Angry with the tone of discussion, PKB walked out of the chamber in protest. The vote went 394 votes to 4 in favour of issuing a memorandum. Things could not have looked worse.

Although, for all of his positive talk, Abdurrahman had half-expected the vote to go against him, it was a heavy blow. He later told friends that he believed that there had been a scare campaign to turn the military against him just as parliament was about to sit, giving him no time to correct misunderstandings and repair the damage before the vote went ahead. According to his analysis, once the military — alarmed by a pernicious rumour campaign that he intended to shake up senior staff positions — had been panicked into supporting the censure motion, it was difficult for Megawati to resist calls from within her party to follow suit. Whatever the veracity of this speculation, the story in the media was almost wholly negative.

'Alone and dangerous' screamed orange headlines across a black background on the 15 February issue of the respected news magazine *Far Eastern Economic Review*. On the cover Abdurrahman was shown head down and facing slightly away from the camera, looking desolate and forlorn as he rubbed his head with his right hand, although in all likelihood he was just adjusting his *peci* (the traditional Indonesian brimless hat worn on formal occasions). The headlines conveyed an impression of a man who was possibly not in his right mind or was at least seriously deluded. The text reinforced this impression. The lead story opened evocatively:

> Cloistered in his stuccoed palace President Abdurrahman Wahid likes to insist he has popular and political backing, but the first week of February saw his parliamentary support collapse in concert with the first mass demonstrations calling for his resignation. Wahid's desperate reaction was to reach for the tools of authoritarian rule. He first suggested to the local media that he might freeze parliament.

Then, behind closed doors, he asked the military to support a state of emergency. The army turned him down. Later, all 38 military representatives stood up in parliament to endorse a memorandum of censure. ...

A senior cabinet minister paints a picture of the president 'living in a world of his own,' where document protocol is often ignored and legal accountability tenuous. The President, frequently wearing slippers and looking dishevelled, is surrounded by a shrinking inner circle of family members and bizarre camp followers — Muslim seers, shady fixers, even a failed meatball manufacturer. During important meetings he falls asleep, and when people dare to criticize him he walks out. At one cabinet meeting in the first week of February, a cabinet member relates, Justice Minister Yusril Mahendra offered Wahid a piece of unwanted legal advice: resign.[29]

The story had a clear bias; and sadly it was reflecting a widely held sentiment among the Jakarta elite and expatriate community that 'Wahid was washed up and finished'.

The Economist, although tough, was kinder. This was the magazine that had run on its cover in October 1999 a large picture of Abdurrahman, with Yenny at his side, beneath the headlines 'Goodness, it's Gus Dur, Indonesia's surprising new President'.[30] In the sixteen months that followed, *The Economist* was consistently sharp-edged in its reporting on the Wahid administration, but it was generally fair and often acknowledged the difficulties of transitional government and the sincerity of the president. In mid-February 2001 *The Economist* reported that the situation in Indonesia had gone from difficult to disastrous.[31] In typically dry-witted fashion it ran across its cover a photograph of Abdurrahman sitting side-by-side in conversation with Megawati, whose outstretched fingers suggest that she was in the middle of explaining something to her companion; in bold letters across the top of the pair is the headline 'Would one of you please start to govern Indonesia?' *The Economist*'s lead story sought to canvass all sides, while acknowledging the difficult situation that faced Abdurrahman. Its concluding paragraphs spoke hopefully of the possibility of a compromise deal with Megawati, but concluded by acknowledging: 'But such a deal is getting harder to imagine. Even Gus Dur's confidants admit that he would rather drive a train over a cliff than admit to his old friend that he had been wrong.'[32]

GRASSROOTS ANGER

The following week saw a development that eroded the credibility of a president who was already being portrayed as cantankerous and desperate. In several large cities across East Java, tens of thousands of NU youth came out on to the streets en masse. They were, they said, outraged that the forces of the former Soeharto regime were seeking to topple Abdurrahman. In their view it was not just a question of losing their president but of losing their democracy. The street demonstrations, although much larger than any of the anti-Gus Dur demonstrations that had been seen in Jakarta, were for the most part remarkably peaceful; what terrified all onlookers was the actions of small groups of demonstrators who broke into the compounds of regional Golkar offices in several East Java cities, defacing the buildings by removing Golkar insignia and trashing offices. Some observers wondered aloud how it was that the supposedly heavily guarded offices were so easily attacked; it was even suggested that the people carrying out the attacks might not have been NU members at all. The military was suspiciously quick to denounce the violence as the work of PRD and other 'Communist' elements who, they said, had infiltrated NU youth.

Golkar was rightly horrified at the damage to its offices but also glad of the opportunity to shift its status from bad guy to underdog. In Jakarta the elite were quick to protest against the 'fanatical supporters' of the embattled president, who they feared would tip the country into chaos. Among opinion-makers in Jakarta it was common to argue that the president was secretly encouraging the protests. Inside the palace, however, it was clear that the reverse was true. Abdurrahman and those close to him, such as his nephew and chairman of Ansor, Saifullah Yusuf, and NU chairman Hasyim Muzadi, tried desperately to persuade regional leaders not to hold demonstrations and especially to discourage the demonstrators from coming to Jakarta.

On Friday, 16 February, Abdurrahman travelled to the regional city of Pasuruan in order to address his angry supporters and encourage them to get off the streets. Much like a labour politician trying to talk round former colleagues at a union picket line, Abdurrahman reasoned with the thousands of assembled protesters, arguing that 'Now was not a time to become emotional and give a chance for other parties to manipulate circumstances to their benefit'. He added, 'We have things under control in Jakarta, but your protests on the streets here only undermine all of the good work we are doing'. He concluded by saying: 'I understand your feelings but please make sure that you keep your heads cool when your hearts are hot ... now please go back home and pray for us — that way you will do the most good.' Back in Jakarta it was reported that the president had made 'token efforts to calm down his fanatical followers' and that he was secretly glad to see them expressing his mass support. There was no question that by this stage Abdurrahman and everyone around him knew that every effort had to be made to cool emotions in NU and stop the protests. They understood all too well that the sight of supporters protesting in their tens of thousands afforded his opponents a field day in the media and made him look all the more desperate and willing to take extreme measures.

FLYING INTO TROUBLE

In the fourth week of February Abdurrahman and an entourage of eighty boarded a leased Garuda aircraft to fly to northern Africa and on to the Middle East to complete the *haj* pilgrimage. Just as Abdurrahman was leaving the country, violence broke out in the Central Kalimantan town of Sampit. Initially it looked as if the fighting between ethnic Madurese transmigrants and local Dayak was small-scale and would be easily controlled. When Abdurrahman arrived in Africa, he consulted by phone with Susilo Bambang Yudhoyono, Megawati and other senior ministers; they assured him that they were on top of the situation and urged him to continue with his trip. Because the trip was organised around the *haj* pilgrimage, which occurs a fixed time each year, Abdurrahman was loath to call it off. His Co-ordinating Minister for Defence and Security also pointed out forcefully to him that, if he were to cancel the rest of the trip and return to Jakarta, it would be seen as expressing a lack of confidence in Megawati and his senior ministers.

Tragically, the violence rapidly worsened. Abdurrahman had been informed by Susilo Bambang Yudhoyono, and other senior military and police officials that the disturbances were of a limited nature and that they would soon have them under control. When questioned at his next press conference, Abdurrahman foolishly relayed this information to the press; he was unaware that as he was speaking hundreds of people were being killed in unstoppable violence. In the end at least 400 people, most of them Madurese settlers, were killed, and some claimed the actual death toll was much higher.[33] In the weeks that followed more than 20 000 Madurese left Central Kalimantan by boat to return to East Java and Madura, and a further 30 000 waited in temporary refugee camps, in appalling conditions, to be relocated.

The news that reached Jakarta and the outside world of events in Central Kalimantan was horrible almost beyond belief. The Dayak were enraged at the Madurese newcomers, whom they saw as tipping the social balance against them; they expressed the anger in the manner of traditional head-hunters of earlier generations by slaughtering their hapless victims most cruelly, sometimes ripping out and eating their hearts and livers.

One of the most serious questions about the whole incident was why the police and military were so slow to respond. Local police were reported to have sat in their stations while the Dayak rampaged unchecked through Sampit. They claim in their defence to have been so hopelessly outnumbered that they dared not stand up to the flood without reinforcements. This begs the question, however, as to why the military failed to come quickly to the aid of their colleagues. Part of the answer might be the military's desire to show the police up as inadequate to the task of maintaining order, which was delegated to them when they were officially split from TNI in early 1999. Also pertinent is the fact that the military traditionally does not post its best and brightest to sleepy provinces such as Central Kalimantan; those who are given a command post on Borneo's wild frontier generally focus on maximising 'business opportunities'. Whatever the case, it is difficult not to see a fair degree of cover-up and denial in the information that was being relayed to the president.

Because of his comments at the start of the violence and because of his failure to call off his trip and return home, Abdurrahman was portrayed in the media as being uncaring about the tragic fate of the Madurese settlers. Significantly, none of the news reports mentioned that most Madurese are members of NU. A few reports in the Indonesian internet media did note Abdurrahman's anguish at the plight of the Madurese and, for the brief few hours that it was posted, one even noted that he had given a sizable personal donation to the refugees, but none of this information made its way into the international media.[34]

On 1 March, two weeks after the violence broke out, Megawati accompanied by Akbar Tandjung travelled to Sampit, where she met with some of the thousands of terrified refugees jammed into camps under horrible conditions. On that day, *The Economist* editorialised under the headline 'Wahid wanders while Borneo burns': 'Indonesia seems fated never to have a good week: no matter how many things go right, the country is too big, too dispersed and too troubled for that.' It might have added that 'Indonesia's president seems fated never to have a good week', for by now scarcely a day passed without more bad news Abdurrahman.

In mid-March Abdurrahman moved to sack a further two cabinet ministers, which did his credibility no good, however justifiable his actions. Justice Minister Yusril Ihza Mahendra was sacked for making repeated public calls for the president to resign. So was Nurmahmudi Ismail, the Forestry Minister, who had previously been the leader of the small, Islamist PK, or Justice Party. As it turned out, Yusril's sacking and his replacement with the well-regarded Baharuddin Lopa did not carry enormous political liability, but the sacking of Nurmahmudi Ismail was much harder to explain. Privately there was talk that he was working to undermine the president and even, some said, siphoning off departmental funds towards those protesting against Abdurrahman. He was also regarded generally as having done a poor job in reforming the notoriously corrupt timber industry. Officially the reason for Nurmahmudi Ismail's dismissal was a difference of vision with the president with respect to forestry management. Unfortunately, his replacement was not as universally popular as the replacement for the Justice Minister. Some of Abdurrahman's friends who supported his sacking of Nurmahmudi privately lamented that Abdurrahman had failed to seize the opportunity to draft a fresh, younger candidate with reformist credentials. Significantly, when Marzuki Usman was sworn into the cabinet, Megawati was conspicuously absent, adding to the sense that she was gradually pulling herself away from the president.

WITH FRIENDS LIKE THESE

Abdurrahman had for some time believed that he was facing a concerted campaign in the media to slander him and to destroy his image and standing. Given that all of the private television stations are owned either by members of the former first family (Tutut alone has significant interests in several stations) or their close associates, and that many of the daily newspapers and weekly magazines also have links to prominent figures from the former regime, this is readily understandable. But there is no denying that Abdurrahman's frank and frequently reckless style was often the cause of his undoing. Often overlooked are the cultural differences that set the rural-based NU apart from urbane elite society, which caused innocent misunderstandings as well as providing convenient ammunition for Abdurrahman's political enemies. This was especially the case in April, when Abdurrahman faced a series of embarrassing setbacks as enthusiastic members of NU came to the fore to defend their beleaguered president. In the eyes of most of NU's poor and rural members, as we have seen, the attack on Abdurrahman was also an attempt by the former regime to reassert itself at the expense of democracy. They feared that, if Megawati were to become president, she would be manipulated and controlled by the military and by Golkar, or if she resisted she would be easily dismissed in the same way that Abdurrahman was. In Jakarta these enthusiastic and spontaneous responses were interpreted as cynical sabre-rattling by the president. Abdurrahman's claims that he was doing his best to restrain his people, and that the senior leaders of NU and Ansor were trying desperately to apply the brakes to a juggernaut fuelled by grassroots anger, fell on deaf ears.

In early April there was a debate within NU about whether moves to topple a democratically elected president were tantamount to treason and therefore could justifiably be met with force. The NU leadership, mindful of the emotional state of many of its members, handled the matter deftly by justifying its position in terms of traditional Islamic jurisprudence in order to win over the rank-and-file of the organisation. The situation, they argued, was in no way comparable with a civil war involving treasonous action, and consequently it was completely wrong to use force to put down attacks on the government. On 4 April Abdurrahman publicly condemned NU supporters who used the language of *jihad*, or holy war, against those who were seeking to impeach him. 'The President disagrees completely with the extreme ways that some people are calling for in his defence,' said his spokesman Adhi Massardi.[35]

Throughout April Abdurrahman, Hasyim Muzadi and Saifullah Yusuf worked hard to soothe and turn around NU's emotional membership. Nevertheless, further developments occurred with fatal effects for Abdurrahman's credibility. In early April a group in Surabaya, without formal connections to NU but made up largely of NU members, claimed that it had list of more than 20 000 people who were 'ready to die' for the president. Several other groups also sprang up to defend

Abdurrahman in what appeared to be spontaneous grassroots responses to elite politics in Jakarta.

As 30 April, the day set for parliament to vote on a second memorandum of censure, drew close, the noisy threats from tens of thousands of NU members to descend upon the capital in defence of the president only exacerbated Abdurrahman's credibility problem. His repeated rebukes of the protesters, as well as his work behind the scenes to stop them coming to Jakarta, did not save him from continuous criticism, in both the national and international press, for his claimed willingness to resort to violence and undemocratic means to support his position.

NU did not shy away from supporting Abdurrahman but did not see itself as blindly fanatical in doing so. NU chairman Hasyim Muzadi explained: 'If Gus Dur is removed via a constitutional process, I think there would be no resistance from the grass-roots but, NU's *kiais* feel that Gus Dur is being "ousted" by force and by unfair means. So, the *kiais* think that they have to defend the President, not because he is Gus Dur, but as part of the effort to fight tyranny.'[36]

After the issuing of the first memorandum against him on 1 February, Abdurrahman promised to redouble his efforts to fight corruption. He was caught, however, in a classic bind — it was a case of 'dammed if he does and dammed if he doesn't'. The arrest of prominent Golkar politician and Soeharto confidant Ginanjar Kartasasmita on corruption charges set tongues wagging around the city, arguing that the president was simply targeting his political enemies. Then in the middle of April came the arrest of Syamsul Nursalim, one of the three major tycoons whom Abdurrahman had said the government was prepared to go easy on, negotiating with them and delaying prosecution. When he was arrested on a long-standing swindling charge, the business and political community rallied to his defence claiming that the recent round of arrests was politically motivated.

While Abdurrahman worked hard behind the scenes to calm his supporters, he often negated his efforts by the manner in which he communicated with the public. For example, on Friday, 20 April, Abdurrahman addressed a major international conference at the Bogor Palace. With a *Who's Who* of the Indonesian elite as speakers and several hundred national and international businessmen in the audience, he spoke of his fear that violence would follow his dismissal from office. 'There are 400 000 people who are ready to descend upon Jakarta,' he said, in a manner which suggested that he supported their presence in the national capital.

The incident that most concerned the media in the final days before parliament's meeting to issue its second memorandum on 30 April was a massive *istigosah*, or public prayer meeting cum rally, planned for Sunday the 29th. Reflecting the mood of the Jakarta elite, *The Jakarta Post* editorialised:

> As noble as the intentions may have been, the Istigosah was nothing more than a political tool of the President and his supporters in the ongoing power struggle against his adversaries. It is no wonder that most other political leaders turned down the invitation to attend the mass prayers. Abdurrahman's Cabinet's repeated warnings that violence would erupt if the House tried to impeach the President sounded more like political blackmail than advice.[37]

In the end, Sunday's *istigosah* proceeded peacefully; after listening to calls for restraint, the NU masses dispersed peacefully. Whether because the initial estimates of an attendance of 400 000 were never realistic, or because the NU leaders had succeeded in their efforts to scale down the event, the final attendance was considerably below what had been anticipated. How much below, however, is a matter of some debate. Reuters reported a crowd of only 20 000, but reliable eyewitnesses said that many more had attended.[38]

In a live television address to the nation on the evening of 27 April via a carefully scripted speech read out by Wimar Witoelar, Abdurrahman spoke warmly of his admiration for Megawati, of his gratitude for her patient support, and of the need to move ahead and work together. He explained his own poor performance as president in the context of regime change and the immense difficulties facing him. If the same sort of conciliatory speech had been made several months, or even several weeks, earlier, it might have been more effective, but at least it did serve to cool things down. Many saw it as 'too little, too late', however, and were in no mood to give him any praise. Besides, Megawati had once again been conspicuous by her absence.

As expected, on Monday, 30 April, parliament debated the motion on issuing a second memorandum late into the night before finally passing it. The TNI–POLRI and PKB factions both abstained, leaving an overwhelming consensus to issue the second memorandum. There were 363 votes in favour, indicating considerable agreement that the president had to be reprimanded. There was no unanimity, however, on what the second memorandum meant. Many, of course, hoped and expected that it would lead to the eventual impeachment of the president at a special session of the MPR. Others, continued to hope that a way out might yet be found, and that some sort of compromise between the president and vice-president might avert the need for impeachment. After all, apart from anything else, there was a serious technical problem with the impeachment process. Whereas the first memorandum had been about alleged corruption involving Bulogate and Bruneigate, the second memorandum was essentially about alleged incompetence, as it was widely recognised that the corruption allegations lacked compelling evidence. This was officially confirmed by the Attorney-General the following month, when the case against Abdurrahman was dismissed for lack of sufficient evidence, just as it had been dismissed by the police for the same reason the previous October.

With no need to attend parliament and no official meetings scheduled, Abdurrahman spent the day at home listening to Beethoven. He met the next day with his senior ministers, and two days later addressed the nation, once again on TVRI. He personally delivered a short unscripted address calling on the nation for calm. He politely thanked the parliament for carrying out its work — and suggested that, with 160 unpassed bills before it, it had rather a lot of work to get back to.

Clearly he was not about to give up. Expectations remained, at least among those who retained a modicum of goodwill towards him, that some sort of compromise might be hammered out which would yet avert the awful precedent of impeaching Indonesia's first democratically elected president on the grounds of political unpopularity.

EPILOGUE
~

As tragic as Abdurrahman Wahid's downfall was, his final three days at the Freedom Palace were marked by a strangely festive atmosphere. From just after dawn until late at night the road through the leafy grounds of his presidential home pulsated with wave after wave of well-wishers arriving to call on the ousted leader. People from all walks of life flooded into the compound, often waiting for hours in line, just to shake his hand and deliver words of support. As news of the 'open house' spread, many of the journalists, intellectuals and activists who had been most vocal in criticising the beleaguered president descended on the palace to express their sorrow at his ousting and to ask for his forgiveness. And amidst the silken finery of Jakarta's elite stood little throngs of ordinary Indonesians, many who had travelled hundreds of kilometres to be there, clad in their best cotton shirts and wearing the sort of smiles that money cannot buy.

Although those last days saw plenty of tears and moments of melancholy, the final hours were punctuated by explosions of laughter from within Abdurrahman's book-lined office where he sat talking to his guests. And as family and friends busied themselves with the task of packing boxes and clearing shelves and cupboards, the mood was more of an end-of-year class break-up than a time of mourning.

In truth Abdurrahman and Nuriyah and their four daughters had never felt entirely at home under the twenty-foot ceilings of the former Dutch governor's mansion. The ever-present security and protocol officers clutching their two-way radios and notebooks made the austere white building more a five-star prison than a family home; after twenty-one months of living in a goldfish bowl, they looked forward to returning to their modest home on Jakarta's southern fringes.

But despite the generally upbeat atmosphere, there was no escaping the sense of tragic loss that marked the end of the Wahid presidency. Although the sad end had loomed for many months, it still hit with a horrible jolt, the jarring made worse by the suddenness of the final collision. Since the middle of 2000, a mere nine months after Abdurrahman came to office, his administration had resembled an ailing hot air balloon: its canopy rent and its burner intermittently failing, it struggled to maintain altitude, the final collision seeming imminent with each successive range of hills that loomed up before it. As it slowly sank ever closer to the ground, every effort to repair the damage and regain altitude was met by a fresh wave of hostile fire from below, and all the while new obstacles appeared.

Even so, there still remained hope of compromise until Friday, 20 July. It was dashed by the announcement by MPR chair Amien Rais that the Assembly was to go into an accelerated special session the following Monday, bringing forward its impeachment hearing from the 1 August date set by constitutional requirements.

By this stage, however, the best hope of compromise had come and gone with the parliament's vote on 30 May to proceed with the special session on 1 August (after the requisite sixty days had passed). In the week before this vote Abdurrahman, finally fully recognising the dire nature of his predicament, offered to hand over all executive authority to Megawati in return for being allowed to remain in office as an essentially symbolic head of state. Understandably, there were concerns about how this might have been implemented, but the details could have been determined in the special session of the MPR, which effectively has unrestricted powers to innovate and interpret on constitutional issues; there was no reason why this compromise could not have been made to work. But the offer to Megawati came too late. She had evidently by this point set her heart not so much on seizing power as becoming president. Megawati rejected Abdurrahman's offer out of hand and on 30 May led the vote in parliament to proceed with the special session of the MPR. It would be interesting to know how individual PDI-P parliamentarians, and for that matter other parliamentarians, felt about impeaching the president, but they were never given a chance to speak. As with all of the major votes in parliament over the previous eleven months, voting relating to the impeachment proceedings was never by secret ballot, though there was a strong precedent for this. Consequently, when PDI-P leader Arifin Panigoro stood up to lead his faction in voting, every member of his faction was obliged to follow suit. Having lost the support of Megawati, Abdurrahman was never going to gain the support of parliament.

Until the eleventh hour Abdurrahman refused to give up the hope of striking a compromise deal. If Megawati, his natural ally, was not interested, he was prepared to talk even with his enemies. On reflection this was not as strange as it first appeared: although Abdurrahman's many enemies in parliament had long plotted his downfall, the prospect of compromise still appealed to powerful figures such as Akbar Tandjung, head of Soeharto's party Golkar. Golkar was above all else concerned with success in the 2004 election, and consequently was desperate to regain the trust of the public. To join in the impeachment of Indonesia's first democratically elected president, on the tendentious grounds that his performance was not up to the miracle-working standards required of him by Indonesia's self-righteous parliament, was a high-risk manoeuvre for a party whose credibility was at an all-time low. Consequently, Akbar had been willing to negotiate with Abdurrahman. Nor was it odd that Marzuki Darusman, the sacked Attorney-General and leading Golkar moderate, had the week before accepted Abdurrahman's offer to rejoin his team as Cabinet Secretary.

Nevertheless, there remained many powerful individuals who had no interest in any sort of compromise, even one in which the president gave up all executive authority to remain as a symbolic head of state. Most notable among these are the improbably wealthy Ginanjar Kartasasmita, golden boy of successive Soeharto cabinets, and his long-time friend and partner Arifin Panigoro, leader of the parliamentary faction of Megawati's PDI-P, and who, despite his unpopularity among old-fashioned democrats in the party, was one of Indonesia's most powerful politicians. Both of these men were facing imminent arrest by the Attorney-General's Office in connection with investigations of their business dealings under Soeharto.

For months Amien Rais, one of Abdurrahman's most outspoken critics, had threatened to bring forward the special session of the Assembly. With most of the Assembly members already in Jakarta, it looked as if on Friday, 20 July, Abdurrahman would finally give Amien the trigger he needed to call a snap session.

In a bid to push party leaders into compromise talks, Abdurrahman had threatened a presidential decree in which he would freeze parliament and call fresh elections. He believed that the only way out of the current impasse, if no compromise could be reached, was fresh elections that included direct election of a new president. This threat, however, was all bluff, for he had no desire to attempt anything so radical, especially as he would be reliant on the military and police, both of which he had alienated, for the plan to work. Nevertheless, frustrated by the lack of response from party leaders, he set 6 pm on 20 July as a new deadline for issuing his decree.

Abdurrahman had also embroiled himself in a conflict with parliament over his suspension of National Police Chief General Suryoro Bimantoro, widely regarded as one of the country's most corrupt police officers. Abdurrahman had moved against Bimantoro because of police violence, including the apparently unprovoked shooting of demonstrators in the East Javanese town of Pasuran. He was also deeply disturbed by Bimantoro's apparent involvement in the Manulife case, in which a Canadian firm, Manufacturers Life Insurance Company, had been victim of a scam when it attempted, in good faith, to purchase shares in its Indonesian operation held by its defunct local partner. After buying the shares, it was informed that they had already been sold to a mysterious third party, Roman Gold, which claimed legal title, having purchased the shares through a West Samoan company and a Hong Kong-based shell company (whose documents were later proved to be fraudulent). The Canadians complained to the police, only to find the investigation turned back on them, with their Indonesian based vice-president being arrested and detained for three weeks. Not only did Bimantoro, as police chief, oversee these arrests, but it also appeared that he had a vested interest in the case.

When Abdurrahman finally suspended him Bimantoro protested, pointing out that the president had failed to seek the approval of parliament, and threatened to stay in office. He then told the president that he was prepared to go quietly provided that he was made ambassador to Malaysia, only to change his mind at the last moment and refuse to hand over power to the Deputy National Police Chief,

General Chaeruddin Ismail. Angered by what he regarded as Bimantoro's insubordination, Abdurrahman announced that he was proceeding with the swearing-in of Chaeruddin on 20 July. Akbar, however, warned the president that to do so would trigger a snap special session of parliament. In a dangerous play of brinkmanship, Abdurrahman decided on the compromise of postponing the decree and swearing in Chaeruddin as 'acting' national police chief. Initially this ploy seemed to have worked, for late on the afternoon of Friday, 20 July, Amien Rais told a Dutch television crew that the president had 'pulled back from the brink' and that consequently he was left without a sufficient reason to call a snap session of the Assembly. Just as the interview was coming to a close, however, Arifin Panigoro approached Amien and called him inside for a chat. Fifteen minutes later Amien reappeared and announced that the Assembly would proceed immediately with a special session, to commence on Monday. The next day the Assembly members convened to plan Monday's impeachment of the president.

Until Friday's announcement by Amien of the move to bring forward the impeachment hearing by ten days, Abdurrahman had remained confident of striking a deal that would at least leave him with the title of president. He was utterly convinced that to hand over the presidency to his deputy, Megawati, who was known to have close links with the military and conservative views about dealing with unrest in outlying regions such as Aceh and Irian Jaya, would lead to the unravelling of the nation at its fringes.

Friday's announcement of snap impeachment hearings threw Abdurrahman into a deep depression. His blood pressure soared erratically and there were signs of thrombosis. His doctors were worried that he might be set to suffer his third stroke.

By Sunday the position of the military could not have been clearer. The weekend was filled with symbolic shows of force, with 40 000 troops taking up positions in the national capital. The marines set up a row of Scorpion tanks in front of the Presidential Palace but, lest it be thought that they were there to protect the president, they were positioned so that their cannon barrels faced towards the Presidential Palace. It was pure symbolism, for security around the palace was in fact comparatively light, in stark contrast to the precinct of the parliament building, where tens of thousands of soldiers protected the people's representatives.

Over the weekend thousands of *ulama*, or religious leaders, from Nahdlatul Ulama, the traditionalist Muslim organisation with 30 million members that Abdurrahman had led for fifteen years, met outside Jakarta to consider his proposed decree. In a tearful meeting on Sunday evening they told him that they supported the decree because they believed it necessary to call fresh elections. Later that evening activists representing scores of pro-democracy NGOs met with him at the palace and also urged him to proceed with the decree, even going so far as helping draft its text. In the early hours of Monday morning, convinced that he was to be impeached within hours and knowing that there was no chance of either the military or the police supporting his decree, Abdurrahman decided on one last symbolic gesture. Knowing that he was signing his political death warrant, he read out his decree in the hope that in doing so he would call attention to illegitimacy of the legislature's move against him.

Later that day a melancholy Abdurrahman sat joking with friends in his palace office as the Assembly sealed his fate. Clearly in deep shock, he spoke about refusing to leave the palace as a gesture of defiance. But remarkably, early the next morning, during his regular early-morning walk around the place grounds, he told friends that he was ready to move on and lead the reform movement from outside government. Earlier that morning, in one of his last walks in the gardens of the Presidential Palace, he made a point of relating a conversation that he had had late the previous night with Nuriyah. 'I am prepared,' he had told her, 'to stay on here whatever they might do — let them cut off the water, let them cut off the electricity, let them come in and cut me down — I am not going to budge.' Nuriyah sagely replied: 'Well, that is all very well and good for you, but what about the people? The people are looking for a leader and as long as you remain here in the palace you can't help those waiting for you outside the palace.' To which Abdurrahman replied: 'Well, since you put it like that, let's move out, let's leave the palace.'

The previous evening, in typical form, the newly sacked president had done something which struck him as entirely natural but produced an unexpected level of contempt from the international media. For days a small crowd of supporters, perhaps no more than a thousand, had rallied in front of the palace. At around 9.30 that evening, the strain of the day's events evident on his tired face, at Yenny's suggestion Abdurrahman made a brief appearance on his front porch to wave to the well-wishers. It was one of the lighter and happier moments of the day for Abdurrahman, but the waiting journalists seized on his appearance in casual attire, wearing the sort of loose shorts and polo shirt that he typically wore when exercising or relaxing late at night. As it happened, he explained the next morning, perplexed as to what all the fuss had been about, he had just finished exercising on his treadmill when he decided to appear on the porch and wave to the assembled crowd before retiring. He was dressed as millions of other ordinary Indonesians are when relaxing at home. The foreign media, however, saw it differently. He had 'appeared to the public in his underwear', they declared, and even waved as if nothing were wrong.

By Thursday morning the palace was all packed up and the former president was ready to leave. Worried about the levels of stress that he was under and the possibility of another stroke, his doctors had decided to bring forward a trip planned for mid-August to Johns Hopkins Hospital in Baltimore for a comprehensive check-up.

Abdurrahman's final day in the Presidential Palace seemed appropriate. It began with an early-morning visit by saffron-robed Buddhist priests, the first of a series of visits by religious and community leaders. As was to be expected, he was later joined by Islamic leaders who prayed for his welfare. More surprising was a visit by a fervent Christian lay worker a little later that day. With a voice quivering with emotion, she read to Abdurrahman from the Bible, then joined him behind his desk and laid hands on him as she prayed for him and for the nation before anointing him with oil (actually a perfume appropriately named 'Eternity'!). Shortly afterwards he went for one last time to sit at the head of the grand ballroom that runs down the centre of the palace with his wife and daughters. Hundreds of palace staff formed a queue that ringed the ballroom four deep to say their farewells. As the tearful goodbyes concluded, Abdurrahman was ushered into his office to meet with his old rival Hamzah Haz, who only minutes earlier had been elected vice-president. Then at four o'clock he settled into the back seat of his large black Mercedes to be driven through the gates of the palace for the last time, though this time he went via the rear exit and the car no longer bore its red 'Indonesia 1' plates. Before proceeding to the airport for a commercial flight to Washington, he was driven to Freedom Square across the road from the Presidential Palace. There he addressed an emotional crowd of thousands belonging to dozens of organisations. Urging restraint, he vowed to continue the long struggle for reform from outside the palace. The banners read: Welcome Home.

CONCLUSION

JUDGING GUS DUR

By the time that the Indonesian parliament had decided to issue its second memorandum at the end of April 2001, Abdurrahman's reputation had bottomed both nationally, at least among the educated elite, and internationally. While few would disagree that his presidency proved disappointing, it is hard to assess to what extent this is because of Abdurrahman's personal failings and to what extent expectations were unrealistically high, given the difficult nature of Indonesia's transition from authoritarian, military-backed government to democracy.

I am convinced that in the long run history will judge Abdurrahman more kindly than did the Indonesian elite and the international media in the months leading up to his two memorandums of censure from parliament. As with any public figure, particularly political leaders, there are many aspects of Abdurrahman's character that are frustrating and perplexing. It is difficult to know whether to read him as, essentially, a flawed and disappointing figure who promised much but failed to deliver, or whether to be more generous and recognise the scale of his struggles and the hard-won nature of his achievements.

Natural gifts

Despite, or maybe because of, the burden of expectations on him, Abdurrahman was from an early age playful to a point of being mischievous and reckless, and in many respects showed considerable lack of self-discipline. He always had a passion for food, and given the opportunity would eat well beyond what was good for him, a tendency made worse by his preference for deep-fried savoury snacks. And in his studies, and later in his professional life, he often failed to achieve all that he could, through lack of discipline or focus. He says himself that he failed a year of high school while in Jakarta because he spent too much time watching football and going to the movies. Later, in the *pesantren* environment of Yogyakarta and Jombang, he excelled. But even there, his academic results seemed to be achieved in spite of, rather than because of, his approach to his studies. Because Abdurrahman is gifted with an extraordinarily sharp mind combined with an almost photographic memory, he was able to get through his studies with little application. His ability to easily memorise large amounts of information served him well in the *pesantren* world, but when he arrived in Cairo his failure to attend classes and generally apply himself became his undoing. After he moved to Baghdad he did much better, both because the environment forced him to focus and because he found what he was doing more intellectually challenging and interesting.

One of his key traits is natural curiosity and, provided his curiosity is sustained, he can focus and apply himself for long periods. If that is not the case, however, he quickly becomes bored, even when the gravity of the task before him warrants more effort.

When Abdurrahman was elected president, many sceptics perceived him as frail and weak (an impression reinforced by the knowledge that he had suffered two strokes and was legally blind). His friends, however, knew better. His ox-like constitution, which like his mental gifts he took for granted and failed to take care of, is combined with tremendous strength of will.

Personality

As already mentioned, one of the dominant features of Abdurrahman's personality, at least for those who know him well, is his strong sense of destiny which produces in him the conviction that he should attempt great things. He has lived most of his life in an environment in which he has few intellectual peers with the same breadth of knowledge and interests as himself. This has produced in him a sense of confidence that many argue is so great as to be dangerous. And yet he is also a remarkably humble and genuinely unpretentious individual. As president he had little time for the protocol of being head of the world's third-largest democracy. In his friends, the attributes he prizes above all else are lack of pretension and genuineness.

Perhaps one of the main reasons why Abdurrahman is frequently misunderstood and thought to be arrogant is his habit of psyching himself up with what might be called 'locker-room talk' when facing a great challenge. He talks himself up as an athlete does before a big match in order to convince himself that he can succeed. Being highly extroverted, he tends to do this psyching up aloud, and being extremely gregarious to boot he typically does it in front of whoever happens to be around. This tendency was intensified by his loss of eyesight in January 1998. Unfortunately, when he became president eighteen months later, he did little to sharpen his discretion and become more careful about the way he voiced his thoughts out loud. Many of his most controversial moments have come about because of this unfortunate combination of habits: talking big to psych himself up, and thinking out loud thoughts that a wiser person would keep to himself.

All of this is exacerbated by his sense of humour. When things are going well this makes him a delightful company and has won him many friends over the years, but when things were going badly it only served to damage him further. A frequent complaint directed at him after he became president was that he failed to appreciate the gravity of his situation. For those close to him this was patently wrong, for he took seriously the issues he was struggling with; but it is his nature to make light of burdens and to talk up his situation, using wit and natural banter to alleviate the pressure in an otherwise impossible situation.

JUDGING PRESIDENT WAHID

From the first months of his administration Abdurrahman faced pressure from a hostile legislature dominated by individuals closely connected to the former regime. As soon as it became clear that he was not a malleable president in the hands of the unlikely coalition that pushed him into the presidency ahead of Megawati Soekarnoputri, his relationship with parliament began to break down. Hostile parliamentarians accused him of a broad array of misdemeanors and failings. For some time the accusations against him focused on two cases of alleged corruption.

When the Attorney-General dismissed both cases for lack of evidence, the cries for Abdurrahman's dismissal did not abate. Instead the campaign against him shifted from claims of corruption to claims of incompetence. In truth the central issue was always his alleged incompetence, or at least parliament's lack of 'confidence' in him, for even among his staunchest enemies few seriously believed that he was a guilty of any serious corruption.

On the face of it, the charges of incompetence and mismanagement seem plausible. President Wahid was a most unlikely president, and his erratic and amateur approach to administration made it easy to write him off as simply incompetent and not up to the task. In fact, his closest friends never wanted him to become president. Those who knew him well understood that he was at heart an NGO activist, not a natural manager, much less a trained chief executive officer. He was always a populist, not an elitist: a major failing in a political system that revolves — at least outside election season — around a tight knot of several thousand middle-class Jakartans.

Moreover, he had gone brilliantly head-to-head with Soeharto in a way that few could during the difficult final decade of the military-backed regime. When the former president seemed prepared to go into any length to squash his rivals, Abdurrahman was always a tactician, not a strategist. Although he was brilliant at short-term political plays — in which his unexpected moves repeatedly caught the Soeharto administration off guard — he seldom showed any sign of planning for the long term. Under Soeharto, this was hardly a serious indictment. It made little sense to think about the long term and risk letting slip what you were planning, when to do so was to invite trouble from the regime. Abdurrahman's tactic of feigning a move to the right only to veer left at the last moment was a perfect method of dealing with an authoritarian regime with totalitarian aspirations. Indeed, it could be said that one of the distinctive features of the Soeharto regime, at least in terms of its impact on nascent civil society, was that it made everyone reactive rather than proactive. In the post-Soeharto era (which for old players like Abdurrahman came much more abruptly than had been expected), the habits of subterfuge and canny brinkmanship were hard to forget.

For Abdurrahman as president there were many situations — particularly in building a coalition with Megawati and PDI-P — where strategic thinking was essential; sadly, on many occasions after becoming president, Abdurrahman followed up a brilliant tactical play with poor strategic planning. This is exemplified in his brilliant success at the August 2000 annual session of the MPR. Although it was widely expected that the MPR would issue a decree greatly diminishing the power of the president, in the end he emerged unscathed, but then snatched defeat from the jaws of victory by forming a cabinet that failed to consolidate his partnership with Megawati and PDI-P. Even his power-sharing with Megawati became more a liability than an asset because of his failure to negotiate a sufficiently robust and substantial deal. As their personal relationship continued to sour, it was easy for Megawati in her silence to give the impression that Abdurrahman had completely reneged on the power-sharing deal; the reality was that the modest agreement was lived out according to the letter, but without consolidating the strategically vital partnership to the extent that was necessary to lift parliamentary pressure from the president.

Abdurrahman compounded his problems with both Megawati and with parliament by repeatedly hiring and firing cabinet ministers and senior officials without offering sufficient explanation for his actions. Were these appointments and dismissals obviously insightful and necessary, he might have been forgiven for his lack of consultation. Sadly, however, he seemed to get these wrong more often than he got them right, particularly during the final year of his presidency. Had he, for example, taken seriously Megawati's concerns about the appointment of Finance Minister Prijadi and Defence Minister Mahfud and stayed his hand, he would have saved himself a great deal of trouble later on. Similarly, had he not sacked National Police Chief Rusdihardjo and replaced him with Bimantoro, he could have avoided an enormous amount of angst and possibly even saved his presidency. Whatever his concerns about Rusdihardjo and the lack of success by the police in arresting Tommy Soeharto, it quickly became clear that he had replaced a moderately good police chief with a quintessentially corrupt one. He made similar errors also within TNI. After years of being manipulated by Soeharto, the military resented being accused of human rights abuses. In the end it did not matter that Abdurrahman was trying to do the right thing and push through reform within the military; his lack of diligence in explaining what he was doing only served to make the villains appear heroes and the corrupt virtuous. If in this one area of his presidency Abdurrahman could have shown greater common sense and restraint, he might well have survived in office with the support of PDI-P. But, beginning with the sudden sacking of Laksamana, he demonstrated a tragic capacity for alienating people through ill-considered or poorly explained dismissals and appointments. Moreover, in these interventions he appeared to be too trusting in accepting the advice of self-serving 'friends'. With a good presidential office staffed by trusted professionals and, most importantly, a strong chief of staff (in many respects Ratih pointed the way to what was required), he might have been spared from at least some of these self-inflicted wounds.

Possibly an even worse failing in the eyes of Jakarta elite is that Abdurrahman is completely unconcerned about appearances. It often seems as if he simply 'does not give a damn'. Indeed, he says as much himself, arguing that in Jakarta too much stock is put in form and not enough in substance. Such disregard for appearances is engaging in its idealism and down-to-earth sincerity, but it is mistaken nevertheless when your day job is being president of a major democracy. As a personal trait, Abdurrahman's dislike of all forms of pretension is admirable and one of his more attractive qualities. It is also a defining aspect of his personality. In fact much of his mischievousness comes from his habit of deflating the pretentious. In politics, however, such disregard for appearances is a serious liability when it prevents communication of your message — which in Abdurrahman's case was frequently. All too often, he would make a public statement about something dear to his heart — the substance of which he assumed was self-evident — only to sabotage himself by failing to explain what he was thinking. In this way he left himself open to the charges of his political opponents that he was erratic and irresponsible. Once again, a strong presidential office could have made an enormous difference in the way that he projected himself. (The appointment of Wimar Witoelar was an excellent start, but it came late in the piece and there was too little time to consolidate on this foundation.)

One well-known example was his often-repeated proposition that if nothing could be done to resolve the political deadlock in Indonesia the best option might be to declare a state of emergency. On several occasions he explained that he meant by this the dissolving of parliament through the declaration of a state of emergency so that fresh elections could be held quickly — and that those elections would involve the direct election of the next president which, under the circumstances, he would certainly not win. In his more reflective moments he explained this would be necessary to give the next president of Indonesia a clear mandate. In principle this argument makes good sense, although many constitutional experts point out that it is of dubious legality. His intention was sound and born of a sincere desire to avoid a 'constitutional coup' and to avert the subsequent slow disintegration of the state. Talk of a state of emergency and the dissolving of parliament, however, made him sound quite the opposite of a democrat. His response to this quandary was simply to say, 'It doesn't matter what people think I know that what I am doing is right'. Such guileless idealism is admirable in an activist, but of questionable utility in a president.

Allied to this lack of concern for appearances is his propensity for commenting on issues that are dear to his heart in a way that makes him sound not just impassioned but almost authoritarian. For example, he spoke out often about his disappointment with the Indonesian media. He occasionally even suggested that it might be necessary to institute legal action if baseless slander of him was repeated unchecked. Objectively he had good grounds for his disappointment with the media, but his talk about suing journalists, like his talk of dissolving parliament, played into the hands of those who claimed that his twenty months in power impaired his judgment and turned a democrat into a tyrant. In fact, his record on press freedom was unparalleled. One of his first actions after becoming president was to dissolve the Department of Information — the bane of many journalists, local and foreign alike. And despite his occasional outbursts of irritation with the press his administration did not once intervene in a substantial way to limit press freedom. On the contrary, the press enjoyed broad access to him as president and to his administration, without precedence in modern Indonesia. Through his openness and candour he went a long way towards demythologising the presidency. Consequently, it can fairly be said that 'his bark is worse than his bite'. But even 'barking' represents a political liability when you don't take time to explain yourself and when you are wilfully nonchalant about appearances.

A strong line of argument in his defence against the charge of incipient authoritarianism is that his political weakness was due to his failure to negotiate ruthlessly and to cut deals with his opponents. For example, he frequently antagonised the generals when he could easily have used them to consolidate his hold on power. He made an enemy when he sacked General Wiranto, who had earlier positioned himself as an ally of the president's against Islamist elements within the military. Similarly, his rebuking of the military for atrocities committed in Aceh in November 2000 permanently shifted the balance of power against him as the military became impatient with his efforts to limit their power. And although human rights abuses continued at an awful pace in regions like Aceh and to a lesser extent West Timor and Irian Jaya, there is little doubt that if he had not restrained the military and the police the abuses would have been very much worse. It would have been relatively simple to have cut a deal in the early days of his presidency with either General Wiranto or another general with political ambitions, and to have played the game that Soeharto played so skilfully of dividing and conquering the military by pitting one section against another. Similarly, it would have been fairly straightforward to negotiate deals with elements within Golkar or PPP to ensure that their votes could be relied upon in parliament. The only downside, of course, with such deal-making would have been the price. For Abdurrahman it was too high a price to be worth paying. It is interesting to speculate what could have happened had a less liberal-minded individual been chosen as Indonesia's first democratically elected president in October 1999. A more ruthless individual could have subverted the vagaries of the constitution and exploited the capricious, self-serving personalities of elite politics so as to make his or her position impregnable.

Consequently, the charge that Abdurrahman is guilty of incompetence rings true, at least at this level. As a would-be dictator, he was hopelessly incapable of putting together the alliances to give him the power that his detractors accused him of lusting after.

To be fair, at another level the charges of incompetence are justified. Abdurrahman's management style was at best erratic and unconventional and at worst seriously wanting. In particular, his frequent reshuffling of cabinet positions in an attempt to find political leverage in his push for reform, like a football coach reshuffling his line-up to make inroads against a tough opponent, provided his critics with abundant ammunition and frustrated his supporters.

Much of the incompetence in his administration had to do with a dysfunctional bureaucracy inherited from the Soeharto era. Nevertheless, there is no denying that a more managerially gifted president would have made a better job of bringing order out of the chaos of post-Soeharto Indonesia. It is easy to imagine, for example, that if Singapore's Lee Kuan Yew had been president, by the end of his first two years in office Indonesia would have become a much more ordered society than it currently is. A Lee Kuan Yew-style president would, of course, not have pushed as hard for democratic reform as Abdurrahman did, but many in the business community would have been more comfortable with such a figure. It is important to recognise — and this reality seems to have escaped some observers — that in October 1999 there was no such figure waiting in the wings, nor is there one now. The argument in favour of Abdurrahman becoming president was that he represented the best of a series of poor choices. It was hoped that his democratic aspirations and liberalism would compensate for his inadequacies in management. Whether they did or not is debatable — for the issues are not as straightforward as many pretend them to be. Still, the first two years of democracy in Indonesia proved disappointing on many fronts. It is tempting to assign most of the blame for this to the nation's maverick president. In doing so, however, we may fail to appreciate the true nature and magnitude of the problems, and consequently mislead ourselves about what is to come.

ABDURRAHMAN'S INHERITANCE: BEHIND THE FACADE OF SOEHARTO'S NEW ORDER

The simplest way of explaining the scope of the problems facing President Wahid — while admitting his weak management and erratic leadership style, together with his propensity for miscommunication — is that as Indonesia's first democratically elected president he faced the difficult task of overseeing the fraught process of regime change. History suggests that any country that has experienced decades of military-backed authoritarian government finds the transition to democracy extremely difficult. At best, the process takes at least a decade before real improvements can be seen on most fronts. Tragically, at its worst, such regime change is unsuccessful, and many countries fail to make it through the transition. The cases of Pakistan and Russia teach us that there is no guarantee of finding light at the end of the tunnel — in fact sometimes it is not even certain that the tunnel has an end. Several aspects of the process of regime change facing Indonesia appear to be unique, but most would be readily recognised by observers elsewhere in the world, whether in Latin America, Eastern Europe or East Asia. Indonesia's unfortunate distinction is that it began its transition to democracy in the midst of an enormous financial crisis. But the major challenge facing it is the one that faces all such transitions: dealing with the cultural and institutional inheritance of the former regime.

It needs to be stressed that in many important respects the Soeharto regime continues to live on long after Soeharto made his exit. The important elements that made the regime an effective, if surprisingly inefficient, authoritarian force are still largely in place, even if the government of the day is no longer the government of Soeharto. One illustration of this truth is what occurred in East Timor in September 1999 — a full eighteen months after Soeharto had stepped down as president. In a sense it was the Soeharto regime that razed East Timor to the ground in the wake of the 31 August referendum vote for independence. It was the same military machine that was the mainstay of the Soeharto regime that vindictively reduced East Timor to smouldering ruins. And it has by no means been pushed from the scene yet. The sad truth behind the empty myth of authoritarian efficiency is that President Wahid took charge of smouldering ruins as surely as did the beleaguered Timorese.

The most debilitating gift from the undead regime that fought Abdurrahman was its insidious cultural legacy, which has eroded the soil that the seed of democracy needs to take root — at least within elite society. Sadly, the rent-seeking culture of the Soeharto regime — which, for all its claims of being developmentalist, was essentially a franchising system of profit-taking and opportunism — still lives on.

The unpaid bills of the Soeharto regime come in many forms and show that 'the Indonesian miracle', once so widely acclaimed in the West, was in many respects — at least by the late 1990s — little more than a scam. Some of these bills take the form of deadly inter-communal tensions, the product of decades of transmigration. This crude attempt, albeit perhaps well-intentioned, at social engineering was unfortunately not accompanied by astute community development to prevent socio-economic cleavages emerging between communities. This is most tragically seen in the archipelago of Maluku, where previously peaceful relations between communities of Christians and Muslims living side-by-side quickly deteriorated into an awful cycle of vendetta. There is good reason for believing this violence was exacerbated by the deliberate efforts of militias sponsored by the military, and by the direct actions of the military itself, but there is no denying that, once the authoritarian lid of the former regime was lifted, countless unresolved issues boiled over.

This in itself would be a big problem for any new democracy, but in many respects it was overshadowed by massive debts in the wake of Indonesian economic meltdown of late 1997. Much of the debt resulted from the failure of Indonesia's numerous private banks, which in some cases were refinanced not just once but twice before being milked of all their assets. This contributed to a crisis of confidence, which made economic recovery extremely difficult. It also left a culture of corrupt practices and deluded mindsets, the reform of which is as difficult as the restoration of investor confidence.

These challenges that faced President Wahid are obvious, but there at least a dozen others which are not so commonly acknowledged.

A DOZEN PROBLEMS THAT PLAGUED THE WAHID PRESIDENCY

Apart from his own failings and inadequacies, most of the problems that plagued Abdurrahman as president can be summed up under the heading of regime change. These problems are so obvious that they are often overlooked. Certainly in some of these areas Abdurrahman could have performed much better, but for the most part these problems would have beset any new president trying to build a democratic Indonesia. When they are enumerated, it becomes apparent that Indonesia's first democratically elected president faced challenges that were not only greater but also more insidious than first thought.

Inflated expectations

The expectations of the millions of Indonesians who greeted his presidency with great enthusiasm and goodwill were grossly inflated. This was partly because under Sukarno and Soeharto the position of president had been built up to mythological proportions — borrowing from the imagery of a traditional Southeast Asia monarch, the president was the state and the state was the president. Moreover, people's hopes about what democracy would bring and how quickly it would bring it went far beyond what was reasonable. The elections of 7 June 1999, the first free and fair elections since 1955, went as well as anyone could have reasonably expected (apart from some strange problems with vote counting), and this good result reinforced the general air of optimism about the process of democratisation in post-Soeharto Indonesia. Even though the transitional Habibie administration had shown that many of the problems, most notably those relating to economic and legal reform, would require a long time to sort out, there was still the false expectation that the new president would be free to inaugurate rapid and substantial change.

It was widely assumed, even by those who should have known better, that during his first year in office the new president would be able to bring peace to warring provinces, rebuild investor confidence, roll back decades of corrupt practice and legal abuse, rein in the military, restore economic growth, and generally deliver Indonesia into a new period of prosperity. Consequently, it was inevitable that disillusionment would quickly replace the euphoria of late 1999.

Formidable opponents

The onset of cynicism and 'reform fatigue' were exacerbated by the formidable array of opponents facing the new president. Some of them were belligerent because they regarded Abdurrahman as a rival; others were desperately afraid that if reform went too far they would be called to account for the deals that had made them wealthy. At the very least, many were concerned to slow the course of reform because they saw it as threatening their interests.

Despite rhetoric about ending KKN, corruption, collusion and nepotism, few people who had enjoyed access to power were keen to see legal reform and the prosecution of corrupt figures. It was all very well to talk about bringing Soeharto to justice, but when attention turned to the dubious business dealings of his associates — many of whom held positions of influence within parliament — and to the human rights abuses committed by the military, Abdurrahman found few allies willing to support a concerted effort at reform. Moreover, many of these opponents of reform had enormous personal wealth and the formidable networks and resources afforded by decades in power.

Weak civil society

While the opponents of reform were generally well-equipped and well-organised, the same cannot be said of those on the side of reform. One of the legacies of the Soeharto authoritarian regime was an enfeebled civil society. Indeed, according to conventional wisdom, Indonesia was nowhere near the point where it was ready to make a smooth transition to democracy. Its middle-class and related civil society were too small to have the necessary means of socialising democracy and setting up the institutional and cultural checks and balances essential to ensuring that it thrived. When the 1999 election went better than had been hoped, this pessimism about the capacity of civil society to cope with reform looked to have been overstated. For a while, it seemed as if the transition to democracy was going to be much easier than had been expected. One year later, however, civil society in Indonesia was powerless to prevent the cronies of the former regime blocking moves for reform at every turn.

A politically charged press

One of the areas in which the weakness of civil society was most conspicuous was the capture of the media by political interests. In many respects, this was to be expected, given the extent to which capital can determine editorial policy. It was particularly evident with the private television stations that are largely owned either by Soeharto's children or by their friends and associates. Controlling capital was also a key factor in the print media and it soon became clear that certain newspapers would take a party line on key issues. What was more surprising, though, was the insidious way in which powerful vested interests were able to influence media output.

This was not the only determining factor, however, for intimidation and threats of violence were also significant in influencing the line taken by many publishers and individual journalists. In some cases this intimidation took the form of attacks by gangs of thugs acting under the banner of radical Islamism.

On the other hand, there is strong anecdotal evidence of considerable financial inducements being offered to run a particular line on certain stories. The cultural practice of giving journalists an envelope containing money for their expenses — lunch, transport and so forth — was established in the Soeharto period, and it was not uncommon for businesses and individuals to use inducements to seek favourable press. Sadly, although the press was ostensibly freer than ever before, the level of inducements appears to have grown significantly as an inflationary cycle took hold. There was much talk within media circles of large sums of money being handed out to journalists by politicians and their associates to ensure favorable coverage, to lock in television interviews, or to block certain stories from running. None of this is surprising in hindsight. What was most insidious and most disappointing was that even quality broadsheets seem to have slowly succumbed to political pressure.

Given the lack of hard evidence, it is impossible to do more than speculate about why the press became so antagonistic towards the president. No doubt to a certain extent it was his own lack of media savvy that set them against him. Moreover, the quality press was long accustomed to feeling that its role as a social commentator was essentially concerned with criticising the government of the day. Nevertheless, there seemed to be much more going on. Given the circumstantial evidence that the elite of the former regime was desperate to deflect criticism from themselves, it is likely that they sought to manipulate the media for their own purposes.

Lack of political capital

From the outset, Abdurrahman's greatest problems was his lack of political capital. In itself this is to be expected, but he experienced surprising difficulty in finding a solution. Indeed, one of his greatest mistakes as president was his failure to recognise the need to build a coalition of support.

In the run-up to the 1999 elections, it was widely expected that defeating Golkar would prove a difficult task. Admittedly by 1999 Golkar's reputation, at least within Java, was at an all-time low. Even so, political calculations showed that Golkar had a strong chance of achieving success in the presidential elections. After all, more than two hundred of the seven hundred seats in the MPR, the electoral college charged with selecting the president, are non-elected positions, and it was thought that Golkar would control the majority of these seats. Golkar was also expected to negotiate a coalition with PPP. In addition, Golkar was the only party that was well-equipped to handle an election campaign and the political negotiations that followed. Thirty-two years of Soeharto had left Indonesia ill-prepared for democracy. When presidential front-runner Megawati refused to co-operate with Abdurrahman Wahid and with Amien Rais of PAN to form a common front against Golkar, Abdurrahman began to consider other options. In the end, against all expectations, he was able to sail into the presidency through the narrowest of gaps on a rickety temporary coalition of former rivals and fair-weather friends. It was inevitable that this coalition would break up within months, leaving him with no natural vehicle. Tragically, he failed to put together the foundation of a robust coalition by neglecting links between his party, PKB, with Megawati's PDI-P.

The need to build political capital became pressing when parliament began to sit. It was soon obvious that the legislature was determined to exert its authority over the executive. It is, of course, natural after forty years of domination by the executive that the legislature should want to reassert itself. Although on paper the Indonesian constitution describes a presidential system, in practice a parliamentary system began to emerge. Unfortunately, however, this embryonic parliamentary system lacked the checks and balances of a bicameral system. Without the numbers in parliament, Abdurrahman was always going to be in trouble.

A divided reform movement

At the same time, opponents to reform had succeeded in dividing and conquering both civil society at large and the political reform movement in particular. Within civil organisations there was considerable disarray and lack of clarity about the way forward. Many student groups continued to call for Soeharto to be put on trial and for justice to be served against those in the security apparatus who had bought so much pain and suffering on Indonesian citizens. These aspirations were laudable, but they were generally not coupled with a sound understanding of the *realpolitik* limitations facing the president. It was not long before many elements of civil society began to turn against the Wahid administration, arguing that it was going neither far enough nor fast enough in its program of reform. Many individuals within Abdurrahman's PKB party were patently exploiting their connection with the president for all it was worth, and even his cabinet ministers were not free from such corruption, further disillusioning many activists. Even when they were convinced of the president's integrity, looking in from the outside on his administration they found it difficult to understand why he was seemingly incapable of controlling his own people.

Even more seriously, the personal relationship between Abdurrahman Wahid and Megawati Soekarnoputri broke down. It had been deteriorating since May 1999 and nothing that had happened over the following twelve months was able to arrest its decline. The relationship went from bad to worse when Abdurrahman made a series of political errors and then failed to correct them. The sacking of Megawati's confidant Laksamana Sukardi from the first Abdurrahman cabinet in April 2000 is widely seen as the beginning of the end for his political relationship with Megawati. Then, when he announced a new cabinet line-up four months later, he was widely viewed as not having consulted Megawati sufficiently. He can argue that he had given Megawati each of the four positions she had requested, but this was hardly an answer to his dilemma. Without the support of Megawati and PDI-P in parliament, there was no way that he could escape constant hounding by the legislature, much less advance his reform agenda.

Islamists used to spearhead opposition

As the relationship between Abdurrahman and Megawati was moving from bad to worse, the other main reformist party in parliament, PAN, began to show signs of division. Amien Rais and A.M. Fatwa began to push the party away from its original liberal charter and towards the exclusivist policies of Islamism, much to the annoyance of liberals within the party such as Feisal Basri. Eventually many of the key liberals abandoned the party, leaving PAN a shadow of its former self.

While the Islamists within PAN were consolidating their position, Abdurrahman was facing opposition from within the moderately conservative PPP along with the small Islamist parties. These forces had been instrumental in putting him into the presidency, and many observers wondered aloud how it was that he had so quickly lost their support. The truth was that he had never really had their support. When Soeharto encouraged the formation of ICMI in 1990, placing it under the patronage of his protégé B.J. Habibie, his backing of this major national organisation marked a significant policy shift. Through ICMI Soeharto courted Islamists and other conservative Muslims from a modernist urban background, the very people he had earlier suppressed. Although he was successful in co-opting some of his staunchest critics, Soeharto was unable to win over to ICMI the largely rural traditionalists represented by NU. In fact Abdurrahman was openly critical of ICMI, warning that its political sponsorship represented the re-emergence of sectarianism in politics. This fact proved critical in Soeharto's growing anger with the outspoken leader of NU, and he encouraged the ICMI conservatives to turn on Abdurrahman.

The surprise was not that early in his term Abdurrahman began to face opposition from conservative modernists and Islamists, but that they had ever supported him at all. They openly rued their 'mistake' in backing him, for a stubborn and non-compliant President Wahid was soon seen to be even less attractive than a secular nationalist Megawati — especially when it became clear that getting rid of Megawati would be much easier than getting rid of Abdurrahman was proved to be.

Elements of the former Soeharto regime may have blocked Habibie's election in 1999, but they were more than happy to enlist the support of his organisation to battle Abdurrahman. Amien Rais and friends were egged on to skirmish on the front line, at the growing expense of their own credibility, while Golkar, which was quietly attempting to rehabilitate its reputation, watched from the sidelines.

The absence of a democratic constitution

The Wahid presidency was marked by the ascendancy of the legislature over the executive. A vigorous legislature is, of course, essential to the functioning of democracy. But a legislature without sufficient constitutional checks and balances that, through its effective control of the MPR, is a law unto itself, is not conducive to the functioning of democracy. It is now apparent that Indonesia's 1945 constitution, which for four decades provided sound service to authoritarian presidents, is unable to ensure that a democratic president is, within reasonable limits, free to do his or her job.

A belligerent state apparatus

If Indonesia had had a well-established tradition of democracy, particularly within the machinery of government, the weaknesses and lack of clarity in the 1945 constitution would not be so significant. The legacy of the Soeharto regime was a dysfunctional, self-serving bureaucracy that resisted reform not because of ideological conviction but because of self-interest. Under Soeharto official wages were low, but so were workloads, and the opportunities for rent-seeking and profiteering were great. The result was a public sector in which efficiency and proficiency were at a very low level.

Not only was the work ethic within the public sector poor, but decades of appointing yesmen had eroded any notion of a meritocracy and left a state apparatus poorly equipped to carry out its core functions.

A dysfunctional public service was an enormous burden on the new administration but the problem went further. Under Soeharto all senior appointments were political, but such arrangements were based on tacit agreements. President Wahid found it extremely difficult to make political appointments because no such tradition was established on paper. Without loyal personal staff and a strong office, it is impossible for any democratic leader to function, much less one whose success depends on reforming the bureaucracy. As a result the president was left without the protective cloak — the layers of carefully fitted state apparatus and particularly a personal office — which is essential to the good performance of any democratic head of government. Without these he stood vulnerable in the full glare of public scrutiny as a naked president.

A dysfunctional legal system

At the heart of the many problems facing the new administration was the non-existence of the rule of law for most people most of the time. Most judges and court officials were corrupt and it was difficult, to say the least, for honest officials to do their job. So while the legal system was not entirely dysfunctional, in many areas it was close to being so.

Sadly, the decentralised nature of power in post-Soeharto Indonesia meant that the nation was probably more lawless than ever before. Frustrated citizens became accustomed to taking the law into their own hands, frequently with tragic results. Mob justice and vigilantism may provide some immediate satisfaction for ordinary people, but the long-term legacy of such behaviour is to destabilise civilisation itself.

It is widely agreed that rebuilding the court system, even in part, will take a decade of stable reformist government. The legal system contributed to the failure of Abdurrahman's administration as the courts worked hand-in-glove with elements of the former regime, including senior parliamentarians, desperate to escape prosecution.

A rentier state in partnership with organised crime

The pathetic state of the Indonesian legal system is a reminder the former regime saw the legal system essentially as a political tool and a means of maintaining social order. Crime in itself was not seen as a problem, provided it was under the control of the regime. Indeed the rent-seeking of the regime extended well beyond 'legal' business and reached into every 'profitable' endeavour in society.

At the same time, the grossly underfunded military (which, until they were separated in 1999, included the police) was forced to make as much as three-quarters of its operating budget, not to mention the enormous private wealth of many senior officers, from business activities. These ventures included, along with illegal forestry and mining, prostitution, gambling, and the drug trade, requiring partnerships with organised criminals, so their corrupting influence was profound. The state and its security apparatus was in partnership with networks of *preman* or gangsters across the archipelago. Some observers suggest that the problem was so extensive that the Soeharto regime can be described as a *preman*-istic regime.

An antagonistic military

The military's partnership with organised crime had a corrosive effect that extended well beyond ordinary criminality. The violence in East Timor in 1999, and in West Timor since, is a reminder of the extent to which the military relied upon *preman*-based militia to do their dirty work.

If such *preman* militia were confined to outlying regions such as Irian

Jaya and Aceh, their existence would be worrying, but there are good reasons to believe that they have been employed in 'dirty tricks' across the archipelago. Military intelligence agents were able to employ *preman* militia to incite violence and destabilise communities; even though hard-liners in the military were in many ways more powerless than ever before, they still had the power to change the course of politics and block reform. Terrorism may be the last resort of the weak, but it is very effective all the same.

In certain respects Abdurrahman's 'taming' of the military was one of his greatest successes but he made enemies of powerful officers and threatened the business interests of many more. His reforms met opposition from hard-line elements within the military and police. Moreover, ultra-nationalist military were outraged by his humanitarian approach to conflict resolution in Aceh and Irian Jaya. It is little wonder that many saw the naturally conservative and nationalistic Megawati as an attractive alternative to the president.

CONCLUSION

No one ever imagined that the transition to democracy in Indonesia would be smooth, but at the outset few reformists, Abdurrahman Wahid included, fully comprehended the overwhelming scale of the task. The legacy of the Soeharto years proved to be even worse than had been imagined. It is reasonable to be disappointed with the Wahid presidency but, given the circumstances in which Abdurrahman had to operate, he deserves more credit than he is generally given.

Few people understand the level of pressure on the president of a large nation in the early stages of transition from authoritarian military rule to democracy. Most people would collapse under such pressure, which takes the form of intimidation at every level combined with impossible expectations and severely limited resources. In this respect Abdurrahman is well served by an unusual combination of attributes, rarely found together. He is unquestionably an idealist in terms of what he aspires to achieve and the values he has espoused consistently through his life, but he also a realist with a sharp sense of *realpolitik*. His conviction that 'politics is the art of the possible' was especially apposite during a transitional period, which by its very nature is messy and cannot be traversed without constant compromise.

There is no question that, whatever else that can be said about Abdurrahman, he remains a rough diamond — in the language of Java he is *kasar* rather than *halus*, he is coarse rather than refined. Indeed he resembles the much-loved *wayang* figure, Semar — the rough, vulgar court jester who underneath his deliberately disarming exterior is sharp and focused. Because I grew up with American television rather than with *wayang kulit* and Semar, he reminds me of the Peter Falk character Colombo. Falk's shabbily dressed detective in a raincoat appears to bumble his way through cases but consistently nails the villains with evidence that they have revealed to him precisely because they made the mistake of underestimating him. Some of the time, at least, Abdurrahman does just that.

There is more to Abdurrahman than meets the eye, but what does meet the eye is often displeasing. His friends and family did their best to groom and polish him for his role as president and, to be fair to him, he too tried hard, but it was only ever an incomplete success.

This aspect of Abdurrahman's personality cost him dearly, for it made it all too easy for his enemies to dismiss him as a self-centred and delusional fool unfit to be trusted with the governance of his country. Sadly, it also made them look good, if not to most Indonesians then at least to some of the watching world's most trusted commentators. In particular, hard-line elements within the military, men who under a mature democracy might have faced long prison sentences for their crimes against humanity, were presented as democracy's defenders.

NOTES

Prologue

1 The episode was recounted to me by the adjutant involved in December 1999. Most of the incidents from 1989 onward described in this book, such as the voting at the 1999 People's Consultative Assembly, I witnessed firsthand; where this is the case, in order to keep the number of endnotes to a minimum, I have not added notes.
2 Adam Schwarz, *A Nation in Waiting: Indonesia's Search for Stability*, Allen & Unwin, Sydney, 1999, p. 191.

Chapter 1: Growing up in *pesantren* and politics, 1940–63

1 It did not occur to his young mother (who, during the first years of her marriage, was literate in the Arabic script, not modern roman characters) that the local registrar officials in her deeply Islamic rural community would record her eldest child as being born on 4 August. This account is based on my interviews with Abdurrahman and his daughters (especially Alissa and Yenny), with whom Solichah often spoke about her early life. Solichah may well have romanticised aspects of the period up to the death of her husband Wahid Hasyim in 1953, but her reputation as a confident, no-nonsense figure would suggest that her recollection is reasonably reliable.
2 There are reasons for doubting this as well. The details of his birth, and those of his five siblings, were recorded in a family prayer-book, but as this was lost sometime in the mid-1960s, and official records no longer exist, we may never be completely sure of the facts.
3 The biographical sketches in this chapter about Abdurrahman Wahid's grandfathers, parents and other family members draw upon material gleaned from numerous interviews with Abdurrahman and friends and relatives. To avoid voluminous endnotes I do not make individual reference to these interviews and conversations unless strictly necessary.

On certain issues Abdurrahman's understanding of matters of family history cannot be verified from other sources, and it is certainly not just possible but likely that on some matters he is mistaken. For example, most historians would view his claims about family lineage with considerable scepticism. It is important that future scholarship should critically examine such matters; in this book, however, I have placed greater emphasis on seeking to understand how Abdurrahman's subjective sense of history has shaped his thinking and behaviour.

Many of the details about the lives of Abdurrahman's grandfathers and father were taken from Saifullah Ma'shum (ed.), *Karisma Ulama: Kehidupan Ringkas 26 Tokoh NU*, Mizan, Bandung, [1926], 1998. Material on Kiai Hasyim Asy'ari is on pp. 67–83.

4 Material about Bisri Syansuri's life can be found in Ma'shum, *Karisma Ulama*, pp. 121–38.
5 An excellent introduction to Wahab Chasbullah's life and times is to be found in Greg Fealy, 'Wahab Chasbullah, Traditionalism and the Political Development of Nahdlatul Ulama', in Greg Barton and Greg Fealy (eds), *Nahdlatul Ulama, Traditional Islam and Modernity in Indonesia*, Monash Asia Institute, Clayton, Vic., 1996, pp. 1–41. See also Ma'shum, *Karisma Ulama*, pp. 139–52. In certain significant respects, such as Wahab's date of birth, these two accounts differ and it seems likely that Fealy's is the more accurate.
6 See Ma'shum, *Karisma Ulama*, pp. 297–315.
7 It was not unusual for some wandering *pesantren* students — *santri kelana*, as they were known — to move from *pesantren* to *pesantren* seeking not just academic knowledge but also the spiritual blessing of the *kiai* that they visited. Wahid Hasyim's quick tour of the *pesantren* represents a more extreme case of this practice.
8 Ma'shum, *Karisma Ulama*, p. 304.
9 Ma'shum, *Karisma Ulama*, p. 306.
10 Ma'shum, *Karisma Ulama*, p. 304.
11 This rather romantic recollection of how the two met comes from Abdurrahman, who grew up hearing the story from his mother (his daughters also recall their grandmother telling the same story). Abdurrahman's mother, Solichah, was a formidable woman but she was also deeply in love with her late husband — something which no doubt shapes her account. In any case, it is likely that Wahid Hasyim knew Solichah, at least from a distance, prior to the encounter described here.
12 It does seem incredible that the daughter of a senior *kiai* should not have been able to read and write in Indonesian at the age of fifteen, but in rural Javanese society prior to independence Malay/Indonesian was much less commonly used than Javanese. Moreover, in culturally conservative *pesantren*, such as Kiai Bisri Syansuri's Pesantren Denanyar, learning to read and write in Arabic was considered more important than learning to write Malay in the roman script, especially when it could so easily be written using Arabic script. In any case, Abdurrahman recalls that his mother made a point of telling him that it was his father who taught her to read and write Indonesian in the roman script and that it was from his father that she developed a love of reading.
13 This is based on Abdurrahman's account to me of his grandfather's treatment at the hands of the Japanese. Australian scholar of NU and an expert on this period, Greg Fealy, points out that there is no corroborating evidence for this claim within the NU literature; given Kiai Hasyim Asy'ari's standing within NU, this seems a strange omission. Perhaps Abdurrahman is guilty of gilding the lily in his recollection of his grandfather, but he certainly seems sure in his own mind that his grandfather bravely resisted pressure from the Japanese to act against his conscience.
14 Ma'shum, *Karisma Ulama*, p. 68.

15 I am indebted to Greg Fealy for pointing this matter out to me. I subsequently raised it with Abdurrahman, but he had little to say on the issue.
16 Ma'shum, *Karisma Ulama*, p. 309.
17 On several occasions during the 1990s I discussed his father's death with Abdurrahman. While he was never unwilling to discuss the matter, it was clear that he did not find it easy to talk about it and our conversations never ran long on this topic. It was only in December 1999, aware of the need to tie up loose ends for this book, that I spoke about the matter at length with him. Even then, it took several more interviews over the following seven months to build up the full picture. Few things that we talked about seemed to move him as deeply as this and yet, typically, he denies any deep emotion. There is no way of being sure of the accuracy of Abdurrahman's recollection of the crowds lining the streets to pay their final respects to his father. He recalls crowds of many thousands stretching along many kilometres of roadside. The reality may well have been much more modest, though there seems little reason to doubt that many people turned out to stand by the road. Whatever the case, what seems most important is that the event left Abdurrahman deeply impressed that his father could have earned such love and respect from the people.
18 See Ma'shum, *Karisma Ulama*, pp. 331–47.
19 Greg Fealy recounts visiting Pesantren Denanyar in the early 1990s and being shown a prized curio by proud Denanyar locals. It was Abdurrahman's old cupboard, replete with the foreign titles that he had read during his two years at Denanyar.

Chapter 2: Islam in Indonesia: modernists and traditionalists

1 It was the American anthropologist Clifford Geertz who first popularised the terms *abangan*, *santri*, and *priyayi* in his 1960 book *The Religion of Java*, Free Press, New York. The paradigm has always been problematic, not least because few *abangan* Muslims would choose to describe themselves as *abangan*, but in the absence of any better way of describing Muslim society in Indonesia the terms became established usage. Today the term *santri* is widely used. An excellent critique of Geertz's tendency in *The Religion of Java* to downplay the Islamic aspects of the *abangan* and *priyayi* traditions is found in Marshall G.S. Hodgson, *The Venture of Islam*, University of Chicago Press, Chicago, 1974, pp. 2.551. For a detailed study of the Islamist aspect of many of the elements of Javanese culture previously rejected as being un-Islamic see Mark R. Woodward, *Islam in Java: Normative Piety and Mysticism in the Sultanate of Yogyakarta*, Association for Asian Studies Monograph No. XLV, University of Arizona Press, Tucson, 1989.
2 An excellent introduction to the Islamisation of Indonesia is Merle C. Ricklefs, 'Six Centuries of Islamization in Indonesia', in N. Levtzion (ed.), *Conversion to Islam*, New York, 1979, pp. 100–128. See also Ricklefs, *A History of Modern Indonesia since c. 1300*, Stanford University Press, Stanford, Calif., 2nd edn, 1993.
3 See Anthony H. Johns, 'Islamization in Southeast Asia: Reflections and Reconsiderations with Special Reference to the role of Sufism', *Southeast Asian Studies*, Vol. 31, No. 1, June 1993, pp. 43–61.
4 For extensive and insightful exploration of Islam and Javanese culture, see Robert W. Hefner, *Hindu Javanese: Tengger Tradition and Islam*, Princeton University Press, Princeton, 1985, and *The Political Economy of Mountain Java: An Interpretative History*, University of California Press, Calif., 1990.
5 Kiai Ahmed Dachlan, for example, was a *pesantren* graduate who had studied in Mecca under the famous West Sumatran scholar Syaikh Ahmad Chatib Minangkabau, who had also taught Kiai Hasyim Asy'ari, Kiai Bisri Syansuri and Kiai Wahab Chasbullah.

6 Abdurrahman argues that his father worked hard to try to rebuild the relationship between the modernists and the traditionalists and, given what we know of Wahid Hasyim, this makes good sense. Greg Fealy, however, points out that there is no known documentary evidence to support this but there is documentary evidence indicating Wahid Hasyim's annoyance with certain Masyumi modernists following the separation of 1952.
7 For a very helpful discussion of these issues, see Greg Fealy, 'Rowing in a Typhoon: Nahdlatul Ulama and the Decline of Constitutional Democracy', in David Bourchier and John Legge (eds), *Indonesian Democracy: 1950s and 1990s*, Monash Papers on Southeast Asia No. 31, Centre of Southeast Asian Studies, Monash University, Clayton, Vic., 1994, pp. 88–98.

The 1.2 billion Muslims in the world today are divided into a Sunni majority and a Shia minority. The Shia account for only 10 per cent of all Muslims and are mostly to be found in Lebanon, Syria, southern Iraq, Pakistan and Iran, with the latter having the only Shia majority population. Until very recently all Indonesian Muslims were Sunni Muslims. One of the main differences between Sunni and Shia Muslims is their approach to leadership and politics. The Shia support a hierarchical model of leadership in which it is more natural for leading clerics to play a prominent role in politics, as was amply demonstrated by the 1979 Islamic revolution in Iran. In the Sunni world, however, political power has historically rested with secular politicians, and the *ulama* became adept at negotiating a stable relationship with leaders that they might not have liked but whose authority they were in no position to challenge. As a result the classical Sunni literature is rich in legal maxims about pragmatic approaches to *Realpolitik* and limited political engagement, making it easy for NU *ulama* to justify their responses to the Sukarno and Soeharto regimes.
8 An excellent account of NU's engagement in politics during the Sukarno period can be found in Greg Fealy, 'Wahab Chasbullah, Traditionalism and the Political Development of Nahdlatul Ulama', in Greg Barton and Greg Fealy (eds), *Nahdlatul Ulama, Traditional Islam and Modernity in Indonesia*, Monash Asia Institute, Clayton, Vic., 1996, pp. 1–41.
9 See Fealy, 'Wahab Chasbullah', p. 25.

Chapter 3: Cairo, Baghdad and Europe, 1963–71

1 I have checked some of the material in this chapter against the accounts of Abdurrahman's fellow students and family members, but the chapter depends on Abdurrahman's own recollection of events as related to me in 1999 and 2000.
2 This account is wholly dependent on Abdurrahman's own testimony, and the facts are difficult to verify from other sources. His critics might well argue that his recall on this matter is selective and that possibly some of his reports on fellow students were not as defensive of them as he maintains. My own assessment is that his recall of the horror of the Communist killings and his personal trauma over the involvement of Ansor is entirely convincing and is consistent with his later actions, including those when he became president, to speak out against the anti-Communist pogrom of 1965–66 and sectarian violence in general. I had not known about his reporting activity at the embassy until he raised it in conversation with me in 1999 and 2000, and it strikes me as significant that he wanted to make sure that it was included in this biographical account.
3 Interviews with Nuriyah Wahid and Yenny Wahid, December 1999 and January and February 2000.

Chapter 4: The *pesantren* and reform, 1971–82

1 Abdurrahman's contributions to Prisma have been reprinted in M. Saleh Isre (ed.), *Prisma Pemikiran Gus Dur*, LkiS, Yogyakarta, 1999.

2   For a good overview of the political changes during this period, see Adam Schwarz, *A Nation in Waiting: Indonesia's Search for Stability*, Sydney, Allen & Unwin, 1999, pp. 24–33.
3   If there were other reasons for Abdurrahman not proceeding with his original plans to study at McGill, he does not mention them today.
4   Many of these articles and essays have been reprinted in Abdurrahman Wahid, *Gus Dur Menjawab Perubahan Zaman: Kumpulan Pemikiran K.H. Abdurrahman Wahid Presiden Ke-4 Republik Indonesia*, Kompas, Jakarta, 1999.
5   Interviews with Nuriyah and with Abdurrahman in December 1999 and in January and February 2000.
6   The Javanese calendar is based on a five-day cycle, so every 35 days the five-day Javanese calendar and the seven-day Western calendar coincide to produce the same unique combination of Javanese and Western days. Many Javanese regard these combinations as spiritually significant.
7   Interviews with Nuriyah and with Abdurrahman in December 1999 and January and February 2000.
8   See Mitsuo Nakamura, 'The Radical Traditionalism of Nahdlatul Ulama in Indonesia: A personal account of the 26th National Congress, June 1979, Semarang', in Greg Barton and Greg Fealy (eds), *Nahdlatul Ulama, Traditional Islam and Modernity in Indonesia*, Monash Asia Institute, Clayton, Vic., 1996, pp. 68–93. See also Martin van Bruinessen, 'Traditions for the Future: The reconstruction of traditionalist discourse within NU', in the same book, pp. 163–89.
9   See Martin van Bruinessen, *NU, Tradisis, Relasi-relasi Kasa, Pencarian Wacana Baru*, LkiS, Yogyakarta, 1994, pp. 101–114.
10 Interviews with Nuriyah and with Abdurrahman in December 1999 and in January and February 2000.

Chapter 5: Abdurrahman and liberal Islam

1   See 'Indonesia: Islam and Cultural Pluralism', in John L. Esposito (ed.), *Islam in Asia: Religion, Politics, and Society*, Oxford University Press, New York, 1987.
2   Interviews with Nurcholish in January 1990, January 1992 and February 1994.
3   For a fascinating portrayal of Pesantren Gontor at around the time that Nurcholish was there, see Lance Castles, 'Notes on the Islamic School at Gontor', *Indonesia*, No. 1, 1966.
4   Castles, 'Notes on the Islamic School at Gontor', p. 205. The English translations of passages from this article quoted here are taken from the translation of Nurcholish's article in the appendices of Kamal Hassan, *Muslim Intellectual Responses to 'New Order' Modernization in Indonesia*, Dewan Bahasa dan Pustaka, Kuala Lumpur, 1982, pp.187–233.
5   The most complete study of the movement to take this position is Hassan, *Muslim Intellectual Responses to 'New Order' Modernisation in Indonesia*. This book helpfully includes translations of four seminal papers by Nurcholish Madjid.
6   In a paper in he wrote while on an academic visit to America in 1976. See Nurcholish Madjid, 'The Issue of Modernisation among Muslims in Indonesia: From a participant's point of view', in Gloria Davis, *What is Indonesian Culture*, Southeast Asia Series No. 52, Ohio University Centre for International Studies, Ohio, 1979, pp. 198–210.
7   For the full, translated text of this paper, see Nurcholish Madjid, 'The Necessity of Renewing Islamic Thought and the Problem of the Integration of the Ummat', in Kamal Hassan, *Muslim Intellectual Responses to 'New Order' Modernisation in Indonesia*, pp. 187–97.

8 For an overview of the way in which Djohan Effendi and Ahmad Wahib pushed the limits of acceptable Islamic thought, beginning with their discussion group in Yogyakarta, see Anthony H. Johns, 'An Islamic System of Values? Nucleus of a debate in contemporary Indonesia', in William R. Roff (ed.), *Islam and the Political Economy of Meaning*, Croom Helm, London, 1987, pp. 254–87.
9 See Fazlur Rahman, 'Islam: Past Influence and Present Challenge', in *Islam: Challenges and Opportunities*, Edinburgh University Press, Edinburgh, 1979, pp. 315–30, and *Islam and Modernity: Transformation of an Intellectual Tradition*, University of Chicago Press, Chicago, 1982. See also Rahman, *Islam*, 2nd edn, University of Chicago Press, Chicago, 1979.
10 For a good summary of Rahman's paradigm and its application to the Indonesian scene, see Awad Bahasoan, 'The Islamic Reform Movement: An interpretation and criticism', *Prisma*, No. 35, March 1985, pp. 131–60.
11 For further discussion of this movement and the contribution made to it by Abdurrahman and Nurcholish, see Greg Barton, 'Indonesia's Nurcholish Madjid and Abdurrahman Wahid as Intellectual Ulama: The meeting of Islamic traditionalism and modernism in neo-modernist thought', *Islam and Christian–Muslim Relations*, Vol. 8, No. 3, Oct 1997, pp. 323–50; Barton, 'The Origins of Islamic Liberalism in Indonesia and its Contribution to Democratisation', in *Democracy in Asia*, St Martins Press, New York, 1997; Barton, 'Neo-modernism: A vital synthesis of traditionalism and modernism in Indonesian Islam', *Studia Islamika*, Vol. 2, No. 3, 1995, pp. 1–75; and Barton, 'The Impact of Islamic Neo-Modernism on Indonesian Islamic Thought: The emergence of a new pluralism', in David Bourchier and John Legge (eds), *Indonesian Democracy: 1950s and 1990s*, Monash Papers on Southeast Asia No. 31, Centre of Southeast Asian Studies, Monash University, Clayton, Vic., 1994, pp. 143–50.

Chapter 6: On the brink of change, 1982–84

1 See Martin van Bruinessen, *NU, Tradisis, Relasi-relasi Kasa, Pencarian Wacana Baru*, Yogyakarta, LkiS, 1994, pp. 110–12.
2 Abdurrahman has often talked with me about Benny Murdani over the dozen or so years that I have known him and has repeatedly made a point of saying that he does not trust Benny and was sickened by his willingness to use violent means. He had justified his contact with Benny on the grounds that it was better for him to be in communication with such influential military figures and to maintain the possibility of dialogue with the military than it was to refuse contact and forfeit the opportunity to explain NU's position on developments and thereby to influence the military's response. It would appear the 'friendship', such as it was, was a very knowing one on both sides. There is also no doubt that the two shared some common concerns, most notably a concern that militant Islamism would one day threaten Indonesia's intercommunal harmony.
3 See Mitsuo Nakamura, 'The Radical Traditionalism of Nahdlatul Ulama in Indonesia: A personal account of the 26th National Congress, June 1979, Semarang', and 'NU's Leadership Crisis and Search for Identity in the Early 1980s: From the 1979 Semarang congress to the 1984 Situbondo congress', in Greg Barton and Greg Fealy (eds), *Nahdlatul Ulama, Traditional Islam and Modernity in Indonesia*, Monash Asia Institute, Clayton, Vic., 1996, pp. 68–109. See also Martin van Bruinessen, 'Traditions for the Future: The reconstruction of traditionalist discourse within NU', in the same book, pp. 163–89.
4 This account is based heavily on Abdurrahman's recollection of the event as recounted in several interviews with me, in particular one on 11 January 2000. It also,

however, concurs with the framework outlined by Nakamura in 'NU's Leadership Crisis and Search for Identity', pp. 94–109.
5 Interviews with Abdurrahman, 6, 11 January 2000.
6 Abdurrahman related this incident to me on several occasions in January (6 and 11) and February 2000 and in February 2001. To many readers the subject matter might seem more than a little esoteric, but clearly Abdurrahman believes that it illustrates the sort of basic flexibility of mind and tolerance that he believes has been a part of the culture of NU for more than half a century.
7 This account is based heavily on Abdurrahman's recollection of the event as recounted in several discussions with me, in particular an interview on 11 January 2000.
8 Abdurrahman often talks about this incident and about his father's involvement in the formulation of Pancasila. Greg Fealy points out that unfortunately no written evidence is available to corroborate Abdurrahman's account of his father's involvement and suggests that this calls into question Abdurrahman's understanding of events.
9 Abdurrahman recounted this to me in several interviews and discussions, in particular an interview on 11 January 2000.
10 This account is based heavily on Abdurrahman's recollection of the event as recounted in several interviews with me, in particular one on 11 January 2000. It also, however, concurs with the framework outlined by Nakamura in 'NU's Leadership Crisis and Search for Identity', pp. 94–109.

Chapter 7: Reform and controversy, 1984–90

1 For discussion of the reasons for NU's withdrawal from the PPP, see Robert Hefner, *Civil Islam: Muslims and Democratization in Indonesia*, Princeton, Princeton University Press, 2000, pp. 168–69; Douglas E. Ramage, *Politics in Indonesia: Democracy, Islam and the Ideology of Tolerance*, Routledge, London, 1995, pp. 47–48; Martin van Bruinessen, 'Traditions for the Future: The reconstruction of traditionalist discourse within NU', in Greg Barton and Greg Fealy (eds), *Nahdlatul Ulama, Traditional Islam and Modernity in Indonesia*, Monash Asia Institute, Clayton, Vic., 1996, pp.182–84; Martin van Bruinessen *NU, Tradisis, Relasi-relasi Kasa, Pencarian Wacana Baru*, LKS, Yogyakarta, 1994, pp. 132–44; and Andrée Feillard, *Islam et armée dans l'Indonésie contemporaine*, Paris, L'Harmatan, 1995, pp. 213–28.
2 I am persuaded from many hours of conversations with Abdurrahman over the past twelve years that, along with all of the practical, *Realpolitik*, reasons for advocating NU's withdrawal from PPP, he was also convinced that NU's direct link with PPP was wrong in principle because PPP was a sectarian Islamic party.
3 For a discussion of Munawir Sjadzali's thought and influence, see Bahtiar Effendy, 'Islam and the State in Indonesia: Munawir Sjadzali and the development of a new theological underpinning of political Islam', *Studia Islamika: Indonesian Journal for Islamic Studies*, Vol. 2, No. 2, 1995, pp. 97–121. See also Muhamad Wahyuni Nafis (ed.), *Kontekstualisasi Ajaran Islam: 70 Tahun Prof Dr Munawir Sjadzali MA*, Jakarta, Paramadina, 1995.
4 On a variety of occasions since 1998 both Abdurrahman and Nuriyah, as well as Yenny, have spoken about this with me.
5 Yenny spoke about this with me in several formal interviews in January and June 2000 as well as in informal conversations in 1999, 2000 and 2001.
6 Interviews with Abdurrahman in January and June 2000.
7 P3M was the first of these NGOs to emerge. It was founded in 1983 with the intention of providing NU with a co-ordinating agency to manage the increasing number of community development projects being funded by foreign aid foundations.

Displaying the Indonesian passion for making acronyms, the organisation's name means the Association for the Development of *Pesantren* and Society ('Perhimpunan Pengembangan Pesantren dan Masyarakat' is a mouthful; 'P3M', pronounced as *pay-teega-em*, is a lot easier to deal with). LKiS stands for Lembaga Kajian ilmu Sosial — the Institute for the Study of Social knowledge — and was formed in Yogyakarta in the early 1990s. Lakpesdam and LKPSM are Jakarta-based NU research and development bureaus.

8 The official director of P3M is Kiai Yusuf Hasyim but he is not involved in its day-to-day affairs. Yusuf Hasyim is a younger brother of Wahid Hasyim and as such can lay claim to a linage almost as impressive as his nephew's. Partly for this reason the relationship between the two men is complex and frequently fraught with difficulties.

9 The chief technical reason for the criticism was that the paying of *zakat* is regarded as one of the five pillars of Islam and is generally classified under *ibadah*, or acts of devotion. There was a general agreement between both modernists and traditionalists that acts of devotion and matters of worship were not subject to change through time, even if other aspects of Islamic teaching were adjusted to suit changed social circumstances. This is because *ibadah* is not seen as being culturally determined. Masdar's work on *zakat* exposed just how difficult it was to draw such neat divisions.

10 Masdar Mas'udi has already been mentioned; others, including Jalaluddin Rakhmat, Komaruddin Hidayat, Muslim Abdurrahman, Fajrul Falaakh and Ulil Abshar Abdalla also played and continue to play significant roles in encouraging critical progressive thought.

11 I am grateful to Greg Fealy for pointing out to me that, decades before Kiai Achmad Siddiq wrote boldly about *ijtihad*, his eldest brother Mahfudz had already broached the topic in his writing. Kiai Mahfudz Siddiq served as chairman of the NU Tanfidziyah alongside his former teacher Kiai Hasyim Asy'ari, who was head of the Syuriah. He was known as a specialist in Islamic logic and reason and was a gifted debater. Tragically, Kiai Mahfudz died at the age of 38 in 1944.

12 The efforts of progressive, younger *ulama* within NU to precipitate a renewal of Islamic thought within the *pesantren* world is described in detail by Djohan Effendi in his 2000 PhD dissertation at Deakin University, Australia, entitled Progressive Traditionalists: The emergence of a new discourse in Indonesia's Nahdlatul Ulama during the Abdurrahman Wahid era. In discussing the *halakah* discussion groups, this chapter draws heavily upon Djohan Effendi's account.

13 See Martin van Bruinessen 'The 28th Congress of Nahdlatul Ulama: Power Struggle and Social "Concerns"', in Barton and Fealy (eds) *Nahdlatul Ulama, Traditional Islam and Modernity in Indonesia*, pp.139–62. The account of the 1989 *muktamar* in this chapter draws heavily on van Bruinessen's article.

14 Van Bruinessen 'The 28th Congress of Nahdlatul Ulama', p. 149.

15 Hefner, *Civil Islam*, p. 169.

16 Hefner, *Civil Islam*, p. 151.

17 Schwarz, *A Nation in Waiting*, p. 188.

Chapter 8: Pushing the limits, 1990–94

1 Nurcholish explained to me on several occasions in the early 1990s that the name 'Paramadina' was a combination of the Spanish (he was an admirer of Andalusian civilisation) *para*, meaning 'for' and the Arabic *madina* with its connotations of 'polis', 'civil' and 'civilisation'. Paramadina quickly became popular with leading members of Jakartan society, including retired military officers and government officials. This was not entirely surprising as Paramadina deliberately targeted middle-class Jakartans. After all, they reasoned, these people were the decision-makers, the opinion-makers;

if they could be persuaded to take Islam more seriously, with a more liberal and tolerant approach, then they could become a greater force for good in society.
2 Robert Hefner, *Civil Islam: Muslims and Democratization in Indonesia*, Princeton, Princeton University Press, 2000, p. 161.
3 See Hefner, *Civil Islam*, p. 161; Douglas Ramage, *Politics in Indonesia: Democracy, Islam and the Ideology of Tolerance*, London, Routledge, 1995, pp. 88–89; and Adam Schwarz, *A Nation in Waiting: Indonesia's Search for Stability*, Allen & Unwin, Sydney, 1999, pp. 191, 239. There is good reason to believe that Nurcholish's surprisingly critical response, as reported in *Tempo*, was partly the result of his being caught off guard by the rapidity and violence with which conservative Muslims attacked Arswendo and *Monitor*. In conversation with me several months after the incident, he explained that his initial reaction was disbelief and shock that Arswendo was willing to risk stirring up sectarian anger for such a trivial cause as boosting circulation of his tabloid magazine. He was, he explained, not so much offended by Arswendo as he was disappointed with his irresponsible behaviour. Nevertheless, he regretted the way in which he had articulated this disappointment to the media.
4 A good account of ICMI's formation and development is to be found in Hefner, *Civil Islam*, pp. 128–66.
5 'ICMI Jangan Ambil Jalan Pintas' (an interview with Abdurrahman Wahid), *Detik*, 3 March 1993, pp. 6–7.
6 Ramage, *Politics*, p. 157.
7 Abdurrahman Wahid, 'Forum Demokrasi sebuah pertanggnungjawaban', *Majalah Demokrasi*, pp. 22–24, 1991.
8 Ramage, *Politics*, pp. 162–63.
9 See Ramage, *Politics*, pp. 57–58.
10 I telephoned Abdurrahman several hours after the rally was over and found him, as ever, relaxed and upbeat. He also added that he was about to write to Soeharto expressing, in the strongest terms, his annoyance at Soeharto's move to block the rally. The letter, which he had referred to with typical nonchalance, was drafted that afternoon and delivered to Soeharto the following day.
11 Schwarz, *Nation in Waiting*, pp. 192–93. See also Ramage, *Politics*, pp. 66–67; and Hefner, *Civil Islam*, pp. 162–63.
12 Interviews with Abdurrahman in January 1993. See also Hefner, *Civil Islam*, p. 169; and Ramage, *Politics*, p. 165.
13 Interviews with Abdurrahman in January 1993.
14 Ramage, *Politics*, p. 164.
15 Ramage, *Politics*, p. 64.
16 Ramage, *Politics*, pp. 59, 136.
17 Ramage, *Politics*, p. 45.
18 Schwarz, *Nation in Waiting*, p. 187.
19 Schwarz, *Nation in Waiting*, p. 188. Adam Schwarz told me that he checked with Abdurrahman three times to make sure that he was comfortable with his comments about Soeharto's 'stupidity' being published. When asked, Abdurrahman was, of course, typically nonchalant but this was probably another occasion when his reckless bravado got in the way of his political acumen.
20 Schwarz, *Nation in Waiting*, p. 190.
21 Schwarz, *Nation in Waiting*.
22 In January 1992 Abdurrahman told me of an odd experience that he had recently had. He would often begin his account of such 'odd experiences' by saying something like: 'Well, I'm a rational man and I don't know what to make of this, but this is what happened.' This time he recounted how, while being driven to a *pesantren* in West Java, he had nodded off, as he often did when travelling. As he was dozing he dreamt

that the car had stopped outside the *pesantren* and that he could see the *santri* playing football in the field across the road. As he sat there two men approached the car. They were obviously wounded for they were limping and leaning upon each other for support. He wound the window down, and he could see that the men were dripping with blood; they had their hands outstretched as if asking for charity. When they came within several metres of the car he recognised their faces as Benny Murdani and Try Soetrisno. Suddenly he awoke. It was clear that the whole thing had been a dream, but as he recounted it the experience weighed heavily upon him. He commented that Benny's and Try's hands were indeed bloody and that it was difficult working with such men.

23 Schwarz, *Nation in Waiting*, p. XX17242.
24 Schwarz, *Nation in Waiting*, pp. 264–69.
25 Schwarz, *Nation in Waiting*, p. 268.
26 Schwarz, *Nation in Waiting*, p. 275.
27 See Greg Fealy, 'The 1994 NU Congress and Aftermath: Abdurrahman Wahid, *Suksesi* and the battle for control of NU', in Greg Barton and Greg Fealy (eds), *Nahdlatul Ulama, Traditional Islam and Modernity in Indonesia*, Monash Asia Institute, Clayton, Vic., 1996, p. 259.
28 Interviews with Abdurrahman in June and August 2000.
29 Hefner, *Civil Islam*, p. 161.
30 Fealy, 'The 1994 NU Congress', p. 259.
31 Fealy, 'The 1994 NU Congress', pp. 261–62.
32 In Indonesia in the 1990s it was difficult, if not impossible, to do business on a large scale without some collaboration with, and assistance from, the first family. When Soeharto decided to oppose a project, its chances of success were virtually nil. Given the Byzantine (and corrupt) nature of Indonesian bureaucracy at the time, it is easy to imagine the ways in which Soeharto may have been able to cripple the Bank Summa venture. Whatever the cause, its 'failure to thrive' was widely regarded as a tragedy because it could have made an important contribution on two fronts. A comprehensive network of such banks could have been effective in providing small-scale credit to the poorest sections of society that most needed it, as well as setting an example of a modern banking approach without the hype that often surrounded Islamic banks and their attempt to distinguish themselves from their Western counterparts.
33 Hefner, *Civil Islam*, p. 173.

Chapter 9: Contending with Soeharto, 1994–98

1 See Greg Fealy, 'The 1994 NU Congress and Aftermath: Abdurrahman Wahid, *Suksesi* and the battle for control of NU', in Greg Barton and Greg Fealy (eds), *Nahdlatul Ulama, Traditional Islam and Modernity in Indonesia*, Monash Asia Institute, Clayton, Vic., 1996, p. p. 275.
2 Fealy, 'The 1994 NU Congress', pp. 272–73.
3 With help from his backers in the regime, Abu Hasan established a NU Central Coordinating Executive (Koodinasi Pengurus Pusat NU — KPPNU) to compete with Abdurrahman's NU Central Board of Management (Pengurus Besar NU — PBNU). Abu Hasan's board faced serious difficulty achieving credibility, not least because nine of its named members declared that they had never been consulted about the board: Fealy, 'The 1994 NU Congress', p. 273.
4 Robert Hefner, *Civil Islam: Muslims and Democratization in Indonesia*, Princeton, Princeton University Press, 2000, pp. 180–81.
5 Hefner, *Civil Islam*, p. 181.

6 Abdurrahman recounted this incident a number of times in my hearing, each time chuckling heartily and slapping his thighs when he got to the last line.
7 Hefner, *Civil Islam*, p. 182.
8 Hefner, *Civil Islam*, p. 183. Hefner notes that Yusuf Wanandi is said to have contributed US$270 000 to finance the Medan congress, and that Adi Sasono was chosen because of his networks among Muslim labour activists and NGOs. Sasono was ideologically more moderate — a pragmatic Habibie loyalist rather than a militant Islamist — and therefore likely to enjoy greater creditability among the PDI rank and file. By this stage Amien Rais had become outspoken in his criticism of Soeharto, and ICMI activists such as Din Syamsuddin, Amir Santosa and Fadli Zon lacked extensive networks outside the relatively small Islamist groups such as KISDI and Dewan Dakwah.
9 Hefner, *Civil Islam*, pp. 183–84; see also Adam Schwarz, *A Nation in Waiting: Indonesia's Search for Stability*, Allen & Unwin, Sydney, 1999, p. 322.
10 Hefner, *Civil Islam*, pp. 186–87.
11 Hefner, *Civil Islam*, p. 187.
12 Hefner, *Civil Islam*, Hefner notes, however, that some of Dewan Dakwah's younger members were deeply disturbed by their organisation's support for the regime, adding: 'One member told me that he felt that Mohammad Natsir would never have engaged in such immoral collaboration' (p. 188).
13 Hefner, *Civil Islam*, p. 188.
14 Hefner, *Civil Islam*, p. 190.
15 Hefner, *Civil Islam*.
16 Interview with Romo Mangunwijaya, January 1997.
17 Hefner, *Civil Islam*, p. 192.
18 Hefner, *Civil Islam*, p. 194.
19 Hefner, *Civil Islam*, pp. 195–96.
20 For an account of Indonesia's economic crisis see Schwarz, *A Nation in Waiting* pp. 337–45.
21 Hilur, Civil Islam, pp. 201–06; Schwarz, *A Nation in Waiting*, pp. 345–48.
22 Writing about the Wanandi bombing frame-up, Robert Hefner notes that 'Wandi was soon to discover that Soeharto had increased the penalties for defiance': *Civil Islam*, p. 204.
23 Schwarz, *A Nation in Waiting*, p. 355.
24 Schwarz, *A Nation in Waiting*, p. 360.
25 Schwarz, *A Nation in Waiting*, p. 361.
27 Schwarz, *A Nation in Waiting*, p. 361.
27 Schwarz, *A Nation in Waiting*, p. 363.
28 Schwarz, *A Nation in Waiting*, p. 309.

Chapter 10: Islam, politics and elections, 1998–1999

1 My own sense was that he had changed little since I had first met him in early 1989. True, he now showed flashes of irritability and clearly didn't have the energy levels that he had before his stroke. But, in the face of what must have been an extremely difficult physical and emotional situation, he seemed relaxed and sanguine, and patiently dealt with the interminable stream of visitors asking his advice. I saw little of the bouts of irritability which, I imagine, might have had more to do with his psychological struggle with loss of eyesight than with his physical condition. By the middle of 1998 the physical signs of the stroke had begun to abate. It seemed that the more he was the centre of attention, received guests, gave media interviews and made television appearances, the more he regained his zest for life.

2 There are widely varying views on what was behind the violence in Banyuwangi. For example, Robert Hefner sees it as possibly representing a calculated initiative aimed at provoking clashes between *santri* and *abangan*: *Civil Islam: Muslims and Democratization in Indonesia*, Princeton, Princeton University Press, 2000, p. 210.
3 Hefner, *Civil Islam*, p. 210.
4 The day before the Jombang rally Ratih was alarmed to see that there was nothing in the 'wardrobe' that Abdurrahman brought suitable for a major public appearance. We immediately set off to Mojokerto in search of some formal long-sleeved batik shirts. Finding shirts in Abdurrahman's size is no easy matter. (Few Indonesian men have quite the robust proportions of Abdurrahman, and I should know as I was the proxy model on the buying trip.) There was nothing in his size in Mojokerto and so we set off for Surabaya, an hour and a half's drive away. There a number of suitably dignified batik shirts were procured. The only challenge remaining was to get Abdurrahman to wear them. Initially he could not see the importance of being so concerned about matters of appearance. 'Why not tell him that its important to look presidential,' I suggested to Ratih. The ploy worked and Ratih was able to persuade him that henceforth he needed to take more care in his appearance. My suggestion about looking 'more presidential' was said not out of any genuine expectation that he would be president so much as recognition of the need to encourage and motivate him. With Yenny, an elegant model of cool confidence under pressure, by his side as de facto first lady, Abdurrahman, in fact, seemed a very credible leader. Always an impressive speaker when in form and not too tired, Abdurrahman campaigned well. Helped by Ratih's innovation of holding regular, formal press conferences, his style of communicating with the media had also improved. He may have been a long-shot, but at least he was looking a little more like a serious candidate for the presidency.
5 I arrived at Megawati's house at 10.30 p.m. and found Yenny, Abdurrahman and Ratih looking troubled. They were waiting downstairs in Megawati's waiting room inside her extensive compound in south Jakarta. 'It would be better if you went on to Alwi's house with the press. There's probably not room for us all to go together, so you go first in my car and send it back. I'll be round shortly,' Abdurrahman said helpfully. I should have realised from the sombre atmosphere that 'shortly' might mean quite a while. At Alwi Shihab's house in the adjoining suburb, over a hundred local and foreign journalists had gathered and beta cams stood poised on tripods three or four deep in a tiered arrangement at the back of the large lounge room awaiting the arrival of Abdurrahman, Amien and Megawati.
6 Brief meeting with Hamzah Haz in the third week of May.
7 *Kompas Online*, 21 July 1999.
8 Abdurrahman repeated this position on several occasions during private conversation during the first half of July 1999. On 14 July I had to leave Jakarta again to return to Australia. When we said goodbye, Abdurrahman was jocular but serious. 'Next time,' he said to my wife, 'you must come and stay with us. Next time it'll be at the palace.'
9 *Kompas Online*, 22 July 1999.
10 It was with some apprehension that I returned to Jakarta in mid-September, unsure of the reception I would get. Australians, most definitely, were popular then in Jakarta. I wasn't even sure of how the firestorm of emotion swirling around the city would affect my relationship with Abdurrahman. As soon as I met him in his hotel room — where, as a member of the MPR, he had been placed in the run-up to the Consultative Assembly meeting — he greeted me warmly and explained to his companions, 'This is my old friend Greg, we're good friends even though he is Australian. It doesn't matter, I have lots of Australian friends, I'm just upset with the government. In fact not the government but one or two people in the government that's all, not with all Australians'.
11 *Kompas Online*, 8 October 1999.

Chapter 11: A brief honeymoon, 1999–2000

1 It was his habit since becoming president to rise each morning at around 4.00 a.m. and do a 20-minute spell on a treadmill before undertaking 45 minutes of walking in the palace compound. Then doctors checked his blood pressure and general health during the first of several checkups during the day. It was to Abdurrahman's credit that he was willing to undertake such a regular schedule of physical exercise. Never in his entire life had he played sport or taken regular exercise. Although his health was in reasonable shape and he showed amazing energy keeping up a gruelling schedule, there were times when exhaustion caught up with him. His schedule was so packed that it allowed hardly any days off in which he could catch up. Even his Sundays tended to be busy with meetings, despite the urging of friends and family to keep the day as a private day of rest.

2 One more indication of the difficulties, both practical and political, that faced the reform process was that there was a severe shortage of cash to meet day-to-day needs. Ratih served four months without being paid in the appropriate accounts, partly because no cash was available to cover her salary.

3 Early in July we were talking in a relaxed fashion about the future when he suddenly began to unfold his plans. 'I'm going to appoint Susilo Bambang Yudhoyono as first Minister,' he said. 'I can rely on him. He is a genuine reformist, maybe not so visionary, but sincere and he is a good administrator.' 'What about Megawati?' I asked. 'Mega will be okay,' he replied. 'I've talked about it with Bambang. He will report to her every day and to me just once a week, although of course we will be in touch by phone all the time.' 'Will Mega accept that, though?' I queried. 'Yes I think so, as long as she's involved.' Abdurrahman continued, 'She will do the things that she doesn't much like doing either and so it's good for both of us'. He went on to outline some of his vision for the rest of the cabinet. 'I want a slimmed-down cabinet who work as a team,' he explained. 'They need to be trustworthy. This current cabinet is torn apart by party political bickering and ego.' Abdurrahman seemed to have a clear vision of the way forward; however, nothing could happen until after the August MPR session. 'Everything is on hold,' he explained, 'until after August. First there's the interpellation, then the MPR session; until that's through, I can't even begin to think of anything else. For now the main thing is to survive.'

Chapter 12: Regime change and the fight for survival, 1999–2001

1 *The Jakarta Post Online*, Editorial and Opinion section, 4 September 2000.
2 Quoted by the official news agency Antara, while on a visit to New York at the beginning of September.
3 *The Jakarta Post*, 1 September 2000.
4 'Our Problems Can't be Solved by Violence: Indonesia's new president speaks exclusively to *Time*', *Time*, 30 July 2001.
5 George Aditjondro, 'Notes on the Jihad Forces in Maluku', posted on the Joyo News Service, 4 October 2000.
6 *Associated Press*, 7 September.
7 *Agence France Press*, 7 September 2000.
8 *The Jakarta Post*, 8 September 2000.
9 *The Australian*, 14 September 2000.
10 *The Australian Financial Review*, 14 September 2000.
11 *Detikworld*, 23 October 2000.
12 *Joyo New Service* [details of original publication unknown], 14 September 2000.

13 *Reuters*, 15 September 2000.
14 *Business Times*, 9 September 2000.
15 *The Jakarta Post*, 7 September 2000.
16 *The Indonesian Observer*, 6 October 2000.
17 *The Indonesian Observer*, 9 October 2000.
18 *The Indonesian Observer*, 10 October 2000.
19 *The Straits Times*, 18 October 2000.
20 *The Straits Times*, 20 October 2000
21 *The Indonesian Observer*, 26 October 2000.
22 *Reuters*, 29 October 2000.
23 *Agence France Press*, 30 October 2000.
24 *Detikworld*, 16 November 2000.
25 *The Jakarta Post*, 29 October 2000.
26 *The Straits Times*, 24 November 2000
27 *The Jakarta Post*, 30 November 2000.
28 *The Indonesian Observer*, 21 October 2000.
29 *The Far Eastern Economic Review*, 15 February 2001, p. 16.
30 *The Economist*, 23–29 October 1999.
31 *The Economist*, 17–23 February 2001.
32 *The Economist*, p. 27.
33 An AFP wire service report on 1 March carried the following quote from an anonymous local official: 'Off the record, in reality based on information that I've got from several local Dayak leaders, I'd say it [the real death toll] is about 3000, with most casualties Madurese.'
34 For several hours Detikcom, one of Indonesia's leading news and current affairs web sites, carried the news that, moved by the plight of the refugees, Abdurrahman had made an immediate and spontaneous gift of approximately US$3000 from his own savings. I later confirmed the details of this story with Yenny.
35 *Associated Press*, 4 April 2000.
36 *The Jakarta Post*, 16 April 2000.
37 *The Jakarta Post*, 30 April 2000.
38 Whereas on 29 April Reuters reported the lower figure, members of the presidential security team said that they estimated that at least 200 000 had attended. Given that the Senayan car park is a venue commonly used for large rallies, it should have been relatively easy to gauge the scale of the crowd, especially as it was stationary for a long period of time.

REFERENCES AND FURTHER READING

The material listed below represents a selection of some of the most useful and accessible sources relating to the subject matter of this book. The list is confined to readily available books published in English, with the exception of a small number of journal articles of particular significance. It is divided into two sections: one on history and politics; and one on Islam.

Indonesian history and politics

Anderson, Benedict R.O'G. (1990) *Language and Power: Exploring Political Cultures in Indonesia*. Cornell University Press, Ithaca, NY.

Budiman, Arief (ed.) (1990) *State and Civil Society in Indonesia*. Monash Papers on Southeast Asia No. 22, Centre of Southeast Asian Studies, Monash University, Melbourne.

Cribb, Robert (ed.) (1991) *The Indonesia Killings 1965–1966: Stories from Java and Bali*, second edn. Monash Papers on Southeast Asia No 21, Centre of Southeast Asian Studies, Monash University, Melbourne.

Crouch, Harold (1988) *The Army and Politics in Indonesia*, revised edn. Cornell University Press, Ithaca, NY.

Emmerson, Donald K. (ed.) (1999) *Indonesia Beyond Suharto: Polity, Economy, Society, Transition*. M.E. Sharpe, New York.

Feith, Herbert (1962) *The Decline of Constitutional Democracy in Indonesia*. Cornell University Press, Ithaca, NY.

Kingsbury, Damien (1999) *The Politics of Indonesia*. Oxford University Press, Oxford, 296 pp.

Kingsbury, Damien and Arief, Budiman (eds) (2001), *Indonesia: The Uncertain Transition.* Crawford House Publishing, Bathurst, NSW.

Robert W. Hefner (ed.) (2001) *The Politics of Multiculturalism: Pluralism and Citizenship in Malaysia, Singapore, and Indonesia.* The University of Hawaii Press, Hawaii.

Lindsey, Tim (ed.) (2000) *Indonesia: The Commercial Court and Law Reform in Indonesia.* Desert Pea Press, Sydney.

Manning, Chris et al. (ed.) (2000) *Indonesia in Transition: Social Aspects of Reformasi and Crisis.* Zed Books, London.

Reeve, David (1985) *Golkar of Indonesia: Democracy, Islam and the Ideology of Tolerance.* Routledge, London.

Schwarz, Adam (1999) *A Nation in Waiting: Indonesia's Search for Stability*, second edn. Allen & Unwin, Sydney.

Schwarz, Adam et al. (eds) (1999) *The Politics of Post-Suharto Indonesia.* Council on Foreign Relations Press, New York.

Siegel, James T. (1998) *A New Criminal Type in Jakarta: Counter Revolution Today.* Duke University Press, Durham and London.

Sen, Krishna and David Hill (2000) *Media, Culture and Politics in Indonesia.* Oxford University Press, Melbourne.

Tanter, Richard (1990) 'The totalitarian ambition: Intelligence and security agencies in Indonesia'. In Arief Budiman (ed.) *State and Civil Society in Indonesia.* Monash Papers on Southeast Asia No. 22, Centre of Southeast Asian Studies, Monash University, Melbourne, pp. 215–88.

Islam

Barton, Greg (2001) 'Islam and politics in the New Indonesia'. In Jason F. Isaacson and Colin Rubenstein (eds) *Islam in Asia: Changing Political Realities.* AJC and Transaction Press.

—— (2002) 'Islam, politics and regime change in Wahid's Indonesia'. In Julian M. Weiss (ed.) *Tigers' Roar: Asia's Recovery and Its Impact.* M.E. Sharpe, New York.

—— (2001) 'A fair measure — assessing President Wahid's first year as Indonesia embarks on the long road of regime-change'. In Damien Kingsbury (ed.) *The Abdurrahman Wahid Government's First Year: An Evaluation.* Monash Asia Institute, Melbourne.

—— (2001) 'The prospects for Islam'. In Grayson Lloyd and Shannon Smith (eds) *Indonesia Today: Challenges of History.* Institute of Southeast Asian Studies, Singapore, pp. 244–55.

—— (2001) 'President Wahid — a realist-idealist?'. In Damien Kingsbury and Arief Budiman (eds) *Indonesia: The Uncertain Transition.* Crawford House Publishing, Bathurst, NSW.

—— (2001) 'Evaluating the Wahid presidency: A response to Marcus Mietzner's evaluation'. In Damien Kingsbury and Arief Budiman (eds) *Indonesia: The Uncertain Transition.* Crawford House Publishing, Bathurst, NSW.

—— (2000) 'Political and social change: The case of Indonesia'. In Andrew Vandenberg (ed.) *Politics and Democracy.* Macmillan, London.

—— (1997) 'Indonesia's Nurcholish Madjid and Abdurrahman Wahid as intellectual *ulama*: The meeting of Islamic traditionalism and Modernism in neo-Modernist thought'. *Islam and Christian–Muslim Relations*, Vol 8, No 3, October 1997, pp. 323–50.

—— (1997) 'The origins of Islamic liberalism in Indonesia and its contribution to democratization'. In Michele Schmiegelow (ed.) *Democracy in Asia.* St Martins Press, New York.

—— (1996) 'The liberal, progressive roots of Abdurrahman Wahid's thought'. In Greg Barton and Greg Fealy (eds) *Nahdlatul Ulama: Traditional Islam and Modernity in Indonesia*. Monash Asia Institute, Melbourne, pp. 190–226.

—— (1996) 'Islam, Pancasila and the Middle Path of *Tawassuth*: The thought of Achmad Siddiq'. In Greg Barton and Greg Fealy (eds) *Nahdlatul Ulama: Traditional Islam and Modernity in Indonesia*. Monash Asia Institute, Melbourne, pp. 110–128.

—— (1995) 'Neo-Modernism: A vital synthesis of Traditionalism and Modernism in Indonesian Islam'. *Studia Islamika*, Vol 2, No 3, pp. 1–75.

—— (1994) 'The impact of Islamic neo-Modernism on Indonesian Islamic thought: The emergence of a new pluralism'. In David Bourchier and John Legge (eds) *Indonesian Democracy: 1950s and 1990s*. Monash University, Melbourne, pp. 143–50.

—— (1991) 'The international context of the emergence of Islamic neo Modernism in Indonesia'. In M.C. Ricklefs (ed.) *Islam in the Indonesian Social Context*. Centre of Southeast Asian Studies, Monash University, Melbourne, pp. 69–82.

Binder, Leonard *Islamic Liberalism: A Critique of Development Ideologies*. University of Chicago Press, Chicago, pp. 399–400.

Boland, B.J. (1971) *The Struggle of Islam in Modern Indonesia*. Martinus Nijhoff, The Hague.

Fealy, Greg (2001) 'Islamic politics: A rising or declining force?' In Damien Kingsbury and Arief Budiman (eds) *Indonesia: The Uncertain Transition*, Crawford House Publishing, Bathurst, NSW.

Fealy, Greg (1996) 'The 1994 NU Congress and aftermath: Abdurrahman Wahid, Suksesi and the battle for control of NU'. In Greg Barton and Greg Fealy (eds) *Nahdlatul Ulama: Traditional Islam and Modernity in Indonesia*. Monash Asia Institute, Melbourne, pp. 257–77.

—— (1994) 'Rowing in a typhoon: Nahdlatul Ulama and the decline of constitutional democracy'. In David Bourchier and John Legge (eds) *Indonesian Democracy: 1950s and 1990s*, Monash University, Melbourne, pp. 88–98.

Geertz, Clifford (1960) *The Religion of Java*. Free Press, New York.

Hassan, Muhammad Kamal (1982) *Muslim Intellectual Responses to 'New Order' Modernisation in Indonesia*. Dewan Bahasa dan Pustaka, Kuala Lumpur.

Hefner, Robert W. (1997) 'Introduction: Islam in an era of nation states: Politics and religious renewal in Muslim Southeast Asia'. In Robert W. Hefner and Patricia Horvatich (eds) *Islam in an Era of Nation States: Politics and Religious Revival in Muslim Southeast Asia*. University of Hawaii Press, Honolulu, pp. 3–40.

—— (1997b) 'Islamization and democratization in Indonesia'. In Robert W. Hefner and Patricia Horvatich (eds) *Islam in an Era of Nation States: Politics and Religious Revival in Muslim Southeast Asia*. University of Hawaii Press, Honolulu, pp. 75–127.

—— (2000) *Civil Islam: Muslims and Democratization in Indonesia*. Princeton University Press, Princeton.

Kurzman, Charles (1998) *Liberal Islam: A Sourcebook*. Oxford University Press, New York.

Liddle, R. William (1988) *Politics and Culture in Indonesia*. Center for Political Studies Institute for Social Research, University of Michigan, Ann Arbor, pp. 1–55.

Nakamura, Mitsuo (1983) *The Crescent Arises Over the Banyan Tree: A Study of the Muhammadiyah Movement in a Central Javanese Town*. Gadjah Mada University Press, Yogyakarta.

—— (1996) 'The radical traditionalism of Nahdlatul Ulama in Indonesia: A personal account of the 26th National Congress, June 1979, Semarang' and 'NU's leadership crisis and search for identity in the early 1980s: From the 1979 Semarang congress to the 1984 Situbondo congress'. In Greg Barton and Greg Fealy (eds) *Nahdlatul Ulama: Traditional Islam and Modernity in Indonesia*. Monash Asia Institute, Melbourne, pp. 68–109.

Rahman, Fazlur (1982) *Islam and Modernity: Transformation of an Intellectual Tradition*. University of Chicago Press, Chicago.

—— (1979) 'Islam: Past influence and present challenge'. *Islam: Challenges and Opportunities*. Edinburgh University Press, Edinburgh, pp. 315–30.

Ramage, Douglas E. (1995) *Politics in Indonesia: Democracy, Islam and the Ideology of Tolerance*. Routledge, London.

Van Bruinessen, Martin (1996) 'Traditions for the future: The reconstruction of traditionalist discourse within NU'. In Greg Barton and Greg Fealy (eds) *Nahdlatul Ulama: Traditional Islam and Modernity in Indonesia*. Monash Asia Institute, Melbourne, pp. 163–89.

Van Djik, Kees (2001) *A Country in Despair: Indonesia Between 1997 and 2000*. KITLV, Leiden. 621 pp.

Ward, Ken E. (1977) *The 1971 Election in Indonesia: An East Java Case Study*. Centre of Southeast Asian Studies Monash University, Melbourne.

Woodward, Mark R. (ed.) (1996) *Toward a New Paradigm: Recent Developments in Indonesian Islamic Thought*. Program for Southeast Asian Studies, Arizona State University, Tempe.

—— (1989) *Islam in Java: Normative Piety and Mysticism in the Sultanate of Yogyakarta*. The Association for Asian Studies Monograph No. XLV, The University of Arizona Press, Tucson.

INDEX

Note
This index is broken down into three separate index lists: People, General and Places. The names and terms used generally reflect usage in the text, which in turn reflect popular usage. This means that in some cases people are listed under their commonly used names rather than their formal names (for example, Yenny Wahid rather than Zannuba Chapsoh Arifah). Most Indonesians do not use surnames, so Indonesian names are listed under their first name (for example, Nurcholish Madjid rather than Madjid, Nurcholish), while foreign names are listed by surname.

People
Abduh, Muhammad 68, 83
Abdul Madjid 122
Abdullah (King of Jordan) 289
Abu Hasan 210–11, 213, 235, 236, 395n
Adi Sasono 103, 239, 249, 259, 376n
Aditjondro, George 334, 335, 398n
Agum Gumelar, General 328
Ahmad Chatib Minangkabau, Syeikh 39, 40, 388n
Ahmad Sumargono 232
Ahmad Wahib 126, 391n
Ahmed Dachlan, Kiai 70, 388n
Akbar Tandjung
   and Golkar 193, 271, 331, 337, 341–42, 361
   and Irian Jaya 339–40
   as DPR Chairman 314–16, 331, 345, 353
al-Banna, Hasan 92
Ali Ma'shum, Kiai 56
Ali Murtopo, General 105–06, 115, 134, 179
Alissa Wahid 107, 155, 157, 225, 276, 386n
Alwi Shihab
   and Abdurrahman 26, 28, 265, 268–70, 272, 281–83, 325, 377n
   and PKB 265
   as Foreign Minister 286, 289, 344
Amien Rais
   and Abdurrahman 238, 239, 242, 263, 265, 272, 275–76, 278, 308, 311, 315, 317, 325, 376n
   and Central Axis 275
   and ICMI 214, 231, 236, 241
   and Islam 211
   and PAN 24, 252–54, 272, 275, 311, 317
   and reform 245, 238, 240, 242
   and the MPR 27, 28, 324
Amir Santosa 214, 236, 237, 376n
Andi Ghalib 249
Anita Wahid 109, 155, 157
Annan, Kofi 335
Aquino, Corry 213
Arafat, Yasser 289
Argo Sutjipto 50, 51
Arifin Panigoro 136, 317, 361, 363
Aristotle 59
Arswendo 181, 182, 394n
As'ad Arifin Syamsul, Kiai 135, 140, 142, 149, 159, 176

Aswab Mahasin 103

Bachtiar Effendy 392n
Bahasoan, Awad 391n
Barak, Ehud (former prime minister) 289
Benny Murdani, General
   and Abdurrahman 133–34, 137, 152, 154, 172–73, 189, 191–92, 239, 391n
   and Islamism 142, 181, 191–92, 391n
   and Prabowo 239–40
   and Soeharto 167–68, 180–81, 194, 248
Bimantoro, General 362, 363
Binder, Leonard 128
Bisri Syansuri, Kiai 37, 38, 39, 40, 41, 43, 56, 61, 64, 387n, 388n
Bisri, Kiai Mustofa 86, 88, 96
Bob Hasan 235
Bondan Gunawan 185, 291
Brawijaya VI 4
Bueller, Willem Iskandar 48

Castles, Lance 390n
Castro, Fidel 278
Chaeruddin Ismail, General 363
Chalid Marwadi 136
Chodiyah (Lily) Wahid 47
Cholil, Kiai 40, 7
Crouch, Harold 335

Dawam Rahardjo 103
Dillon, HS 330
Din Syamsuddin 214, 236, 237, 376n
Djadja Suparman, General 335
Djaelani (Johnny) Naro 115, 133, 134, 138, 147, 152
Djohan Effendi 126, 162, 166, 183, 198, 314, 302, 391n, 393n
Donne, John 85
Dorodjatun Kuntjorojakti 177
Dostoyevsky, Fyodor 92

Edi Sudrajat, General 252
Eggy Sudjana 259, 260
Emil Salim 310
Esposito, John L 390n

Fadli Zon 237, 243, 248, 376n
Fahmi Saifuddin 135, 202, 204
Faisal Tanjung, General 194, 203
Fajrul Falaak 393n
Fakhi, Kiai 139

Falk, Peter 385
Fatwa, AM 380
Faulkner, William 85
Fazlur Rahman 127, 128, 391n
Fealy, Greg 387n, 388n, 389n, 392n, 393n, 395n
Feillard, Andrée 23, 24, 30, 42, 48, 393n
Feisal Basri 329, 381
Friedman, Thomas 341
Fuad Bawazier 317, 319, 329, 334

Geertz, Clifford 63, 388n
Ginanjar Kartasasmita, General 243, 244
Gunawan Mohammad 253
Guruh Soekarnoputra 193
Gusmao, Xanana 297

Habib Ali Baagil 337
Habibie, BJ (former president)
   and Abdurrahman 277–78
   and East Timor 261
   and Golkar 251–52
   and ICMI 182, 194, 201, 212, 236–37, 241, 259, 276, 381
   as President 18, 19, 29, 244, 247–49, 254–56, 281–82, 376
   as Vice President 244, 238, 242
Hamengkubuono X (Sultan of Yogyakarta) 256, 316, 324
Hamzah Haz 272, 283–84, 377n
Hanuman 121
Hardoyo 30–31
Harmoko 181, 194, 201, 241, 244
Hartono, General 210–11, 235–37
Harun Nasution 126, 153, 162
Hashim Wahid (Abdurrahman's brother) 309–10
Hassan, Kamal 390n
Hasyim Asy'ari, Kiai 38–40, 42, 44–46, 53, 61, 387n
Hatta, Mohammad 45
Haziz Bisri 60
Hefner, Robert 172, 230, 234, 388n, 392–97n
Hemingway, Ernest 85
Hodgson, Marshall GS 388n
Howard, John (prime minister) 261, 279
Hussein (Crown Prince of Jordan) 289
Hussein Umar 232

Idham Chalid 113, 115, 147, 148, 149, 150, 152, 159, 173, 176, 215, 263
Imam Ardyaquttni 268
Inayah Wahid 116, 155, 157
Iqbal, Mohammed 130

Jalaluddin Rakmat 174, 393n
Johns, Anthony H 388n, 391n
Joplin, Janis 101
Junaidi, Kiai 54, 55, 57
Jusuf Kalla 311
Juwono Sudarsono 306, 336

Kafka, Franz 85
Kastor 334
Khofifah Indar Parawansa 263
Khomeini, Ayatollah 62
Khudori, Kiai 56
Kivlan Zein 243, 255
Komaruddin Hidayat 393n
Kwik Kian Gie 286, 303, 319

Laksamana Sukardi 286, 302–05, 311, 313
Lee Kuan Yew (former prime minister) 373
Lenin, Vladimir 59
Lopa, Baharuddin 354

Mahfud MD 328, 330, 337, 370
Mahfudz Ridwan 95, 98, 100
Maksyur, Kiai 139
Malik Fadjar 241, 248
Mandela, Nelson (former president) 278
Mangungwijaya, Romo 234, 376n
Mao, Tse-tung 59
Marcos, Ferdinand (former president) 213, 258
Marimutu Sinivasan 346
Marsillam Simanjuntak 25, 185, 227, 291, 295, 312, 314, 315, 318, 323, 328
Marx, Karl 59, 60
Marzuki Darusman 286, 307, 354, 361
Masdar Farid Mas'udi 161, 165, 393n
Matori Abdul Djalil 252, 262
Maulana Maududi 129
Megawati Sukarnoputri (president)
  and Abdurrahman 18, 19, 27, 211, 229, 235, 238, 243, 245, 248, 250, 256, 258, 262–63, 269–70, 278–79, 281–82, 296, 311–14, 316–17, 302, 325, 327, 330–31, 340, 350, 354, 337, 360–61, 368, 370, 379, 380
  and Golkar 315, 341, 379
  and Islam 211, 258, 262, 381
  and PDI 193, 199, 211–14, 230–32, 253
  and PDI-P 255, 254, 302, 328–29, 361, 369–70, 379, 380
  and Soekarno 288
  and Taufik Kiemas 303, 349
  and TNI 343, 355, 363, 384
  as Vice President 284, 286–87, 312, 323, 339, 342–43, 352
Mochtar Buchori 255
Moerdiono 173, 235
Mokodongan 240
Mozart, Wolfgang Amadeus 246
Muchdi Purwoprandjono, General 248
Mukti Ali 106, 126, 152
Munawir Sjadzali 48, 153, 166, 177, 392n
Munib Huda 27, 28, 266, 299
Murdoch, Lindsay 280
Muslim Abdurrahman 393n
Mydans, Seth 25

Nafis, Muhamad Wahyuni 392n
Nakamura, Mitsuo 390n, 391n, 392n
Nasser (former president) 84, 86, 92, 93, 94
Natsir, Mohammad 124, 125, 130
Nurcholish Madjid 121–28, 131, 151, 153, 162, 163, 181, 182, 390n, 393n
Nuriyah Wahid 20, 60, 61, 103, 104, 107, 108, 109, 112, 116, 265, 276, 389n, 390n, 393n
Nurmahmudi Ismail 341, 354

Plato 59
Poe, Edgar Allan 85
Prabowo Subianto, General
  and Abdurrahman 236–37, 239
  and Habibie 244
  and Islamism 239, 243, 245, 248–49
  and PDI 230, 240
  and Suharto 238–39, 247
  and violence 236–40, 243, 254–55, 262
Prajogo Pangestu 346
Prijadi, Praptosuhadjo 328, 330, 370
Pushkin, Alexander 85

Qutb, Sayyid 92, 93

Ramage, Douglas 185, 392n, 394n
Ramin 99
Ramos-Horta, Jose 297
Ratih Hardjono 27, 29, 265, 266, 268, 271, 371, 376–78n
Ravana 121
Rizal Ramli 325, 328
Roosevelt, Franklin D. (former president) 59
Rozi Munir 302
Rudini, General 173
Rusdihardjo, General 337, 345, 370
Rushdie, Salman 21, 182

Saifullah Yusuf 268
Salahuddin Wahid 10
Schwarz, Adam 40, 190, 390n, 393n, 394n, 395n
Semar 121, 385
Shari'ati, Ali 92
Siddiq, Kiai Achmad 132, 393n
Siddiq, Kiai Mahfudz 164–65, 167, 393n
Sin, Cardinal Jamie 213
Sobary, Mohamad 29, 30, 108, 109, 302
Soeharto, Muhammad (former president)
 and Abdurrahman 148, 153–55, 158, 170, 172, 174, 178, 180, 186, 187–88, 191, 195–96, 200–01, 209, 229, 235–36, 238, 242–43, 258, 270, 286, 290, 292, 369
 and ABRI 99, 158, 168, 194, 240, 237, 336, 370
 and corruption 257, 304–05, 317, 337, 356, 377, 380, 382
 and dissent 115, 151, 158, 172, 179, 187–89, 191–93, 195, 202, 205, 237, 241, 235–36, 248, 377
 and Golkar 133, 170, 193, 341, 361
 and Islam 67, 127, 130, 167–69, 174, 180–83, 190, 194, 238–40, 243, 248, 381
 and Megawati 212–14, 229–32, 237
 and NU 148, 150, 170, 172–73, 177, 186, 241
 and Pancasila 114, 137–38, 153–54, 187
 and succession 26, 199, 205, 229, 243–45, 237–44, 246–47, 249–52, 283, 373, 383

 and Sukarno 89, 113, 121, 287–88, 376
 and the 1971 elections 104–05
 and the Chinese 177, 200
 and the New Order regime 23, 29, 30, 31, 125, 130, 134, 151, 159, 179, 245–46, 254, 260–61, 263, 291, 301, 310, 323, 329, 335, 345, 351, 369, 374, 378–79, 382, 384
Soeharto, Tien 229
Soeharto, Tommy 336–38, 370
Soeharto, Tutut 236–37, 235, 354
Soeryadi 193, 212, 230, 231
Sofyan Wanandi 248
Solichah 43–44, 46, 52–53, 218, 228, 386n, 387n
Sonny Keraf 328
Sri Bintang Pamungkas 191
Sri Mulyani 329
Subagyo 241
Sudharmono, General 173, 194
Sudjono Humardhani, General 105
Sudomo, General 189
Sukarno, Ahmad (former president)
 and Abdurrahman 90, 212, 287–88, 297
 and Islam 74, 76–77
 and Megawati 193, 288
 and Pancasila 75, 141
 and PKI 87, 89
 and Soeharto 31, 113, 121, 376
 and Wahid Hasyim 38, 45–46, 75
Sultan of Brunei 304, 305
Sultan of Yogyakarta see Hamengkubuono X
Sumitro Djojohadikusumo 238
Susilo Bambang Yodhoyono, General 294, 325
Suwando 304–05
Syafi'i Anwar, Muhammad 253–54
Syaikh Ahmad Chatib 39, 6
Syamsyul Nursalim 346
Syaril Sabirin 329
Syarwan Hamid, General 201, 213–14, 230, 237

Tamizi Tahir 201, 242
Tan Malaka 11
Taufik Kiemas 303
Thoenes, Sander 280
Tolkhah Mansur, Kiai 140–41
Tolstoy, Leo 85
Truman, Harry (former president) 59

Try Sutrisno, General 167–68, 173, 191, 192, 194, 203, 252

Ulil Abshar Abdalla 393n

van Bruinessen, Martin 171, 173, 390–93n

Wahab Chasbullah, Kiai 40, 41, 56, 386n, 388n
Wahid Hasyim, Kiai 38, 41–53, 56, 61, 73, 74–76, 386n
Wanandi, Yusuf 230, 376n
Wimar Witoelar 310, 312, 336, 337, 371
Winters, Jeffrey 317
Wiranto, General 247, 249, 252, 255, 260, 283

Yenny Wahid
  and East Timor 280
  and her dad 23, 24, 27, 157, 386n, 389n 392n
  and the election campaign 221, 266, 269, 271, 377n
  and the President 20, 29, 299, 312, 350
  and time management 451
  as a child 108, 155
Yusril Izha Mahendra 328, 350, 354
Yusuf Hasyim 263, 393n
Yusuf Kalla 302

Zastrow, Al 266

General
abangan
  and mysticism 67, 121, 180, 211
  and pancasila 74, 137, 140
  and pluralism 185, 254, 258
  and *santri* identity 64, 159, 180
  and urban life 70, 72
  vs. *santri* 43, 63
ABRI (Angkatan Bersenjata Republik Indonesia) 99, 210, 240, 244, 245, 248, 240, 244, *see also* TNI, military, police
Ansor 58, 89, 90, 91, 203, 267, 268, 351, 355
army *see* ABRI, TNI
asas tunggal 136, 137, 138, 139, 151, 521
Australian Financial Review, The 398n

Australian, The 398n

Bank Indonesia 244
Bank Rakyat Indonesia 329
Bruneigate 305, 309, 313, 316, 342, 345, 358
Buddhist 38, 40, 63, 67, 68, 120, 365
Bulog (Badan Urusan Logistik) 304, 305, 338
Bulogate 342. 345, 358

Central Axis 28, 275, 277, 281, 283 *see also Poros Tengah*
Chandra Asri 346
Chinese
  and Abdurrahman 20, 177, 267, 290, 308, 346
  and Amien Rais 254
  and business 107, 142, 155, 176–77, 181, 200, 238–39, 248–49, 245, 267, 290, 346
  and *cerita silat* 24
  and Christianity 177, 181, 233, 238–39, 346
  and mainland China 290, 308
  and NU 169, 176–77, 200, 233, 238–39
  and violence 233–234, 238–39, 247, 236–37, 245–46, 249
Christian
  and Abdurrahman 20, 177, 232–33, 234, 239
  and Amien Rais 254
  and Chinese 20, 177, 233, 254
  and Maluku 259, 305–06, 333–34
  and NU 235, 239
  and Poso 326, 333
  and TNI 239, 247
  and violence 233, 235, 239, 259, 305–06, 326, 333–34
CIDES (Centre for Information and Development Studies) 236
CPDS (Centre for Policy and Development Studies) 202, 236, 237
CSIS (Centre for Strategic and International Studies) 105, 230, 236, 248, 307

Dewan Dakwah Islamiyah Indonesia (DDII) 130, 184, 232, 376n
Dipasena 346
DPR (Dewan Perwakilan Rakyat) 105,

256, 263, *see also* Parliament

Economist, The 38, 350, 354, 399
Editor 22
Elections
  1955 74, 76
  1971 104–06
  1977 114–15, 150
  1982 132–33, 150, 158, 181, 192
  1987 155, 159, 170, 180, 192
  1992 185, 187, 192
  1997 214, 230, 237
  1999 251, 256, 260, 272, 310, 376, 379
  2004 331
  call for accelerated election 348, 362, 364, 371

fiqh 6
FPI (Front Pembela Islam) 332, 333, 335, 337

Golkar
  and Abdurrahman 155, 170, 189, 192, 201, 237, 241, 276, 283, 302, 311, 315, 317, 302, 328, 330–31, 341–42, 345, 351, 355–56, 361, 373, 381
  and Habibie 19, 182, 282
  and ICMI 182
  and opposition 214, 252, 254, 269, 273–76, 379
  and PPP 114, 133, 170, 251, 253–54
  and Soeharto 105, 193–94, 251
  and the 1971 elections 106
  and the 1977 elections 114
  and the 1987 elections 155, 170
  and the 1992 elections 192
  and the 1997 elections 237, 241
  and the 1999 elections 273–74, 379
GPM (Gereja Protestant Maluku) 334

hadith 5
haj 40, 49, 63, 76, 83, 180, 291, 352
halakah 165–67, 175, 393n
halus 23, 385
Hindu 38, 40, 63, 67, 68, 120, 121, 306
HMI (Himpunan Mahasiswa Islam) 123, 125, 126, 251, 342

IAIN (Institut Agama Islam Negara) 66, 100, 102, 123, 152–53, 162, 163

ibadah 164, 174
IBRA (Indonesian Bank Restructuring Agency) 293, 309
ICMI (Indonesian Association of Muslim Intellectuals) 210, 211, 212, 214, 230, 231, 232, 236, 238, 239, 240, 241, 248, 241, 242, 381
ijtihad 69, 128, 129, 132, 153, 164, 165, 166, 174, 393n
IMF (International Monetary Fund) 243, 244, 245, 235
Indonesian Observer, The 398–99n
Interfet (International Force East Timor) 280
IPS (Institute for Policy Studies) 237
Islamism/Islamist 3, 60, 61, 92, 119, 130, 134, 151, 181, 184, 191, 192, 194, 198, 232, 235, 237, 246, 235, 236, 251, 253, 254, 254, 275, 289, 305, 317, 335, 354, 372, 378, 381

Jakarta Charter 75, 149
Jakarta Post, The 181, 330, 331, 332, 341, 337, 398n
jihad 259, 334, 355
Joyo News Service 398n

KAHMI (Korps Alumni HMI) 342
kasar 23, 385
Khittah 1926 138, 140, 143
kiai 20, 37, 40, 41, 42, 44, 46, 52, 54, 56, 58, 64, 71, 72, 73, 89, 100, 107, 108, 113, 121, 132, 133, 135, 136, 139, 141, 142, 143, 164, 166, 171, 174, 176, 200, 204, 211, 262, 263, 267, 269, 281, 284, 338
KISDI (Komiti Indonesia Solidaritas Dunia Islam) 232, 239, 243, 376n
KKN (Korupsi, Kolusi & Nepotism) 290, 302
Kompas 107, 181, 265, 377n
Kopassus 239, 238
Kostrad 343

Lakpesdam 161, 393n
Laskar Jihad 305, 306, 333, 334, 335
LKPSM 161, 393n
LP3ES (Lembaga Pengkajian Pegetahuan, Pendidikan, Ekonomi dan Sosial) 103, 104, 107

madrasah 42, 43, 55, 56, 61, 69, 70, 71,

104, 108, 110, 122, 126, 127
Masyumi
  and conservatism 124, 126, 130, 150, 182–83, 253
  and Islamic state 74
  and NU 45, 55, 73, 75–76, 122
  and Parmusi 105–06
  and Sukarno 76, 77
mazhab 68, 128, 164, 166
MIAI (Majlisul Islamil a'laa Indonesia) 11
modernism/ists, Islamic 20, 55, 66, 68, 69, 70, 72, 83, 122, 127, 128, 129, 131, 153, 184
MPR (Majelis Permusyawaratan Rakyat)
  and 1966 decree on communism 345
  and Abdurrahman 18, 19, 26, 27, 155, 180
  and government appointees 105, 379
  and Suharto 137
  and the 1993 session 186–87, 192–94
  and the 1998 session 242, 248, 255–57
  and the 1999 session 238
  and the 2000 session 309–10, 312–13, 315–18, 319–20, 323–24, 331, 340, 370
  and the special session 342, 358, 360–63
  the authority of 105, 155, 310–11, 320, 322, 382
Muhammadiyah
  and Abdurrahman 56
  and Amien Rais 184, 231, 236, 241, 254
  and communism 91
  and *madrasah* 71
  and modernism 20, 54, 66, 70, 72, 160
  and NU 55, 73, 151, 158, 248, 268
  and PAN 253
  and Suharto 167, 241
muktamar/national congress
  1979 Semarang 134
  1984 Situbondo 148, 150–53
  1989 Krapyak 159, 169–73, 176, 178, 182
  1994 Cipasung 195, 199, 201–04, 209–10, 230, 238–39, 242
munas 140, 143, 241, 242

neomodernism, Islamic 127, 131, 153,
163, 167, 190
New Order 104, 105, 127, 150, 151, 152, 209, 212, 232, 374
New York Times, The 25, 26, 43, 44, 341
NU (Nahdlatul Ulama) v, 1, 8, 22, 23, 30
  and Abdurrahman 20, 23, 107, 111–13, 116, 132–44, 147–67, 169–77, 183–88, 191, 192, 193,162,163,164,165,166,167,168,169, 204, 209,176,177,180, 232–39, 241–42, 246–47, 248, 250, 252–54, 257–58, 262–66, 272–76, 281–82, 284, 302–03, 351–57, 381
  and *pesantren* 104, 192, 210, 211
  and politics 30, 281–82, 284, 291, 302–03, 351–57
  and PPP 113–15, 134,158, 199, 270
  and Soeharto 183–88,158, 193,165, 200, 201, 202, 203, 204, 209, 210, 211, 213, 214, 230, 232–39, 241, 235, 240–41, 257–58, 381
  and the 1971 elections 106
  and the 1982 elections 134, 181, 192

P3M (Pengembangan Pesantren dan Masyarakat) 161, 165, 392n, 393n
PAN (Partai Amanat Nasional) 2, 252, 253, 254, 272, 254, 275, 281, 311, 317, 345
Pancasila 46, 114, 181, 186, 187, 190, 191, 247, 392n
Paramadina 181, 393n
Parliament
  and Abdurrahman 302, 304, 309, 313–15, 318, 340, 342, 344, 358, 368, 370, 373, 379–80
  and censure of President 356–57, 360–61, 366
  and Golkar 114
  and legislation 293, 339
  and MPR 105, 310
  and party discipline 311
  and PKB 263
  and PPP 115, 133
  and Soeharto 240, 244, 377
  and the military 256, 349–50
  and Wahid Hasyim 49
  appearing before 312–14
  dissolving of 348, 362, 371–72
PBB (Partai Bulan Bintang) 275, 317
PBNU (Pengurus Besar Nahdlatul

Ulama) 20, 28
PDI/PDI-P (Partai Demokrasi
  Indonesia/ — Perjuangan)
  and Megawati 193, 199, 211–14,
    230–31, 237, 253, 255, 275, 283,
    302, 313, 315, 334, 342, 343, 349,
    361, 369, 379–80
  and NU 258
  and PKB 267, 271
  and PPP 133, 151, 189
  and Soeharto 193, 212–14, 230–31,
    237, 240, 248
  and Soeryadi 193, 230–31
  and Sukarno 193
  and the 1992 elections 192
  and the 1999 elections 272
  and the 2004 elections 341
  and the cabinet 286, 302–03, 313,
    319, 328, 342, 345
  and the Islamists 306, 334
  and xxv, Abdurrahman 192, 268, 283,
    345, 349, 361, 369–70, 379–80
People's Consultative
  Assembly/Assembly *see* MPR
Pesantren
  Al-Munawwir 56
  and Abdurrahman 46, 53, 57, 60–61,
    85–86, 103–04, 109–10, 116,
    120–21, 132–33, 137, 171, 175,
    195–96, 266, 309, 367, 394n, 395n
  and IAIN 66
  and innovations in teaching 39, 84,
    104, 110, 122, 139, 153, 162,
    164–66, 169, 175
  and *kiai* 41, 54, 58, 71, 89, 132–33,
    164–66
  and *madrasah* 42, 55–56, 61, 69–70,
    104, 108, 110, 127
  and NGOs 161, 163, 165, 167
  and NU 38, 72–73, 90, 152, 155, 158,
    172
  and Pancasila 137
  and rural life 70–71, 72, 77, 89, 103,
    105, 147–48
  and *santri* 63, 64, 66
  and secular society 107, 116, 140,
    147–48
  and social change 64, 66, 106, 161
  and social networks 44, 64, 158
  and traditionalist Islam 37, 78,
    120–21, 123, 127
  and women 6

Cipasung 203
Denanyar 37, 40, 110
Krapyak 171
Probolinggo 235
Situbondo 140, 149, 170, 174, 234
Tambakberas 40, 99–100, 108, 110
Tebuireng 39, 40, 42, 141
Tegalrejo 56
PK (Partai Keadilan) 275, 276, 281, 317
PKB (Partai Kebangkitan Bangsa)
  and Abdurrahman 19, 253, 263, 270,
    273, 276, 281, 303, 349, 379–80
  and Alwi Shihab 265, 281
  and Megawati 276
  and NU 250, 252, 258, 262, 270, 281,
    302–03
  and PDI-P 267, 271, 254–55, 303,
    349, 379
  and PPP 263–64
  and the Central Axis 281
  and the Parliament 349, 337
PKI (Partai Komunis Indonesia) 87, 89,
  90, 232
PNI (Partai Nasionalis Indonesia) 105,
  106
Police 133, 134, 187, 189, 231, 234,
  237, 238, 256, 258, 267, 269, 301,
  305, 318, 329, 334, 337, 338, 339,
  345, 346, 349, 352, 353, 337, 358,
  362, 363, 364, 370, 373, 383, 384
POLRI (Polisi Republik Indonesia) *see*
  police
Poros Tengah 275, *see also* Central Axis
PPP (Partai Pembangunan Persatuan)
  and 1982 elections 181
  and 1987 elections 155, 159, 170
  and 1992 elections 192
  and 1997 elections 237
  and Abdurrahman 147–52, 155, 159,
    170, 192, 197, 199, 283, 290, 318,
    328, 342, 345, 373, 381
  and Golkar 251–54, 373, 379
  and NU 106, 113–15, 147–52, 189,
    199, 214, 263–64, 270, 272
  and Soeharto 230, 237
  and the Central Axis 275–276, 283
PRD (Partai Rakyat Demokrasi) 231,
  232, 240, 351
priyayi 63, 67, 69, 70, 71, 72
PRRI (Pemerintah Revolusi Republik
  Indonesia) 77

Rapat Akbar 186, 187, 188
RMS (Republik Maluku Selatan) 334

santri
  and communism 90–91
  and community 55, 72–73, 159, 180, 182, 253
  and mysticism 70, 211
  and outlook 49
  and *pesantren* 66, 71, 175
  and politics 106, 253
  and rural life 71
  and social change 64
  and Soeharto 180–83, 236
  and the military 168, 173
  and the state 74–75, 114, 137
  traditionalists and modernists 66
  vs. *abangan* 20, 43, 63, 70, 258
SekNeg (Sekretariat Negara) 288
Semar 121, 385
Shia/Shi'ites 174
State Secretariat *see* SekNeg
Straits Times, The 399
Sufism 66, 67, 109
Sunnah 67, 120, 132, 138, 164, 165, 166
Sunni 77, 78, 174

tarekat 173
Tempo 22, 40, 107, 112, 126, 394n
Texmaco 307, 346
Time 309, 398n
TNI 280, 292, 349, 353, 357, 370, *see also* ABRI, military
traditionalists/ism 20, 38, 42, 53, 54, 55, 57, 64, 67, 68, 70, 73, 77, 120, 122, 127, 128, 131,126, 163, 164, 165, 166, 167, 174, 235, 254, 269, 364

ulama 9, 31
  and NU 113, 134, 135, 136, 140, 141, 142, 147–52, 241–42
  and *pesantren* 37, 38, 54, 64, 70, 148
  and politics 78, 87, 94, 114, 115, 133, 158, 257, 270–71, 305, 364
  and scholarship 31, 39, 67, 73, 83, 128, 139, 161, 165–67
umat 124, 125, 199, 242
United Nations 280, 335, 337, 338, 339

wayang kulit 57, 58, 59, 92, 120, 121, 324, 385

zakat 63, 161, 393n

Places
Aceh 8, 30, 260, 270, 271, 272
Africa 65, 84
Al Azhar 61, 83, 84, 85, 87, 88, 91, 93, 94, 95
Amman 289
Ambon 6, 28, 259, 260, 300, 305, 306, 325, 329, 333, 334 *see also* Maluku
America *see* United States of America
Australia 261, 265, 279, 397n *see also* Melbourne, Sydney, Perth

Baghdad 94, 95, 96, 97, 98, 99, 100, 101, 102, 123, 132, 367
Bali 171, 255, 283, 310
Bandung 50, 51, 72, 321, 329, 343
Bangkok 294
Banjarmasin 321
Banyuwangi 257, 258
Beijing 290, 294
Berlin 294
Borobudur Hotel 338
Brunei 294, 304, 305

Cairo 60, 61, 132, 236, 239, 240, 241, 265, 308, 367
Canada 102
Canberra 261 *see also* Australia
China *see* Beijing
Ciganjur 112, 174, 188, 195, 196, 247, 235, 239, 246, 256, 273, 276, 277, 280, 287, 311, 316
Cilandak 116
Cimahi 50
Cipasung 203 *see also muktamar*
Cipete 135, 136, 210
Ciputat 123
Cuba 297, 298

Damascus 123
Denanyar 37, 40, 56, 387n, 388n *see also pesantren*
Dili 280, 297, 326

East Timor 134, 239, 237, 261, 262, 278, 279, 280, 292, 296, 297, 301, 334, 335, 343, 375, 383 *see also* Dili
Egypt 61, 87, 92, 94, 104, 123, 127, 265 *see also* Cairo

France 2, 101 *see also* Paris, Sorbonne University

Germany 101 *see also* Berlin

Halim Airport 51
Havana 297, 298
Hilton Hotel 2, 3, 4, 24, 25, 322
Hong Kong 298, 362

IAIN Sunan Kalijaga 99, 126, 163
IAIN Syarif Hidyatullah 123, 127, 153, 162, 163
India 49, 65, 69, 294 *see also* New Delhi
Iran 62, 128, 182, 258 *see also* Teheran
Iraq 97, 99, 100 *see also* Baghdad
Irian Jaya 241, 292, 293, 311, 339, 340, 343, 345, 347, 363, 373, 384 *see also* Papua
Islamabad 308
Israel 198, 199, 203, 289
Istana Merdeka 291

Jalan Gatot Subroto 296
Java 37, 38, 39, 41, 44, 50, 51, 52, 57, 64, 65, 66, 69, 70, 71, 72, 102, 103, 104, 106, 107, 120, 121, 122, 126, 187, 189, 191, 203, 257, 258, 259, 263, 269, 270, 273, 274, 277, 281, 332, 333, 334, 351, 353
Jayapura 340
Jombang 37, 38, 39, 40, 41, 44, 45, 46, 51, 56, 57, 59, 60, 61, 103, 104, 107, 108, 268 *see also* Denanyar, Tambakberas
Jordan 198, 289

Kalimantan 38, 233, 240, 272, 321, 332, 352, 353 *see also* Pontianak, Sambas, Sampit
Kedung Ombo 154, 158, 170
Krapyak 56, 171, 176 *see also* pesantren
Kuala Lumpur 244
Kupang 297
Kuwait 289

London 294, 298

McGill University 102
Madura 39, 40, 41, 353
Magelang 56, 58, 59, 156 *see also* pesantren

Malang 291
Malaysia 240, 244, 362
Maluku 28, 259, 300, 306, 310, 311, 332, 333, 334, 335, 347, 375 *see also* Ambon
Manila 198
Matraman 45, 49, 51, 52, 102, 103
Mecca 39, 40, 41, 42, 49, 83, 86, 95
Medan 230, 236
Medina 63, 83
Melbourne 265
Menteng 45, 47, 138, 230, 238
Mexico 298
Mexico City 298
Middle East 8, 30, 53, 54, 83, 86, 88, 89, 90, 91, 93, 99, 352
Mojokerto 396–97n
Mulia, Hotel 322

New Delhi 294
New York 3, 4, 197, 335, 337, 341

Pakistan 374
Papua 292, 293, 301, 317 *see also* Irian Jaya
Parliament Building 245, 247, 296, 363
Paris 23, 30, 294, 298, 308
Perth 245
Philippines, The 258, 316 *see also* Manila
Pontianak 272
Poso 325, 326, 333 *see also* Sulawesi

Qatar 289

Russia 99

St Louis 308
Salatiga 95
Salt Lake City 278, 289, 290, 308
Sambas 272 *see also* Kalimantan
Sampit 352, 353 *see also* Kalimantan
Saudi Arabia 294 *see also* Mecca, Medina
Semanggi 256
Semarang 134, 263
Seoul 294
Singapore 245, 262, 303, 337
Sorbonne University 83, 308
South Korea 294, 346
Sulawesi 259, 325, 332, 333, 334, 347 *see also* Poso

Sumatra 38, 269, 270, 341 *see also* Aceh, West Sumatra
Surabaya 40, 41, 51, 126, 306, 327, 342, 355, 296n
Switzerland 294
Sydney 245, 265, 280
Syria 123 *see also* Damascus

Tambakberas 40, 56, 61
Tebuireng 39, 40, 41, 42, 122
Tegalrejo 56
Teheran 308
Thailand 243, 244 *see also* Bangkok
Tokyo 289, 308
Trisakti 236

United States of America/USA 123, 244, 260, 265, 294, 297, 298, 304, 310, 333, 338 *see also* New York, Salt Lake City, St Louis, Washington DC

Washington DC 289, 297, 308, 365
West Sumatra 69, 77
West Timor 259, 335, 336, 339, 373, 383 *see also* Kupang

Yogyakarta 54, 55, 56, 57, 58, 59, 70, 72, 85, 99, 100, 101, 103, 125, 126, 140, 156, 161, 163, 235, 256, 301, 315, 316, 324, 328, 367